# RIVER TEETH

# RIVER TEETH

*Twenty Years of Creative Nonfiction*

EDITED BY Joe Mackall & Daniel W. Lehman
FOREWORD BY Robert Atwan

University of New Mexico Press | Albuquerque

Library of Congress Cataloging-in-Publication Data

Names: Mackall, Joe, editor. | Lehman, Daniel W. (Daniel Wayne),
1950– editor. | Atwan, Robert, writer of foreword.

Title: River teeth: twenty years of creative nonfiction / edited by
Joe Mackall and Daniel W. Lehman; foreword by Robert Atwan.

Other titles: Twenty years of creative nonfiction | River teeth.

Description: Albuquerque: University of New Mexico Press, 2020.

Identifiers: LCCN 2019037141 (print) | LCCN 2019037142 (e-book) |
ISBN 9780826361394 (paperback) | ISBN 9780826361400 (e-book)

Subjects: LCSH: American prose literature—21st century. |
Prose literature—21st century. | Reportage literature, American.

Classification: LCC PS659.2. R48 2020 (print) | LCC PS659.2 (e-book) |
DDC 818/.5408—dc23

LC record available at https://lccn.loc.gov/2019037141

LC e-book record available at https://lccn.loc.gov/2019037142

"The Best Fried Chicken," from *Kitchen Yarns: Notes on Life,
Love, and Food* by Ann Hood. © 2019 by Ann Hood.
Used by permission of W. W. Norton & Company, Inc.

"Going Back to Plum Island" by Jill Christman. © 2015
by Jill Christman. Originally published in *River Teeth:
A Journal of Nonfiction Narrative*, Volume 17, Number 1,
Fall 2015. Used by permission of Brandt & Hochman
Literary Agents, Inc. All rights reserved.

Cover and interior designed by Mindy Basinger Hill
Composed in Aldus LT Std, Acumin Pro, and Rosella

THIS BOOK IS DEDICATED
TO THE MEMORY OF HAROLD D. LEHMAN
a faithful reader and discerning critic who for more than ninety-eight
years believed in truth and in a world where peace might
pass all understanding.

I'D LIKE TO DEDICATE THIS BOOK TO JIM MACKALL
a renaissance man for eighty-eight years and a kind
and loving father for sixty years and counting.
Thanks for showing me the way home.

# Contents

# Foreword

"The fact is the sweetest dream that labor knows."
ROBERT FROST | "Mowing"

Imagine *River Teeth* existed in 1853. And that one day Joe Mackall and Dan Lehman receive an unsolicited manuscript—handwritten of course—that begins as follows:

> When I wrote the following pages, or rather the bulk of them, I lived alone, in the woods, a mile from any neighbor, in a house which I had built myself, on the shore of Walden Pond, in Concord, Massachusetts, and earned my living by the labor of my hands only. At present I am a sojourner in civilized life again.

Messrs. Editors, the cover letter begins,

> I humbly submit to your esteemed periodical the enclosed essay, which I have titled "Economy." It is the opening chapter to a longer work, concerning my recent experiments in solitude, which I hope will one day find a publisher. In the meanwhile, my friend and neighbor Ralph Waldo Emerson considered the first essay quite ready for publication and suggested I send it to you with his endorsement.

Signed *Yours Truly, Henry David Thoreau*. Not a name that Joe and Dan are familiar with. But—despite the unruly penmanship—they like what they see. Right off, Joe admires the way the author immediately corrects himself so as not to imply that *all* the pages were written at Walden Pond. Dan wonders if "a mile from any neighbor" can be verified. They especially like his excuse for relying on the first-person singular:

> In most books, the I, or first person, is omitted; in this it will be retained; that in respect to egotism, is the main difference. We com-

monly do not remember that it is, after all, always the first person that is speaking. I should not talk so much about myself if there were anybody else whom I knew as well.

And as they read they realize that "Economy" perfectly encompasses all the principles of narrative nonfiction they hoped *River Teeth* would advance.

Except, of course, that the term "nonfiction" didn't exist then. The earliest use of the word, according to the *Oxford English Dictionary*, goes back to 1858, just a few years after the discouraging publication of *Walden*, when the Boston Public Library used the hyphenated term "non-fiction" in a circulation report to distinguish certain books from works of fiction. It may have been a useful term for categorization but it had little descriptive value. And it still doesn't, which is why we like to add to it such positive modifiers as "creative," "literary," or "narrative." And even then the usage is vague, that is, *literary* works that are *not* fiction.

If not fiction, what are they? And here the whole business gets thorny, as we hope that words like "creative" or "narrative" will suggest that a piece of nonfiction possesses undisputed literary value. That, like *Walden*, it has as much right to be called a work of literature as does a poem, story, novel, or play. So allow me right now to introduce the key term that troubles both our assessment of nonfiction and the ways we go about writing and evaluating it: *imagination*.

By calling a work imaginative we can mean that it is fanciful, made-up, unrealistic, not to have ever happened, not to be believed. To say that someone's memoir or travel account is quite "imaginative" may not be considered a compliment. In this sense, imaginative contrasts with truthful, honest, accurate, candid. But imaginative can also mean that a piece of writing is inventive, original, innovative. In nonfiction, to be inventive does not necessarily mean that we have made up story lines, incidents, or facts. We have simply found an effective and creative way to convey them. Compositional ingenuity in no way indicates a disregard of truth or

a compromised honesty. Literary techniques aren't in themselves lies but artistic methods of arranging, selecting, designing, and shaping. Would we call the intricate crafting of clay on a potter's wheel deceitful? The future vase may be fabricated but it's not a complete fabrication.

Much recent criticism has become overly suspicious of creative nonfiction (still an oxymoron to some) and disinclined to see how significant a role imagination plays in its crafting. I'm not speaking here of lyric essays or hybrids, where prose poetry bubbles clearly at the surface, but of the large variety of nonfiction works that depend on an accurate presentation of facts. I wonder if as writers and readers we're overly influenced by standards of journalism that ought to apply to news and reporting but that don't necessarily apply (and never had until recently) to personal essays, memoir, and other forms of creative nonfiction where talented writers may strive for literary effects that challenge the boundaries of ordinary verifiability. This doesn't mean turning the actual sunny day into a rainy one to describe the breakup of a romance just because the effect would be gloomier. Imaginative nonfiction can easily accommodate the essential facts of any story, but there are literary and documentary effects that can't be achieved without some requisite artifice.

Please excuse a little close reading. Here's a specimen of imaginative nonfiction I very much like. It's by no one of any literary prominence today, though the author, John Bartlow Martin, a biographer of Adlai Stevenson (and his major speechwriter), was a diplomat, a veteran journalist, an award-winning true-crime reporter, and a lifelong champion of the underdog. Martin also pioneered what one day would be called "The New Journalism." He opens his first book, *Call It North Country* (Knopf 1944), an account of the land and the people of Upper Michigan, with the following passage:

> Peter Moore—nobody ever called him Pete—stood apart at the bar, and his heavy shoulders drooped and even his full gray beard looked sad. Down at the end of the bar a bunch of miners, money in their

fists, and their clothes red with iron ore, were punishing a bottle of George Voelker's best tanglefoot; this was payday in the mines and tonight the boys would lower the boom in Ishpeming. But not Peter Moore. He leaned over the bar alone and frowned at his liquor and scuffed his hobnailed Chippewa boots savagely on the iron plate that protected the floor at the bar. The country was going to hell.

The narrative tactic is a kind of "cold open": Martin drops us into the scene before we know where we are and what's going on. We gradually discover it is the turn of the twentieth century and we are inside the head of a real North Country inhabitant, Peter Moore, a trapper in his fifties, a loner, having a drink at George Voelker's saloon on Main Street in the iron ore town of Ishpeming, Michigan. The country is rapidly changing and Martin decides to document those changes as seen through the eyes and experiences of one tough woodsman.

Although Martin based his account of the Upper Peninsula on extensive research and interviews over a period of years during his vacations from Chicago, he doesn't begin with origins but with a concrete moment—a particular person and a particular place. And, I should add, a particular point of view rendered in that popular fictional mode called "free indirect style" that allows a writer to employ the third person and still retain a first-person perspective. We see Peter Moore—more or less objectively depicted—from Martin's perspective, but the language and voice also allow him to render Peter Moore's subjective feelings; or, to put this another way, the description is Martin's, though much of the vernacular is Moore's: "The country was going to hell." Martin works both outside and inside Peter Moore, instinctively employing imaginative techniques the New Journalists would within a few decades perfect.

In fiction, techniques like cold openings and free indirect discourse are important tools of the trade. But Peter Moore is a historical figure, albeit an obscure one, and Martin has no idea how the trapper thinks or what he's thinking. He has pulled into that dangerous intersection where journalism, history, and imaginative nonfiction can easily collide. The journalistic standards of our time no longer permit this sort of creative reconstruction of a real person's thoughts and feelings. The old creative and street-smart

columnists, like New York's Jimmy Breslin, would not be able to report today the way they once did. But does this invalidate Martin's approach? Does it make *Call it North Country* fiction? Not at all. Any sensible reader knows this is not a novel or story but narrative nonfiction intended to recreate dramatically a time, a place, and an individual character. Martin is not deceiving anyone nor falsifying anything: we realize the scene is imagined—not for fictional, but for expository purposes.

<p style="text-align:center">❧❧</p>

There's another way that imagination helps us encounter reality. How do we describe the indescribable? Take one example: how do we depict the absolute present, the fleeting moment we inhabit, our consciousness of "right now"? Surely an instant of time is real, some might say the only reality, since the past exists only as memory and the future only as specu-lation. Early on in *Leviathan*, Thomas Hobbes contends that imagination and memory are "divers names" for "one thing." Mary Warnock, one of my favorite contemporary philosophers (she is now ninety-four), argues in her study *Imagination* (1976) that the faculty is intimately connected with memory, time, and our interpretation of the world. We use it not only in the creative arts but also for "our ordinary perception of the world." Asleep or awake, attentive or distracted, we are always imagining. The literary issue for us should not be how imagination distorts the truth, but how we could write a personal essay or memoir without it.

In several books on the subject, Warnock investigates the role of imag-ination in Wordsworth's groundbreaking autobiographical poetry. But we could also learn how the imagination works in nonfiction by paying close attention to the brilliant prose of Virginia Woolf, whose personal essays continually struggle to express the inexpressible. Woolf knew that reality comes to us both distinctly and indistinctly, and she was a genius—in both her fiction and nonfiction—at exploring the blurred boundaries between these two modes of perception. In the enigmatic and posthumously pub-lished essay "A Moment: Summer's Night" she engages in what may seem artistically impossible: the depiction of a fleeting instant flickering through our being. It opens:

The night was falling so that the table in the garden among the trees grew whiter and whiter; and the people round it more indistinct. An owl, blunt, obsolete looking, heavy weighted, crossed the fading sky with a black spot between its claws. The trees murmured. An aeroplane hummed like a piece of plucked wire. There was also, on the roads, the distant explosion of a motor cycle, shooting further and further away down the road. Yet what composed the present moment?

Woolf wants nothing less in this essay—with its spooky details and ominous sights and sounds—than to capture the elusive present moment and to "compose the truth of it, the whole of it." She offers us a wonderfully succinct way of describing the work of imaginative nonfiction: composing the truth.

Thoreau thoroughly understood imaginative nonfiction and discovered that it was perfectly adapted to our stubbornly factual world. *Walden* is full of numbers, measurements, ledgers, and calibrations. (Its author, remember, could always find day work as a surveyor or carpenter.) And yet all the calculations we encounter there—the specific outgoes and income of raising beans, the varying seasonal temperatures of the pond—contribute in the end to the overall imaginative power of the book. Facts need not stifle the imagination. Indeed, as Thoreau intended to demonstrate, they can inspire it.

For twenty years, since the first issue of *River Teeth* came my way, I've applauded the range and quality and the editorial standards of this very special literary journal. For twenty years, Dan and Joe have consistently provided readers with some of the finest nonfiction of our time. And, as this book so amply and admirably proves, they have done so without compromising either truth or imagination.

**ROBERT ATWAN**

JOE MACKALL &
DANIEL W. LEHMAN

# Introduction

For twenty years now, *River Teeth: A Journal of Nonfiction Narrative* has published what we believe to be a compelling blend of memoir, essays, literary journalism, and critical commentaries on the nonfiction form and its authors.

The signature obsession of *River Teeth* during these two decades is to explore the deepest implications of writing and reading nonfiction. We've said it all along the way: Because nonfiction purports to capture the lives of real people and events, it pits the characters and narrators who live inside the text against those same characters and actual authors who cast shadows in the outside world. What exactly is at stake when an author sets out to capture the life of a real person on the page? How do such narratives affect privacy and identity? Even if the narrative is scrupulously true, how do both parties face the recognition that secrets will be told and lives will be altered?

When we started this adventure, almost on a dare in each other's offices, we knew we were swimming against a pretty strong critical tide. All around us, the rush to expose false binaries was the critical rage, and one of those false binaries was said to be fiction and nonfiction. All knowledge is representation, the thinking went; all is culturally and ideologically produced, no fact can be solid, and the very idea of truth is a conceit. While we were the last to argue that the notion of truth was fixed and innocent, we insisted that the distinction between truth and invention mattered.

What made nonfiction interesting for us was the very difficulty in pinning it down. What counted was the ever-complex relationship between

the character on the page and the character in life, the event as represented and the event as remembered by others.

We weren't after innocence; we were after implication.

So we asked these sorts of questions in our writing, reading, and editing: Even if the narrative is scrupulously true, how do both parties face the recognition that secrets will be told and lives will be altered? How does a text change when its characters inhabit the real world or when literary death or pain opens the flesh of actual wounds? In fiction, when characters die and live, *characters* breathe or stop breathing; in nonfiction, when characters die and live, *people* breathe or stop breathing.

In one way or another, the essays, memoir, reporting, and critique you will discover in this book create that sort of lasting conversation. We bring writers who work in literary journalism into community with memoirists and essayists more comfortable in the MFA world of Associated Writing Programs. We sprinkle in a bit of theory and criticism. We have much to learn from the other. From winners of the Pulitzer Prize to reporters for small-town dailies, the journalists and writers published by *River Teeth* combine compelling stories with old-fashioned reporting to enliven stories with precise description, memorable dialogue, sure scene writing, and challenging narrative structure.

Along the way, we wanted *River Teeth* to focus on what matters about nonfiction: characters, events, and memories that precede the written text. Uncovering the deep relationship between sources and texts—particularly when real names are used—explodes more formalist notions of writing style. Technical arguments about what can or cannot be done in nonfiction hit dead ends because they normally are obsessed by the classification of narrative rather than by its power. Therefore, ostensibly nonfictional texts about private events, especially when names are altered or obscured, turn out to be largely indistinguishable from fiction. The genre distinction in those cases depends mostly on the author's good-will promise to live up to some standard of factualness. So when "facts" inside the nominally nonfiction text cast little or no shadow on the world outside the text, the traditional generic boundary largely becomes a distinction without a difference. What really counts, we would argue, is not a safe realm of

generic certainty, but the dead reckoning of nonfiction's potential ability to affect actual lives.

How does that happen on the page?

Deft voice, sparkling scenes, targeted research, and a sure sense of audience are the blueprint for shared discovery. Most of us will have to lay aside the idea that a story or memory is automatically important to us as a writer because it happened to us as a character. We need to shed a certain shortsightedness that focuses only on our own traumatic (or even triumphal) experience. Instead, we will cultivate a recognition built on readers: how a reader might breathe in our story and how we can build a common, empathetic experience through the magic of text.

*River Teeth* prowls for edgy, compelling nonfiction, crafting volumes that regularly make our readers take an extra breath and blink. At heart we always ask two questions: Is this the sort of piece I would want to call the other editor in the middle of the night to say we have to have? And would we die if we saw this piece in someone else's journal and knew we could have had it for ourselves? Those are the criteria, nothing else really. Some of the pieces you find here are the work of friends and acquaintances, but we publish them without apology if the pieces meet our standards.

Only then. That's all. That several Best American Essays in this volume come from writers with close ties makes our case. Both were among the best dozen or so essays we saw that year in ours or any other journal; it would have killed us to see them win those prizes for someone else. And we confessed that fact in writing when the pieces were published and before the prizes were won.

We know all this sounds more than a little intuitive, even presumptuous, and quite a bit less than arm's length. That's the nature of love, we guess.

Still, we probably owe our readers some articulated standard for what you will find here; heck, we owe it to ourselves. One of the best we've heard comes from Cheryl Strayed in her introduction to *Best American Essays 2013*. "Behind every good essay there's an author with a savage desire to know more about what is already known," she says. She terms great nonfiction writing part philosophy, confession, recollection, reimagination,

clarity, and conjecture. Ultimately, Strayed says, "the essay's engine is curiosity; its territory is the open road."

How do we find such pieces?

*River Teeth* editors consider some three thousand submissions a year, each one of which is read by at least one founding editor. Beyond that, we prowl for even more publishing possibilities at conferences, at readings, and by word of mouth. We are part of an ongoing community of writers. We will go after anything we consider to be good—even (especially) if we have no business asking for it.

We often are asked how we manage to choose from so many possibilities from so many fine writers. Fair question, indeed.

The first thing we look for is something urgent. We aren't interested in publishing an also-ran piece by a good writer. We want to publish something that a writer was born to write. We want something that is the most important thing he or she has ever written; we want to prize the fact that they've trusted this thing to us. Even if that's not strictly the case, it has to read with that sort of urgency.

Beautiful language and fresh material aren't enough in themselves, though that certainly helps. It's always hard to pin down, but here it is: Something about the writing has to be vertical, has to feel like something has been ripped open viscerally. And we're not really talking about subject matter. It doesn't have to be traumatic; it can be quiet and beautiful. But it has to mean something important, and the writer has to communicate that to us with everything she has.

We read so many manuscripts in which the things that happen clearly mean a lot to the writer, but the writer has not yet found a way to make the story mean a lot to the reader. It might need more compelling depth. It starts, for sure, with giving a moment or a passage a purpose beyond itself. And it means searching for the perfect word, the perfect sentence, and the perfect scene to convey that purpose. Something has to reach beyond. The underlying idea is that the kind of writing we are after will make us see something about the world in a fresh way or will remind us of something important that has an arguably public dimension, even though the content itself may be personal and private.

In short, if you are going to write a memoir, or really any nonfiction

that matters, you have to be willing to let the truth ride on its power all the way to the end. What sinks a piece is when one detects that the writer is afraid to let the reader see the truly dark matter—or at least the truly important stuff. You'd be surprised how many writers flinch at exactly that moment. A writer sometimes gives with one hand and takes away with the other.

And, finally, there is an essential difference between experience and meaning making. If we read for a while and this happens and this happens, and we still don't know why it is important, then we know the writer might not be up to it. As our great, dear friend Judith Kitchen once said, paraphrasing, "Nonfiction writers don't make up, we make of." So just writing about something that has happened to you is never enough. It's what the writer does with her own experience, what she *makes of* it that counts.

Ultimately, it is the writer's business to help to create a reader who can read his work at its best and deepest level. And the first thirty pages or so in a book manuscript or the first page or two in an essay is often where that perfect reader is created—or not. All sorts of negotiations are happening here: Is this a voice that can last for me over the course of the piece? How is scene conveyed? How does language work at the sentence level, paragraph level? Tense? Diction? What can I expect from its style? Its structure? Is it going to get somewhere for me? Somewhere surprising that yet was there all along?

In these two decades we have said a couple of things again and again in much the same words in describing what we do.

Truth matters—never more than now. It is seldom easy to pin down facts and represent them, but that's the point. And what began as a largely academic assault on the concepts of truth and factual reference has metastasized in our nation. Daily we hear the label "fake news" applied to solid documentary reporting and writing that simply exposes or inconveniences the name-caller. And the ones we publish and reprint here are the pieces we simply had to have—whose loss we would mourn if we saw someone else get it and knew that we could have had it.

That's the feeling we are always seeking—whether it's a sketch of one or two pages, a standard-length submission, a long piece, or a 250-page

manuscript for the River Teeth Literary Nonfiction Prize. It's gotta be there. It's gotta be love.

That's what makes it work.

And so, we promise to remain feisty, outspoken, committed to the truth, no matter how complicated and difficult, ready and eager to publish all those writers who accept that challenge and who write with craft and beauty, who pull us in, who change us, who enlighten us, who make us weep and squirm.

We nearly wept and squirmed when choosing pieces for this book. How would we ever choose the pieces that would represent some of the best work of the last twenty years? Our first draft of this collection contained nearly sixty works and came in at a ridiculous yet sensible 289,000 words. Because we publish only what we love and when we love something we'll go to the ends for it, we wanted so much more in this volume. So many of the essays, memoir, and literary journalism we've published over the last decade could not make the cut. We said no to so much we loved. This volume contains thirty pieces by thirty-one writers. That was the tough thing about putting this volume together, but we believe it's also what makes it so compelling.

Two of the most gifted writers and wonderful people we've known are no longer with us. Our dear friends Judith Kitchen and Brian Doyle departed this world too damn soon. I thank God we knew them and that we're able to include them here and read their work for the rest of our lives.

For us *River Teeth* has always been about the writing, of course, but we never imagined how many truly good people would come into our lives because the two of us happened to start a journal almost on a whim in 1999. It does seem that we're living in a different time than when we started out. We were still pre-9/11, before Iraq and Afghanistan, before family separations at our southern border. But much, of course, has not changed. We still love and laugh and weep and work and rear our children and become grandparents and bid good-bye to people we love. And we still need to tell our stories. Without stories it can feel as if we have nothing, as if everything is out of reach. With our stories, all of our stories, something else happens, some alchemy of experience and meaning making that renders us somehow more than we are. To paraphrase our friend Cheryl

Strayed, after reading the best stories we ought to then believe "that nothing will ever be the same again." Acts of creation transform us; we're made anew. If this sounds a touch grandiose, we'll ask your forbearance. That's just how we feel about the power of literature. We always have.

When we're worried about our passion for the written word perhaps embarrassing us or our readers, we often cite a couple of sentences from Tim O'Brien's "The Lives of the Dead" from *The Things They Carried*: "And this too is true. Stories can save us." Or as Leslie Marmon Silko writes about the enormity of stories in her novel *Ceremony*: "They are all we have, you see, all we have to fight off illness and death. You don't have anything, if you don't have stories."

So here we have a little something.

JUDITH KITCHEN

# Breath

"The breath of the mind is attention."

**JOSEPH JOUBERT** | *The Notebooks of Joseph Joubert*

*In with the good air, out with the bad. In with the good air, out with the bad. One thousand and one, one thousand and two. One thousand and one, one thousand and two. Push down on the back, lift up with the arms.* However we chanted to ourselves, this was how we learned what they then called artificial respiration. How to save someone who had drowned. Push, then lift. Push, then lift. This was not CPR. No lips met other lips. *One thousand and one.* We went on counting as we practiced bringing breath back to the body before us.

It's been forty-five years since that one bout with pneumonia—the one where I drowned without drowning. There was no cough, just the sledgehammer of pressure, the ache in the lungs. And the fever. For days I saw things on the bedroom wall, like a movie playing over and over. The soldiers rose in unison and walked into the swamp. In unison, their heads disappeared beneath the sluggish water. And then, as though I were there, under water with them, I stared as their hair began to swirl and float, like seaweed, among the seaweed. This was the era of Vietnam. This was the terror: that it was beautiful. That their hair made intricate patterns on the wallpaper.

"Help me!" I shouted. "*Me ajuda,*" I called, in the world's worst Portuguese. No one moved. And there he was—a body grown heavy the more he was out of the water, and I was struggling to haul him the last few feet onto the sand. "*Me ajuda,*" but no one helped as I pummeled his back and

lifted his arms and counted my count until suddenly he sputtered and spit and my job was over. I looked up at the circle of people who stood there with candles at the ready—to light if he didn't make it—looked up to see who had made no move even to help me drag him beyond the waves. Yet they had candles. What kind of faith in fate did they share?

I see her now—there on that beach—that young woman I used to be. The minute she hears the cry from beyond the breakers, she begins to run. She doesn't think. She just runs. And by the time she reaches the water, the two men who were trying to save their friend are lying half in, half out, exhausted, chests heaving. So she wades in and struggles to drag the man a few inches forward, a few inches more into the air that surrounds them all. She tugs and pushes, and no one steps forward. No one wants to touch this man who has forgotten how to breathe.

If the breath of the mind is attention, then what is the breath of the body? The autonomic inhale/exhale that tugs at the air as though it were self-sufficient? And it is: in, then out, fill, then empty, over and over, without thought. You hardly notice the slight rise of the chest, the twitch of the nose. The prodigious body at work, attending to nothing more than its essential needs.

If the breath of the body is behind the scenes, then attention brings the scene to the forefront. What is attention but a complete entry into the here and now? The present moment, lived to its fullness? There are people capable of that, but I am not one of them. It seems to me that I live so often in future tense—that my focus on the future determines what I notice in the present. And, already, I find myself planning for how—in that future—I will remember this present. Which thrusts me into a premature past, a future memory. But what are we without memory? Doesn't memory shape what we become?

Where was her husband? Back with the boys, far up the beach, shielding them from what they might have to face. And what did she notice? The day. The spark of sun on the water. The beach so white under the sun's lethal drip. The umbrellas, casting their circles of shade. Red-and-white stripes, green-and-yellow stripes, turquoise spirals on white, plain blue, plain red. The glint of oil on glistening bodies. The man. His brown skin turning gray. The man. Like something foreign. The man. His back. His back suddenly heaving.

Somewhere on the streets of Rio an old man knows that he has lived his borrowed decades in the shadow of a woman whose name he does not know. His friends tell him she was there, but he finds it hard to believe. A woman who did not speak his language, but knew, somehow, the language of breath.

Hold your breath. Don't hold your breath. Out of breath. Under one's breath. Save your breath. Waste your breath. All in one breath. In the same breath. Bated breath. Breath of fresh air.

If breath of the mind is attention, what did they see as they watched her pushing the water out of his lungs? What did they hear in her foreign dismay? How did the candles fit into the hands, and the hands—how did they decide when and how to pray? Was it as simple as breathing? And why did she run, without thought, toward their turning away?

Somewhere on the streets of Rio, she learned the art of attention. She opened her eyes to an unfamiliar world and she listened to its sounds. The soft scraping of the broom along the patio across the *praça*. In the doorways of the shops, the rising inflection of the maids buying milk, bananas, rolls for the morning breakfast. The strange twist of the tongue, the nasal tint of the words, *tudo bem*? how are you? all well? She was not well. Not at all. She was in over her head. This would be the death of her. She wanted to go home, though just where "home" was she didn't know. She could not breathe the thick air of loneliness. She could not draw in breath without a wish for a different life, something she would recognize.

Today, so many years later, the breath of the body is compromised. It does not retain its shape but slips down a narrowed tube, defies the CT scans, is scarred and broken. "Just breathe normally," says the pulmonologist. But what does that mean? She is tied to a slim green tube, oxygen making its way to her wherever she goes. Stuck with her lack of elasticity. Today she is aware of breath as never before. Its lack of odor, its hunger for tense. She will attend to it. In with the good air, out with the bad. She will pay it respect.

And memory? What good will it do her now? Memories sorted in piles, like laundry, memories twisting their way back to back then, but how to bring them forward? She tells stories to her grandsons. Someone needs to have heard them. Someone needs to know that this—these discrete moments brought to life in image and sound, breadfruit and waterfall,

the popsicle man walking the beaches calling Kibon, Kibon, that innocent word conjuring a future where someone calls, and calls—is the sum of a lifetime. The sum of walking through this world, parting the air with the body, parting the thought of the air with the mind.

Here, in the present, the ice cream truck one block away. Ding, dong, ding, dah. Up, down, up, down. The universal tune, spelling cold, spelling sweet, spelling summer. Though now it's not quite summer. It's dark when we wake in the morning. The berries on the mountain ash have turned to orange. A few leaves drift in the air. Ding, dong, ding, dah. Oranges and lemons—say the bells of St. Clement's. When I grow rich—say the bells of Shoreditch.

Near Cedar Breaks, Utah, it was the altitude—over eleven thousand feet. The breath came in hiccups. I found I couldn't walk. The ranger said she understood, that it had taken her a year to become acclimated. But I had a day, and I wasn't going to walk, so we drove instead, past an alpine meadow where tiny plants were blooming: yellow, purple, blue, red—red because those plants can convert the sun's rays into heat. We rolled down the windows to listen to the wind as it swept over the rocks. Yellow, purple, blue, red, in tiny incremental steps along the mountain, and the stunted pines, like old men, bent and almost lungless. The sound of the marmot, his tin whistle trailing him, though just where he was we could not say.

Or the strip show in Harrogate, two rows of benches on the sides of a narrow hall, rows of folding chairs in the center, ending under the balcony—a cave full of men. On the bright stage the women dance, so far away you can't tell if their breasts are bare or decorated with sequins and fringe. Their bodies ripple and flow. You can hear the breathing quicken, hard, in unison. Then, there in the dark, one man throws back his head and makes a sigh. Involuntary chain reaction as up and down that final row the fusion of eye and lung and ear conspires to set them free.

Who are we without the memories that make us individual? Even when memories are shared, they diverge. A second opinion, so to speak. Who would she be if she did not know what, and when, and to whom? If she could not call up the hefty feel of a jackknife in her pocket, or the sound of that old maroon Dodge, or the purple of heather and the yellow of gorse? If she could not hear her sons still lifting their voices as they

fished for crabs in Maine? If she could not hear her inner voice above the noise of the lungs? That inner voice that says *yes, that was how it was*. The things you carry: the present, along with an ever-present past. And a future that may or may not be yours.

Wheeze. Gasp. Rasp. Gurgle. Huff. Puff. Pant. Cough. And crackle. Always, they hear a crackle.

Purse the lips, tighten them, breathe across the aperture. The flute comes to life. Or would come to life in the right person's hands. In mine, it makes its sounds, but they have very little in the way of mood. I understand the notes—the math—but not the emotion. Music eludes me. The making of music. Though I hear it well enough, hear Alfie Boe—*any way you do-oooo*—have his fun with Elvis, hear Elvis—*take a walk down lonely street*—delve into his private sorrows, hear Orbison—*cry-y-i-y-ing*—give voice to public pain. These are voices that carry the windswept wail of the fipple flute, the centuries that take us back to the Iron Age whistle made from bone found in a Yorkshire field. These are the voices that catch at the heart. They have no need of training; the lungs fill with air, and the body, as it has always done, asserts itself.

Here's what astounds me. I plod on. I do not think. I simply plod on. Because what else is one supposed to do? I still have work to do, still have a body to bathe and feed, still have the craving to see and listen and touch. When will even the senses fade? When will the sheer effort to breathe take over, take charge, take precedence?

So savor. Breathe in the scents. The clean smell of rain. Pages of old books. Pine tar's smell of lumberyard, acid tang of orange peel, amber's artificial musk.

Memory encases us in its resins. Picture this: a camp in the Adirondacks—tent, campfire, clothesline, canoe. Picture the canoe in a placid blue lake, our father paddling farther and farther from shore. Picture the way he stands and sways, tipping the canoe, tipping himself into the water. See the canoe, upside-down, still as a rock above the surface. See the way the water does not part, and our father does not appear. Imagine the panic rising, filling the body, filling the space between us and the canoe. Where is he? Where? What should we do? Our voices begin to shout. *Oh no, oh no*. And then the laughter—from underneath, from where the air was

waiting all the time. This is not funny. Doesn't he know that? This is a terrible lesson in breath, invisible breath stopped in the spaces of the mind.

My father's last breath came when they turned off the machine. We had begged and begged, and now it was done. He died alone, as we all die alone. But he was more alone than many, and anyway, he wouldn't have been able to hear the music of our hearts, or the rhythm of our concern. All his attention had been paid, and now he was taking it with him. But I have the stories: ours, and his. Sometimes we repeat them: how his father would wait at the door, listening in case his mother wanted something from the store. How, hearing nothing, he'd go down the steps and wait at the gate. How he'd open the gate with its hoarse wheeze, and only then would it come—"Oh Geoooorge"—and the back of the brain would fly into gear as he hurried away, pretending not to hear. Our father's fists, thumbs down on the back of his neck, showing how the medulla's reflex set his father going, and going.

I have been shaped by sound and sight. By sunlight pouring off rocky ledges. By babies' insistent flailing, their fists saying "no" before they can talk. By the green-tipped leaves of the bamboo outside the window. By the memory of white gloves on Sundays. Hats with tiny veils. Moors stretching wide with rust-colored bracken. The winding stairs to the upper level of the Edinburgh buses, wet cobblestones, dusk by 3:00 p.m. Fish and chips, greasy waxed paper and newsprint on the fingers like a murky sifting of coal dust. Minnows in a shallow pond, all skittery shadow, scurry and skirmish. The smell of hot dogs on the grill. The slush of March. Sound of the merry-go-round spinning its tune down to a drawl. I have been shaped by memory until memory shapes a life of its own. My sons skate the ice of time. Their hair flows backward, fluid and unpredictable. Their jackets are red, purple, green. Their eyes are blue. Their skates make a swishing sound—leeeeft, riiight, leeeeft, riiight—whoosh, they sweep past me and are almost lost as I catch them now—here—catch my breath at their beauty—back there, back then—in memory's amber stone.

Think about it. There are many ways to revisit respiration. I remember watching my breath—white—preceding me up the hill in winter air. My father blowing smoke rings, doughnut breath, rounded and shaped, growing ragged as it vanished. The soccer player's heaving diaphragm. Fraction

of a second before a sneeze. Slow sip of air over a hot bowl of soup. *Humpf* of jealousy. Voice husky with regret. Kiss that takes your breath away.

Who knows when the last breath will be? It seems so sad, beforehand. Not to have to pay attention. Gone, the mind taking notes at the surge of autumn red. The mind with its open memo to the body. You are gone, while they stay on—the blue glass goblet on the windowsill, the wooden box with your grandmother's letters, all outliving you. Will your last clear breath make its own whistle—intake or exhale—or slide softly, softly into a whisper, then nothing? Air diffused by more air, until the colors of the world come clear: yellow, purple, blue, red. And green. The breathing green of what goes on.

TED KOOSER

�֍

# Small Rooms in Time

Several years ago, a fifteen-year-old boy answered the side door of a house where I once lived, and was murdered, shot twice by one of five people—two women and three men—who had gone there to steal a pound of cocaine. The boy died just inside the door, at the top of a staircase that led to the cellar where I once had set up my easel and painted. The robbers—all but one still in their teens—stepped over the body, rushed down the steps, and shot three people there, a woman and two men.

Somebody called the police, perhaps the people who rented the apartment on the second floor. The next day's front-page story reported that the three in the basement were expected to survive. The boy's father, who was somewhere on the first floor and out of the line of fire, had not been injured.

It's taken me a long time to try to set down my feelings about this incident. At the time, it felt as if somebody had punched me in the stomach, and in ways it has taken me until now to get my breath back. I'm ashamed to say that it wasn't the boy's death that so disturbed me, but the fact that it happened in a place where my family and I had once been safe.

I recently spent most of a month building a Christmas surprise for my wife, a one-inch to one-foot scale replica of her ancestral home in the Nebraska sandhills. The original, no longer owned by her family, was a sprawling fourteen-room, two-story frame house built in 1884. Her great-grandparents and grandparents lived there. Her great-aunt, still living and 108 years old at the time I am writing this, was born there. Her father and his brothers and sister chased through those rooms as small

children, and as a girl my wife and her younger sister spent summers there, taking care of their invalid grandmother.

Day after day as I worked on this dollhouse, pasting up wallpaper, gluing in baseboards and flooring, I would feel my imagination fitting itself into the little rooms. At times I lost all sense of scale and began to feel grit from the sandhills under my feet on the kitchen linoleum, to smell the summer sun on the porch roof shingles. I had never lived in that house, but I lived there during those moments, and as I worked, the shadows of wind-tossed trees played over the dusty glass of the windows. Now and then I would hear footsteps on the porch, approaching the door.

Immediately upon seeing the dollhouse on Christmas Eve, my wife began to recall the way it had been furnished when she was a girl, to talk about this piece of furniture being here and that one there. I watched her feed the goldfish in the dirty aquarium and sit down on the stiff, cold leather of the Mission sofa. I saw her stroke-damaged grandmother propped in her painted iron bed under the eaves. Listening to my wife, watching her open the tiny doors and peer into the tiny closets, I began to think about the way in which the rooms we inhabit, if only for a time, become unchanging places within us, complete in detail.

I clipped the article about the shooting and must have read it a hundred times those first few days. In a front-on photograph, like a mug shot, there stood the house, sealed off by yellow police tape, looking baffled, cold, and vacant. Next to the picture was a row of slack-faced mug shots of the five arrested. They looked as empty as the house.

I mailed a copy of the article to my first wife. I wanted her to share the shock that I was suffering, like a distant explosion whose concussion had taken years to reach across a galaxy of intervening happenstance. At the site where only the most common, most ordinary unhappiness had come to us—misunderstandings, miscommunications, a broken marriage like thousands and thousands of others—there had been a murder, three people had been wounded, and five were on their way through the courts and into prison, all for the want of a pound of cocaine that the article reported had never been there.

For several years in the early 1960s we'd rented the first floor, which

included the use of the cellar that I used as a study. We'd been married for three years and were then in our early twenties. Diana was a schoolteacher in a nearby town, and I worked as a clerk at an insurance company. While we lived there, Diana became pregnant, our son was born, and when we brought him home from the hospital we carried him in through that same side door where the murder took place.

I remember matted orange shag carpet inside the door and continuing down the steps to the cellar, and more of the same carpet on the damp concrete floor and glued to the walls. (I can't think of it now without seeing bloodstains.) At the foot of the stairs, in a mildewed, overstuffed chair I'd bought at a thrift shop, I studied for night classes at the university. In that room I painted a few amateur pictures by bad basement light, one of a towering grain elevator that I thought was pretty good but which I mislaid long ago. A life-sized nude of Diana disappeared while we were packing to leave that house for another across town. I wonder if someone doesn't have it nailed up over their basement bar. Perhaps over cocktails on football Saturdays their guests try to guess who that pretty young woman might have been.

Two quiet, Latvian women rented the upstairs apartment. They had emigrated from Europe during the Second World War and spent spring, summer, and autumn on their knees beside beds of annual flowers they'd put in along the driveway. Olga was the older, then I suppose in her sixties. She had a badly curved spine, a shy smile, and from a forest near Dresden had seen wave after wave of Allied bombers. She told me that a thousand feet over the city the atmosphere stood in red columns of flame. Alida was handsome, dark-eyed, dark-haired, younger than Olga. Of the two, she was the less approving of the young couple who lived downstairs, who drank too much, who had a very barky dog.

When I think of the exterior of that house, their flowers are always in bloom—petunias, asters, pansies, bachelor buttons, phlox—but when I remember Diana and me living there, it is always winter and we are closed in by heavy snow. The side door where the boy was killed opened onto the driveway, and the first thing I did on those blizzardy winter mornings was to open it to let out our black Schipperke, Hagen, and watch him

wade through the snow to pee and then turn back, a miserable look on his sharp little face. It was a cheap, aluminum storm door with loose glass panes, icy to the touch. As I waited there I could hear the kitchen radio behind me, turned up loud so that Diana, who dreaded the twenty-mile drive when the roads were bad, could catch the list of schools that were to be closed for the day.

In a few weeks' time I could build a miniature version of that house, using the approximate measurements of memory, and as I worked with plywood and paper and glue I would be able to gradually remember almost everything about it. But I won't need to do that; since the murder I have often peered into those little rooms where things went good for us at times and bad at times. I have looked into the miniature house and seen us there as a young couple, coming and going, carrying groceries in and out, hats on, hats off, happy and sad.

As I stared at the article, every piece of our furniture took its place in the rooms. I could have reached in through the door of that photograph and with the tip of a finger roll our antique dental chair over the floor. A friend's big painting of the Rolling Stones hung on the opposite wall. On the living room floor was the plush, white carpet I bought with money from a literary prize. It was always dirty. Down the hall and through a door to the left, our bed, rumpled and unmade, stood right where it stood when we were young parents, with Jeffrey's crib nearby, and by leaning a little forward I could hear the soft, reassuring sound of his breath.

It has been more than thirty years since we lived at 2820 "R" Street, Lincoln, Nebraska. I write out the full address as if to fasten it down with stakes and ropes against the violence of time. I hadn't thought about it often, maybe a few times a year. But it was our house again the minute I opened the paper that morning and saw its picture and the faces of the people who had struck it with terrible violence. They didn't look sorry; they looked like they'd do it again if they could.

Now and then since the murder I find myself turning into that decaying neighborhood and down that street, slowing to look at our house. The

window shades are drawn on what were once such bright, welcoming rooms. Nobody lives there now, as far as I can tell. On snowy days there are no tracks up the drive to that flimsy side door.

I lean down, I try to fit myself inside. Even after thirty years there still might be the smell of Olga and Alida's salt herring being cooked upstairs, and on the first floor the fragrance of phlox, a few stalks in a water glass. For thirty years I had put it all firmly behind me, but like a perfect miniature it had waited in a corner of my heart, its rooms packed with memories. The murder brought it forward and made me hold it under the light again. Of course I hadn't really forgotten, nor could I ever forget, how it feels to be a young father, frightened by an enormous and threatening world, wondering what might become of him, what might become of his wife and son.

Only a year after Diana, Jeff, and I moved away and into another house across town, our marriage came apart, and I began to learn to be a single father. From time to time Jeff came to visit me at the home of friends who had taken me in. The dead boy, too, had gone to visit his father.

If my luck in this life had been worse I might have been that other father, occupied by some mundane task, perhaps fixing a leaky faucet when my son went to answer the door. But I was lucky, and my son was lucky, and today, long after the murder, finding myself imagining that damp cellar room, peering down into it as if looking into a miniature cellar, I don't hear shots or see blood on the steps. I hear only soft sounds: my breath as I sit with my book, Diana's stocking feet as she pads along the hall above me, and water running into the bathtub as she gets ready to give our baby a bath.

The landlord, who owned a little doughnut shop, died many years ago. They had once lived in that house. His wife had Alzheimer's disease and sometimes arrived bewildered at our door, wanting us to let her in. She too is gone. If I were building a miniature of that house I would stand her at the door, clenching her purse in both hands, her hat on crooked.

The flowers that grew along the driveway are thirty years past their season, and their beds are only dust today. My friend who painted the

Rolling Stones has died. Olga and Alida, having survived the horrors of war to come to the new world and take a little pleasure in simple flowers, they too are gone. I've noticed lately when I've driven past that the porch has begun to slope toward the street as if to pour our ghosts out the front door and onto the buckled sidewalk. And I am not that young father any more, but a man in his sixties who is slowly becoming a baffled old woman who hammers and hammers at a door, wanting to be let in again, knowing by instinct that something good must still be waiting just inside.

SYDNEY LEA

# Black Marks

On this Sunday morning in March, I've been walking the Snake Road, its tar prematurely dry; our winter was small this year. I kneel to consider twinned, dark marks on the pavement, snakelike themselves. They were probably made last night by some adolescent burning rubber, as my buddies and I used to say as beer-crazed boys.

I won't continue another mile or so to the turn where a beater Ford Ranger went out of control two decades ago. A pair of kids—the one named Willy driving, Evan his passenger—slid across the macadam and smacked into a pine there. My wife, to whom I'd been married only twelve years back then, was heading the other way in the very next car on the scene, our two-year-old daughter with her. How sadly different my life would have been if those two had turned up mere seconds earlier.

Wife and child watched Willy as he shook his friend by the shoulders, crying, "Evan, wake up!" Evan would not wake up.

I rise to my feet and feel my stomach pitch. How sadly different, too, some other lives might have been if a certain child had walked ten feet more closely behind the small, car-chasing terrier I ran over at seventeen. I see that girl clearly, mouth gaped in a wail. I think of the fear that must have gripped her mother, behind her, clutching a trowel.

Spring's familiar flocks of snow geese have begun to course over. Their doglike yelps sound woeful enough, yet the birds strike me as icons of life. Those that survive will come by again in late October. I imagine an autumn rain, this buckled roadbed a welter of mud and yellow leaves. I will smell that chamois odor of decaying sweet fern, which certifies the absolute death of summer.

I sometimes think we endure, if we do, by accident. Evan's drunkard grandfather had given the underage boys their liquor. One afternoon, years earlier, the old man knocked his wife out cold on the broken ground where she tended her flowers. Or so I'd once heard from Luther, the wretched couple's son, like his own wretched son gone to a too-early grave. Luther, black sheep among black sheep, overdosed on OxyContin, and Evan gone now too. The sins of the fathers, indeed, as is written.

Today's March 1, which happens to be my wife's birthday. By now there have been twenty of which she might not have been conscious, nor that daughter either. I turn from these tracks on this tiny roadway, having been reminded how everything in this world awaits a defining moment.

# The Book of Knowledge

In 1952, when I was three, my parents bought a set of *The Book of Knowledge*, ten hefty volumes bound in maroon leather, each filled with questions from "The Department of Wonder." Like sentinels posted at the gates of wisdom, the books stood proudly on a shelf between the glossy forelocks of equestrian bookends, each volume embossed with a golden torch. It was, my mother explained in one of the hundreds of letters she wrote to my grandmother, a purchase as much for her as for her boy: "I have really been enjoying it. I've been studying the subjects of music and art so far." Reading in *The Book of Knowledge* was one of the ways she fended off the depression that swept over her during these years, especially when my father traveled. "That is how I've been spending some of my evening while Max is away."

*The Book of Knowledge* evolved from *The Children's Encyclopædia*, the inspiration of Arthur Mee, born to a working-class family in Stapleford, England, whose formal education ended when he was fourteen. Questions posed by Mee's daughter, Marjorie, were the direct inspiration for the encyclopedia. In his letter "To Boys and Girls Everywhere," published in the first volume of *The Children's Encyclopædia*, Mee writes that Marjorie's mind was filled with "the great wonder of the Earth. What does the world mean? And why am I here? Where are all the people who have been and gone? Where does the rose come from? Who holds the stars up? What is it that seems to talk to me when the world is dark and still?" Mee's wife had "thought and thought" about these questions "and answered this and answered that until she could answer no more. Oh for a book that will answer all the questions!" she complained. *The Children's Encyclopædia* was born.

What set his book apart, Mee explained, was the belief in children's eagerness for knowledge and their capacity for wonder. But he knew that his book also filled an important gap for adults. It "had the power to make plain to the average man, woman, and child the aspects and imports of the problems which the very men who had wrested them from nature could not make so plain." It offered up the mysteries of the few for the rest of us. By the time *The Children's Encyclopædia* had evolved into *The Book of Knowledge*, Mee had added the "Department of Wonder," and each volume contained sections devoted to "wonder questions" like the ones Marjorie posed to her perplexed parents.

For my mother, who had dropped out of nursing school when she was nineteen to marry my father, the gaps in her education were becoming an embarrassment. Born Roberta Maxine Reinhardt and called Bobbie, she had been the darling of her parents and of the small Kansas town of Glen Elder where she grew up. Pretty and bright, she made nearly perfect grades but not without help. "As I remember I used to make A on every theme you wrote for me," she mentioned in one letter to my grandmother. A little unsure of herself when she entered nursing school in 1946, she created elaborate study schedules, but soon she found that she was good at school and liked her classes, which included American literature as well as courses in child guidance, microbiology, the history of nursing, nursing arts, physical education, home economics, and something called "the Home Project." As she pursued her studies she became more confident: "I'm so thrilled about my subjects. There is an awfully lot of reading to do, but it is interesting." Anxieties about how hard the classes would be proved unfounded and she flourished in the program. "I've been wondering how I would like my nursing subjects—it is play to study them."

After marrying, that confidence in her abilities slowly eroded, especially when my father joined the pharmaceutical company American Cyanamid as a managing director and our young family moved from Dodge City, Kansas, to Nanuet, New York, a suburb of the city. In the 1952 letter about buying *The Book of Knowledge*, she describes a lavish dinner party served by maids. "Of course the conversation got around to operas and plays," she complains, "as it always does here"; she did not feel comfortable again, she adds wryly, "until they all started talking about the pigs in Missouri." She admits that it was "an educational evening"

and, after it was over, "a nice experience to have" but laments that she was caught off guard: "had I known beforehand I would have studied up." *The Book of Knowledge* was her way to 'study up.' "I've done very little brain work since I got out of school," she writes. "All you have to do is move around and meet new people to realize how dumb you really are." For my mother the gilded volumes of *The Book of Knowledge* served as a self-help textbook on culture.

For me they were simply wondrous. I liked to lie on my stomach on the floor in front of the bookcase, my feet kicked up behind me, just taking in the strange and glorious pictures: color illustrations in soft pastels from *The Book of the Dead*, which was left, the caption inaccurately tells us, "in the tombs of Egypt for the dead to read." A black-and-white cartoon of the globe in a ball cap, beaded in sweat and pulling down on a scale, to illustrate "Volume, Mass, and Weight." A four-page spread called "The Glory of the Grass" with detailed colored drawings of foxtail, rye, oat, timothy, manna, bearded darnel, broom, barley, reed, and wheat. Another four-page spread of "Beautiful Birds of the World," with a peacock in full array on the first page, surrounded by a Blue Crowned Motmot, a Leadbeater's Cockatoo, and a Groove Pygmy Goose, along with nine other brightly colored birds. And in Volume Eighteen, the fourteen-page spread of butterflies and moths and beetles that begins with a Peacock Eye, an American species of butterfly, and concludes, 236 individual illuminated drawings later, with the European beetle called the Great Agrilus.

The famous frontispiece to the first edition of *The Children's Encyclopædia* shows a boy in knickers and girl in bloomers looking into a universe: a system of eight planets, alongside comets, stars, and galaxies, surrounding the sun, which sends a halo of sunbeams out into the darkness. But the inside cover illustration of each volume of *The Book of Knowledge* that I grew up with suggests a similar grandeur with a modern twist. In it, a boy in shorts and girl wearing a skirt stand alert and excited on a red book floating toward an island of worldly wonders, including a telescope, a pagoda, totem poles, a factory, the faces of Mount Rushmore, and a giraffe. Overhead soar a rocket, a dual-propeller commercial airliner, a helicopter, and some sort of futuristic V-shaped spacecraft. "Here is a gift to the nation," Arthur Mee wrote to the readers of *The Book of Knowledge*.

"It is a story that will never fail for children who will never tire; and it is the best of all stories, told in the simplest words, to the greatest of all ends."

And what is the end? On April 6, 1961, when I was twelve, my mother drove into a park near Deerfield, Illinois, where we lived at the time, and killed herself with a gun. Whatever knowledge she had gleaned from those books, as well as all that was left in her heart and mind of love, joy, sorrow, and agony, was swept away too. The obliteration ripples out from there. My father did not talk about the past, and the subject of my mother rarely came up after my father remarried and the family began anew. I remembered almost nothing of my life or her life before the suicide except a few vivid flashes—images, really—with the rest blown away by her death, and for years I was resigned to my ignorance and, perhaps, even content with it. I grew up, raised by a caring stepmother who probably got more than she bargained for when she took on, along with my dad, my brother and me, and I acquired a wonderful older stepsister who socialized me, and we did not dwell on our history. I went to college and married, and when I was in my thirties, my grandmother gave me the letters of my mother, but by then I had a job and a family with four children. I worked hard and was not depressed or suicidal. Why would I want to read the letters of a mother who killed herself before I could even get to know her?

When I turned sixty, I was given a new office at work, and I used that change as an opportunity to discard files, magazines, and correspondence— the stuff that I had accumulated over the years. I threw away books that I thought I would never part with. My wife, Barbara, gave me a rule of thumb: if you feel the urge to sneeze when you open it, toss it out. In the end I threw away or recycled fourteen large plastic bags of junk, and I drove back from the transfer station feeling lighter. But when I got to the boxes of my mother's letters, I could not throw them away. I held them in my hand—they were dusty and definitely gave me the urge to sneeze—but I could not shove them in a plastic trash bag.

I made a vow that if I kept them I would read them.

So, at the age of sixty-one, I bought a set of the 1952 edition of *The Book of Knowledge*, like the ones that I'd had as a child, and I read my

mother's letters. Barbara raised an eyebrow when I mentioned *The Book of Knowledge*, a twenty-volume set bound in ten thick books, since she had been trying for several years to weed old books from our shelves at home, just as I had at the office.

"Are you going to *buy* them?" she asked. I think she was making soup or maybe spaghetti.

"They have a set for $350 at Amazon."

Barbara, poker-faced, just kept stirring the pot.

Eventually I found a complete set available at AbeBooks online for $150 and put in my order. Sheepishly, I promised Barbara that I would keep the box they came in and resell them online as soon as I had finished with them.

When they arrived they were as magnificent as I had remembered, each handsome volume feeling heavy in the hand. Substantial, I thought, cracking open the cover of Volume One. Quotations by the likes of Louis Bromfield, Eleanor Roosevelt, aviation pioneer Captain Harry F. Guggenheim, and Lou Little, the head football coach at Columbia University, added authority to weight.

"The poet Marlowe might have been thinking of *The Book of Knowledge* when he spoke of 'infinite riches in a little room,'" Mrs. James P. McGranery, a member of the National Executive Committee of the Girl Scouts of the USA, explained.

"There is only one good. That is knowledge," John S. Knight, the publisher of Knight Newspapers, announced, quoting Socrates while glowering at me from his photograph. He added a stern admonition:

"There is only one evil. That is ignorance."

We fanned the books out on the floor and began leafing through them, stopping at the colored spreads, Barbara running her fingers over the brightly illuminated pages. The books spoke of a time after the Second World War when knowledge and progress and hope were allies, a time that she and I remembered dimly now as we ended the first decade of the twenty-first century. Barbara found a page that asked, "Could We Ever Travel to the Moon?" and I cringed at the outdated question, but she smiled. "Listen to this," she said later, reading at random an article in Volume Thirteen called "Government and Taxes," which argued that

simply taxing in proportion to income, as the Constitution says, is unfair. "Taxes should be levied in such a way as to establish equality of sacrifice between rich and poor."

"Equality of sacrifice," she repeated, "imagine that."

Before long she was eyeing the bookshelves we had been hoping to clear. "We'll make space right there."

"These books are pretty out of date," I said apologetically, opening a volume and resisting the urge to sneeze.

She was thinking about our new grandchildren.

"They could stand to read this."

She rapped the book with her knuckle. Decision made.

In retrospect I regret that I waited so long to read my mother's letters. There were 406 in all, carefully arranged by my grandmother in shoeboxes. Over time, as the family leafed through them, they had gotten out of order and had been placed in different areas of the house before most were carted off to the office. It was not until six months after I finally brought them home that I spread them out on a pool table and put them in order. I boxed them and marked off each of the years with strips of manila cardboard, tickets to the past extending back in time from 1960 to 1945, and one chilly morning in November 2010, some fifty years after my mother's death, I started to read the entire set through.

My mother's writing style is direct and friendly, and—since she saw my grandmother as a confidante, especially in the early years of her marriage—often candid. As she got older, and more troubled, she tried to hide her depression, but she had become so used to confiding in her mother that the truth comes out anyway in the letters. As I read about her life, my memories, lying like ashes in me, were sparked. The steady chronology of a letter or two each week allowed me to place the few vivid memories I had left in a context so that I saw how they fit and understood why they, of all in my lost past, had remained as a glowing remnant. My dad, in that time before I remembered him, came back clearly as well. Most of all, I got to know my mother at last—not the stereotypical fifties mother forced to play an uncomfortable role, though she was that, but the real person with her achievements and flaws and hopes and many, many fears.

As she married, left college, moved away from home, and had children of her own, I watched her change and grow, darken and retreat. The return addresses evolved from "Bobbie Reinhardt," a young nursing student in 1942 at the University of Kansas Hospital in Kansas City, to "Mrs. M. J. Harvey" in Dodge City in 1947. By the time the family had moved to New York, she dropped the "Mrs." altogether, and in Chicago in 1959 she retreated entirely by writing the return address using my father's name and title: "Dr. M. J. Harvey."

Every letter stood alone—capturing a particular time and, more important, mood—and yet each danced in consort with the others. As my mother married and had children, the mobile of her life grew heavier and more complicated, with many moving parts, and by the time of her death the structure groaned under the weight of accumulated anxieties and regrets. Armed with letters and a children's encyclopedia, I was determined to know who this woman was, and, with luck, claim a legacy of beauty and wonder from a devastating event.

Wonder Question: "Does the earth make a sound as it rotates?"

"No," *The Book of Knowledge* answers, the "earth spins silently in space. It spins all in one piece, and that means not only the solid earth and the waters but the blanket of air above us as well. All spins round, never pausing." Like some enormous Carny ride, the globe rotates at a thousand miles per hour, and yet the mobile over my shoulder hangs motionless by a thread and going nowhere, expectant and watchful as an acrobat holding a pose. "If the air stood still we might hear the earth whooshing through it," but the "air is part of the earth and moves with it," creating the illusion of stillness.

Even if we could step off of the earth—like the boy and girl in the illustration for *The Children's Encyclopædia*—and stand on some promontory separate from the planet and listen hard, we would not hear the earth spinning. The scene would unfold like a slow-motion silent film, the incredible rush of the whirling planet registering on our eyes like the imperceptible motion of the slow hand on a watch and on our ears as a held breath. The other celestial objects would lumber along in mute procession with vast stretches of nothing at all between them. To hear any

sound, "we must have vibrations, or waves, or trembling." But space is a nearly empty vacuum, and no matter how dark and gloomy and terrifying emptiness may be, trembling requires "something substantial" to be felt.

In space there is "no substance to be set trembling."

When she was five or six, Roberta trembled beside a toy tricycle that was built to look like a single-prop airplane. My grandparents took a Brownie photograph of her standing beside the new toy, with the shingled side of their house as the background. The front of the trike had a propeller with a circle of pistons behind it and the tailpiece at the end had numbers stamped in it to make it look authentic. The cockpit swooped down so that the rider could sit down completely and pedal. The toy is large—longer than she is tall—and it is clearly made of metal, with dimples where bolts attach the wheels to the body. The wheels are inflatable rubber tires with shiny metal hubcaps. In the photograph my mother poses proudly, wearing Mary Janes, stockings, a pleated dress, a V-neck sweater, a beaded necklace, and a knit cap. She is dressed for cold weather and, since she was born in June, this is probably not a birthday gift but a Christmas present. A shadow of some sort, perhaps the shadow of a tree, rises like a thin stream of smoke from behind her shoulder and spreads across the shingles of the wall, the adumbration folding ominously, like the black contrail of a plane in trouble, and turning on her. Hurtling through space at a thousand miles an hour, my mother may be trembling a bit from the cold, but otherwise she does not feel the future rushing toward her. She cannot see the crash ahead. The air, after all, is moving too, at one with a planet of rocks and stones and trees and spinning silently in a universe largely without substance. The girl who is my mother leans casually with her open hand on the wing of the toy while a ribbon of black smoke billows across the shingles behind her. Unaware and smiling, she looks directly at me.

Wonder Question: "Why do faces in some pictures seem to follow us?"

"The rule is very simple," The Book of Knowledge says. "If the sitter is looking at the painter or at the camera, then wherever you stand, he will seem to be looking at you." I lift the photo of my mother beside her new toy and tilt it under the lamp, first to the right and then the left, and her eyes stay on me even though the nose of the airplane seems to bob away

and return, the world of the photo turning on the axis of her eyes. And her smile—yes, it also seems to keep smiling at me, no matter which way I turn the stiff and fading image.

But this rule, as stated here, is not as simple as *The Book of Knowledge* likes our wonders to be. There is the word "seem" in the phrase "he will seem to be looking at you," which is never simple. It drains the ink out of the words around it, appropriating them subjunctively. The little mood shift created by that one word invites supposition, hypothesis, possibility, and desire into the mix, leaving the facts behind. It is the 'seem' of what is not, the 'seem' of absence and longing and despair that these pictures in the end make me feel, a magical 'seem' bringing in its wake the black smoke of an apparent accident that has not happened yet in the photo, but has already happened a long time ago in life. Nothing is looking at me in this photograph, although it is smiling broadly into the camera and trembling slightly in the cold, a trembling I can't feel because of the nothing she is and the nothing between us, and this nothing follows me no matter which way I turn.

Thirty years later, in November 1960, my grandmother "got word" that my mother was in the hospital. I was eleven and we were living in Deerfield, Illinois. The phrase "got word," taken from notes that my grandmother wrote near the end of her life, is portentous. It means that my mother was in no condition to write to her or call her and that my father, whom my grandmother never trusted, had to break the news. If I grow still and close my eyes, I can imagine the sound of the conversation, him offering up the facts through the mixture of sympathy and complaint he used to calm anxious colleagues, and her, with her Kansas reticence, replying in tight-lipped, staccato phrases. I cannot even begin to imagine their words. She and my grandfather "left immediately by train for Deerfield." They stayed with my brother and me until my mother killed herself five months later. My grandmother never talked to me about what happened when my mother was institutionalized for depression, but she did talk to Barbara, who wrote letters to her on a regular basis until my grandmother died in 1986, and who was probably my grandmother's dearest confidante at the end of her life. She told Barbara that when they

released my mother from the hospital, the doctors said that they "had done everything that they could" and were still pessimistic. "When she left the hospital your grandmother knew she would do it," Barbara said when I asked her about it again this morning. She had told me about the conversation before but to make her point clear now she put it this way: "when she left *that morning*" on the day she killed herself, "your grandmother knew she would do it."

After I graduated from college, I asked my father about my mother's death. We were riding in silence in his car early in the morning. It was still dark outside, the only light the blue glow from his dashboard. I know he didn't want to talk about her suicide, but he wanted to answer my questions. Nothing made her happy, he told me, and the doctors could do nothing for her. "They tried everything," he said, an echo of my grandmother's words. He said that she bought a .44 caliber gun, which is a large bore. "She *meant* to do it—to end things." So she drove to the lake and killed herself. It pained him to say this, I could tell. I do not want to underestimate the difficulty of living with someone who is clinically depressed. I know, now, from reading her letters that he tried to make her happy, and he was very good at making others feel happy, but in the long run he could not work that charm on her. He took a long drag from his cigarette, squinted, and stuffed the butt in his ashtray, slowly exhaling the smoke as the car hurtled down the highway, waiting for my next question, but I did not ask any more. We rode silently into a predawn darkness illuminated by the blue light from the dash.

I turn to *The Book of Knowledge* for the answers to questions I didn't ask.

In its 7,606 pages, *The Book of Knowledge* has no entry for 'suicide.' It has no entry for insomnia, alcoholism, or addiction either. There is an entry for ragweed, but not for rage. In the age of anxiety there is no entry for anxiety. No entry for depression without 'Great' in front of it. The entry on sex is limited to plants and flowers. There is no entry for conformity or blandness or dullness or insipidity—and this was the 1950s! Sometimes I wonder about *The Book of Knowledge*. I find an entry for Peter Pan, of course, but none for Cyril Ritchard. No entry for either "Fever" *or* Peggy

Lee. Nothing on the doldrums, the dumps, the mulligrubs, or the blues. No blue funk or the blahs. Nothing on grief—*grief*! No entry for funeral, burial, interment, last rites, cortège, mourners, pallbearers, or pall. No entry for self-murder, self-slaughter, self-destruction, and no entry for self. No entry for hara-kiri (which is a little surprising) or suttee (which is not). There are several entries under medicine, but no cure for despair, despondency, sadness, sorrow, unhappiness, melancholy, or gloom. Doom does not make the pages. Nor agony nor suffering nor woe. In *The Book of Knowledge*, no *woe*!

Wonder Question: "What is everything?"

In the late 1950s, after the doctors try everything else, they strap the patient to a gurney in a hospital room and tape the leads of a heart monitor to her chest. They do not inject her with an anesthetic for pain or use muscle relaxers to reduce the chance of bone fractures and other injuries when the arms, legs, and chest rise against the restraints, but they do place a block in her mouth so that she cannot bite her tongue while the procedure is performed. They attach electrodes on either side of her face at the temples after applying a conductive jelly so that an electrical current will pass into her head and brain more easily. Once she is ready, the doctor turns on a machine that sends a steady stream of electricity into her skull, the current running between the right and left lobe of her brain for twenty seconds, inducing a grand mal seizure and leaving her unconscious, usually for about a half hour. No one knows for sure what happens in her brain as her eyes roll back and her body stiffens. The shock of electricity may slow overly agitated mental activity or dull the brain receptors altering her mood. It may release neuropeptides that ease depression. Or it may cause brain damage. Electroshock therapy helps many people, but, as one critic put it, the procedure is "like playing Russian roulette with your brain."

What is everything in the late 1950s?

It is a very sad figure of speech come true.

When I was a boy, I lay in bed at night listening to my parents fight downstairs. The arguments began as conversation mixed with the clinking sound

of ice in glasses, the words spoken softly, clipped and brittle, dipping to inaudibility when whispered. The clicking of tree branches that is prelude to the storm. Eventually the voices rose until the two were shouting and finally screaming furiously, the sound coming through the walls in unarticulated growls. I don't think they ever hit each other, but sometimes they broke glasses and ashtrays. Dad may have caught her arms when she took drunken, limp, and futile swings at him. I think I saw that once.

I was too afraid when they fought to move and lay wrapped under a cocoon of sheets and blankets that felt like safety but acted like an echo chamber, amplifying and distorting the low rumble until the roar, punctuated now and then with a slam or a crash, spilled over me in torrents. I waited, understanding nothing, absorbing it all. It was only when the yelling was done that the silence after the curses brought me out of bed to the top of the stairs to be sure that they were all right. I usually walked down a few steps and leaned forward, peering between the balusters in order to see into the kitchen, blinking at the fluorescent glare. One night, they caught me. I can picture the tableau even now. My dad, his sleeves rolled up, facing a wall, my mother sitting bent over in a kitchen chair with her back to him, crying in gasps, mascara running down her cheek.

"Oh, no," she says when she turns and sees me running back upstairs.

The next day my father pulled me aside and asked what I had heard.

"You were fighting," I said.

He corrected me. They were not having a fight, but a "discussion."

"That's what adults do," he said.

The memory of the fight followed by the conversation with my dad glows like a lit match in the darkness that is my past. Here is another lit match. From my bedroom I see a light in the hall, soft this time like the glow of a candle. Drawing the twisted sheets up around my shoulders, I hear the clank of the changer and the long wavering whoosh and whir when the needle hits the disc. Clink of ice in a glass. Swoosh of a magazine dropped to the floor. My mother turns up the volume, and soon Peggy Lee's voice fills the house to the corners, beating back gathered silence. I slip out of bed and hide at the top of the stairs to watch. Snapping fingers, slapped cymbal, thud of a double bass and drum, and a lone, plaintive

female voice. Mom's there, her back to me, her face partially visible, lit by the glow of the console. She sways, drink in hand, and sings, watching the record spin, holding the notes out for no one, trying to sound good.

"What a lovely way to burn," she croons. "What a lovely way to burn."

The fights and my mother singing "Fever" happened before my grandparents moved in with us in November 1960. Peggy Lee's new song, "Fever," was the rage, and my parents had the album in their record collection, and this record followed my family long after my mother died. I remember it because of the distinctive cover photograph of Peggy Lee in a black cocktail dress, her pale skin and platinum-blonde hair set against a blue background. The album was released in May 1960. So the fights and the drinking alone while singing into the stereo console must have happened between May of 1960 and November 1960, in the time just before my mother was hospitalized for depression.

During 1959 and 1960 my dad was gone most of the time on business trips and to take courses in business management in St. Louis. My mother thought he was pushing himself too hard. He had developed an ulcer and the doctor recommended that he cut back on his work. "Sometimes I think we are crazy," my mother wrote on June 24, 1959. "The men work at such a pace and under so much pressure." During that time she must have confronted him about the burden that the maddening pace and heavy responsibilities of his job placed on him and the family: "We discussed this when he was sick and I suggested a change, but he said he liked his work and seems to have the ability so we decided it would be a matter of adjusting our leisure time to make it workable."

I know what those 'discussions' sounded like.

In the end my dad had his way. The trips continued. "Max has been in St. Louis," she writes on March 26, 1959, and on July 9 she mentions that "Max has been to St. Louis since Tues. will be back tomorrow." These business trips to St. Louis run like a refrain after 1959 until the letters come to an abrupt halt in June 1960, within a month of the release of the album that contained "Fever." The memory of that song may be the last message I have from my mother since it probably came after the last letter.

My stepmother tells me that she met my father in St. Louis.

My mother seems unaware of infidelity during 1959 and early 1960. In the letters she appears to be genuinely concerned about the problems related to Dad's job. What upset her was the pressure that it put on their lives. It did damage to their friends, some of whom became alcoholics; made my father ill; and saddled my mother with social responsibilities she could not, given her tendency to depression, handle. I sense in all of the letters from that time a desire to live in a way that reduced the strain on everyone, and I suspect that the conversation about leaving the company was real. Dad's ulcer and her exhaustion only reinforced the idea that their loveless marriage had to do with the demands of his career, not another woman, but sometime in June of 1960 she must have figured out that Dad had found love elsewhere, and the letters stopped.

"Captain Smith loved Pocahontas," Peggy Lee sings in a verse that she wrote and added to her version of the song. They "had a very mad affair."

The depression that perched on my mother's life and led to her suicide on April 6, 1961, had many sources, but here is one black wing: On April 29, three weeks and two days after my mother's death, Dad married my step-mother.

"What a lovely way to burn," Peggy Lee growls four times at the end of "Fever." "What a lovely way to burn." In the penultimate line her voice rises in desire on the first word—"What"—before it slides down "a lovely way" to the last note, "burn," dying like the flicker of a heartache.

And the final line? It is a scorched whisper, a beckoning, and a come-on. It is a raised eyebrow. "What a lovely way to burn."

Wonder Question: "Who holds up the stars?"

The stars only appear to be nailed into fixed positions in the dome of the night sky, and no one really holds them up for us. According to *The Book of Knowledge*, "all the stars—in fact, everything in the universe, asteroids, stars, galaxies of stars—all are moving through space at unbelievable speeds of many miles a second." The "great force of gravitation" holds them in check. "Each bit of matter in the universe pulls upon every other particle of matter," and this mutual attraction can cause collisions. "If one body comes too close to another body, the lesser is drawn into the greater and destroyed." But when the velocity of the objects and the

distance between them is right they move in consort. In the end this apparently accidental dance of forces is "responsible for the balance and state of equilibrium in the universe."

On the day of my mother's death, I stared into trembling stars nailed into the night sky of my own making in the hope of achieving some equilibrium. I liked spinning in our newly renovated downstairs den, holding a Jetfire balsa-wood plane that I kept in my hiding place under the stairs. I usually got the planes at the five-and-dime when I visited my grandparents in Glen Elder, but they must have brought the plane to me because this memory is in Illinois. I can still clearly picture these planes that I assembled myself and studied for hours. The wings were stamped with red designs marking the ailerons and flaps and labeled on one side with the name of the company, "Guillow's," and on the other with the name of the plane, "Jetfire." The cockpit was embossed on the fuselage and inside a pilot with a red helmet leaned forward. Meant to ride breezes, the glider is light in my hand. It has a small piece of metal folded over the nose for protection when it crash lands against the walls of the house or the concrete driveway, which is most of the time, but I'm not allowed to fly it indoors, so I hold it and spin, making airplane noises and getting dizzy. When I stop, the room seems to keep on spinning and I wobble a bit as if I have taken a blow. I'm almost twelve. Too old to be doing this sort of thing.

My mother died on the day that my father planned to leave the family for good. In retrospect I know that he intended to start a new life for himself in Kentucky without my mother or my brother and me. Was he anxious or exhilarated when he left the house that April morning, relieved or scared? Or some other emotion I cannot even imagine. If on that day my grandmother knew what my mother would do, he may have too, but I'm not sure because, unlike my shrewd grandmother, he was an optimist. After he left, my mother bought the gun, drove to the park by the lake, stepped out of her car, and pulled the trigger. My grandparents, who knew it would happen, were taking care of my brother and me. When Dad found out, he came back for us.

In memory I was alone downstairs in the newly renovated den, killing time with this spinning game, when my dad arrived and the house began

to fill with neighbors and my parents' friends. I heard the ringing doorbell of each new arrival. The hushed greetings. The whispers. The shuffle of feet over carpet as adults overhead approached each other. I am pretty sure that no one had told me what had happened yet. Dad would do that when we were on the train going to Kentucky. But I knew *something* because I hid under the stairs in my favorite hideaway, where I kept some toys like the balsa *Jetfire,* and sat there a long time before anyone noticed my absence. The points of the nails that had been used to secure the treads to the risers of the stairway protruded overhead. Like stars they glittered in the crawl space, and I looked into them as I listened to the groan in the floorboards. Suddenly it grew silent, and I heard my father call for me. At first his voice was a question, but then, freighted with all of the tension of that day, it became a barked command. Soon others joined in, their anxious voices a keening chorus on my name.

A shadow passed over the risers.

"Who holds the stars up?" Marjorie Mee asked her perplexed mother.

I covered my ears.

Last September, when Barbara and I visited my stepmother, Lou Harvey, in Kentucky, we spent a Saturday morning looking through pictures. Lou—who is nearly eighty—pulled them out of boxes one at a time with her arthritic fingers, stopping occasionally to talk, and the subject came around to my mother.

"No, honey," Lou said, when I asked if my mother bought the gun before that day. I'm sitting across from her at the kitchen table. Barbara, who is standing, stops flipping through pictures, and listens. "She bought it that morning. She killed herself in the park. A policeman saw her and thought it unusual so he watched. She stepped out of the car and then."

Lou puts her finger to her temple and lifts her eyebrows.

"Bam."

I look away. A cat waits in a crouch under the bird feeder in her neighbor's yard.

"Neither of us had anybody," she says, explaining that her first husband was impossible to live with, too. "I had nobody. Your dad had nobody."

Silenced for a moment by that story, we return to the pictures. Many

of them show Lou with my dad through the years, but I pause over one in particular. In it, the two of them are preparing dinner. They both are young, in their thirties. My dad, heavyset in a dark shirt and white warm-up pants, has turned, startled by the picture, and his face, picking up the full impact of the flash, wears a customary carefree and bold look. He's making a salad and is, no doubt, about to tell a joke. The flash explodes like a supernova on the sliding glass door behind him, turning the rest of the glass black.

It is the image of my stepmother that holds my attention, though. She stands in the wood-paneled room, looking young and very pretty in a striped sweater and tight slacks, her nose aquiline and her hair all dark curls. She leans toward my father from behind as if she has some secret to share, but the easy-going intimacy of the photograph keeps no secrets. He came to her in St. Louis for fun, happiness, love, and sex. He came to escape a home full of woe, some of it, no doubt, of his own making—some, but not all. He was leaving us for this, that was the secret, and when my mother figured it out, she gave my brother and me to him, to them, with a single gunshot.

Wonder Question: "What is the sound of everything happening at once?"

"When a gun goes off," *The Book of Knowledge* says, "the flash and the report of the gun occur in the same moment." If we stand at a distance, the flash appears first, as a silent flare in the darkness, and the muffled blow of the sound arrives later, in an echo of the flash. So, if you stand at a safe distance half a mile away when the gun is fired, "you will not hear the sound for nearly half a minute."

"And yet," *The Book of Knowledge* adds, because it is also fond of 'and yet.' "If we are very near the gun, we see the flash and hear the noise at the same time." At that range, you miss nothing. If you hold the gun to your body, you feel everything happening at once, and it reverberates until the trembling stops somewhere at the edge of nothing.

Turning the self into a nothing is a moral conundrum too difficult for *The Book of Knowledge* to crack. A literal self-contradiction, the answer even eluded Jesus. The Catholic poet Dante may have planted the suicides with other violent sinners in a deep ring of hell and tormented the poor souls with winged harpies, but the golden rule is about doing unto oth-

ers, not doing the self in, and on suicide Jesus is silent. It wasn't until the nineteenth century that Immanuel Kant, whom some consider the wisest European philosopher, explained the immorality of suicide with his "categorical imperative." When faced with a moral dilemma, Kant argued, you should act so that your action becomes universal law. When you lift a gun to your temple to pull the trigger, you must imagine that the hands of all of the people in the world are required by your version of the moral law to lift a gun to their temples too. No one escapes the bullet in this game of Russian roulette. "Do you like this vision of the world?" Kant asks.

I give it a try and see my mother in the hall of mirrors within her moral imagination, every hand in the world holding a .44 lifted at her command, and she pulls the . . . but, no, that is not right.

Suicide is about the survivors.

Suicide is two boys and a father hurtled into darkness at the speed of a locomotive. The boys, sitting on the plush pile seat of a railroad car headed away from their home in Deerfield, Illinois, will never see their mother again, rarely speak of her again, rarely think about her again. Their father—a big man, bulging out of his suit—sits down on his haunches in front of them. Facing into the darkness ahead, he has been through hell and has been given one more impossible task, but he is a man who believes in taking charge and wants to fix things even when he can't, so he will do his job. The boys are headed backward into the night, the lights outside the window floating away from them, and I don't know if they are afraid or in shock or just tired. Who knows what the younger one remembers? He is eight years old and has penetrating blue eyes. The older one remembers his dad looking down but only for a moment and then, as he always did when he spoke to people, looking directly into his sons' eyes and saying the impossible. I remember him speaking, his voice a mesmerizing low rasp conveying confidentiality this time as well as command, and I remember him reaching out with his arms to kind of hem us in as he spoke, his large arms coming out of the sleeves of his suit a bit as he extended them. I remember—or I think I do—the maroon plush of the seats in the Pullman and the windows black as we rode into the open fields of Illinois at night.

But I have no idea what he said.

Someone took pictures at my mother's funeral. I found them in a wicker basket with other photos and memorabilia. Several show the graveside service conducted on the open prairie of Kansas, the land that my mother wrote of "going back to" in her memory while living in New York. The photographs are mixed in with a nearly identical set of pictures from my grandfather's funeral, which came three weeks after hers, including a particularly sad one of my mother's and grandfather's graves side by side, her blossoms windblown and slightly wilted beside his new batch of greenery and white.

But the hardest pictures for me show my mother's open casket surrounded by a shower of flowers, a mound of red and white carnations, daisies, and pink mums. The coffin is draped in a spray of red roses, and my mother's body lies in a bed of satin, the opening of the casket draped in a transparent mesh. The picture of her face is very small, but I can see that her hair is pulled back from her forehead in tight curls. She wears a suit with a silk scarf at the neck, exposing the base of her throat. I find a magnifying glass that I keep with my dictionary, and examine the picture up close. The cotton and plaster of Paris that the morticians used to reconstruct the face make her cheeks look puffy and the dermal wax and restorative cosmetics hide her wounds and bruises under a shiny pastiness betraying the illusion of life. There is something wrong with the mouth, which has been stretched wide into a smile after the mortician pulled together the scalp, and the eyebrows are heartbreaking, dark and perfectly arched like wings, as if, after all, death took her by surprise, and maybe—who knows?—it did.

My gaze settles at last on her eyes. Leaning forward into the lens to see more clearly, I tilt the page this way and that for a better look, before slumping back into my chair.

Faces in photos don't follow us if their eyes are closed.

Until I read her letters, those closed eyes were my mother's story, an image that I carried until I became a sixty-year-old man. And yet—because there is always this 'and yet'—there is more, much more, and it is in the letters, not the photographs.

"We took our first drive yesterday," my mother writes on Monday, November 20, 1950, from a brick bungalow in Monsey, New York, when

she and Dad first moved away from Kansas to live in the Northeast. "The scenery around here is gorgeous. We took the Hudson River Drive on the way up." She explains that she is sending pictures, and I find the colored postcards in my wicker box, stiff and pretty colorized photographs of West Point and the river, but her words say more than the pictures. "The river is very large, calm, and beautiful," she writes. Having lived in the prairie all of her life, she is unaccustomed to seeing large bodies of water and is filled with wonder. "Saw the ships and were quite thrilled—first large ones I've ever seen. We took Bear Mountain Drive home. We were sorry we didn't get to see all of this because it got dark before we got home. It is completely dark by five here."

My mother weathered the mental cyclone of depression much of her adult life, but there are moments in the letters when she paints, in words, another self—whole and wonder-struck—and the whirlwind stops. These moments often happen outdoors, or while looking outdoors, and record a joyous embrace of a wide and open sky that may have evoked feelings of the family farm in Kansas where she and my grandparents picnicked while she was growing up. They are sublime glimpses of grandeur, often bounded by darkness—the blackness that finally claimed her, creeping in at the edges—but they are also marked by a brilliance of light and an expansive vista that is exhilarating. The sights transported her, lifted her momentarily out of the troubles of life; they helped her to be her best self and reengage with family.

In one letter she describes a flight back from Kansas in prose reminiscent of her descriptions of seeing the Hudson River for the first time. "Had such a smooth flight from K. C. to N. Y. Slept part of the way. The plane was very crowded when we boarded so I had to sit on the inside seat of the three[-seat] row which was fine except I couldn't see out too well but thought the view of K. C. and Chicago were gorgeous. Looked like a huge Christmas display." She explains that she arrived early at LaGuardia and took the time to freshen up before meeting us. "When I walked out I saw Max & boys—called to them. The boys were so surprised for a second—I squatted on my knees—Ronnie said, 'Mommy' and gave me a big hug. I hugged Steve with my other arm. He put his arms around my neck and said 'Hello, Mommy.'"

After my mother died I forgot the sensation of her touch and the sound of her voice. I could not hug a shadow. I could not fill her silence with my words.

Who is suicide? She was suicide.

She became her death.

And the pictures, hundreds of curled shavings of the past in a basket, did not bring her back. Even when my mother gazed directly into the camera, I knew that she was looking into a future that was already over, with shadows like gun smoke folded into the glossy black-and-white. I needed a voice speaking in her present, not one whispering to posterity, a voice animated by the desire to capture the present for someone alive. *That* is the voice I heard in the letters. When I read them, I got to know her—for the first time, really—know her and miss her. Miss *her*, not some made-up idea of her. The pain, which had been nothing more than a dull throb, changed in character, becoming softer, more diffuse, and ardent like heartache.

"They each held on to my hands," my mother wrote, describing our triumphal exit from the airport at LaGuardia. "They kept talking to me about how happy they were that I was home—and sorta beamed."

Wonder Question: "Could we ever travel to the moon?"

"We know everything we need to know for the planning of such a trip," *The Book of Knowledge* claimed optimistically in 1952. Its writers argue that the first real problem will be creating a rocket with enough thrust to allow a "space-ship" to reach "escape velocity," the speed required to lift the ship beyond the gravity of the earth and let it float, unimpeded, toward the moon. The formula for determining this velocity is too complicated for *The Book of Knowledge* to make clear, so it asks that we accept on faith that by means "of a computation belonging to the realm of higher mathematics" the velocity required for a rocket to rise into space and escape the gravitational pull of the spinning earth is "7 miles per second." Once a rocket can attain that speed the "earth's gravity is powerless" to pull it down, and the rocket can drift into the vast emptiness of silent space, leaving the weight of its earthly burdens behind.

Five years later, the Soviets rocketed a satellite into orbit.

At midnight on the last day of January in 1957, my mother and father

woke me to watch Sputnik 2 cross the dome of the sky, and I don't remember it happening at all. I do remember Sputnik 1. We were still living in our house on Caravella Lane in Nanuet, New York, and many from the neighborhood, including my mother and me, had lined up on the dead-end street in front of our houses to see the first satellite propelled into orbit, but the memory of the second satellite is gone.

It was an anxious time internationally, causing Americans, like my mother, to have mixed feelings about the space race. "It is a shame," she wrote, that "the great event of launching a satellite into space has to be overshadowed with the fear that the Russians are a great deal ahead of us scientifically." At the dawn of the nuclear age, she lamented that the Soviets had "perfected the intercontinental missile" and wondered about the ability of America to prevail. "It makes us all realize we have been complacent." Despite these anxieties, she wrote that we were all "very excited" and that Sputnik 1 was a "spectacular sight."

Sputnik 2 caused a stir because it carried Laika, the dog, but by this time our family had a new set of anxieties to deal with. After seven years of living in New York, we had moved out of our house in Nanuet and were living somewhere near our new house on Warrington Road in Deerfield, Illinois. Construction had been delayed and my parents had not yet moved in, but they were checking on it daily. "This is the finishing work that makes a house a home," my mother wrote. I am sure, with the move, the delay, and the new house, that this was a busy and exhausting time for my father and mother, but I must have pestered my parents to let me see Sputnik 2 and they relented. "Steve has been so interested in the satellite that we promised him we would wake him if it did orbit."

In my imagination they both wake me, my mother nudging me quietly while shushing me so as not to wake my brother, my father standing behind her holding my coat. I rub my eyes awake and see their faces glowing in the half-light of the room, my dad waving us toward the bedroom door. Outside it is cold—this is February, north of Chicago—but it must have been clear. The three of us walk into a grassy clearing away from trees and train our eyes on the evening sky.

Dad lights a cigarette for my mother and then for himself, the glow from the match illuminating their faces against the night sky for a moment

like two crescent moons. He shakes out the match and takes a long draw, letting the smoke out slowly. My mother fiddles with her cigarette before taking a quick puff, pulling her coat around her. We wait in the cold briefly, me standing between them, my mother pulling me toward her for warmth.

Suddenly, it appears. "Over there," my dad says, squinting from the smoke, and we turn to face east. The tree line forms a black horizon and above it the Milky Way shimmers in the chilly air.

Dad kneels down, pointing up for me to see. The cigarette at the tips of his fingers traces the arc against the sky. My mother sees it too and, putting an arm on my shoulder, she leans forward to be sure that I have found it. I follow my dad's arm to the spot among the stars and locate it at last, not the satellite itself, which is too small, but the casing, a tiny oblong of light, tumbling silently across the constellations nailed into the night sky. It flip-flops in a regular rhythm, like a heartbeat, without glittering, and, despite its size, glows with a white-bright incandescence. In her letters my mother calls this satellite "Muttnik"—a phrase in the press at the time—because of the dog inside, but it is hard to think of a dog now, or anything else, living in this slug of pure light.

I cannot imagine that night sky now without creating metaphors from the time three years later that I hid under the stairs and looked at the nails driven into the treads overhead, that coffin-lid of stars that still haunts me as one of the few vivid memories of that time. Thinking of it now, the other memories come flooding back as well. Of me at the top of the stairs watching my mother crying at the kitchen table, while my dad stands off to the side. Of me stepping out of my bedroom to see my mother sing "Fever" into the record console with a drink in her hand. No, those thoughts—those precious and horrible clues—don't go away, but they also don't erase that night, lost to memory but captured in a letter that I almost didn't read, when my parents and I, somewhere in Illinois, stood in a darkened field together and looked into the heavens. I picture the tableau now like some illustration out of *The Book of Knowledge*, with me standing in my coat and flanked by my parents, my dad pointing and my mother with an arm around me, while the three of us gaze into the night sky with wonder.

"This is," my mother wrote, "a fabulous age."

ANGELA MORALES

# Riding in the Dark

Typically, I wake up before dawn. I can't help it. Most mornings my eyes open at 4:45 without an alarm clock and then my legs start twitching. The best solution I've found to my early morning angst is to get on my bike and start riding. Usually I'll ride my bike in the dark to the base of the mountains near my house, and because the road slants uphill, it's slow and grueling. Each revolution of my feet requires conscious effort, and some mornings, I wonder what fool tendencies live inside me to make me want to give up the safety and warmth of my down comforter, all for the thrill of creeping through the darkness like some criminal. I pass through deserted intersections, no need to stop. The only people out now: a few solitary runners, newspaper delivery drivers, and the random insomniacs. In the silence of morning, the streetlights change from red to green with a low hum and two clicks. Farther up the road, though, it gets wilder. Cars disappear, thank goodness, for nothing spoils good darkness like the shock of headlights in the eyes. The only light comes from the dim amber street lamps over which tower cobweb-covered pine trees, over which tower pinpoints of stars. Here I must hone in on the senses: my vision narrows to the white disc of light in front of my tire produced by my bike light, and my ears tighten up. If I shift my light upward a bit, my vision expands to a crescent that reveals the undersides of bushes and the full width of the street, but only faintly, as if looking through a thin, lacey veil.

Skunks, from what I've seen, don't care a thing about humans. I've ridden close to many foraging skunks, though they barely even glance my

way—too busy are they rooting for black widows and earthworms and searching for pizza crusts and rotten bananas in people's yards. Some mornings, I'll come upon a skunk—easy to spot in darkness, that white stripe waddling next to the curb, nose to the ground—and I'll ride alongside it until it notices me, evident by a tilt of whiskers and small black eyes in a sidelong glance. If a skunk glances at you, you'd best move away, but slowly, coolly. You've got to love skunks for their adorable natures: one second they're ambling along, cute as stuffed animals, and the next second their tails shoot up, heads draw back and whoosh! A skunk spray is the equivalent of an involuntary scream. And skunks, like absent-minded professors, startle easily. They sink so deeply into their business that they forget to notice the big picture. Then, if one sprays—usually at some rogue raccoon—I'll have to pedal right on through, choking my way into the cloud of doom—no choice but to breathe it in and marvel at the potency of their skunk-y weapon.

Month after month, our sky—tight as a drum with only a few meager twists of clouds—refuses to rain. Even the oak trees creak and moan with thirst, and if you live near oak trees, you know that nothing short of a blast of napalm can kill an oak. (For years, I've been trying to kill a volunteer oak that's been growing in a bad spot in my backyard. So far, the oak is winning.) The rivers and creeks have dried up long ago. If you knock on the ground it sounds hollow, like an old, clay jar.

One time, just as I round a bend into the darkest, most strenuous stretch of my ride, three full-grown coyotes appear in my headlight. They stand in the middle of the road, hackles raised, fur billowing in the breeze. What had they been up to? Their eyes glint red as they look at me—a weird, slow-moving mess of helmet and wheels. In previous run-ins with coyotes, they, always skittish, dart off nervously into the darkness—embarrassed, almost. But these, these three—they stand their ground. They look perfect as a museum display—poised, regal. How beautiful and how terrifying they are in my circle of light, daring me, almost, to come closer. What dream could be better than this? Anything you see at 5:00 a.m. has the

qualities of the subconscious—both vivid and remote, real and unreal. What if I ditch the bike, grow fur, and run away with them into the canyon? Ah, but then there's this: Who would take care of my human children? Who would teach my morning classes if I turned into a coyote and disappeared without a trace?

As I enter pitch darkness, I pull my headphones off. My own ragged breathing fills my ears—that, and the sound my tires make as they grind into the asphalt. I've learned to rely much more on my hearing. My mother, who lives nearby, does not approve of my morning rides, but what can she do? I am an adult, after all. So whenever I'm up here at the scary juncture, I hear her voice: Do you have a death wish? Are you sick in the head? One morning, as I'm struggling along next to a long stretch of foliage—sagebrush, oleander, nightshade—a botanical hodgepodge of native and non-native, I'm focusing on the illuminated patch of asphalt in front of my tire when I hear a quick rustling of leaves, and some snapping twigs. I jump, thinking, *What the hell was that?* I've never heard such a noise. It's a big noise, and it feels like a warning.

Then I see it. Maybe ten feet beyond my right arm, nestled in some bushes, appears a pair of luminous golden eyes. These eyes, almond-shaped and glowering, are big—much bigger than the eyes of any animal I've seen here before. The pale creature crouches low in the bushes, though its eyes remain fixed on me—utterly focused. And it's BIG. Then it registers. In such moments, your synapses fire up, traveling deep and quick into the recesses of your brain like fast-motion root filaments in search of water. In a second, you attempt to connect what you see with what you hear and what you've learned in a human lifetime: tattered library books, National Geographic, a zoo cage, a past life, whatever you can conjure up.

Before you: yellow eyes, crouching form.

Mountain lion.

Error. Error. Error.

In the time it takes for my brain to spark this thought—five or six seconds at most—I twist my handlebars away in one violent jerk and my

left foot hits the ground. I fumble for the pedal as it spins around, and I struggle to regain my balance. Then I hightail it back down the hill wondering how much pounding one human heart can take before it implodes.

Later, I study up on mountain lions and read that they are attracted to moving, sparkling objects, much in the way that housecats lunge at twine and plastic balls. In Southern California, nearly all the mountain lion attacks have been on hikers, joggers, and mountain bikers. Reports of these attacks often include testimony from family members or friends who commonly note, with surprise, the outstanding health of the victim—how he or she had been in great shape—strong, capable of running. It's the movement that attracts the animal. Imagine the lion's perspective: a clumsy creature ambling up a hill—half-human, half-machine, twinkling lights, squeaking gears—a big fat toy, an invitation to play.

Just to clarify: I'm much more afraid of humans than of any other animal. Once I watched a true crime show about a woman out riding her bike in a wooded park when a guy leaps out of the bushes, whacks her with a baseball bat, drags her behind a tree, strangles her, and then steals her bike. What kind of animal does that? One morning a pickup truck, old and rattly, slows, passes me, slows again. Truck stops. Idles. Just me and him and a mountain road. *That fucker's gonna kill me*, I think indignantly. I know that a very fine line separates stupidity and bravery, but nonetheless, I put my foot down. Literally. My little light shines on his dented bumper. I cross my arms and glare at his rearview mirror. Then I send him my strongest fuck you vibes. For a minute it's a standoff. Foolish on my part, but I swear I won't move another inch. *I'll be goddamned if some sick bastard is going to kill me today*, I say to myself. This is for me and for her, that woman who ended up behind the tree. Luckily, the truck rumbles on its way.

A popular saying: It appeared as if out of nowhere. Recently I read about a teenage surfer who was mauled by a great white shark. His friend, who

Check Out Receipt

Wednesday, June 1, 2022 12:31:44 PM
80834

Item: 31183200047543
Title: River teeth : twenty years of creative no
nfiction
Call no.: 818.5408 R
Due: 06/22/2022

Total items: 1

You just saved $24.95 by using your
library today.
Free to Be All In
Late fees no longer
assessed for overdue items
Ask for details or visit bcpl.info

witnessed the attack, told reporters, "Suddenly it [the shark] appeared as if out of nowhere." But really, everywhere is somewhere. Even nowhere is somewhere. Nowhere is the dark space outside the edges of your light and, most likely, many somethings lie in that somewhere. This is my thinking when it comes to my early-morning bike rides. There is no such thing as out of nowhere. Something can and will appear and it will have come from somewhere. And as for the poor boy who was mauled by the shark—I see an update in the newspaper that this morning his friends held a funeral at sea. In the sea. In the photo, a group of teenagers sits atop their surfboards at the approximate spot where the boy was torn apart by the shark. They've bowed their heads in prayer, ankles kicking just beneath the waves. But where is the great white shark? Is he still nowhere? We now know that the great white is, in fact, somewhere. Will a large, shiny, and very visible fin appear, first from a distance, and will it approach slowly, zigzagging though the water? Will those kids on their surfboards then mentally associate a triangular shark's fin with an actual shark? At this point will they perceive danger? Will they then imagine the music from Jaws? Will they then swim frantically back to shore? Will they then be safe? If so, we will have a situation in which the shark did not appear out of nowhere.

In the city, this is how we learn about local wildlife. I spot an unfamiliar bump on the side of the road—most likely an animal hit by a car. As I pedal closer, I see what is, indeed, an animal and that the animal is moving—though unnaturally, as if it is being moved. Quaking. I get off my bike and lean it on its kickstand, positioning my headlight down onto a mass of rumpled, bloodied fur. Dead opossum. Her pointed, opened snout exposes razor-sharp white teeth, and her lips have drawn back in a frozen snarl. But something wiggles beneath the fur on her belly. Her fur shifts and ripples, and for a second I think in a panic: *zombie!* Then a tiny pink head pokes out from the opossum's pouch. Small as a snail, the pink, hairless possum claws at the air, nudging its head back into her belly, eyes still sealed shut. A few seconds later, another visceral pink head pushes out, and then another. They squirm against her body, mewling, so young

that delicate blue veins appear beneath their skin. I crouch low, peering at them. I count seven babies in all. Maybe eight. I can't move. I am looking at the mother's feet—the delicate curve of the nails, the undersides unexpectedly pale and soft. In a few minutes, a car slows and pulls to the side of the road. I hear tires in gravel and a door opens. Footsteps. A man calls out over the running engine, "Hey, is everything okay?"

"Dead possum," I say. "She has babies." The man peers down with me, crouching on his heels, his profile then illuminated in my light. We stare at the squirming, now-doomed baby possums. He sucks his breath in. Sighs a slow, soft whistle. "Poor things," he says. "What a shame." As if held there by some force, we keep staring at the wriggling mound of life and death.

"What should we do?" I ask, finally, as if I know him, as if whatever happens will be done together. The man doesn't say anything for a few seconds. He looks apologetic in the spotlight. I think he must be a good man. He shrugs. "Probably best to just leave it alone," he says. "Yeah," I say. My head agrees: Nature will take its course. Still, I wonder how long it will take for the opossum's body to cool, before her warm pouch will turn cold and stiff, and how long those babies will push their snouts at her useless teats, and what it feels like to struggle like that. My heart: Pick them up and put them in your jacket pocket. In my dealings with animals, the heart and the head never agree. Finally, I stand up, angling my light back at the road, leaving the dead mother possum and her babies in darkness.

You can see the fires burning up the mountains, even from miles away—deep red, glowing scabs that fester and worm their way lower into the foothills. Riding uphill is difficult now—the smoke is getting bad, and I know I'm stupid for doing it, like smoking three packs of cigarettes in a row, maybe worse. But I can't resist. Coughing and wheezing all the way, I make it to Rubio Canyon. At the top of the closest peak, yellow-orange tongues dart and explode just over the ridge. Bits of burned sagebrush and yuccas drift through the air, the ash falling like snow. Firefighters have blocked off roads and forced residents to evacuate, and when the sun comes up, helicopters will drop loads of red powder over this hill.

The bears are coming down from the mountains now. In the paper I read about a guy who chased one out of his garage. I read about a woman who said that while she was cooking dinner, a bear had tried to knock down her front door. The pictures are of overturned garbage cans, claw marks on a tree. My mother tells me that a bear swam in her swimming pool and then took a nap on her patio furniture. She shows me the muddy tracks leading out of the water, the overturned cushions, the bear scat on the grass. On my usual route I find much more bear scat—piles of it that trail back into the canyon. My headlight becomes like a microscope—I pause and note the red berries, bits of fur, gristle. Then, suddenly, I smell something overpowering—a musky, piney, meaty, heavy, barnyard, rotting-grass smell. I hear low shuffling, scuffling, possibly breathing. Here's a phantom, and which part of him I've crossed, I just don't know. He's outside my light now, in the nowhere.

How I long for nowhere, but I hop on my bike and get the heck out of there.

On my way down, I startle a doe as she stands eating grass in someone's front yard. It occurs to me that those people, these residents of the big city, may never know that a deer visits them in the morning before the first light, not five feet from their front door. The doe trots away in front of me with a funny sideways gait, her front legs and back legs misaligned. She keeps looking back at me, so I wave at her.

Then I coast home at twenty-five miles per hour, wind running through me like chilly river water. In the winter, I'm half-frozen, my chin a veritable ice cube. But this is it, man! I stand up on my pedals, a prayer for the wheelchair bound, and if it's a clear day, sunrise comes—the still-distant sun will paint a pastel streak across the horizon. Then, back on Asbury Drive, I bump into my driveway, dismount my bike, and kiss my handlebars. I give my bike two pats and thank it for not failing me. Call it idolatry, but each morning, that thing saves my life, allows me to widen the boundaries. Later, when I'm standing in front of a classroom, hemmed in, pacing before the chalkboard, I will recall the darkness and the edges of everything.

JON KERSTETTER

# Triage

October 2003, Baghdad, Iraq. Major General Jon Gallinetti, US Marine Corps, Chief of Staff of CJTF7, the operational command unit of coalition forces in Iraq, accompanied me on late-night clinical rounds in a combat surgical hospital. We visited soldiers who were injured in multiple IED attacks throughout Baghdad just hours earlier. I made this mental note: *Soldier died tonight. IED explosion. Held him. Prayed. Told his commander to stay focused.*

In the hospital, the numbers of wounded that survived the attacks created a backlog of patients that required immediate surgery. Surgeons, nurses, medics, and hospital staff moved from patient to patient at an exhausting pace. When one surgery was finished, another began immediately. Several operating rooms were used simultaneously. Medical techs shuttled post-op patients from surgery to the second-floor ICU where the numbers of beds quickly became inadequate. Nurses adjusted their care plans to accommodate the rapid influx. A few less critical patient beds lined the halls just outside the ICU.

The general wanted to visit the hospital to encourage the patients and the medical staff. We made a one-mile trip to the hospital compound, late at night, unannounced, with none of the fanfare that usually accompanies a visit by a general officer in the military. After visiting the patients in the ICU, we walked down the hallway to the triage room.

One patient occupied the triage room: a young soldier, private first class. He had a ballistic head injury. His elbows flexed tightly in spastic tension, drawing his forearms to his chest; his hands made stonelike fists; his fingers coiled together as if grabbing an imaginary rope attached to his

sternum. His breathing was slow and sporadic. He had no oxygen mask. An intravenous line fed a slow drip of saline and painkiller. He was what is known in military medicine as *expectant*.

Some of his fellow soldiers gathered at the foot of his bed. A few of them had been injured in the same attack and had already been treated and bandaged in the emergency room. These fellow soldiers stood watch over the expectant patient. The general and I stood watch over them. One soldier had a white fractal of body salt edging the collar of his uniform. One wept. One prayed. Another quietly said "Jesus" over and over and kept shaking his head from side to side. And another had no expression at all: he simply stared a blank stare into the empty space above the expectant patient's head. A young sergeant, hands shaking, stammered as he tried to explain what had happened. The captain in charge of the expectant soldier's unit told the general and me that this was their first soldier to be killed—then he corrected himself and said this was the first soldier in their unit to be assigned to triage. He told us that the soldier was a good soldier. The general nodded in agreement and the room fell suddenly quiet.

The general laid his hand on the expectant soldier's leg—the leg whose strength I imagined was drifting like a shape-shifting cloud moving against a dark umber sky—strength retreating into a time before it carried a soldier. And I watched the drifting of a man back into the womb of his mother, toward a time when a leg was not a leg, a body not a body, toward a time when a soldier was only the laughing between two young lovers—a man and a woman who could never imagine that a leg-body-man-soldier would one day lie expectant and that that soldier would be their son.

As I watched the soldiers at the foot of the bed, I noted their sanded faces, their trembling mouths, their hollow-stare eyes. I watched them watch the shallow breathing and the intermittent spasm of seizured limbs and the pale gray color of expectant skin. I took clinical notes in my mind. I noted the soldiers—noted the patient. I noted all the things that needed to be noted: the size of the triage room, the frame of the bed, the tiles of the ceiling, and the dullness of the overhead light. I noted the taut draw of the white linen sheets and the shiny polished metal of the hospital fixtures. A single ceiling fan rotated slowly. The walls were off-white. There were no windows. The floor was spotless, the smell antiseptic. A

drab-green wool Army blanket covered each bed. Three beds lay empty. I noted the absence of noise and chaos, the absence of nurses rushing to prepare surgical instruments, and the absence of teams of doctors urgently exploring wounds and calling out orders. There was an absence of the hurried sounds and the hustle of soldiers in the combat emergency room one floor down. Nobody yelled "medic" or "doc." Nobody called for the chaplain. Medics did not cut off clothing or gather dressings. Ambulances and medevac helicopters did not arrive with bleeding soldiers.

The *Merriam-Webster Online Dictionary* defines *triage* as "the sorting of and allocation of treatment to patients and especially battle and disaster victims according to a system of priorities designed to maximize the number of survivors." All dictionary definitions refer to the origin of the word, *triage*, as deriving from the French verb *trier*, to sort. The essence of the meaning is in the sorting. In the context of battle, a soldier placed in a triage room as *expectant* has been literally sorted from a group of other injured soldiers whose probability of survival was deduced by a sort of battlefield calculus implemented by a medical officer or a triage officer. The sorting occurs rather quickly—usually with minimal, if any, deliberation.

A military physician trains for triage situations. I trained to make combat medical decisions based on the developing battlefield situation and limited medical resources. I read about triage. I role-played it in combat exercises. When I first learned about the role of triage in combat, I reasoned: *of course, triage is necessary. It's part of war. You do it as part of the job of a medical officer.*

More than twenty years ago, when I was a newly minted captain, I attended the two-week Combat Casualty Care Course at Camp Bullis, Texas. The course was designed to teach medical officers combat trauma care and field triage techniques. The capstone exercise included a half-day mass casualty scenario complete with percussion grenades, smoke bombs, and simulated enemy forces closing on the casualty collection point. The objective was to give medical officers a realistic setting in which to perform triage decisions and to initiate medevac protocols according to standard operating procedures. About twenty moulage patients mimicked battlefield casualties ranging from the minimally injured to those requiring imme-

diate surgery. Each medical officer in training was given five minutes to perform the triage exercise and to prepare an appropriate medevac request. Providing treatment was not an option: the exercise focused exclusively on making triage decisions.

All the participants could have easily completed the role-play within the time limit. Nothing, of course, is that straightforward in Army training. There is always some built-in element of surprise to test how well trainees cope with chaos. In this case, the element of the "unexpected" was a simulated psychiatric patient who was brandishing an M16 rifle and holding a medic hostage while threatening to commit suicide. In order to maintain the element of surprise, the doctors who had finished their turn were whisked out the back of the triage tent, not to be seen again until the after-action review some hours later.

My turn. I entered the tent at the shove of my evaluator. The mock "psych" patient was screaming and threatening to kill a nearby medic. Other medics were pleading with the disturbed patient to lay his weapon down and let the wounded get on a helicopter. I was to take charge and get control. I did. I approached the screaming patient with quick confident steps. I got about halfway through the triage tent when he pointed his rifle directly at his hostage medic and yelled, "One more step and the medic is dead." I backed off slowly, turned sideways, and quietly pulled my pistol. In an abrupt and instantaneous movement, I reeled around and shot the psych patient with my blank ammunition. "Bang—you're dead!" I yelled. A nearby evaluator took his weapon and made him play dead. One out-of-control psycho eliminated. I finished the triage exercise within the five-minute time limit. My evaluator laughed. "Damn," he said.

I felt great. I had control.

In the after-action review, I was asked about my decision to shoot. "Time," I answered. "I only had five minutes, so I maximized my effectiveness by eliminating a threat. It's combat," I argued.

One fellow doc asked if I would really shoot a patient in combat. A debate ensued as to the ethics of my decision. Nobody else had shot the psych case. Nobody else finished the exercise in the allotted time. Some trainees had considered shooting the crazed soldier but failed to act. Some managed to talk the psych patient into giving up his weapon. Those physicians

had taken nearly fifteen minutes to complete the exercise—minutes in which some of the simulated patients died a simulated death. In the end, it was decided that my decision to shoot, while potentially serving a greater need, may have been a bit aggressive, but that it was in fact *my* decision, and my decision met the needs of the mission. All ethical considerations aside, I felt that I understood the necessity and the theory of triage. I understood it as part of my job.

Military triage classifications are based on NATO guidelines and are published in numerous websites and Department of Defense publications. "The triage categories in the third edition of *Emergency War Surgery*, the Department of Defense bible of military medicine, are listed below:

> IMMEDIATE: This group includes those soldiers requiring lifesaving surgery. The surgical procedures in this category should not be time consuming and should concern only those patients with high chances of survival.

> DELAYED: This group includes those wounded who are badly in need of time-consuming surgery but whose general condition permits delay in surgical treatment without unduly endangering life. Sustaining treatment will be required.

> MINIMAL: These casualties have relatively minor injuries . . . and can effectively care for themselves or can be helped by nonmedical personnel.

> EXPECTANT: Casualties in this category have wounds that are so extensive that even if they were the sole casualty and had the benefit of optimal medical resource application, their survival would be unlikely. The expectant casualty should not be abandoned, but should be separated from the view of other casualties. . . . Using a minimal but competent staff, provide comfort measures for these casualties.

The text of *Emergency War Surgery* further notes, "The decision to withhold care from a wounded soldier, who in another less overwhelming situation might be salvaged, is difficult for any surgeon or medic. Decisions of

this nature are infrequent, even in mass casualty situations. Nonetheless, this is the essence of military triage." Triage requires assigning patients to those various categories based upon a rather quick and semi-objective assessment of a patient's injuries. If the triage officer calculates that a patient falls into the *expectant* category, treatment is withheld in order to allow medical teams to more efficiently concentrate on those soldiers with potentially survivable injuries. Preserving the fighting force is the central tenet of the process.

I have read and reread the official triage definition. I suppose I might have used it in a classroom of medics that I instructed. I am intimately familiar with the words that describe each category and with the professional commentary about the mechanics and ethics of sorting injured patients, yet I repeatedly come back to those words that try to clarify exactly what might be involved in the process of triage. I find the words weak and innocuous. They undercut the gravity and scope of a real-time triage experience. Here's the rub: the official commentary about the decision process focuses on the essence of triage as being the difficulty of making that decision. The difficulty is a given, but I think there is more. I think the essence of military triage is the necessity of making the decision when the combat situation demands it. It is the necessity of triage that requires medical staff to assign expectant soldiers to their death in order to provide an accommodation to a calculated greater good—a cause measured by the number of combat survivors. It is an accommodation that has not changed since the trench warfare of World War I.

Modern military medicine provides battlefield casualties with more sophisticated treatment and much faster aeromedical evacuation than in prior wars, but the process of triage remains essentially raw and unrefined as a standard combat operating procedure. Combat physicians encounter an overwhelming number or complexity of casualties. They make a rapid medical assessment, render a decision based on incomplete information, assign a triage category, and move to the next patient. Done. If they are particularly adept, they can triage several critical patients simultaneously.

Saving lives is the endpoint of all triage. Let one life go, save three others, or five, or maybe ten. The ratios don't matter, the benefits do. And

a benefit in war always comes at a cost. On the surface, of course, the ultimate cost of a triage decision is a soldier's life. One decision, one life, perhaps one decision, several lives. But there are other costs not so easily calculated, like the emotional cost to survivors or the psychological cost to soldiers who make triage decisions. Textbook definitions are silent on how military physicians prepare for, or react to, the demands of making a triage decision. No chapter in a military textbook instructs combat physicians in the multidimensional complexity of decision-making that serves to deny life-saving interventions for soldiers. There are chapters on why triage decisions must be made and chapters on how to apply established medical criteria in making those decisions. But what to do next, after the triage decision has been made—not covered. And that vacuum of knowledge leads to a feeling of exposure and vulnerability, both of which cannot be tolerated in war.

The act of triage is subsumed under the assigned duties of medics and physicians. I am not suggesting that the process fall to someone else or that the criteria used to make triage decisions should be discarded for a different process. I know of no other way of quickly sorting and categorizing patients when the critical nature of combat demands that it be done. I am, however, declaring that the practice of triage obligates doctors and medics, whose principle duty is the saving of lives, to perform tasks that share in the brutality and the ugliness of war—tasks which are tantamount to pulling a trigger on fellow soldiers.

In the final analysis, the decision to withhold medical care is not a decision that can be practiced, and rehearsed, and fully prepared for outside of the realm of combat. How could that ever be accomplished with any modicum of reality? Could a medical officer simply say, as I did in training, "Bang, you're dead" or "Put the black tag on this one," and with that, feel the same gut-ripping tension that combat evokes? No, the reality of triage tends to hit more like the force of a bomb blast. In an instant, fragments of stone and metal explode through the air with such velocity that when they hit a human target, even if the target is not killed, it is stunned and bleeding and breathless. It is that environment in which a military doctor or medic makes a live-fire triage decision and then must stand against the ballistic force of its consequences.

Somewhere in the process of making notes about the expectant patient, I paused and moved toward the middle of the bed. I put my hand on the patient's leg, just as the general had done. I laid it there, let it linger. From where I stood, I stared directly into the expectant soldier's face. I watched his agonal breathing, a long sighed breath followed by an absence of movement, and that followed by three to four shallow breaths. I matched his breathing with my own breathing. I timed the slowing pattern with my watch. I made some mental calculations, then looked away. Once again, I noted the quiet of the room and the whiteness of the walls. I noted the empty beds, and the ceiling, and the antiseptic smell. Again, I watched the expectant soldier who was oblivious to all of my watching.

I stood at the triage bedside thinking if this were my son, I would want soldiers to gather in his room—listen to his breathing. I would want them to break stride from their war routines, perhaps to weep, perhaps to pray. And if he called out for his dad, I would want them to become a father to a son. Simply that: nothing more, nothing less—procedures not in Department of Defense manuals or war theory classes or triage exercises.

I moved to the head of the bed, placed my right hand on the chest of the patient. And my hand rested there with barely any movement. I turned to the other soldiers, gave them an acknowledgment with a slight upturned purse of my lips, then looked away. I lifted my hand to the patient's right shoulder and let my weight shift as if trying to gently hold him in place. I half-kneeled, half-bent—closed the distance between our bodies. I noted the weave of the fabric in his skullcap dressing and the faint show of blood that tainted its white cotton edges. I lingered. I prayed for God to take him in that very instant. I whispered, so only he could hear, "You're a good soldier. You're finished here. It's okay to go home now." I waited. I watched. I saw the faces of my own sons in his: was glad they were not soldiers.

I finished, stood up, and walked to the foot of the bed. One of the soldiers asked me if there wasn't something I could do. I said no. I meant no. I wanted my answer to be yes. I faced the captain and put my hand on his shoulder, told him that we were finished, that his soldier did not feel pain, that he would be gone soon, and that everybody had done everything they could. The tone of my voice was neither comforting nor encouraging,

neither sorrowful nor hopeful. It was, as I remember, military and professional.

I think about that expectant soldier so often. I know I would have seen his name in his hospital chart or been told his name by his commander. I did not take the time to write it down anywhere and that bothers me. It bothers me because years later he remains nameless—just like so many other soldier-patients I encountered—and I think I equate that namelessness with a form of abandonment for which I feel personally responsible. I do understand, in a professional sense, that the patient was not abandoned, that his triage was purposeful, and that it allowed an ascent to medical efficiency that, in the end, saved other soldiers' lives. But I also understand that the theoretical basis of triage quickly erodes when confronted with the raw, emotional, human act of sorting through wounded patients and assigning triage categories. In my mind, the theoretical and the practical wage a constant battle, so that whenever I participate in a triage decision, part of me says *yes*, and part of me says *no*.

I sometimes find myself wanting to speak with the expectant soldier's mother and father. I want to tell them that their son did not die alone in a triage bed—that he was not simply abandoned or left as hopeless in a secluded corner room of a distant combat hospital. I want to assure them that he died in the company of men who stood watch over him as if guarding an entire battalion and that we tried to give everything we could give—that we tried to be more than soldiers or marines or generals or doctors.

When I tell the story of this particular soldier to my medical colleagues, I always mention that triage is a necessary part of war. I tell them it's a matter of compassionate medical necessity and the entrenched reality of combat—that it's the exercise of a soldier's final duty.

Occasionally though, I think about telling them how I wished I could have done something: anything. But then I realize I cannot tell them that, because in fact, I did do something, and I am left with the nameless face of an expectant soldier and countless sheets of history filled with decisions

made by doctors at war. I am left with my own understanding that we who are soldiers are all triaged.

I want to remember the expectant soldier as a person with a name, but I have come to accept that I cannot. I remember, instead, the triage room. I recall the general who placed his hand on a young man. And I see the drifting once again—the fading of a soldier back into the womb from which he was born into life. I see him loved. He is a soldier. Wounded. Triaged. Expectant.

KIM BARNES

# The Clearwater

I take the river a step at a time. My feet slide from the shoulders of rock; my toes wedge between boulders. I am timid about this, moving out toward the center, where the water is deepest, where the big fish might lie.

Here, at Lenore, the Clearwater is not easy. Too wide to cast from shore, too swift, too pocked with hidden currents and sudden holes. I go at it anyway, still without waders, determined to find my place of stability, the water at my belly, my thighs numbing with cold.

My husband fishes below me. On shore, our daughter and son dig pools in the sand. I watch as they flash in the sun, and I feel a rush of gratitude, the joy of living only minutes from water, the same water my brother and I played in as children. It is as though I am reliving my own young life, there on the banks of the Clearwater, as though I exist in two dimensions and know the pleasure of each—the child's pure delight in the moment; the woman's recognition of continuance, of nostalgia, of the water around her and the sun on her face.

I choose a fly I think the fish might favor, its color the color of the day's light and leaves and wings. I praise its tufts and feathers, its hackle and tail. I load the line, thinking not of the S I must make through air but of the place above and where the water eddies, the V above whitecaps, the purl below stone.

I do not think of the line or the fly or the fish as much as I think about the water moving against and around me, how the sky fills my eyes and the noise-that-isn't fills my ears—the movement of everything around me like the hum of just-waking or sleep, blood-rush, dream-rush, the darkness coming on, air.

I forget to watch for the fish to strike, forget to note the catch, the spin, the sinking. I pull the line in, let it loop at my waist, sing it out again, and again. The trout will rise, or they won't. The nubbin of fur and thread will turn to caddis, black any, stone fly, bee, or it will simply settle on the water and remain a human's fancy. Either way, it's magic to me, and so I stay until my feet are no longer my own but part of the river's bed. How can I move them? How can I feel my way back to shore, where my family is calling that it's time to go home? They are hungry, and the shadows have taken the canyon. They are cold.

From my place in the water, they seem distant to me. I must seem like a fool, numb to my ribcage, no fish to show. But I am here in the river, half-in, half-out, a wader of two worlds. I smile. I wave. I am where nothing can reach me.

North Fork, Middle Fork, South Fork, Main: see how the flow of the sounds is smooth, so lovely. The rivers themselves flow together this way, spilling down from the mountains. They drain the north Idaho land my father and others like him logged and loved so easily in the years before it seemed to matter.

And now it matters and we all know it, though we may come to our understanding in different ways. The timber companies worry about access and shareholders' profit; the mills worry about viability and foreign markets; the loggers worry about the land and life they know and ways to feed their families; the foresters worry about the politicians; the politicians worry about the timber companies; the environmentalists, some more, some less than radical, worry about the whole of it. Meanwhile, while the sales are being staked and the trees are being spiked, the land slumps from beneath its covering of burned slash and razored stumps, slides off the hills and down the draws, sloughs off its dying skin like an animal readying itself for another season.

And all of it moves toward water. Always, the run-off of rain, the soil it carries, the ash and cinder, the dry bones of trees. Maybe this is why I think of water as woman: it takes what it can, takes the land in its lap, holds the eggs in its belly.

Here, where I live with my husband and children above the Main

Clearwater at Lenore, twelve miles from where the forks have all come together, we see the movement of land in the water's flow. Spring thaw, and the trees come fully rooted, ungrounded by the wash of high current. Old logjams from previous floods break loose; new ones pile against the bridge footings and small islands. Each becomes a nest of lost things: fishing lures, loops of rope, men's undershirts, women's shoes.

I wonder, sometimes, if my own life's mementos are contained in those tangles, perhaps a hair barrette I lost while fishing Reeds Creek, or one of my mother's pie tins that my brother and I used to pan for gold. Or the tree itself fallen from the riverbank I sat on as a child, searching for the mussel shells we called angel's wings, though they were mahogany brown and often broken.

What the river takes, the river gives, and so it is with my life here. Each hour I spend with my feet near water, I feel more deeply rooted; the further I get away, the less sure I am of my place in the world. For each of us, there must be this one thing, and for me it is the river. Not just the river, but the composition that begins as the North Fork and flows into the Main. I have known this river from its feeding waters to its mouth where it meets and becomes the Snake. I have known it before the dams, and after. I have known it as a child knows water, have known it as a lover knows water, and now as a mother knows and recognizes water as she watches her own children who are bent at the waist, leaning forward to bring up the sandy wings.

I am closest to the Clearwater when I am closest to its origins, and to my own. Reeds Creek, Orofino Creek, Weitas Creek, Deer Creek, the Musselshell—they feed the river as the river feeds me. It has taken me longer to feel intimate with the stretch of river that curves into *omega* below our house. I watch it each day, uneasy with its width and deep holes. I realize, too, that I distrust this length of the river because it no longer moves of its own volition: Dwarshak Dam controls a great part of it now. The North Fork, the river I once knew as a tree-lined stream the color of turquoise, now ends in a man-made reservoir covering over fifty miles of land that was first logged for its timber before being flooded. The river bulges at its base, its narrower neck seemingly unaffected by the

distant, concrete obstruction. People drive northeast for hours to reach the Bungalow, Aquarius—places where the water remains swift and the fish are often native.

But I know better. The river's betrayal sometimes shames me, the way it carries on as though what it travels toward is not a state of near stasis, depositing sludge along miles of riprap dikes, piling its dross against the pylons and locks and turbines. It cannot rid itself of what it is given, cannot carry its silt and timber and ash to the mouth of the ocean where it can be broken down, taken to great depths, washed and sifted into sand and dirt. Instead, the silt falls from the slow current, depositing itself in great layers, narrowing the river's channel. The river becomes murky, the flat color of pewter. The trout are replaced by bottom-feeders, lovers of warm water. Every year, the Corps of Engineers sponsors a trash-fish derby, paying the fishermen to catch and kill what their dams have spawned.

Like so many others who love this land, it has taken me some time to understand that the place—the rivers and streams, the forests and mountains and high meadows—does not absorb but reflects what we bring to it. Perhaps what I see in the river is some mirror of the contradictions that make up my own life—the calm surface, the seeming freedom. Certainly, the river is a metaphor for memory. "I am everywhere I ever was," Stegner wrote, and so it is with the river—water and rock, metal and mineral, stick and bone, trout-flash and deer-lick. Perpetual, even in the face of destruction, I think, even as I read the sad stories of pollution and poisoning, fish-kill and disease. Perpetual because the rain must fall and the mountains must accept and the water must run toward oceans. A comfort, knowing that the amount of water in our world never changes, that there is never any more nor any less, only the same and in various forms: ice, liquid, steam. I trust that water will withstand, given its basic demands—to fall, to move, to rise, to fall again.

This, then, may be my final recognition: the inevitability of movement. We slow, we go forward. We age. We rise to greet each morning. We fall into sleep each night. Constant as rain, perpetuated in death and birth and rebirth.

It has taken me time to understand the need I feel to be consumed by the river. Raised a stoic, I am seldom given to need. Need is a weakness,

a loss of control, the Achilles' heel of human existence. My connection to the river is complicated by its pull; I resent the power it possesses to draw me. Yet I want its sound in my ears, its smell, its taste. I want to be immersed—my hands, my feet, my hips. Like all seductions, it necessitates surrender.

I am learning to let go.

I bring to the river my love and those that I choose to love. I bring to it my child's memories and my woman's life. I bring to it hunger but always joy, for whatever it is that weighs on me dissipates in those few miles between our house in the canyon and the water's edge.

I understand how water can become something grim, how it can rise and take and swirl and drown. How it can become something to fight against, something to resist. The dam on the North Fork, the largest of its kind, was not built for electricity or simple recreation, they say, but for flood control in Portland, four hundred miles west.

There's less flooding now, although three springs ago, in 1996, not even the dams could keep pace when the temperatures rose and the snow-melt came down with rain. We watched from our house above the river, stranded between washed-out roads, watched the roofs and porches, the dead cows and refrigerators and lawn chairs, the still-intact trailer house that slammed against the Lenore Bridge.

How can I cheer such destruction? For that is what I felt, an overwhelming sense of boosterism. I wanted the river to win in some essential way, wanted to see it rise up and lash out, pull down the dams and drain the reservoirs, ferry away the docks and cleanse itself of silt. I wanted it to show a god's righteous anger, a larger reflection of my own frustration and resentment.

I didn't mind then, that we couldn't get out. My husband had made a last, grand effort to snatch our children from their school in Orofino twenty miles east, hauling them back over bench roads not yet torn away by the massive run-off, roads that crumbled and disappeared behind them. Other rural parents with children in school were not so lucky: it would be a week before any travel was allowed in or out, except by helicopter. Our family was together, protected by our place high on the canyon wall. We had food, water, wood. We had days ahead of us without school or

teaching, weeks before the roads would be cleared, and now the sun that had started the rain was back out and warming the air into spring.

We packed sandwiches and cookies, cheese and crackers and a fine bottle of red wine. We hiked to where we could watch Big Eddy, the place where the river curled against itself and created an enormous back current that caught and held the debris. While the river ran thick with trees and fence posts, goat huts and wallpapered sheeting, we ate and drank and gathered ladybugs for our garden. Certain logs were red with their hatching, their coming out of hibernation. We scooped them up in handfuls and carried them in bundles made of paper towels and candy wrappers. Their odor was strong, dry, astringent—a promise of summer.

We watched a jet boat make its way down the river. Foolish, we thought, for risking such danger. The river was running at a near-record high; the water was choked with flotsam, some larger than the boat itself. The two men inside were not wearing life jackets, and I shook my head. What were they thinking?

The boat pulled in at a smaller eddy downstream, and there we saw what they followed: a large raft of finished lumber, floated loose from the mill at Orofino. Scavengers' rights. If they were willing to risk for it, the lumber was theirs.

One man kept the helm while the other bent over the gunnels to grab the wood. They pulled it onto the boat's bow one plank at a time until the craft sat low in the already threatening water. We held our breath, knowing that if they went over or capsized, we could do nothing but watch.

They loaded the wood. They let the current swing them about, turn them upstream. They made their way slowly, navigating through tangles of barbed wire still stapled to barn doors, past trees three times the length of their boat. They had the booty. They were gone.

I couldn't imagine such nonsense, such greed. What desperation could bring on the willingness to risk so much for so little? I felt content, driven by nothing other than the warmth on my shoulders and the love I felt for this land and my husband and daughter and son, who gathered around me to show what they had found: a mantid's egg case, triangular and strangely textured, like meringue hardened and fired to a ceramic glaze. We would take it home as well and put it in the garden, where it would hatch its eaters of grasshoppers and aphids.

I must have believed, then, that it was love that would see me through the long hours of darkness, that would keep me grounded during the wild summer heat. I must have believed that, like the river, what we love may surge and wane but remains nonetheless constant, giving, taking, carrying on.

And doesn't it? Perhaps it is we who fail love, refusing to allow its seduction, its pull and sway. Love is a river we stop into, like the waters of baptismal rebirth. We close our eyes. We bow our heads. We allow ourselves to be taken as the water closes over our heads. For that moment, we must believe.

"I don't think we can make it." I looked at what was left of the road, stretching down before me into a dusk of low tress.

My daughter and son moaned. After a day of writing, I had picked them up from the sitter's in Orofino, promising a late afternoon along the river. My husband was in the mountains near McCall, hiking the upper lakes, safe with friends he'd known since high school. There was a place I'd heard of, just down some side road, where Ford's Creek met the river, a place with sand and stiller water, where Jordan and Jace could swim and I could spread my blanket and think The stretch of river we were after mattered to me: it was a section of the last few miles of the Main Clearwater, the last free-flowing water between the headwaters and the ocean.

I needed the river in a way I had not only hours before. It wasn't fishing I was after. I was sour with bad news, begrudging even the rod, line, and fly their pacification. That afternoon, I'd gotten a phone call from across the country and learned that our close friends' marriage was in sudden and serious peril, rocked by confession of a particularly insidious spate of· infidelity. The levels of betrayal had shocked me, and the narrative of contentment and ongoing friendship that I had trusted was suddenly gone.

The anger that I felt surprised me. I am not comfortable with anger, having been taught from the cradle that anger, like other unmanageable emotions, is best kept under lock and key, somewhere in the heart's deepest chamber. The river would help, sweep away the confusion of emotions with its own ordered chaos. The river would help me find my footing, my point of rest.

But now this: I'd chosen the wrong road. Even after having made the decision to put the car into reverse and back our way out of the ravine, we were going nowhere. The tires of the front-wheel drive Toyota spun and chattered in the gravel, unable to push the weight of the car up such a steep incline. The dirt and basalt-studded bank rose close on my left; the road crumbled away on my right, slumping into a gully of black locust, poison ivy, blackberry brambles thick with thorns.

"*Now* what." I said it in the way my mother always had. Fatalism. Tired resignation.

I eased the clutch, tried again. Nothing but smoke and the bitter smell of burning rubber.

"I think we'd better get out of the car," Jace said. At seven, he's the cautious one, always sensing the adult's boundless capacity for error.

"No," I said. "It's okay. Let's just go on down. We can turn around at the bottom." I had no idea if this were true, but my choice was to keep going or for us all to begin the long walk back to town for a tow-truck. I also felt a kind of apathy: what was the worst that could happen? The river was only five hundred yards away. We'd find our way out.

What we found instead was an increasingly narrow once-road. I saw that, for years, the rain had washed down the path scraped from the hill-side, taking what dirt remained with it to the river. What was left was a deep schism that forked and meandered its way around rocks too large to be moved. I concentrated on riding the ruts' shoulders until there was no rut to straddle but only a series of woven ditches. I kept thinking it would get better, that the road would even out. That *someone* had made it down here because the vegetation was scraped from the center. I kept wishing for the Suburban with its high clearance and granny gear, but I doubted that the path we traveled would have allowed its girth.

We bounced over boulders the size of basketballs. The skid plate caught and dragged. Jordan and Jace whimpered in the backseat. I tried to act as though this were nearly normal, to be expected. If I stayed calm, in control, they would feel safe.

"Mom, please." Jordan had her hand on the door handle, as though she meant to jump.

"We're almost there," I said. "We'll get to the river and be glad." We

were far into the darkness of trees now, the yellow pine and locust, the dense undergrowth of vine maple. I jostled the car around a corner, then stopped. I could see ahead to where the road leveled off, where sunlight broke through. Between us and that point of flat ground was a final pitch downward, where the road hooked a ninety-degree right angle. The bigger problem was that the trail became narrower still, hedged in by the bank on the left and, on the right, an old tanker truck settled into a bog of brambles.

I examined my passage. A boulder twice the size of our car protruded like a tumor from the eight-foot dirt bank. The abandoned tanker, its red paint faded to rust, was just as intractable: steel and stone, and only the space of a small car between them.

*If I stop here,* I thought, *the tow truck might be able to reach us.* But I had begun to doubt the plausibility of such a rescue, given the right turns and narrow corridor down which we had traveled.

I thought cable, winch, but could not imagine the logistics of being dragged backward from the ravine without damaging the car beyond repair.

"Mom?" my son's voice quavered.

"What?" I was snappish, weighing our chances, calculating the risk.

"Can't we just walk from here?"

I thought of the brambles, the probability of rattlesnakes, what unseen dangers might wait around the corner.

"Just hang on." I inched the car toward the passage, like Odysseus steering his ship through the straits. I sucked in and held my breath, giving the air what room I could. One scrape and we were through and bumped into the clearing.

Whoops and hollers from the backseat. "We made it!" Jace shouted. Jordan crowed. I stopped the car, got out and circled it twice, looking for damage. Nothing but a few shallow scratches. No dripping oil. The muffler remained miraculously intact.

"Watch for snakes. Wait for me." I gathered our water bottles and bag of sandwiches, taking in the lay of the land. Between us and the river was the railroad track, built high on its ridge of rock. To the left, I saw remnants of a gold mine, its entryway framed in old timbers. To my right was a settling pond, green with algae. As we began our short walk, two blue herons rose from the still water, awkward on their wings.

There was a game trail that we followed to the tracks and over. What we found was a long beach of rocks and a smaller one of sand. The children had all but forgotten the trauma of our trip and stripped themselves of shoes and socks before wading in. I felt the heat, then, the sweat gone sticky at my collar and waist.

I walked a few yards upstream, found a rock close to water, where I could dangle my feet and keep an eye on my son and daughter. I tried not to think of the sun's low slant, the hard way out. I tried not to hear what I was thinking: there *is* no way out of here except to leave the car and walk. No way I could make that first climb and twist between the rock and truck.

I closed my eyes. The river filled my ears, and I began to float with the sound. I needed to find something to dislodge the fear—not only of the trek ahead of us, but the feat that had come while listening to my friend's grieving. It could happen, any time, any place, to anyone. One minute, you're on solid ground, the next moment the earth has cracked open beneath you. You get up in the morning and look in the mirror and tell yourself what the day will consist of, and then the light jerks sideways and you are left falling through the dark.

Behind me, a dog barked. I came back to my vision slowly, not willing to give up the cool place behind my eyes, the blindness, the deafness of water.

I turned to see a large yellow Lab, and then an older man walking the tracks. He stopped and raised his hand in acknowledgment of our presence. I hesitated, suddenly aware of another danger: a woman, two children, alone.

*He could help us,* I thought. He might live close by, have a tractor or winch. I thought, *I can't let him know we're stuck here, can't let him see how vulnerable we are.*

"How's it going?" he yelled.

I nodded and gave him a thumbs-up. He stood for a long time, and I thought he might decide to walk toward us. And then what? For all I knew he was one of my father's old logging friends. For all I knew, he was a transient bent on some evil.

He stayed on the track, and I watched him disappear around the bend. There was too much to be afraid of, too much to fear. I rose and waded the rocks toward my children, suddenly distrusting even the river, its currents here strange and unpredictable.

They were making a catch basin for the small minnows they caught in the net of their hands. They hardly noticed my presence. *I should have them gather their things*, I thought, *hustle them toward the car, or herd them in front of me up the rag of road, where we could walk the asphalt into town.* It would take hours, I knew, hours into dusk, a woman and two children on a rural road where few cars traveled after dinner. I could hear my mother's scolding voice, the one I have known all my life, consistent through all my unwomanly adventures and forays: "What in the world were you thinking? What could have made you take such a risk?"

Risk. I looked across the river, where Highway 12 tied east to west. Cars flicked through the trees, distant and quick. I knew the benefits of being where I was: the water comforted me, the sand and rock and cottonwood leaves turning golden in the last rays of the sun. I needed this, often and sometimes desperately. I believed, too, that my children were made better by such a landscape, that every handful of water they dipped from the river was an hour they would later remember as good.

But why here? Why hadn't I been content to take the easy way, pull off the road and find the familiar beaches and banks: Pink House Hole or Big Eddy, Myrtle or Home Beach?

I looked up, then down the far bank. This part of the Clearwater was different than farther downriver. Not so big. The rocks on the other side seemed still part of the canyon wall, huge and jagged from the blasts of road making. Maybe it was good to be in a place I had not memorized, to be surprised by stone and current. I ran my hand through the water, patted the back of my neck. I needed to remember what I believed in, remember that things might just as easily go good as bad.

I called my children in. They refused to be hurried, reluctant as I to face the trip out, though it would be much easier, I had cozily assured them, going up than down.

Mosquitoes clouded around us as we walked from the river toward the pond. My daughter swatted frantically: they are drawn to her especially, and their bites leave her swollen and miserable.

"Hurry," I said. "It's getting dark. We need to get out while there's still light."

We crowded in, full of sand and river smells. I made a last check of the

ground beneath the car: no oil or other inappropriate leakage. We made a tight turn, and I sighed as we faced the hill. What was it worth to attempt the ascent, lose the muffler, bash in the doors? We wouldn't be killed. What were my chances? It seemed an impossible decision.

I thought of the mosquitoes, the long walk out with two tired children, our feet rubbed raw by wet stones and sand. I said, "Buckle your seatbelts and lock your doors." I gave the engine more gas than usual.

The first pitch was not dirt and rock but a dick of muddy clay beneath a thick layer of pine needles. We spun, then began sliding backward, back into the long thorns of locust, over boulders and humps because the car could not be steered in such muck.

When we came to a stop, I leaned forward, rested my forehead against the wheel. I thought I might cry.

"Mom?" My son's voice was high, nearly shrill.

"Yes, Jace."

"I'm out of here."

He opened the door before I could stop him, slammed it shut and ran for the railroad tracks. Jordan was fast behind.

I rolled down my window. "Okay," I said. "You stay right there, this side of the tracks. Don't you move. If I can get past this first pitch, we'll make it. When you hear me honk, come running." They nodded, miserable among the mosquitoes, shaking in the suddenly cool air.

I backed up as far as I could, put the car in first, gunned the engine and popped the clutch. I hit the hill with my tires screaming, went up, careened sideways, bounced off the boulder, lost traction and stalled, then slid all the way back down, cringing with the screech of metal against rock, wood against metal.

*I need to focus on the initial few yards instead of the dogleg corner at its summit,* I thought—the boulder bulging from the hillside, the tanker truck with its sharp edges. If things went well, we could get out with minimal damage. If things went bad, I might slide down into the gully with the truck, be swallowed by blackberries, have to fight my way out of thorns and lord knew what else.

I got out of the car, tried to pull some of the larger rocks off the road, broke off what branches I could. I scuffed at the pine needles, realizing

the uselessness of it: the ground underneath was saturated with moisture. I backed up, got a stronger run. Black smoke clouded around me. I got a foot farther before sliding back down.

I went at it hard then, again and again, as the sun settled lower in the west and the sky darkened. I was still afraid, still fearing too much power, too much speed. It was best to keep control, stay steady. But I got no farther. Always, almost to the top, and then the sudden spin and slide.

How many times? Twenty? Thirty? I didn't care about the car anymore, hardly heard the worried cries of my children. I was feeling something building inside me, something I hadn't felt for a long time. It was hard and headlong, heedless in a way that might be brave. I'd felt it often before, when I was younger and wildly free. No husband. No children. Only my own life in my hands. I'd felt little fear of anything then, and it was a comfort. Now, with so much to love and lose, I'd come to cherish the expected, easy ways. Risk came in larger increments: sickness, infidelity, divorce, death. I'd begun to live my life as though, by giving up the smaller risks, I could somehow balance out the larger, keep the big ones at bay with a juju bargain-the sacrifice of whatever independence and strength such risks brought me.

Sitting there, the car smelling of rubber and fire, the heat and the mosquitoes and darkness coming on, I felt something else, and it was anger. Anger at what I feared and must fear, anger that I was where I was and in possible danger.

I felt suddenly and awfully alone, not because of the isolation, but because I was a woman where I should not be, having risked too much for the river.

The car idled. I hit the dash with the heel of my hand. I let all of it come into me, then-the anger I felt at love and death, at men who might hurt me and the men who would never, at the car and the land in its obstinacy. I felt the quiver in my belly and the rush of heat that filled my ears. I needed speed, momentum to carry me through.

I revved the engine, popped the clutch. I made the turn and didn't slow down. I kept it floored. I hit the boulder, jerked the wheel hard to the left, hit the truck. The tires spun. I didn't know what was behind me now, what I might slide into. I turned the wheel this way, then that, seeking purchase.

I yelled at the top of my lungs, "You son-of-a-bitch, go!" And then I was up that first pitch and breathing.

The kids came running, screaming, shouting. They piled gleefully into the car. We were going to make it. Everything was okay.

But it wasn't, because now there was another pitch, and then another. We spun. We stalled.

They got out. They ran all the way back to the railroad tracks.

I rocked the car back against the tanker. Bounce, spin, back. Bounce, spin, back. Each time a little farther, and when I found my ground and started careening up, I didn't stop. I bounced the car out of the canyon, figuring the exhaust system was already gone, figuring it had all been decided hours ago and this was the final scene.

When I got the highway, I set the emergency brake and jogged back down. Jace and Jordan were coming to meet me, exhausted and still frightened. I batted at the mosquitoes and hurried us all up the hill. I was laughing, giddy with adrenaline. They were weepy, a little confused by my gaiety. They never wanted to do it again.

"It was an adventure," I told them. "And see? We are fine."

As we drove the highway home, I felt vibrant, exhilarated. The moon rising was the most beautiful thing, the wind through the windows a gift. I'd check the car for damage tomorrow, but for now nothing could touch us.

My children would sleep well, and I knew that in years to come, they would tell this story and the story would change and remain the same. Always, there would be the road we traveled, the rocks, the ruts, the mine to the east, the tanker to the west. There would be the night and mosquitoes, the smoke as they watched the car beat its way out of the canyon. There would be their mother's foolishness or her bravery, her stubborn refusals. The words might change, and maybe their fear. But always, there would be the river. It would run cold and loud beside them, the water they cupped in their hands and held above the sand to be sieved and drained and cupped again.

It will keep them near me. It will carry them away.

# As a Boy I Dreamed
# Often of a Tiger

Rippling, immense, long back rubbing with liquid force against the doorway, it steps from the bathroom and turns down the hallway, padding—slowly and without sound—toward the room I share with my little brother.

My three-year-old daughter isn't sure, but my five-year-old son thinks Tigger is *half-tiger*. He cites as evidence Tigger's whiskers, stripes, and tail, as well as the fact that Tigger's *almost-scary*. Pooh, Piglet, Owl: no one else in the Hundred Acre Wood is even close to scary. "But Tigger is *almost-scary*. That's why he's *half-tiger*, Dad."

Shoulders filling the doorway, the tiger lifts its great head and gathers its weight—haunches flexing, yellow eyes going dark and thin.

Movie night, the four of us snuggled up on the couch, munching walnuts and popcorn, and Kaa, the python, is no problem. King Louie and his jazzy orangutans, too, pass with more delight than worry. But Shere Khan, the

tiger, the impossible wings of his shoulder bones shifting through the grass—Shere Khan has us all pulling the blanket over our heads.

A single great in-suck of tiger-breath, hot wind pulling across me for the force of it, and I wake into the same night-black room I have just been dreaming of—and I scream, scream, scream.

Despite its fuzzy softness, its bright stripes, funny whiskers, and cartoon smile, most nights the tiger pillow-pet the kids caught at the Christmas parade last year ends up kicked under the bottom bunk.

The house I grew up in—with its uneven ceilings, L-shaped rooms, and closets that worked like hallways—was stitched together from the scraps of abandoned homesteaders' shacks. Nothing was where it was supposed to be, least of all my parents' room, which was on the other side of the bathroom, the bathroom the only way in or out. After tuck-in, I lay awake for hours and in my mind's eye traced backward the tiger's dark path, from my room through the hallway and the bathroom and into my parents' room. And I knew—could feel it in the hollows of my groin and gut and up into the slick, aching places behind my heart—that was where the tiger came from: nowhere but there: the tiger rising and remuscling, each night, in my parents' room.

While my son catalogues and categorizes, lists the planets from biggest to smallest, his cousins from youngest to oldest, my daughter daydreams, wanders off by herself and invents intricate worlds of sticks and grass

and fallen blossoms. She regales us with tales of her sister, Sha-sha, who is sometimes younger and sometimes older, who doesn't always do what she is supposed to do and is often—too often, I wonder?—sick or hurt or otherwise distressed. Like all good storytellers, my daughter shamelessly cannibalizes her world—her child discoveries, our daily comings and goings and conversations, whatever narrative scraps she gleans from books and kids' shows—all of these she refashions and breathes into life in her breathless tellings.

The dreams started before my father died. I say this and wonder if it's true, wonder why all these years I have believed it to be true. Is it because I can't imagine myself screaming so as a ten-year-old, an eleven-year-old, a young man? Do I have a memory of my father coming to me in the night, following the dream-tiger's route, stepping into the very space the tiger occupied? I don't know, but I can anyway see it: my father in a tight white T-shirt and underwear, my big, black-haired father shushing me, comforting me, hard hands laying me down. Was the dream-tiger, I wonder, my child's way of reckoning the cancer even then gnawing at my strong father's bones?

Walking home, we see a light on in the upstairs hallway. Packing up her menagerie of screens, the harried babysitter tells us our daughter wouldn't go to sleep, that she kept talking about a tiger, was scared of a tiger. I go upstairs and find our daughter sitting up in the bottom bunk, blue eyes dark and wide. She tells me she can't sleep. I hug her, tuck her in, tell her of course she can sleep. She looks up at me, then turns her little face into the pillow, says, "Well, now I can."

My fear? That the tiger preceded both death and sickness. That the tiger is the most truthful of us and was always there, is still here.

MARY HAUG

# Standing Naked in a Pool of Her Clothing

In a softly lit gallery at the Chicago Institute of Art, portraits of women bathing hang on the stark, white walls. The women are slender and sinuous, stocky and sturdy; they are blonde and fair skinned, brunette and bronze; they kneel or lie in shallow tubs twisting their bodies in awkward, yet somehow graceful, poses as they scrub or dry themselves with plush towels.

In one painting, a woman lies on her side facing a copper bathtub, one leg lifted and resting on the tub's edge. A maid, in a white blouse that balloons above her starched cuffs and a red skirt that billows over the floor, lifts the woman's hair with one hand and with the other dries her back. I marvel at the women's comfort with touching and being touched by one another.

In another painting, a slight woman leans over the narrow edge of a slipper tub. A towel drapes over the back of her neck, over one shoulder, and across her chest, leaving one breast exposed. Her silky auburn hair falls over her face, and she raises one arm to lift it away. As I study the painting, I feel a pleasurable guilt—not that of a window peeper, but more like someone who has been invited into an intimate moment in a stranger's life. I am fifty years old, and for the first time in my life, I grasp the difference between sensual and sexual, a distinction that my prudish girlhood had not prepared me to appreciate.

Years later, as I soak in a pool of hot water at a Korean bath, I look across the room where four young women sit on their stools, studying

their naked bodies in mirrors as they scrub themselves with rough cloths, making small, slow circles over elbows, hands, legs, feet, breasts, and neck. Their hair is gathered at the tops of their heads and cascades in shiny black rivers down their long necks; their slender bodies curve in at their waists and out at their hips. Holding their arms above their heads, they sway like dancers as they caress first one arm, then the other, with the porous scrubbing cloths. With no sense of voyeurism, shame, or uneasiness, I watch them scrub for several minutes. Not even Degas had captured such beauty.

I come from a family that dressed in bathrooms and closets. So I was glad none of them was watching when I walked up the stairs at the Boryeong Mud Spa, took off my shoes, set them on a wooden mat outside the door, went into the women's bath, and bought a ticket for four thousand won (about six dollars) from the attendant. She gave me an expandable bracelet with a small metal disc numbered 368 and pointed to several rows of lockers. After wandering a bit, relieved I was the only one in the room, I found my locker, but I couldn't open the door. I was fumbling with the bracelet when the attendant came around the corner, grabbed my wrist, and held the disc to the lock, which made a grinding noise, and popped the door open. She gestured that I should take off my clothes and put them in the locker.

As I struggled to decide whether I should strip or flee the room, I heard my mother's voice: *You are actually planning to get naked in front of other people?*

My Irish-Catholic mother had such an aversion to the naked body that she once took my little brother's crayons and scribbled clothing on the nude women in our illustrated Bible. "Whoever decided Eve was naked?" she said as she colored a dress on the picture of Eve leaning against the apple tree in the Garden of Eden. Years after her death, I still hear my mother's voice.

The attendant pointed at the locker, so I took off my jeans, my socks, and finally my turtleneck sweater, folding and stacking them in a tidy pile in the cubbyhole. When I was done, the attendant pointed at my bra and panties and then again at the locker. I shook my head "no," hoping that she'd let me wear my underwear in the bath.

*What are you thinking?* I heard my mother say.

I was willing to ride home in wet, muddy underwear rather than answer Mother's question.

I shook my head "no" once more, but the woman stood her ground, glaring at me with her hands on her hips.

Then she reached over and tugged at my panties, muttering and pointing at the locker. Finally, while she stood just inches away, I took off my undies and threw them in the cubbyhole. She handed me a towel the size of a newborn baby's diaper and pointed to a door on the opposite side of the room, a distance I estimated to be four hundred yards, although as I consider it now, it was more likely forty feet.

Mustering my dignity, I straightened my back and shoulders, clutched the towel to my middle—somewhere between breast and pubic bone—and walked across the room to enter the bath, feeling the attendant's eyes on my bare back.

I was an exchange professor from South Dakota State University, teaching conversational English at Chungnam National University. My discomfort with nudity kept me from the public baths, or spas, for the first few weeks Ken and I lived in Daejeon. Ken, however, had always been more comfortable with his body. The morning after we were married, I walked into the bathroom, where he shaved naked in front of the mirror. "Good morning," he said. I was stunned. I had never seen my father wearing less than a white cotton t-shirt and gray work pants. What kind of man stands naked in front of a mirror? What kind of man had I married? Unlike me, Ken easily immersed himself into the bath culture, going often to the public spa at the Yuseong Hotel.

We had only been in Korea two weeks when Dr. Nho took us to the seaside town of Boryeong, famous for its beaches and the restorative power of its mud. While we were there, a mud spa was celebrating its grand opening, and Dr. Nho suggested that we visit it. We walked down the beach toward a large building of concrete and glass, up the wide steps, and into the foyer where photos of the annual Boryeong Mud Festival hung on the wall. There were pictures of men and women relaxing in mud bathtubs, sliding down a muddy slide, wrestling and playing softball in the mud. One of the photos showed the winners of the Mr. Mud and Ms. Mud contest wearing mud crowns and mud bathing suits. We studied

the pictures for a while before Dr. Nho recommended that we try the bath "for the experience."

I stalled. I heard my mother's voice: "*Are you nuts?*" But I also heard my own voice saying, "Ken, let's promise that we are going to accept every invitation to experience Korean culture." I had already kept my promise the day a little boy named John looked at the dried, silvery fish, eyes and scales intact, lying at the bottom of my metal bowl and asked, "Don't you like our fish?" I grappled the fish between my chopsticks, popped it in my mouth, chewed, swallowed, and mentally crossed eating shiny silver fish off my to-do list. In that same spirit, I walked naked into a mud spa.

Previous exchange professors had told us that Koreans scrub themselves meticulously before entering the baths, which seemed pointless in a mud spa. Erring on the side of caution, however, I entered a shower stall, picked up a rough scrubbing cloth and a bar of soap from the shelf, and turned on the water. I quickly ran the cloth up one side of my body and down the other, shampooed my hair, rinsed, and scurried into the misty spa, wanting to get into the water before other women came into the room.

I walked over to a large pool with gently rolling waves and saw a sign that said it was a seawater pool. I walked down two steps into the water, thinking that because it was the largest pool in the room, it would also be the deepest. But the water only reached my knees. As I soaked in the bubbles, I could hear water gurgling, steam pipes hissing, and a lazy plopping sound like a Yellowstone mud pot. I peered through the steam and saw a pool of muddy water and a long rectangular tray filled with mud.

Oh, why not?

I climbed out of the pool, walked over to the tray, smeared myself with the soft, pasty mud, and sat on the pool's edge for several minutes letting the mud dry until my skin puckered. Then I slid into the tub. As I sat in the mucky water, I heard her voice once more: *Oh, for the love of Mike, have you lost your mind? Only pigs wallow in mud.*

After we left the spa, we followed Dr. Nho down the beach to a tented restaurant with enormous glass fish tanks, from which he selected several fish. The chef scooped them out of the tank, slapped their heads against the sidewalk, scaled them, and chopped them into big chunks. Five minutes

later, we stared at platters piled with fish, *hweh*, so fresh they seemed to wiggle on the plates. We dipped the raw chunks into little bowls filled with horseradish paste and seasoned soy sauce with sesame seeds. Then the waiter brought a platter of shellfish. Dr. Nho threw them on a tabletop charcoal grill until they sizzled. We pried the shells open, slurped the briny seawater, and then dipped the flesh into hot chili sauce. As we drove home that night, I felt relieved that I could now cross eating raw fish and going to the baths off my to-do list, and I was thankful that I wouldn't hear my incredulous mother speaking from the grave again.

The next class period, I said to my students, "Well, guess what. I went to a mud spa this weekend." The women covered their mouths and giggled behind their hands. The men grinned.

I said, "I have never been to a public bath before, and I probably won't go again. But I am happy I tried it."

Bora asked, "Don't you have baths in America?"

"We have spas," I told her, "but I don't know of any public baths where everyone is naked."

"But you American women more free than Korean women," Honey said. "American women wear sexy clothes and dance sexy."

I laughed. "Well, this American woman doesn't wear sexy clothes, and she's too stiff to swivel her hips and prance around the dance floor."

But I understood her confusion. These students had watched the exhibitionism of Britney, Paris, and Madonna on MTV, and they couldn't reconcile those images with a Western woman's professed modesty, no matter how old she was.

Even young women raised in a hyper-sexualized American culture are more modest than my Korean students might have expected. During our time in Korea, several students from SDSU came over to tour the campus and the country. At a university banquet, a couple of the coeds wore slinky silk gowns with necklines that plunged to their waists, yet when I asked them if they had tried the spa at the hotel where they were staying, they flushed and stammered, until finally one admitted, "We went to the bath last night, but we swore we wouldn't tell anybody back home. We don't want anybody to know we were naked in a room full of women."

I overheard one of the women whisper, "I'd rather be naked in front of a man than a woman." Good lord, I wondered. What does that mean?

In contrast, the shy and modest young Korean women in my conversation class wore baggy t-shirts or blouses buttoned at the neck, with loose fitting jeans, or tights under short skirts. Yet they were at ease being nude with other women. Weeks later, when I started frequenting the baths and watched giggling, naked little girls jumping in and out of the water, chasing each other across the concrete, or holding hands as they sat on the pool's edge, oblivious to the naked women around them, I understood how the women had acquired their ease with nudity.

My Korean students insisted I try the baths one more time.

Bora even said, "I go with you to Yuseong Hotel spa and show you how."

For the first time since I'd arrived in Korea, I refused an invitation. Anonymous nudity was one thing; nudity with a girl I'd have to face in class the next day, quite another. I now regret saying no. Bora might have taught the teacher a lesson, might have instilled in me a healthy attitude about the body. But overcoming sixty years of modesty was challenging enough; I wasn't prepared to reduce myself to the vulnerability of naked flesh in front of my student. However, she did convince this reluctant woman to try the baths, alone, one more time.

The next week, at the Yuseong Hotel, I followed my routine of methodically removing each piece of clothing and folding it neatly. Then I cowered behind the locker door for several minutes, clutching the tiny towel to my middle until I worked up the courage to walk across the dressing room, past the beauty shop, where a stylist wearing only her underwear sat on a stool cleaning hair brushes, and over to the door that led to the baths. I peered through the steamy window and saw several women scouring themselves with rough cloths as they sat at the edge of a large, kidney-shaped pool.

When I opened the door, I heard loud SPLATS, like the sound of my mother slapping bread dough on the counter. In one corner, a masseuse in bra and panties used her closed fists to pummel a naked woman's back; in another corner, several naked women napped on slatted wooden floors, their heads resting on rolled-up hand towels.

As I walked across the room toward a scrubbing stool, I saw heads turn. My stomach tightened. Suddenly, I was an awkward seventh-grade giant

walking into the locker room after gym class, the eyes of tiny girls sitting on benches scrutinizing me, the girls who were elected to be cheerleaders and went home from basketball games with the starting guards, while the chunky girls crowded together in the bleachers waving our pompoms and going home alone.

But the women returned to their scrubbing and soaking, chatting quietly, or gazing across the room. Westerners are still an oddity in much of Korea, and I may have been the first naked Western woman they had ever seen. Perhaps these women were simply curious.

Women integrate the baths into their daily lives. Young mothers dangle their feet in the water as they nurse their babies by the poolside. Others wander around the spa brushing their teeth, sipping bottled water, nibbling on slices of apple they cut with a knife they carry. Young girls gently scrub the backs of elderly women too stiff to reach around and wash themselves.

I once watched a frail, silver-haired woman kneel at the edge of the pool for forty-five minutes as she scrubbed herself, dipping a bowl into the pool and pouring the water over her head. There was something ancient about this woman and her scrubbing, and I imagined her years ago leaving the children and the cooking pots, the man in the rice field, and the small hut filled with smoke and grease, to gather by a stream with other women, to strip off her filthy, tattered clothes and wade into the cold, rushing water, to sit on the pebbles glittering beneath the stream, scrubbing off the dirt and grime of her daily life. In that moment, I felt as if I had joined a venerable ritual practiced by women for centuries.

When my sister Jeanne came to visit, we took the train to the resort town of Gyeongju. By now, I relished the luxury of sitting on a stool studying myself in the mirror, free of shame or judgment as I tenderly scrubbed my bends and curves, freckles and dimples. But I couldn't imagine undressing in front of my sister.

"Sorry, Jeanne," I said, "but I'm just not ready to be naked with you."

As we made our spa reservations for separate times, Jeanne asked, "Could you have ever imagined that at age sixty you would walk naked in a public bath full of women?"

"Are you kidding me?" I said. "In high school I lied to my gym teacher

at least twice a month that I had a visit from my 'friend' just to avoid showering after class."

Even in college I'd avoided the gang showers in gym class by sneaking into the bathroom stalls, where I changed out of my orange bloomers into a skirt and sweater and waited for the room to empty before dashing off late to class. In the dormitory, I'd stayed awake until midnight to shower so I could have the shower room to myself.

Jeanne laughed. "Well, I think we've shocked Mother today." *Those two girls don't have a lick of sense.*

I put my luggage in my room and rushed to the spa. I bought my ticket, scurried into the dressing room, threw my clothes in the locker, and skated over the wet floor to a scrubbing stool.

Later, I walked down the steps into the largest pool. A chubby woman came over, took my hand, and led me to a pulsating waterfall. She stood under the waterfall with her head down while the jets of water battered her shoulders. Then she gestured to me and watched while I stood under the pounding water. She took my hand again and led me to a spot where water spurted just below the surface, turned her back, scrunched down, and moved her body back and forth through the streams of water. Once again, she watched as I imitated her. At another spot, she floated on her stomach and let the churning water bounce her body in the bubbles. Then I did the same, riding the waves like a jellyfish. After a while, she patted my shoulder, said something I didn't understand, and left. The next day when I returned to the spa, she was soaking in the hot pool. We smiled and waved like old neighbors greeting one another over the back fence.

The outdoor pool nestled in a rock garden surrounded by a tall stone fence with fragrant purple and white hibiscus growing out of the cracks. I walked up steps to a patio with a bubbling hot pool and several lounge chairs. I soaked in the hot pool for a bit and then sat at its edge, feeling the sun warm my bare back. I could hear bees buzzing around the flowers, a cuckoo bird in the rustling leaves, and the whoosh of the waterfall hitting the pool below. The soft breeze whispered against my skin, while above me, white clouds drifted across a brilliant blue sky. A pollution-free day in Korea was rare, and I intended to enjoy it, even if it meant ignoring my mother's command: *Are you crazy? Get back inside and put on your clothes.*

After a while, two women came out, naked except for small towels wrapped like turbans around their heads, and lay down in the lounge chairs next to me, laughing and chatting as they sunned themselves. What were they saying? Were they laughing about grandchildren's antics or their husbands' foolishness? Were they sharing secrets of love affairs? Gossiping about neighbors and family?

I tried to envision sitting naked with my friends talking casually about politics or books, but I couldn't.

When I returned to South Dakota, I asked my friends, "If there were public baths in America, would you go to one with me?"

One woman said, "You mean in our swimsuits, right?"

"No, we'd be naked."

"Absolutely not. I'm not getting naked in front of anybody."

The rest of the women added qualifications.

"I'd probably go with my sister."

"Maybe if I had enough to drink."

Only one said, "Sure. That sounds great."

I said, "I'd go if the spa were in another state and the room were full of women I'd never see again."

As I uttered those words, I suddenly pictured a vignette on canvas of brown-skinned, dark-eyed, naked little girls, teenagers, young mothers, and old women soaking in pools of bubbling water, talking and laughing, sharing slices of apples, and scrubbing one another's bodies with rough cloths. At the edge of the painting, a gray-haired, pale, and heavy-breasted woman peers through a window. I realized with sadness that the baths were a part of the life I had left behind in Korea.

Now that I'm home, I think often of young girls washing the bodies of old women. In the time and place of my childhood, people were not often physically affectionate. Perhaps this reserve came from the teachings of repressive Old World churches, lessons people packed in the trunks they carried to the Great Plains. Or maybe people were simply too exhausted from working an unpredictable land to take time for cuddling. Whatever the reason, many of us grew up uncomfortable with touch. In Korea, I came to understand that scrubbing an old woman's back is an act of generosity, as is accepting the touch of another woman; these are gifts that Korean

women have passed on through the generations, the legacy offered by an ancient sisterhood. This is the gift they offered me when they invited me into their community.

I saw my mother naked for the first time when she was eighty-one years old, after she had undergone open-heart surgery following a major heart attack. I had wheeled her to a room at the nursing home where she was to begin rehabilitation. An aide came into her room saying, "We need to document Marie's condition on admission to make certain she doesn't have any bruises."

She slipped off Mother's clothes, dropped them on the floor. Mother stood by the twin bed, shivering, her clothes in a pile around her feet, her withered, naked body defenseless as a baby's, while the aide circled her, checking off the items on a list in her hand like a rental-car salesman looking for dents and scratches on returned vehicles.

In that moment, my mother, who had guarded her modesty all her life, looked helpless and defeated. She glanced at me and then turned her face to the wall. I bent over, picked up her clothes and underwear, slowly folded them, and put them in a neat pile on a chair by the bed. Then I fumbled in her overnight bag for her pajamas and handed them to the aide. I drove home that night weeping with regret and guilt that I had stood by and watched a stranger dress my frail mother. But I also knew it was too late for such physical intimacy between us. Some patterns have been etched too deeply in our lives to be worn down by time or reworked by tears.

I remember my tired, sick mother standing naked in a pool of her clothing. Had we been less inhibited in our family, I might retain a memory of her naked body during her younger years, when power flowed through her heavy breasts, ample hips, and calves sturdy as fence posts. Instead, I remember her at her most vulnerable. Had I been more comfortable with touch, I might have cared for my mother the way Korean girls cared for the old women at the baths. It might have been my hands that scrubbed her back in her final years, my hands that caressed her fragile skin with small, soft circles; it might have been my hands that comforted in her suffering, my tender hands that eased her dying.

CHRIS OFFUTT

# Someone Else

By the time I was fourteen, my family was accustomed to my absences—wandering the woods, sleeping in town, eating at other people's homes. What mattered to my parents were academic grades. I maintained all A's, an easy task in Appalachia during the sixties and seventies. Of equal importance was granting utter obedience to Dad, and never causing my mother public embarrassment. With this veneer of civility thus attended to, I was free.

I don't remember how I met the fatman. I assume he approached me. He lived in town on the second floor of a small building, where he rented a single room with a bathroom in the hall. He was nice. He bought me candy bars and bottles of pop, which my parents never allowed me to have. I told him about my life and girls I liked. At four feet eleven inches, I was the shortest kid in high school with the longest hair, reputed to be the smartest but lousy at sports. The fatman listened to me. He offered a kind of sympathy and attentiveness that I needed. He accepted that I wanted to be an actor or a comic book artist when I grew up, and he believed such aspirations weren't ridiculous. He didn't talk about himself but implied that he'd experienced life beyond the confines of Rowan County, and that I would like it out there when I finally left.

I was vulnerable, I suppose, although not a dire misfit. I was open and friendly, having gone through eight years of grade school with the same small group of kids, then riding the bus ten miles to high school. One by one, my classmates began losing the habit of attending school. It was not expected but certainly accepted, and of little concern. After all, we were from Haldeman, the community farthest from town, site of the main

bootlegger, weekly drag strips, occasional shootings and arson. We were at the bottom of a pecking order that didn't start very high. Bused into town, we became aware of our status. Some of us responded by staying at home, changing our style of dress, or becoming withdrawn. I explored town.

The fatman's room was small, with no chair, and we both had to sit on the bed. The whole time I pretended it was happening to someone else. Afterwards, the fatman said he liked me. He gave me money. I left the room and walked to the drugstore, where my mother picked me up after shopping for groceries. I bought a lot of comic books at the drugstore. She didn't ask where I got the money.

I don't remember his name or what he looked like. I don't recall the print on the wallpaper or the color of the bedspread. What I do remember is the overhead light fixture, a plain bisected globe in a ceramic setting that emitted a dim yellowish light. Surrounding the globe and painted over many times were plaster rosettes with narrow leaves. I remember the light because I spent all my time staring at it and waiting until I could leave.

When I returned, I climbed the steps very slowly, trying not to make any noise because I didn't want to get the fatman in trouble. A clot of tension rose along my spine, vibrating like an embedded blade. I felt hollow—my heart pounding, sweat trickling down my sides, mouth dry, my stomach congealed to stone. The fatman opened the door and ushered me in. The bed sagged when he sat down. The money lay in sight on the bedside table. Time stopped as I slid away from my body to rove the air, imagining a life beyond the hills. I would be a movie actor. Beautiful women would throw themselves at me as I left French cafés. I was the mayor's son, the governor's nephew. I was secretly adopted. I inherited a Lexington horse farm. I was anyone but a lonely kid feeling the dampness of fat fingers.

Just before I started being someone else, I decided my parents would be proud of my open-mindedness in such a small town. They considered themselves progressive. My mother wore miniskirts and my father had a tidy beard. They traveled often, leaving me in charge of my younger siblings for a few days at a time. They went to exotic locales for science-fiction conventions—Cincinnati, Louisville, St. Louis, Nashville, once even Florida. I thought that what I was doing with the fatman made me similar

to my parents. They wrote porn. They had affairs. If they knew about the fatman, they would respect me, maybe even like me.

The fatman took me to the movies. We stood in line but didn't have to buy tickets. The fatman looked at the owner, put his hand on my shoulder, and nodded once. The owner looked at me without changing expression and let us in free. I felt important.

The fatman bought a large buttered popcorn and gave it to me. I was not allowed to have popcorn at the movies because my father said it was too expensive. Occasionally Mom made popcorn at home, but she never put butter on it. I felt special eating buttered popcorn and watching *The Godfather*, which affected me in a very powerful way. I'd never seen a movie that long or that slow. The world was utterly foreign but I understood its insular nature, the power dynamics, the violence and loyalties. After the movie, the fatman gave me a dime because I insisted on calling my father and telling him that if anything ever happened to him, I would avenge his death. I was crying into the phone. My father said little.

The fatman wanted me to touch him in his bed, but I refused. I explained that I liked girls, though I'd never been with one. I'd kissed three and touched one's bra strap, but never got any further. The fatman offered me two hundred dollars to help him make a movie. They'd shoot the whole thing in a hotel room nearby, but I'd have to touch a man, maybe another boy about my age. I told him that I really wanted to be with a girl, and suggested we make that kind of movie instead. He said if I made a movie with a man, he would provide me with a girl to be with afterwards. I told him no. He told me to think about it, but I didn't. Instead I looked at the light fixture and went away in my mind. I'd developed the ability to go rapidly, to vanish from the circumstances and enter a trancelike state in which I was a prince with a personal garrison at my command, a lavish kingdom to rule, and a harem of lovely women. I fell in love with a commoner and abandoned all my riches for her. We lived by the sea in Italy. Our eyes never left each other. We were together throughout the ages, each era presenting its version of our love. Abruptly I was back in the dim room. My legs were bare and cold, my body tense. The fatman was breathing hard. I took the money and left.

The last time I went to the room, I encountered another boy on the

steps. He was a year older than me, with long hair, new to school. I'd seen him before, outside the building, but we pretended like we didn't see each other. This time he was crouching on the steps. He motioned me to be quiet. I joined him, moving silently. We were midway up the staircase. The bathroom was at the top of the stairs and the door was not fully closed. Through it we could see the fatman standing in the shower, his vast naked bulk exposed. He was vomiting and defecating simultaneously. It was a sickening sight, so repulsive that it was hard to stop staring. I realized the fatman was crying. Not just weeping but an uncontrollable sobbing that made his shoulders quake, his torso ripple. He leaned on the wall as if in surrender.

The other boy and I slipped down the stairs and laughed about what we'd seen. What else could we do? We laughed at the hideous sight. We never talked about it later and he soon quit school. It took me many years to wonder if the other boy made a movie at the motel. By then he was dead of an overdose. The fatman had once suggested I bring my brother to visit, and I got very angry. The only good that I can find in all this now is that I protected my brother. At least I did that.

The fatman left town as suddenly as he'd appeared. I didn't speak to anyone about him. Instead, I began to shoplift. Every time I entered a store I walked around as if browsing, while secretly examining lines of sight and avenues of getaway. I was a meticulous planner. The best technique was to set what I wanted to steal near the door, then buy something cheap that required a shopping bag. On my way out of the store, I'd surreptitiously slip the preset goods into the bag. I got very scared as I walked to the door, my body encased in the same adrenalized state as when climbing the steps to the fatman's room. I breathed slowly through my mouth, sweating inside my clothes. On the sidewalk outside, I felt the euphoria of relief at having gotten away. Stealing supplied an intensity to life that was absent. It later left me feeling bad about myself, but that didn't matter because by then feeling bad felt normal.

I skipped school and began spending all my time at the pool hall. I learned to shoot a good stick. I also learned to make marijuana pipes from an empty toilet paper tube, a Coke can, an apple, anything I could punch two holes in. Some cool older boys gave me acid. Next I tried Valium. I

began taking amphetamines and breaking into cars. I never got caught. I never stole anything good. I dropped out of high school and joined the army, but they didn't want me. I went to college.

In a psychology class, I read an article that defined victims of sexual abuse. This made me feel uneasy because I knew the whole fatman business was my fault. I didn't like the idea of being a victim. Nobody forced me to enter that building and climb those stairs and push open the dark wooden door. I went there freely. I went there more than once. I felt special. I felt bad. I wondered if I was gay. I dropped the psychology class and got stoned, then drunk, and stayed that way for a good while.

Twenty-five years later I began talking about the fatman. I thought I might feel relieved, or unburdened, but I didn't. I told my wife. I told my parents and siblings in a group letter, which I suppose was cowardly, perhaps even cruel. It was shocking enough that no one knew how to respond. My father, surprisingly, called. He wanted to know if the fatman still lived in the county. In fact, Dad evoked the Godfather, saying that he would send Vito and Luigi to kill the man. I didn't have the heart to tell him how that particular movie figured into things so long ago.

After revealing my old secret, I mainly felt embarrassed. Worse things happened to other people, and much worse things happened to women. I was never forced or hurt. It was a long time ago. I understood the fatman had probably been abused as a child. I also knew that I should find it in myself to forgive him, an act that would ultimately benefit me. But I couldn't do it. I'd spent too many years hoping the fatman went to prison. I hoped every inmate spat on him in the corridors. I wanted them to fill his food with poison, smack him around in the yard, and ambush him in the shower. I wanted him to be scared and alone. I wanted his life to be so miserable that he spent every day wishing he was someone else. I wanted him to memorize the dim flat light fixture in his cell. I wanted him as dead as I felt, as dead as I still feel sometimes, as dead as the other boy I saw on the steps will always be.

LEE MARTIN

# Heart Sounds

### ARTERY OCCLUSION

I'm sitting at the breakfast table reading the newspaper when my vision closes in at the edges for an instant and then clears. It's a Sunday morning in late September, and I've just come up from lifting weights in the basement. I try to move my right arm and find I can't. It's dead weight, as is my right leg. I try to call for my wife, who's in the kitchen, but I can't form the words I want to say. I'm nine days away from my fifty-seventh birthday, and, when I got out of bed this morning, I thought I was in perfect health.

### BRAIN BLEED

At the emergency room, the neurologist says he'd like my permission to give me the tPA (tissue plasminogen activator), the clot-busting medicine that has to be started within three hours of the first symptoms of a stroke. He wants me to understand there's a three percent chance that the tPA will cause a bleed in the brain. Still, this is my best chance for recovery. I offer my approval by raising my left arm and giving the neurologist a thumbs-up. The iv drip of tPA begins. I don't know, then, that statistically the odds are still against me. tPA only cures one out of ten stroke patients.

### CEREBRAL INFARCTION

Also known as an ischemic stroke, it results when there's a disturbance in the blood vessels of the brain. After my CT scan, my neurologist tells

me he suspects a piece of plaque has come unhinged in my brain and is blocking a blood vessel. He tells me that as the tPA does its work, this piece of plaque may flip around, causing momentary periods of recovery and relapse as I regain and lose again the use of the right side of my body and my ability to speak.

## DEATH

Hemorrhagic stroke—bleeding in the brain—is less common but more frequently deadly than ischemic stroke.

## ECHOCARDIOGRAM

I get lucky. The tPA works its magic and by evening I'm able to lift my right arm, able to stand, my right leg steady. My speech is back to normal.

The next morning, my neurologist comes into my room in the Neuro ICU, and I greet him with a wave of my right arm.

He says, "Well, that looks much better today." Then he admits that he was very concerned about me. "Now," he says, "it looks like you're on the mend."

The problem is he doesn't know what caused my stroke. He does know, though, that it wasn't a piece of plaque as he originally thought. It was a blood clot that somehow moved to my brain. But how? It will be a day of tests, he says.

A while later, I lie in my hospital bed as a technician moves a transducer around my chest. The transducer sends out high-pitched sound waves and records the echoes they make as they bounce off the internal structures of my heart. A computer converts the echoes into moving images on a monitor I can't see. The sound waves bounce off blood cells, and, when they do, their pitch changes. I listen to the swoosh and swirl, the thud and thump. The computer colorizes these Doppler signals and gives an image of the direction and velocity of my blood flow. That's how I find out that I have what the doctors suspect is a hole between the atria of my heart.

## FORAMEN OVALE

"A PFO," my cardiologist tells me. "A patent foramen ovale."

During fetal development, a hole in the septum between the atria of our hearts allows blood to move from the right atrium into the left. Since our lungs are nonfunctional when we're in the womb, we don't need the blood to pass through them. We get our oxygen from the placenta. The opening between the atria, the foramen ovale, is crucial then to our well-being in the womb. We have a layer of tissue that acts as a valve over the foramen ovale. After we're born, the pressure in the right side of the heart drops when the lungs start working, and this decrease in pressure causes the foramen ovale to close entirely. In approximately twenty-five percent of the population, though, the foramen ovale doesn't seal, and then it's known as a patent foramen ovale. An increase in pressure in the chest—from coughing, sneezing, straining to have a bowel movement, or, as I suspect was the case for me, lifting weights—can cause the foramen ovale to open, allowing blood to shunt from the right atrium to the left. If that blood happens to contain a clot, it can travel to the brain, causing a stroke.

"About forty percent of people who have a stroke from no identifiable cause," my neurologist says to me in the hospital, "have a PFO."

These cryptogenic strokes, he goes on to explain, usually occur in patients younger than fifty-five.

"I was always a late bloomer," I tell him.

### GOD

My mother took me to church and taught me to love Jesus. God, she said, was watching over us. He knew everything we said, everything we did. God loved us so much he sent his son to die for our sins, to redeem us, to offer us a chance at grace and eternal life. My mother was a devout woman who endured much: her father's drinking problem; the Great Depression, during which she taught at various country schools in southeastern Illinois, bringing her wages home to help her parents, with whom she, a spinster, lived; and much later, the farming accident that cost my father both of his hands and the anger he brought into our home. She married him when she was forty-one, and he was thirty-eight. A last chance at

love for both of them. Four years later, I was born. Oops. A surprise baby, never meant to come along, but there I was, with a patent foramen ovale, a fact that my mother and father never knew. There I was, a baby with a holey heart.

### HELP

"I'm counting on you to tell me the right thing to do about this PFO," I say to my cardiologist.

"Well, here's the thing," he says. "No one really knows."

It's a question of whether to close the hole via a heart catheterization procedure or instead to manage the situation with anticoagulants.

"I hate stroke," my cardiologist says. "That's why I want to close every hole I find. I long for the day when a clinical study proves the undeniable effectiveness of PFO closure. I'm not a quack. I know what can happen if there's a hole between the atria, and I know how to stop it from happening again."

"Cardiologists are surgeons," my neurologist tells me. "They want to close holes."

### INSURANCE

The only clinical trial completed thus far showed no significant difference between PFO closure and management with medication. A second study, this one using a different closure device, will make its results known late in October. Some insurance companies won't cover the cost of PFO closure unless a patient suffers a second stroke.

"I want you to wear an event monitor for three weeks," my cardiologist says, "so we can see if you have any atrial fibrillation. Then we'll go from there."

### JOGGING

It's a glorious Indian-summer day in Columbus, Ohio. Red and yellow leaves twirl down from maple trees along the street. I enjoy their leisurely descent as I take my morning walk. I feel their lazy rhythm in my stride.

Soon, I'll break into a run, the pace that's been more familiar to me for years.

I left the hospital after my stroke with no impairments. My family doctor says I can begin running again, but only five minutes to start. Then, after four days, I can add another five minutes. It seems like a long way back to my normal hour of running. I'm struggling with who I am on the other side of my stroke. I remember lying in my hospital bed in the Neuro ICU, unable to make myself say the words, even if only to myself, "I had a stroke."

Words have been my life. Some I've manufactured in stories and novels; some I've recalled in memoirs and essays. Still others I've never been able to bring myself to use. So I know that what we say is who we are, even those unspoken words that echo just beneath the sounds of the ones that we allow ourselves. Our heart sounds pulsing in the silence.

My family was often an angry family; my father filled our house with his temper. My mother kept quiet and endured. Sometimes I tried to make a noise of my own, but often I let my father's voice swallow up my own.

### KNUCKLEHEAD SMIFF

When I was a kid, I loved watching the ventriloquist Paul Winchell. I was fascinated by the fact that Winchell could make it appear that his dummies were talking when really it was his own words giving them voices. No matter how hard I tried, I couldn't see his lips move. Knucklehead Smiff was one of his dummies. He wasn't as intelligent as Winchell's featured dummy, Jerry Mahoney. Winchell gave Knucklehead a crooked mouth, eyes that didn't move, and painted-on hair to reinforce the persona of a true "dummy." Winchell was anything but that. He was also an inventor who held the first patent for an artificial heart. The basic principle that Dr. Robert Jarvik used in the Jarvik-7, the first artificial heart to be successfully implanted into Barney Clark in 1982, was exactly the same as the one in Winchell's design.

## LATIN ROOTS

*Venter* (belly) *loqui* (speak). This belly talk was thought to be the voices of the dead who took up residence in the stomach of the ventriloquist. People believed that the ventriloquist could speak to the dead and foretell the future.

## MONITOR

To my students and friends who come to see me after I'm home from the hospital, I must seem fine, but the truth is I'm a mess. My anxiety level is so high I can't sleep. I worry about what might happen during the night, that another clot might pass through the suspected hole between my atria and travel to my brain. When I left the hospital, the doctors and nurses watched me with smiles on their faces. One of them said, "This just doesn't happen here. In this critical care unit, we rarely see someone go home without some sort of impairment."

I came home with orders to take a baby aspirin every day to keep my blood from clotting. I'm also on a low-dose statin to lower my bad cholesterol, which was slightly elevated. I'm a worrier by nature, and I go to my family doctor to talk to her about my anxiety and my depression.

"Your body is in full fight-or-flight mode," she tells me.

"I'm a fighter," I say.

Then I weep. I can't help it. I weep because my students have brought me wind-up toys to add to the collection they know I have. I weep because of Chirpy Bird, and Robot Guy, and Nunzilla, and Knight on Horse. I weep because colleagues have come to help with my classes, because friends have called with words of encouragement. I weep because of how differently this story might have ended, because in spite of that fact love is all around me.

I do my best to get used to the weight of the heart monitor sliding around with me when I roll over in bed, the electrode pads that irritate my skin, the fear that the monitor will detect something abnormal. Meanwhile, my cardiologist receives a report each day. People are keeping watch over my heart, but I have trouble finding confidence in the future. I struggle to find a rhythm.

# NOTHING (AND MAYBE EVERYTHING)

The heart monitor records no episodes of atrial fibrillation. The results of the second clinical trial for the PFO closure device manufactured by St. Jude Medical, the Amplatzer PFO Occluder, are released. They show a forty-six percent to seventy-two percent risk reduction in recurrent strokes if the PFO is closed with the device as compared to medical therapy alone.

Still, there's a mixed response to these findings. Those in favor of PFO closure—that is to say, the cardiologists who perform the procedure—have emphasized that the findings reaffirm that carefully selected patients with a history of cryptogenic stroke and PFO may, indeed, benefit in stroke risk reduction from device closure over medical management. Others—that is to say, the neurologists who are typically more conservative and prefer medical therapy—are quick to point out that this evidence is inconclusive given the lack of statistically significant primary endpoint results demonstrating superiority of one therapy over another.

Bottom line? Even though the study's results are favorable for closure, they haven't achieved statistical significance, which assesses whether the findings of a clinical trial reflect a pattern or merely chance. Bottom line? No one still knows for sure that PFO closure is preferable to medical therapy. I make an appointment with my cardiologist to discuss our next steps.

# OCCLUDER

A catheter-delivered device that blocks a hole in the wall of a heart. Often the occluder has a clamshell design and is folded up until the catheter arrives at the area of the defect. Once in place, the occluder is unfolded on both sides of the defect so that pressure keeps it in place.

# PATENT

Not blocked; open. Long before I knew about my patent foramen ovale, I learned to seal things inside me, to go mum. There were words I could say, and words I couldn't. I could make a joke with my father, but I couldn't tell him I loved him, nor could I say those words to my mother, whom I loved dearly. We weren't that kind of family—no hugs, no kisses, no

whispered terms of endearment. We managed to find our ways toward occasional happiness, but when it came to utterances from the heart, we were tightlipped, closed off. We had to become practiced, then, at listening to the silences around our words. Only in those silences could we know how much we meant to one another.

When I was twenty-four, my father had a heart attack. As he lay in the ICU—this gruff man with whom I'd had such a difficult time, now retreating inside himself where I'm sure, knowing what I do now on the other side of my stroke, he was perilously close to surrendering to despair—he barely said a word. He'd been poleaxed by the reality of his own mortality, and what vocabulary was sufficient for all that did to a man?

I wrote him a letter. I told him all the things I'd never been able to say to him in person. I told him I loved him. Despite the history of trouble between us—too much temper, too much bullheadedness, too much violence and hurt—I'd always loved him. I'd always felt his strength, this man who'd lost both of his hands in a farming accident when I was a baby and had come through all that with a steadfast determination. Steel in his blood; fire in his eyes. I told him that whenever I'd been weak or stupid, I'd eventually drawn from his strength as a way of getting myself back on the right path. I gave this letter to my mother and asked her to deliver it.

"He asked me to read it to him," she told me later, "but he couldn't listen to it all."

"That just makes me cry," he'd said, and he was not a man who allowed himself that. I'm not sure that he ever heard everything that I had to say.

## QUACKSALVER

Charlatan. From the Dutch word, "kwakzalver," a hawker of salve. In the Middle Ages, "quack" meant to shout. Quacksalvers hawked their salves in the public marketplace by shouting out the often unfounded claims for the benefits of their products. In current times, accusations of quackery often rely on the polemics of one group as it attempts to establish the truth of its belief by claiming the falsity of another group's opposite belief.

When I meet with my cardiologist, I ask him straight out, "What would you want done if it was your heart?"

He doesn't hesitate. "I'd want that hole closed," he says. "In a minute. Wouldn't even think about it."

I can't imagine being able to live my life without fear if I know the hole exists and at any minute a clot might pass through it and again travel to my brain. I let myself trust my cardiologist's confidence. I tell him yes, and just like that a date is chosen three weeks in the future for the procedure that will be necessary to confirm the suspected hole, assess its size, and, if feasible, close it.

Sometimes, I think, the only choice we have is to dummy up, keep quiet, surrender to the claims and the care of others.

### RECURRENCE

If my cardiologist doesn't close my PFO, I have a one percent to three percent chance every year of having another stroke.

He tells me he'll use the Gore Helex Septal Occluder, which the FDA approved in 2007 for the treatment of atrial septal defect. The membrane of this occluder has been used for more than twenty years in open-heart surgery with a history of proven safety. This is how my cardiologist can close my PFO without having to wait for the FDA to approve a device particularly designed for that job.

Much to my relief, the procedure will be minimally invasive. My cardiologist will thread a catheter through the femoral vein in my groin to deliver the occluder.

He tells me I'll be awake for the procedure and I can watch it on a monitor if I wish.

"What will I feel?" I ask.

"You won't feel a thing," he says. "Not even when I tug on your heart."

### SYSTOLE

The word, in ancient Greek, meant "a drawing together." The systolic number in a blood-pressure reading is the top number, the one that measures the maximum arterial pressure during a contraction of the heart's left ventricle. We're talking about the pressure exerted on the walls of

the blood vessels as our blood circulates. The bottom number measures the diastolic pressure, when the heart refills with blood after systole. A normal blood pressure is 120/80.

I'm the sort who's never liked to think about what's going on inside my body. I've preferred to trust that everything is working exactly as it should. Not that I make unhealthy choices, mind you. I'm a good patient who believes in annual physical exams and preventive medicine. But when it comes to the beating of the heart, the pumping of blood, and everything that has to happen to keep me alive, I've preferred to leave that curiosity to someone else. I've always thought the cable television channel right before the one that shows surgeries, etc., should carry a warning so folks like me, who'd rather not be reminded of the delicate and intricate systems we are beneath our skins, can skip on by.

Now an invitation to watch my heart while my cardiologist implants the occluder? The writer in me says, "You have to know the facts; you have to bear witness." The person I am, though, wants to close my eyes and say, "Doc, just let me know when you're done."

### TRANSESOPHAGEAL ECHOCARDIOGRAM

On December 10, I report to Riverside Methodist Hospital, where one of my cardiologist's associates attempts to put a probe down my esophagus. This transesophageal echocardiogram will either confirm the presence of the suspected hole between my atria or else show that the surface echocardiogram performed when I was in the hospital after my stroke was in error.

"These surface echoes sometimes show holes where there are no holes," my cardiologist told me then. "A TEE will let us know for sure."

If the hole is there and it turns out to be large enough to close, my cardiologist will do just that. The occluder he'll use will be a small patch made of a polytetrafluorethylene material held inside a wire frame made of nitinol, a metal alloy of nickel and titanium. Once the patch is in place, tissue will begin to grow into the patch, allowing the occluder to function as a permanent implant. My blood flow will return to its normal path, no longer able to shunt from my right atrium to my left, thereby significantly reducing my chances of having another stroke.

I'm sedated for the TEE, but I have to be able to respond to commands—to swallow the probe, to cough so the doctor can access the shunting of blood from right to left. The probe has an ultrasound transducer at its tip. The heart rests directly upon the esophagus, so the ultrasound beam will have only millimeters to travel. The proximity will reduce the attenuation, or the weakening, of the ultrasound signal, generating a stronger return signal, which will enhance the images received. Sound waves will travel to my heart. As these waves bounce off my heart's structures, a computer in the echo machine will convert them into pictures on a screen. These images will show the size and shape of my heart and how well the chambers and valves are working. My cardiologist will get a much clearer look at the structure of my heart and will know for sure whether the suspected PFO exists, and if it does, whether it's of a size that he can close.

He doesn't know that my heart has secrets. Will he hear them in the beats it makes—the quavers left there by my father's anger, the pulsing of all I tried to say and everything I wanted to hear? My heart, my heart. Will my cardiologist know how it's always longed to be whole?

## UMBRELLA

The shape of each disk in the occluder that will seal my heart.

My mother owned one umbrella her entire life. She rarely used it. An umbrella with a wooden tip and pleats of red and green and blue. She preferred a rain bonnet instead. A pleated plastic rain bonnet that she kept folded neatly in her purse, at the ready whenever she might need it.

That was my mother, practical and prepared. She also had clear plastic rain booties that slipped over her shoes and buttoned across the top of her foot. She knew how to protect both head and foot, but when it came to my father's anger, she was helpless . . . except the night she threatened to walk out. I was five or six, the possessor of a black eye thanks to my cousin and a baseball bat, and my mother was trying to apply a warm compress to it. I was fussy, which made my father angry, which led to loud voices and shouting. It was pouring rain outside, and finally my mother had had enough of my father's temper, and she said she was leaving. She threw on her coat, grabbed her umbrella, and started toward the door.

I ran to her and threw my arms around her legs. "Don't go," I said. "Don't go."

I couldn't bear the thought of being left alone with my father. Who would I be without my mother?

She couldn't turn away from me. She stayed. We never spoke of that night again. We lay down in our house and the rain beat on our roof and against our windows, but finally we fell asleep on this night when my mother came close to walking out.

As I grew older I started to sometimes wish that she would take me and we would go away and start a new life without my father. In time, I came to understand that, though she never said it, she loved him.

I remember how she wept when he died, how she said, "All my life, I've taken care of someone." She'd cared for her elderly grandfather, the Civil War veteran. As the oldest child, she'd cared for her brothers and sisters. Finally, she'd cared for my father in spite of all he asked of her and how difficult he could be, and, when he was finally gone, and her quiet days of widowhood began, all she could say was, "Now what am I supposed to do?"

## VENTRILOQUISM

The illusion that voices come from sources other than the speaker. A technique known as the ventriloquial drone, or the bee drone, allows the ventriloquist to create distant voices. The ventriloquist, as he or she practices the ventriloquial drone, takes a deep breath and while holding it makes a retching sound at the back of the throat. Then the ventriloquist utters a prolonged "Ah," exhaling slowly. That "ah," as it's prolonged, will begin to sound like the hum of a distant bee drone. The farther back in the throat the sound is made, the more distant it will seem. Move the sound forward in the throat, and it will seem nearer.

A PFO between the atria, the two upper chambers, can affect the force, volume, and direction of blood flowing through the heart. As a result, patients with this defect may develop abnormal heart sounds and rhythms.

In healthy adults, there are two normal heart sounds, a *lub* and a *dub* that occur in sequence with each heartbeat.

The noise of a heart that has a septal defect such as a PFO should tell its

tales to the listener, but for nearly fifty-seven years doctors have listened to my heart and heard nothing that alarmed them.

One doctor, who visited me in the hospital after the surface echocardiogram gave an indication that I might have a PFO, pressed the diaphragm of his stethoscope against my chest and listened for a good long while.

"I can't hear it," he finally said. "I can't tell it's there at all."

Which brings me to another *V*—the vanishing point, that point at which something disappears or ceases to exist.

### WISHING WELL

On the grounds outside a hospital in a town near my very small hometown in southeastern Illinois, there was a wishing well. I remember my aunt taking me there once when I was a small boy. My aunt was a nurse's aide at the hospital. I can't recall whether someone from my family was a patient there at the time, or whether we had just stopped by to visit my aunt. What I do remember is her giving me a penny and telling me to throw it in the well. It was a summer Sunday. The wind stirred the leaves of the oak and maple trees, the sun warmed the bricks of the well, the smell of freshly cut grass was in the air. For what did I wish? I have no idea. How many people over the years came to toss in a penny and make their own wishes? How many prayers and pleas were said silently in the time it took those pennies to arc and drop into that well? Where was my mother on this day? Why was I with my aunt? These are all questions I can't answer. My mother and father are gone. My aunt is gone. My family has disappeared and here I am unable to talk to them, just barely able to recall the sound of their voices.

### X

Marks the spot.

### Y

A fork in the road. Choose. Walk toward the vanishing point.

My cardiologist enters the cath lab in his scrubs. He puts a hand on my shoulder. "Okay, buddy," he says. "Let's get to work." A few minutes later, I hear him say, "I'm definitely in the left atrium now."

Earlier, even with sedation, I failed to swallow the transducer tube for the transesophageal echocardiogram. I've agreed to let my cardiologist go ahead with the PFO closure procedure, convinced as I am that the hole will be there waiting for him.

I'm wide-awake, watching the procedure unfold on a screen. My cardiologist was right; I don't feel a thing.

"There's the PFO," he says, and I can't imagine sweeter words. If he found no hole, I'd have a week's recovery period ahead of me, all for nothing. Plus, we'd have no idea what caused my stroke or when it might happen again. But there's a hole. Hallelujah! There's a hole, and this man is going to close it.

"I'm done," he finally says. He comes to me and lays a hand on my shoulder. "There was a hole," he says. "I closed it. You're going to be fine." Then, like a rock star, like Elvis leaving the building, he's gone.

I ask my nurse about the size of the hole. She shows me the device they used to close it, and it appears to be slightly larger than a nickel, slightly smaller than a quarter. I ask her about a fluoroscopic image still left on the screen.

"Is that my heart?" I ask her, and she says it is.

She shows me where the occluder is located, the titanium rings of mesh locked in place to keep blood shunting from right to left. Such a light thing, such a beautiful thing.

"Can I have a copy of that image?" I ask.

As they wheel me to my recovery room, I clutch it to my chest.

In the image, my heart looks like a face in profile. It looks, I decide, like my father's angry face. The ridge of his forehead, the hook of his nose, his slightly open mouth, his clenched chin.

This must be the face he put on when he first heard the news that my mother was pregnant. My mother told me years later, after he was dead, that the first thing he said to her doctor was, "Can you get rid of it?"

Maybe somehow he knew. The damage, the abnormality, the violence, everything that was to come. He didn't have a word for it, but he knew. I hear it in the silence after the question, that moment of pause, as the doctor leans forward in his chair, as my mother looks down at her hands resting on her belly, as I take root inside her. In the amniotic fluid, my heart beats. Do I feel the silence in my pulse, a silence I'll strain to hear the rest of my life? The doctor clears his throat. Then he tells my father, no, he can't. He can't get rid of it.

What can my father do, then, but wait as the months go on? What can he do now that he's tried to save us and failed?

Son. The word for who I was to him feels incomplete with its one syllable, a first heart sound waiting for its second. I listen for it. I've always listened—thinking, *there*, no, *there*. Any noise will do—even an echo—no matter how distant, no matter how faint.

JULIE MARIE WADE &
BRENDA MILLER

# Telephone

In the beginning was the gray, and it was called Elisha. In the beginning was the bell, and it was called Alexander. In the beginning was an office in Highland Park, a classroom in Boston, competing laboratories. One future hinged on the "harmonic telegraph"—better than a letter, better than a message in a bottle. Think of it: *your own words in real time, your own voice coming through the line like music, and there on the end, your beloved rapt and eager, listening, waiting to hear!* In this beginning, as with all: a diagram, a caveat, a rival creation story.

Imagine the bell chiming in the gray. Imagine the loud moon of sound rising through the clouds. Now Alexander whispers to Elisha on the courthouse stairs, "We can't all be famous, man." In this version, he has a pipe and pretty hair, soft like taffeta on a woman's dressing gown. "Give it a century or so. History might turn this all around."

"Since when?" Elisha spits. He tugs his beard to a narrow point, then tucks his hands inside his trouser pockets. "Since when has history ever been kind to the underdog?"

When the red curtains sweep closed, the gold tassels swish this way and that, almost an echo. Over the clatter of applause, everyone hears it—that loud moon of sound, so unmistakable now: a bright silver telephone ringing.

Can you hear it? The song of a loon—voice echoing across a bright sliver of lake, disembodied. Like the voice on the other end of the telephone. In the beginning, that voice mingled with static, especially long distance, and long distance was expensive. My mother hissed the words to us as she spoke with her mother in Brooklyn—*long distance*—when we made a racket in the kitchen. She stood at the tall counter as she talked, the long coil of the telephone looped around her fingers. Her fingers twirled the loops tighter until her knuckles bulged, and then she let the strand uncoil, bouncing ringlets, like the hair on the girls I admired in novels.

I tried to imagine it: long distance, and how a voice could traverse that territory to reach us there in the suburbs of Los Angeles. My mother's voice, as she talked, became increasingly inflected with New York-ese, an actual dialect recorded by linguists; she seemed to take on the persona of a different person, the girl I never knew.

When my cousins came to visit they spoke a foreign language, tough and hardy, a rollick through the streets. They said I had an accent too—a California twang—but I couldn't catch it. Can we ever hear ourselves clearly? How others hear us? Say hello to your grandmother, my mother said, and handed the earpiece to me. Hello? I said into the static, my greeting always a question, each word that followed echoing across the distance between us. The telephone warm with my mother's ear, her fervent listening.

My father's palm warms the receiver with sweat. His dime slides down the phone's cool throat. As he waits for a dial tone, he peers through the grate on the hospital window. It's late evening, September in Seattle, plump pigeons mingling on the ledge. It's his wife's mother he's calling, a woman they haven't seen or spoken to in years. His voice wavers when she answers, but then he says it, clear as a bell, "You're a grandmother!" Silence: looping back on itself like a snake's tail. "Did you hear what I said, Teena?" She sighs, begins to uncoil. When she speaks at last, her tone is merely curious: "Boy or girl?" This is the first time my father has ever mentioned me aloud, and she can hear the hope and love and fear passing

through his teeth like water over rocks. This is an actual dialect recorded by linguists, as is disappointment, as is grief. "We have a daughter," he tells her proudly. Now the pigeons have moved on to other perches. A lone taxi glides through the street like a pat of butter. My grandmother lays the phone back in its cradle.

Grief: does it forever swing over the cradle? We listened for it, knew by heart this dialect: a phone ringing in the middle of the night. A phone ringing at 9:00 a.m., 1:00 p.m., 6:00 p.m., even 9:00 p.m.: these calls had an aura of polite questioning (*who's calling please?*). These calls were interrogatives. But a phone ringing at 4:00 a.m.: these calls used the syntax of the imperative (*who's calling?!*). Jerked from the warm confines of sleep, my mother fumbled for her glasses (*I can't hear without my glasses on*). In our bedrooms, we heard the phone jangling, water over rocks gaining in volume, the roar of the rapids approaching. The noise before a phone answered at 4:00 a.m., and then the quiet, the murmured words, *oh no*— water easing out into ripples against the shore. Sleepwalkers, we huddled in our parents' doorway, the light from the bedside lamp wan in the wee hours. The phone sitting now innocent in its cradle, stubborn and silent, while my mother wept in my father's arms. They sat upright against the headboard, in their pajamas, the covers still demure against their legs. *Go back to bed.* This moment: not meant for us to witness.

So we went back to our beds, in rooms that held no phones, not yet. Our rooms contained only the present, could not be intruded upon via *long distance.* Our rooms connected to no other place or time—sported no cables or wires, inlets or outlets. The air: undisturbed, but for our own errant interrogatives, imperatives. We wondered the precise words murmured through the telephone line at that hour: who called and what language could they possibly speak?

My little pink room that held no phone yet: pink as a pencil's head, pink as an esophagus. The wicker chair where my mother rocked me, undis-

turbed, by the wan lamplight of the early years. There were roses on those walls—almost an imperative, instructing me how to be a daughter. Girls like frilly, delicate things (*don't they?*). The doll with the velvet dress and tatted shawl who kept watch from a corner shelf—whose tiny porcelain nail beds we painted. Girls always do as they're told (*don't they?!*). The bed made every morning, the still-warm pajamas slipped down the chute, the hairbrush and powder puff on the vanity table, stubborn and silent, in the room where no phones rang, not yet.

My mother had a French telephone on her nightstand, ivory and gold. She conducted important business on the bed with her shoes off, her steno pad poised. (*Can I put you down for a casserole?*) (*Flower-arranging is set for the morning program.*) (*Just a small donation would be much appreciated.*) Her voice was never demure, always an imperative. I crouched in the hall, listening to the rotary spin, picturing the seven numbers flying like a carnival ride at the fair. She worked late into the night sometimes, for Delta Kappa Gamma and the Garden Club, for Bingo and Bunco and AAUW. I thought if I listened long enough, I might learn the secrets of ladyhood: how to speak only like you mean it, polite and precise, but never wavering. Even a question is never a question. A request only cloaks a demand.

Sometimes I fell asleep, and my father would find me, crumpled against the grandfather clock he had come to wind. His back was not so bad yet that he couldn't lift me, cradle me in his arms as he carried me back to bed. "You're going to be a little wilted flower tomorrow," he'd say, not quite scolding, pulling the mauve sheets up to my nose, then the quilt like a patchwork blush, a wave of cotton. In the room without inlets or outlets, I slept like the pink pearl I was, soon to erase everything.

Erasure: the sound of a telephone ringing in an empty house. A request becoming a demand becoming disappointment. The phone rings 5 (*polite*), 7, (*precise*), 9, 11 (*peeved*) times, almost giving up, then 12 (*resigned*), the quiet afterward like a sigh. It's a mystery now, words unspoken but held suspended, pearls in the groove of a tongue.

Sometimes you could hear the phone ringing as you pulled up in the station wagon, your mother hurrying out of the car, fumbling with the bags and keys, rushing inside to pick up . . . and nothing, just the echo of a *click*. She stood there a few moments, the earpiece in hand, warbling *hello?* into the silence, as if the question, the repetition, could be an incantation, recalling the caller from oblivion. The house vibrated in the aftermath of a missed call; the rooms, after all, had heard the insistent ring, and they'd inclined toward the phone, wondering. They would have picked up, if they could, would have taken a message.

Messages written on the chalkboard in the kitchen. Coming home from a night out, you automatically swiveled your head to the chalkboard to see if anyone had called, if anyone wanted you. But those messages were imprecise: *Kevin called.* You imagined your mother talking to the boy, saying *May I take a message?* like the career secretary she'd been. She was an expert at answering the phone, had just the right inflections, the accent of professional courtesy. And even those simple words made you blush: the thought of your boyfriend's voice in her ear, and then her careful transcription in chalk on the board. She couldn't say what he wanted, couldn't have really known.

You often declined to go out, instead sitting by the telephone—no, not by it, but as close as possible, the phone in your lap—willing it to ring. You didn't dare move, didn't even go to the bathroom, because what if you missed it? That jangly bell summoning you, and you lunged to get it (*I've got it!*), your voice cracking with panic and hope. If it wasn't the person you expected, you yelled *I have to keep this line open!* and hung up, still waiting. Once you got the call you wanted, *if* it finally arrived, you stayed on the line for hours, speaking in various positions: sitting up, lying down, rolled onto your back, your hand caressing the cord.

Your house had one line, two phones, so sometimes you heard the surreptitious click of someone picking up—intentionally or by accident— eavesdropping on your intimate pauses. Your mother or your brother might butt in to say they needed the line (*get off the phone!*), and you hissed *okay! Just a minute!* And you occupied the line, the only line, a few moments longer to say your awkward good-byes.

You remember the sound of a busy signal: that loud, brash, staccato

buzz—almost angry, indignant, saying: *you can't get through.* If you were desperate, if the line had been busy for hours, you could ask the operator to break in, an emergency, and those conversing—your boy-friend and another girl?—heard the distant, officious voice of the operator telling them to *get off the line.* And there you'd be, embarrassed, with your non-emergency. What was worse? The busy signal—signifying life, someone home, but unconcerned about you? Or the phone ringing in an empty house, the echo of your insistence (*pick up, pick up*) to be there, to answer?

It's a mystery now, how the world your parents love is lost, how the world you think you love is empty, shallow as water slipping through the lips of Puget Sound. They keep eavesdropping on your heart (*how they do this, you'll never know*), then breaking in with their loud, concerned voices: *So many false prophets,* they warn. *So many paths to perdition!*

Your father has two telephones in his basement office: an old brown rotary for home, a slick new push-button for work. *Two lines.* Plugged into their respective wall ports, the phones sit side by side like rivals, or worse—married people who no longer touch each other. You envy the way your father has another life where he is important, the glimpses you have of it: graph paper, a swivel chair, a desk light that bends to various positions, a black-handled, magnifying lens.

Sometimes you play a game where he calls you on the home line from his work phone in the office. You stand at the top of the stairs in the kitchen by the big, yellow phone, the one you call the *mothership.* Mostly, it belongs to your mother. This phone is big like a blimp, yellow like a submarine. You love answering this phone, stretching the cord long as a jump rope, straddling it, then trying on inflections the way some girls try on shoes: the interrogative, the imperative, softening your voice to a whisper or making it whistle-sharp, precise.

Your parents say one day boys are going to call asking for you, wanting to take you out on dates, to restaurants and dances—but you don't believe them. Your parents also say you must never call boys, regardless of your

generation's lax morals, its empty, desperate search for *quick fixes* and *instant gratification*. None of this means anything to you yet. You like to play with Shawn across the street, so you call him sometimes in secret. Mostly, his mother answers. Her name is Adele, which reminds you of *addled*. She has sadness you can hear in the pauses between her words. She is all line breaks, like a very sad poem.

Your own mother intercepts you at the threshold. "Who was that you were talking to?" You tell her you and Shawn are going to play tennis, you and Shawn are going to climb trees. You tell her yes, *he* called *you*. What you don't tell is that you and Shawn are going to double back to his family room and prank-call all the neighbors for hours—until the officious operator cuts in to report, "We've had some complaints associated with this number." You will roll on your backs, howling with laughter. You will close the White Pages, toss them back on the shelf. Everything is still funny then, and for no good reason. Even when you grow up, you will never touch each other.

The Yellow Pages arrived every year, predictable as migration: that heavy thump on the threshold, as if something had crawled to your porch to die. Whether you wanted it or not—if there had been big changes or none at all—you had to drag the directory inside and find somewhere to put it. For some reason, your mother kept the old books for a while, stacking them under the counter like building blocks (*you never know* . . .). Maybe it seemed a shame to toss out something so big, so substantial—something that wanted only to be of use.

Whenever you needed anything—from an auto mechanic to a zoo—you pulled out the Yellow Pages and thumbed through the slick listings, trying to discern from the language and format of the entries which company might serve you best. You always wondered about the one-line listings in pale, non-bolded font: they announced themselves hardly at all, gave you no reason to call. These companies nestled like secrets between the display ads—loud promotions that held pictures of smiling tradesmen kneeling with their children, proclaiming *Family Business! Serving you*

*since 1959*—and for that reason alone you wanted to call the quiet ones and see who might answer, what they'd have to say for themselves.

Public phone booths used to have the Yellow Pages dangling by a chain, protected by thick, black plastic covers. When you tried to use these directories, they thwarted your efforts; you had to twist and turn to get them to open and lie flat. You had to find a nickel, a dime, a quarter, rummaging in your pocket or purse, your elbows banging against the glass. You had to hold the phone wedged between ear and shoulder while you deposited change and kept your finger pointed to the number you wanted to call. You often dropped your coins. You had to disregard those people standing outside the booth, peering in, waiting impatiently for their turn. Watching you there, boxed in—private but public, your need for help on display.

Once, in a phone booth at a beach park, you kept a long line of people waiting for a half hour while you cried to a friend. *I don't know what to do*, you repeated, clutching the receiver, keeping your gaze narrowed to the metal shelf dusty with grit, studded with chewed gum. Someone had stolen the Yellow Pages; the chain dangled empty. People grumbled, and one boy banged on the glass. They thought you were addled, or simply rude. But you had to hold onto the voice at the other end of the line. The voice talked you down, told you to take deep breaths, move one foot at a time to a café, where you would eat a bowl of brown rice and vegetables with peanut sauce. The store next to the café sold crystals and amulets. You might find something there to see you through into your next life.

Whenever you drove long-distance—another broken relationship funneling out behind you—you noticed every phone booth you passed, or every opportunity for a phone booth, exits blinking by like pauses in your sadness. Every phone booth setting off a ping in your chest, igniting that desire to call, to hear a voice one more time, to get some *closure*. But you could never have enough change to bridge these particular distances, these breaks in the line. You'd need to call collect, and what if no one accepted the charges after the operator asked?

❧

And then there were calling cards, cheap and prepaid from Costco. Times were changing. Even change was changing. Coins no longer jangled in your purse or pocket. You had the card, see. It was sleek and white with a silver stripe you scratched off like a lottery ticket. You called your parents with it—from the beige standard-issue dorm phone, from the greasy payphone after work at the mall, from your first apartment on the push-button receiver with numbers that glowed in the dark.

Flash to an episode of *Matlock* where Conrad, the chief PI, breaks into a suspicious efficiency. There he finds an empty room, a gritty floor, three Yellow Pages stacked askew. "What do people do on a stakeout?" he muses aloud, following the phone cord to a rotary on the windowsill. You can still hear the echo of his boots in that barren space, still remember the trick that delighted you: how he paused to lift the phone book on top, then dropped it so the pages splayed wide. "You order a lot of pizza," he answers himself. And sure enough, the book yields its secrets like a primed confessor, falling open to the food section—Italian eateries, the bold-stroke slogan WE DELIVER!

You were lucky no one could do that with your mind: rifle through your repeated wishes, peer inside the little jukebox of longing cloaked in thinking where you spent the most time. You had become so good at being quiet by your college days, tamping down and tucking in, collecting sadness like pennies in a well. Everyone remarked how your voicemail greeting didn't even sound like you, so you replaced it with music, then learned how to screen your calls.

You could make them wait, but you couldn't escape them—their questions bridging the distance you had built: book by book and mile by mile. *What are you eating? What are you learning?* (And under those questions nestled the real ones: *What is your weight? What are your grades?*) It wasn't until the night you didn't call back at all that they decided to drive north. All night the little green numbers glowed on your phone alone. You were glowing, too, until the urgent ring, your father's voice cutting in like too-bright light through morning curtains. "Why are you not sleeping in your own bed?" he demanded to know. "What do you have to say for yourself?"

"How did you find me?" I asked, voice still croaked with sleep, or not sleep but the aftermath of sex. I squiggled into my pants, couldn't talk to my father while naked from the waist down. We'd known the minute the bedside phone jangled in that white apartment that it was my father calling, the ring as insistent and angry as his voice. *Never mind that*, he said, *just get home*.

And, of course, that had never been the right question to ask.

There were years, I know, when my parents couldn't find me. I moved away to college, lived in an old Victorian house with ten other people. I called from a payphone on a Berkeley street—surrounded by the scent of falafel and patchouli—and said I wanted to come home. *Hang in there*, my mother said, but I know she must have cried when she hung up. After college, I drifted from state to state, and I remember no phone calls then, though there must have been: truncated calls, where I hid all my secrets, said everything was fine. I lived in a campground, lived in a trailer, lived on strangers' couches. I never had a phone. I must have called from various booths, must have slipped once and said, *all I want is to go home*, and my mother asked, *where is home?*

That has always been the right question to ask.

When I rented my first apartment, with my own phone, I bought a little cassette answering machine. It took quite a while to record the outgoing message, to time all the clicks, to figure out what I wanted to say and to say it just right. I erased and erased, ended up finally with the officious *You've reached . . .* and *Please leave a message after the beep*. But the truth was: those callers had not reached me.

It became a reflex to look for the light of messages as soon as I walked in the door, the way I had swiveled my head to the chalkboard in my mother's kitchen. And a reflex too: the glad lift when the machine blinked its green light, the heavy drop at nothing. I still pushed the button to hear *you have no new messages*, just to make sure. I rewound the tiny cassette and played old messages, just to have other voices in the room. My mother. A friend. An official from school.

Once, an obscene phone call, a message under the cheerful green light: *I want to fuck your brains out.* The man's voice gravelly in the throat, gritty in the room. Even then, I thought it strange that the man would leave a message, would wait so politely for the beep. I played it twice, to make sure I'd heard right, then erased it. You could do that then: erase what you didn't want. Could watch the tape go back to its own beginnings and start again, start again, until it broke.

In the beginning was the gray, and it was called weather. In the beginning was the bell, and it was called school and church and dinner. Always a summons to one thing, away from another, and just as we were settling in, time to change again.

We had seven phones in our home by the time I was grown, and one would always ring first, sounding an alarm. The others followed, like rivals or worse—a family that yammered constantly with nothing substantial to say.

One year we got an answering machine. My mother said they were all the rage. After that, when a call came during mealtime, we sat stiff as mannequins: *one ring, two rings, three rings, four.* We waited for my father's canned voice to rise up through the vents, sweep across the kitchen floor: "We are unable to answer the phone at this time. Please leave your name, number, and the reason for your call, and we'll return it just as soon as we can."

Before long, my mother never wanted to answer the phone, its ring suddenly presumptuous, an imposition on her time. Instead, she ran to the landing, crouched on the stairs—static, her body silent, as though the caller could hear her if she moved.

"I know you're there!" her friends sighed, echoing each other. "Pick up!" my father insisted. "I need to talk to you."

Soon, she forbade us to answer the phone, even if we were *expecting a call.* "If it's so important, they will leave a message," she hissed. "And if it's not important, why are we wasting our time?"

Eventually, my mother proposed a code: let the phone ring twice, hang up, wait ten seconds, redial. Then, and only then, would the person at home lift the receiver, clutch it in his sticky palm, press it to her addled ear.

I didn't use this code the last time I called my mother. Were her knees too sore to crouch? Did she lean against the wall instead, steady herself on the railing? It was still my father's voice that followed the beep, but did I detect a waver, the deep moon of sound slowly waning?

What I might have said: *You aren't home to me anymore.* (Too harsh.) *We're history.* (Too curt.)

What I did say, clear as a bell: "I love her." Were they listening as I dangled on the line?

Are you listening? Words dangle midair as they pass from child to child: a mouth to an ear, the head inclined, a smile of attention. Then the head swivels to the next in line, words already morphing into new meaning or nonsense. How many children? As many as you want there to be. They line up and shuffle in place, already giggling. The last one delivers the message in its mutant form, and laughter somersaults through them.

The man in the Verizon commercial struts from place to place, phone pressed to his ear. *Can you hear me now? Can you hear me now?* Yes, we can hear each other everywhere. Words whiz through the air, from ear to ear—imperative, interrogative—disembodied as the moon. We overhear: *where are you?* We catch: *love you.* Thousands of *love yous* before the phones click off. *Love* without the I.

Before Alexander invented the telephone, he worked with deaf children; Helen Keller was one of his pupils. His own mother was deaf, and his future wife, Mabel, came to him first as a student. She wrote: *Have no recollection of hearing except of a soft low sound I always called the singing of the frogs.* Bell invented the telephone for her, that they might speak. She could already see his love in his lips, but not feel it in her ears. His rival, Elisha, and his "harmonic telegraphs" couldn't reach far enough, could convey only music. Music, in this case, was not enough.

But the first words over the telephone line are not directed to Bell's wife.

His assistant becomes the recipient of this oft-repeated, often misquoted line: *Mr. Watson, come here, I want to see you.* Or perhaps it was just *I want you.* Or maybe the only intelligible word: *want.*

Imagine: all language is code, and we spend our lives on the line, waiting for the right voice to reach us. A voice we can understand. And every message, decoded, means: *I love.*

RICHARD HOFFMAN

# Love & Fury

My father is explaining that he thought it best to name my brother as executor of the will since he is local. He has also given him power-of-attorney when it comes to medical decisions. Well, he hasn't actually filled out the paperwork, including a Do Not Resuscitate order, but he assures us he is going to do so. His signature there will ratify something he'd said to me on the phone a week or so earlier. "Just promise me that when I go you don't let them bring me back, you hear? For Christ's sake, it's bad enough to have to die once." I know he's had a similar conversation with my brother, so there's something about this meeting at the scarred and wobbly table that is formal, official, like closing on a house. My father is "passing papers." Earlier he'd said, "After supper tonight I'd like to sit down with my sons and go over some things," as if we were not the sons he was referring to. And in fact there is something detached and ceremonious about the way this is unfolding. "So. Any questions before I close up this box? Anything unclear you want me to go over again? No? Good."

Then, the silence uncomfortable, I start to gather the remaining dishes, rise to take them to the sink. "Sit. Sit," he says. "There is something else. Something else I want to talk to you boys about." Joe and I sneak a look at each other: you boys?

But whatever my father had planned to say, or at least the words he'd planned to use, won't come; tears, which he stanches with difficulty, arrive in their stead. "I'm sorry," he says, "I made a mistake once, a big mistake, and I don't want it to cause any more trouble. Joe, I think you know a guy named Beerman. I think you went to school with him." My brother is nodding, his brows knit, wondering what's coming. "Well, his aunt

is a woman named Amanda Schuler. I don't know if that name means anything to you."

It does. To me. And I can see my brother knows where this is going, too.

I can remember my father slamming the door on his way out to visit her. He and my mother had been arguing. It was right before Christmas, either the first or second since our move to this house, so I would have been fourteen or fifteen. I've never considered this before, but thinking back to my father in a coat and tie—something he never wore—groomed and cologned on his way out the door to his girlfriend's house, further west even than our house on 13th Street, further into the wealth of the city, I wonder if my father was, perhaps, trying desperately for the bourgeois life denied him in the semi-squalor of our family. There was not only the heartbreak of my two brothers wasting away in their wheelchairs, doomed by Duchenne muscular dystrophy, not to mention their constant need for care, but also my mother's less-than-respectable family: Helen, Cory, Etta, and Kenny—without education, alcoholic, vulgar, poor. My father's prospects had just improved: he was hired as recreation director for the city. For years he had worked as a coach at the Boys' Club, as a laborer, then as a city health inspector, all the while umpiring and refereeing for extra cash and his love of sports. Now he was finally getting to do what he loved. I imagine it felt as if a new life were possible.

"Well, you might someday hear from this guy Beerman that your dad had an affair with his aunt, so I wanted you to know that it's true. I'm not proud of the fact. I was selfish and weak and I know I hurt your mother terribly. But I just wanted you to know so you don't someday get in a brawl or something with this Beerman kid trying to deny it." The look on my brother's face, my fifty-four-year-old brother who I don't believe has ever been in a fistfight in his life, is perplexed. When my father turns to talk to me, Joe allows himself an amused shake of the head.

"And Dick, the worst thing is that I let you down." I was ready to protest, but his hand came up in the STOP sign. "You were dealing with a lot back then, and I wasn't there for you. You needed your dad, and I wasn't there for you." He was biting his lower lip, eyes welling again. "I'm sorry. I want to apologize to both of you boys."

Some fifteen years earlier I had told him about being raped by my little-

league coach—what he meant by "dealing with a lot back then." I had written about it in a memoir that sent that coach, who was still violating young boys, to prison. My father had been instrumental in putting the book in the hands of people who knew where the coach was. He took it on himself as a moral failing he had to put right, and I'd considered the account more than squared.

While my father was with Amanda Schuler, I'd stayed home in the evenings, watching TV with my brothers, helping my mother care for them, and sometimes trying to console her as she wept and raged at my father.

"And I imagine, I don't know, but I imagine that it's good for you to know that your mother and I got through that okay. She took me back. She forgave me. And we were in a real good period in our life together when she got sick. That's the hell of it." He took a moment to steady himself. "But I want to apologize to you two boys."

I remember thinking that yes, it was the boys to whom he wanted to apologize.

I waited until I was sure he was finished, not wanting to risk the hand again. I recounted the enormous pressures he faced, day after day, caring for two sick and dying children, the financial pressures, the emotional pressure, the knowledge that there was only one end to the story. I said I didn't blame him.

"Aw, you're just trying to let me off the hook. You don't need to do that. I don't want you to. Not just like that"—he snapped his fingers. "I don't want you making excuses for me."

He was right. As I was speaking it had occurred to me that my mother had been under all those pressures, too, had felt that despair, that terrible doomed love for her hopeless children, and had to feel his rejection and betrayal besides. I am also my mother's son.

I remember her leaning on the sink, weeping over a stack of dirty dishes. I'd seen her from behind and her posture drew me to her. I placed a hand on her shoulder and she went on crying. Behind us, in the next room, my brothers were watching TV: Bobby, fifteen, in his wheelchair; Joey, eleven, hugging his knees on the floor; Mikey, nine, in the wheelchair that used to be Bobby's. "What am I going to do?" my mother sobbed. "What am I going to do?"

Before my brother Bobby grew weak, falling down, unable to get up, before he was diagnosed with Duchenne, and before my brother Joe was born, and Mike, who never walked, my mother was a singer. She sang the whole day long: *Shine, little glowworm, glimmer glimmer. Bewitched, bothered, and bewildered. Don't sit under the apple tree with anybody else but me.*

My mother sang in clubs during World War II. My aunt told me this was how my parents met. Of course I always imagined it Hollywood-style: my mother at the microphone, spotlit in a sequined dress, a band behind her in the semi-darkness, singing some torch song while my father, looking handsome in his dress uniform, medals above his heart, his tie knotted just so (as he had tried to show me time and again before finally giving up and buying me a clip-on) listened appreciatively from a small table across the smoky room. Mood indigo.

But recently my father told me the story a little differently. Oh, I'd long since understood that my version was fantasy. My mother in a slinky sequined dress? Please. And my father was a private back from basic training, awaiting orders. And a "club," in Allentown, is a barroom, dark, with usually only a diamond-shaped, face-sized window in the door and a few frosted glass bricks to let in some light. A couple of years ago I asked him about it and he smirked and waved his hand in that way of his that means "Bah." Or "Go on," a kind of erasure to make room for what he would say.

"It was up at the VFW, and your mother was in there with her mother and Kenny, her stepfather. Kenny was a blowhard when he was drunk, a loudmouth. He was a regular and had a kind of gang there. Him and Etta were up there all the time. And that night he was on his feet and telling everybody to pipe down, pipe down, his daughter was going to sing. Your mother didn't want to. She asked him to stop. 'My daughter's going to sing a song!' he kept saying, and I believe if she hadn't got up to sing it would have got ugly. So she did. She was a little shy but she had a great voice. You know your mother could always sing. And I don't remember if I asked her out that night or called her later." I asked him if he remembered what she sang that night and he said he didn't.

Her songs, her singing, hung on for a while, though not for long. I remember my mother singing and ironing:

(clump) Come onna my house, my-eye house,
I'm gonna give you ca-an-dy. (clump)
Come onna my house, my (clump) house,
I'll make you feel (clump) da-an-dy.

Come onna my house:

My mother is stirring soup made from boiling half a dozen franks in salt water, two or three potatoes and half an onion cut up in it, with parsley and a dash of pepper. Supper after supper of this. Supper is our word. We eat supper. "They" have dinner. Out in the "west end" of town, where "the Rockefellers" live, they have dinner.

Or "hamburger soup": meat boiled till it is gray, floating in the water it's been cooked in, not skimmed, lenses of slick fat floating and rainbowing the fluorescent kitchen light, two or three potatoes and half an onion cut up in it, with parsley and a dash of pepper. Supper.

On Mondays (also the day my mother did laundry and hung it, billowing, on clotheslines the length of the yard) we had a supper called "cream-dry-beef." And every Monday my father would explain, again, that this creamed and dried beef was also called "shit-on-a-shingle," the shingle being the slice of toast over which the salty thick goop was ladled. I loved it because it was army food. I loved it like my father's paratrooper regalia and his bayonet in its sheath. I used to look at the stains on that blade, wondering if they were blood, if my father had killed Nazis with it. I only ever saw my father use the bayonet to open old paint cans that had crusted shut; eventually the tip snapped off, and the bayonet became even more useful for that task. I had the chance, recently, to order it—Creamed Dried Beef—in a southern diner, and although they plopped it on a biscuit and garnished it with a sprig of parsley, it still tasted good to me. Whether I acquired a taste for it via my father's emphatic belly-patting pronouncements each week ("Man, that's good!") or would have found it tasty anyway, I can't say. So much of my life is history, I don't know if anything, any soul or essence or self preceded it. I'll leave that to the geneticists, since by the time I became aware of myself as someone distinct from the person my parents believed they were speaking to—by the time,

that is, that I had enough inside to try to manipulate the outside—I was already brimful with history.

Home from the store, my mother divides up the S&H Green Stamps between Bobby and me so we can paste them in their squares in the redemption booklet. For five thousand points we can get a set of tea towels. For ten thousand, a set of cups and saucers. Fifty thousand will get us a floor lamp that would "go nice" in the living room.

*Que sera, sera*, my mother sings, *Whatever will be, will be. The future's not ours to see. Que sera, sera.*

"Your mother and I got through that okay. She took me back. She forgave me."

What could she do? What choice did she have? I wonder sometimes what choices she ever had. My mother grew up in rural poverty during the Depression, illegitimate, with a drunken stepfather and three younger sisters, and school ended after eighth grade. And yet she sang. What love—is there another word for it? Courage? Generosity?—to have been ever kept from opening the gift, but to pass it along to her children just the same and not demean it or throw it away in frustration. What wisdom, astonishing in its offhandedness, to have passed along also the wish to open it, the yearning to be able to one day open it, the longing to live beyond mere duty and endurance.

My father would most likely have encountered the word *patriarchy* as a ten-letter gap in one of the crossword puzzles he did with a pencil sharpened with a knife so the lead had a sculpted quality, rounded at the tip and smooth, not pointy, so it wouldn't tear the soft paper, and so it wouldn't incise the letters onto the page, which would make it harder to erase. Erasing, correcting, changing your mind when you were wrong, was a given; in fact, if you didn't have to do this at least several times to complete the puzzle, it was too easy. That's why each of his whittled pencils was capped with a pink wedge of eraser, soft rubber that didn't wear away the surface of the page, that gave you as many chances as you needed.

No one outside a marriage can really know its features—its ecstasies and regrets, its disappointments, reassurances, tendernesses, cruelties, secrets, truces, promises, compromises—least of all a child of that marriage.

I can only say how it seemed to me; when I was young, before the future became a source of dread and inevitable grief, my parents were happy. They were in love: I recall enough of their touching and joking and kissing and flirting back when Bobby and I were young to feel sure of this. And I believe that "in love" or not, they loved each other continuously, even when their angers burned hot as hatred.

This will not come clear. It can't. There is no binary good/bad, glad/sad conclusion to be reached. When I have spoken of my family in the past, there is always someone who wants to know how such love and fury could coexist, and I don't understand the question. It seems either naïve or disingenuous. Families seem to me to be *made* of love and fury. The world is mostly water; we are mostly water; life itself is mostly water, but we don't ask how hydrogen and oxygen can coexist. We just drink it and live. Maybe we wish it were champagne, or root beer, or cider, but we're not foolish enough to wish it were liquid hydrogen, or liquid oxygen.

When my mother was dying, my father proposed to her again. My aunt Marie told me this coming from my mother's room where she lay struggling for breath. My aunt blew her nose in a tissue and smiled through tears: "Your mother said yes." I have no business dismissing that as sentimentality, nor is it any of my business what either of my parents said. And yet, if my mother had had no choice years earlier, she certainly didn't have one then. And there is always, intrusively and insistently, the thought that she had in fact already made her choice, moving smoke by smoke, pack by pack of Chesterfields, toward the only escape available to her. And even if she were still hurt and angry, wounded and furious, she could not have refused my father the consolation he was seeking; she didn't have it in her.

And neither do I. I am also my mother's son.

"It's a great relief," my father says, rising from the table and reaching for his footed aluminum cane, "a great relief to me to get that off my chest." The meeting is over. Joe and I sit there and watch him make his way slowly into the living room to his recliner. He reaches for the remote, and in a moment the TV comes on, loud enough to feel it through the floor.

JESSIE VAN EERDEN

✣✣

# Among Women

Women breathe questions into one another. They question with their hands, with their fingers, slipping in and out of jeans pockets. A woman tosses her hair back over one shoulder as if to ask the other at the table, *Am I alluring? Should I braid it? Color it?* The woman at the table hums a quiet song and nudges the Mason jar by her plate, posing the cut daffodils in the light: *Will I always set just one place for supper? Will he come?* A daffodil bends left. This is how she asks for comfort, and her song grows softer.

I live with three other women, all of us breathing young and inquisitively. Our questions whiz past each other as we hurry off to work or class. We leave mixtapes and clementines as little presents for each other. We leave phone messages in blue on the dry-erase board, maybe in red if it was a boy who called. We leave our bedrooms cluttered with the day's assignments, with dirty laundry crumpled in a heap: a pair of jeans sprawled into a question mark on the floor. We sometimes hold our breath when the phone rings.

I have always lived in a community of women, watching them closely, sometimes even trying to shut them out. In my girlhood I lived in the Whetsell Settlement where women warmed their homes just over the ridge or across the fencerow from mine. Most of them seemed ancient to me. Many lived alone, widowed. I grew up in oversized T-shirts, grew up plump with the love of those widow women all around me in work dresses. I suppose I come from a sad place, from a community of mourning. But that's not how I remember it. The widows didn't wear their losses on their dress sleeves where I could see them. They gave me kisses and yogurt candies and red apples. My mouth dripped with the sweet milk they offered,

as though they lived lives of plenty. How could they have had any milk left in their jugs for me? How much had they given, how much had they lost? Why did they hold my plump face in their dishpan hands and tilt me to see that love in their eyes instead of the weary redness? These are the questions that I ask with raspy breath.

I am slimmer now, not gaunt with age like some of them, but more aware of my waistline. I cook for myself and have to think twice before stuffing yogurt-dipped malt balls in my mouth. I am older. And my face has turned blue with questions. I remember the plump T-shirted girl who took eggs to the woman at the crest of the hill. I remember the things I saw in the company of widow women. And I need to look again. And to ask, as though breathing hot breath onto the glass of their portraits and wiping them clear.

I remember staring at black butter. It scared me over there in the dark of the Jeffers' kitchen. A warm lump, black with coal stove dust under the porcelain lid of the butter dish. I didn't know if it was real. I had only known fresh pats of salty butter. I helped churn our cow's milk during Saturday morning cartoons, pressed it in the butter mold, and ran it under a cold faucet till it was firm enough to wrap in freezer paper. I knew butter that went limp on hot biscuits on clean plates. But black butter was hard. Mom took me with her to help clean Don and Eliza Jeffers' place, and on the way over, in the cab of the truck, she told me that Eliza had once been a pristine housekeeper. I just stared and sniffed back my fear as Eliza drew me to her and kissed me somewhere between my neck and my jaw, wherever she could reach.

Don had had a severe ear infection as a boy, so severe it had seeped into his mind and speech. I was afraid of Don. He shuffled into Beatty Church in his only brown suit coat on Sundays, his wife, Eliza, tucked by his side. When I or another kid passed him, he poked our toes with the rubber tip of his cane and laughed, saying something in words all mushed up together. We just had to smile and sweat and nod till he unpinned our toes, and we could bolt out the door to play freeze tag or to pick up chestnuts. Sometimes Mom and Dad were the ones to give the Jeffers a ride to church. When Don got sick and had to labor getting out of the truck, Mom said

low, "Isn't it hard, Eliza? Isn't this almost impossible for you?" But the weary woman just answered, "Not when you love him."

The house slumped into the hillside on Butch Mayfield's property. As Mom and I passed Butch's trailer on the way, we saw his son Wayne tinkering with a tractor, and I waved with my mop handle. Mom and I couldn't carry our buckets, mops, and jugs up the front steps because the whole front of the Jeffers' house had sagged and threatened to give under our weight. Sometimes Don spit his tobacco juice onto the floor, and I wondered if it just sat there till Mom and I came. Several rooms in the house were curtained off, and I was afraid of rats scurrying behind the threadbare-sheet doors. Cold air leaked out from under the hem. Mom said that all Don's mother's things were piled up in there, dressers and newspapers and plastic flowers.

Mom cleaned up the commode that sat behind a curtain in the bedroom, while I stayed at the kitchen table, fiddling with the lid of that butter dish. When I saw the black mush, I wondered right away how the coal dust that had seeped into Don and Eliza's clothes and crept up the walls, how it could have gotten under that lid onto the butter. But I didn't ask. Instead I asked if I could bring in some wood. I asked if I could take the stove ashes outside and dump them. I lifted the latch of the door that opened out to the wood stack, I lifted as *if* to ask, *Is this it, Eliza? Is this how love is?* My stomach coiled while my voice offered up the little girl questions. The old couple just smiled and nodded.

Eliza said Don died of a broken heart. The doctors wouldn't let him come home, and he died longing for company. Eliza listened to the local news program on WFSP so that voices filled the kitchen. I wondered if she sang to the radio songs when she was alone, like I did. She did dishes sometimes, at the sink where a framed sketch of the biblical Ruth hung duct-taped on the wall, Ruth the Moabite woman whose husband up and died. Up and died. Every time I came to help Mom clean, to bring in some wood or coal for the kitchen stove, Eliza drew me to her and untucked another kiss for me.

Now I live with these three women. Now I keep margarine wrapped neatly in the Blue Bonnet box in the refrigerator door. The yellow sticks stay

pale and rigid till I unwrap them for baking, or till I cut off slivers for our hot dinner rolls. None of us have yet tucked ourselves by a man's side for good. In my mind I see black butter and I get scared. "For rich or for poor. Till death do us part." Give all, lose all. Just lay the butter out in the coal-dusty kitchen and expect it to go black. Or expect the tobacco juice to brown the floor because you love him. That kind of love sops up the heart like a dishrag. I don't want to wax hard and cold with fear. I don't want to wrap butter in freezer paper and tuck it away in a cool corner, never tasting, never being tasted.

I remember dirty leather. The dirty leather of an old baseball I found in my brothers' closet. I handled it like an orange ripe for peeling. I put it to my lips like a malt candy shell, fingering its red stitches. And then I saw that floppy worn mitt shoved back behind worn-out sneakers and I yanked it out. The mitt stank. It had "MACE" in game-worn ink along the inside. It had once belonged to my uncle. It was a glove flimsy from boys' punches. I loved it.

The ball glove gave me power and spunk. I struck out this boy Matthew in fifth grade gym class, my left palm sweating inside that mitt. I flung the ball, then clasped it with the glove, flung, and nabbed. Matthew asked me to "go with him." To hold hands. Up and asked me outright. I struck him out. I didn't put his name next to mine in my notebook: "Matthew loves Jessie, together forever," in ink. I kept my name covered with my hand.

I got my name from Jessie Beatty Shaffer who lived within hearing distance down over the hill. She must have heard us kids when we hollered "Red Rover!" or punched our mitts or pummeled each other in a game of longtown-shorttown, our two-base version of whiffle ball. Jessie was seventy-nine when I was born.

Hers was the name on the front flap of my journal, and on her own journals, shelved together on a bookcase after she died. "Sam came today," I read in one short entry. Sam and Budz were the boys who had squeezed out of her womb, who came to see her and drive her to town. Her husband, Rufus, was long dead.

Jessie asked me once to read her a poem from my journal. I read her one

about moonbeams that danced, and another about a boy who kissed a girl behind a big oak tree. She was nearly ninety then, and I wanted to ask her, *Who were you as a young "Jessie"? Who kissed you?* But I didn't ask. I kissed her. I asked her for milk. I asked her who permed her hair. She lived alone with her feather-white hair and that womb there: like a floppy mitt.

I made butter deliveries to Jessie Shaffer. I tucked the cool, wrapped package under my arm and walked down to her white gate and lifted the lever. She usually had an ironstone bowl of scraps set out for Jack, her slow beagle. She was the widow who kept a glass Christmas tree candy jar filled with yogurt-covered malt balls and raisins, stuck together mostly. Jessie insisted I pluck one from the gummy mass each time I offered up the butter. The candy was stale and tough to chew. I loved it. I loved her for it. And for her powdery smell, for her white kitchen sink and her garden so soft and rockless she might've tilled it with a comb. For her advice to my mom on late Saturday nights when Dad called for her to come home and his voice carried down dear to Jessie's and the women kept talking till four in the morning. For the daffodils she planted around the flat rock for Mom in May. For every time she patted her Queen-Anne's-Lace hair when my stringy, darkening hair was pulled up wet.

For never forgetting my name when I visited, all the way up till she died like a whisper after ninety-eight years: a name on the palm of the inside of a mitt, ink thin, but dear. For the malt oozing into my spit, so sweet down the back of my throat.

I want to savor it now, tonight. I and the three women living here with me splash sweetness on our arms and necks, none allowed inside us. Skim milk like water, reduced-fat peanut butter, sugar-free tea in the fridge. One woman squirts on cucumber-melon body fragrance, one smoothes sunflower silk lotion over the cuts on her shaven legs. One candies her cheeks with blush. I smear on vanilla lip balm just to taste it. We gloss ourselves up. Up and down.

With these gestures we ask each other, *Are we alluring?* As we ask, another woman-friend comes to visit. She is older, but not old. She's come for a glass of watery milk and to share a secret about "allure." I smooth my hair that can't be smoothed and listen as she flips through pages of

her Bible. She points in Hosea's Book and reads what God has whispered of His people: "I will allure her, will bring her into the wilderness and speak comfort to her. I will give her her vineyards from there, and the Valley of Achor as a door of hope; she shall sing there, as in the days of her youth." My friend smiles at my expression, as if she knows that I have been remembering my youth, as if she knows that I, at twenty, am not young and not old. She reads the rest of God's promise: "I will betroth you to Me forever." I admire the beauty in Hosea, but I still feel my hand struggle from my jeans pocket to touch my hair. I work loose a tangle. My friend has scribbled a holy epigraph for my list of questions, as though I'll understand when I'm older.

I remember the spokes. The spokes with fluorescent plastic decorators snapped on. When I rode my bike I "click-clacked," a steady bike chatter, all the way down the road as the plastic slid up and down the spokes in bright whorls. A yellow bike with a banana seat, a basket attached with sandal straps. Wind lifted the straw hair off my neck and the shirt off my hot skin. I was a girl on a chattery bike like a fastball, shedding the spit of a pitch, feeling flung. But the seat, even a stretched out banana seat, accommodated just one, a detail youth wouldn't notice. The singleness was simply necessary for a steady ride and a dear vision of the road. To be alone was necessary.

Mary Jane was a woman down the road whose driveway gate I passed on my bike. Mary Jane who had lain alone with tuberculosis as a high school girl, who had lost a baby daughter from the curve of her arm, who had lost George Schmidle from her bed, from her grove of pines. Pieces of her life had been erased before I ever knew her, or blew past on my bike, clacking.

Once I skidded to a stop in the gravel and leaned my bike against the fence along the road by Mary Jane's house. I pushed through the gate, with her mail under my arm, and walked up to her porch. She thanked me and held back her little dog from biting my leg. I wondered if that poodle was her only company. I asked if she wanted me to bring the mail again the next day. I waved and walked to the gate, pushed back through to the road. I eagerly picked up my bike, as though to ask my widow friend, *Did*

*you spend years alone and clear on a bike out here, in the wind, like me?*
*Were those the best years?*

Twice, when I was an older girl, I rode on a motorbike behind a kind
boy named Billy. We were not in love, and the wind slapped in between
us even though we pressed together, pressed hard when the street curved.
"Lean into the curves," he told me over the bike's unsteady roar, drowning
out the simple clack of my banana bike, so I shut my eyes and let my
body sink left with his.

George had been the Gum Man, passing out bubble gum to kids in the
"Whetsell Settlement on his way home from work I was too young to
remember that, but I'd heard about it, and it was the only thing I could say
about Mr. Schmidle. I knew Mary Jane. She did everything on her own. She
drove her corn-yellow car to town, sometimes dropping a birthday card or
money for eggs and butter in our mailbox. She drove herself even after
she'd had one of her legs amputated. She mowed her grass on a lawn trac-
tor, and she crinkled her face into a perpetual smile. I always kept my eyes
on Mary Jane's smile from my seat up front in the youth choir at Beatty,
as I sang with the other squeaky sopranos. "Praise the Lord," she said for
our singing. "Praise the Lord," she said for an early Sabbath morning, for
an early evening, for light, for the wilt of the world in rain. For the brain
tumor that massed under her bob of gray hair. One Sunday she told the
whole congregation about those festering cells in her head. She said she
would have to cut her hair when they operated. It was necessary for the
removal of the tumor. We all bit our lips and cried and prayed in a circle. I
tugged my fingers through my own straw-shade locks. "Praise the Lord."

"Bless your heart," Mary Jane said, when I brushed up against her
polyester salmon suit or took in her mail or grabbed a Milky Way from
her paper sack on Halloween. "Bless your heart." One Sunday morning,
our choir sang "The Beatitudes" straight from the King James Version:
Matthew, chapter 5. I don't remember where the melody came from, but
we sang the "blesseds" of the Sermon on the Mount, word for word.
"Blessed are the poor in spirit: for theirs is the kingdom of heaven." Blessed
are the meek. The merciful. The persecuted. And then right out into Mary
Jane's smiling face, I sang, "Blessed are those who mourn: for they shall
be comforted." I sang it to every widow in the oak pews, while I shifted

weight on loafers and didn't see their tears. I tugged at my jumper for the end of the worship hour, for the bike ride waiting for me in the wind.

I pedaled past, streamer tassels added to my handlebars. I waved to the widow whose tendency it was to weep through a smile, and I never feared wrecking in a ditch or gravel patch.

But I'm afraid now. I know gravel hurts. Blessed are those who mourn. I am not as sure of Christ's promise as I was in my youth. I don't sing it as loudly. But my widow friend is sure somehow, and she wants my heart to be plump with faith and with blessing, for the day when I will need it. From this aging evening, I hear a whisper from my lips follow into the dip in the road in front of Mary Jane's: "I love you," I say to her. I love you as best I can. And it is raspy, almost a whisper, deflating as it trails the gravel and potholes. I'm not sure what's necessary for those words.

The women I live with are too old to whorl clackers into the town streets. And we are too nervous to hitch a ride on a roaring motorbike that leans us down. So we make noise with the key in the car ignition, with the knob on the tape deck turned up full blast. A mixtape flings a song to the wind out the window, and a somber girl sings to a steady guitar riff: "Now I am sitting here on the best years of my life, wondering where I'm going next and who's coming along, singing a song of a summer night." I rewind and play it again.

I remember watching Gladys scratch in the dust. She was our prize hen before she died. She laid eggs with tough olive-green shells that stuck out from the other freckled brown ones in the cartons my mom filled to sell. Gladys cocked her head around the corner of the house whenever she flapped over the rusted wire of the chicken coop fence or squeezed through the space between the coop door and the cinder block that held it shut. Gladys and her chicken sisters scared me from the other side of that fence, with the constant garble in the back of their throats, the putrid yellow eyes and jerky motions. Still, when I sneaked past their stares the day I got engaged, they kept my secret. We were five-and-a-half, Timmy and I, and we raced to the woods behind the chicken coop, making up engagement vows. He slipped a Mayapple-stem ring on my finger and

kissed my hand, because I had told him I was not allowed to kiss boys on the mouth, not till I was a woman. I lost the ring somewhere on the race back to the house.

I sometimes had pity on the hens and fed them grass over the fence because their scaly toes had scratched the coop floor to gray dirt and rock, with only the occasional orange peel to offer any color. The hens fed me, too. Their warm eggs swirled into the bowl of flour and sugar for a chocolate cake or banana bread. "Girls," my mom always called the hens. "My girls." Girls losing eggs that I took and juggled around inside me, their yolk-and-white working into my body. Maybe into the secret parts of my own girlness, harboring a nest of tiny eggs, sealed off, waiting.

When our bird dog Gabe killed Naomi Close's best setting hen, Naomi didn't get angry with us. She didn't really let her loss show. Even when her husband, Toots, began losing limbs. It wasn't all at once. First there were the weekly drives to the hospital for dialysis, then the darkening of the foot, the leg. When he died, the big gray farmhouse down the gravelly road from mine looked so big all of a sudden, so big and stark on the ridge, with Mrs. Close hidden inside.

The Closes had a long, trailing driveway and a mud-caked cattle bridge without a gate. With my delivery in my sack, I played back and forth on the iron ridges until my sole almost got stuck in the dip between them, and I pressed on up the drive. A breeze always blew through Naomi's kitchen when I stood there and handed her the sack, asking if that was all she needed. Asking if that was all I could give her, as if to ask, *Can a girl really give anything to a woman, can I offer any secrets? How much am I like you, if I am like you at all?* If I delivered a jar of elderberry jam or apple butter, I expected a similar jar to turn up in our mailbox a few days later. Sometimes she filled it with jam, too, or cracked walnuts for cakes. She slipped us her special recipes for treats, like lemon sugar cookies the size of quarters. I had a sweet every time I stopped by. I stood in the breezy kitchen and Toots's enormous voice boomed from the living room, "Give that girl something from the freezer." I licked my lips all the way home. I didn't know Toots very well, but I knew Naomi, and I knew he left her alone in that kitchen for good.

I loved to say Naomi's name. It sounded secret. "Ny-oma" is how I said it. The only other place I heard that name was in Sunday school, when they told the story of Ruth the Moabite woman whose husband died. Naomi was Ruth's mother-in-law, and Naomi lost her husband first. Ruth clung to her for breath and promised, "Wherever you go, I will go." She sweated in the sun and gathered strands of barley in bundles for Naomi, for their small company of two. I just whispered that name and watched for jars of jam in the mailbox. "Ny-oma."

When I buy eggs at the store I split the cost with the women I live with. The eggshells are pale and colorless, except for the veiny web of cracks in a few of them. They sit right beside the Blue Bonnet. There's no way to tell whether the chickens that laid that dozen eggs were prize setting hens. But I have my doubts. I just spill the store-bought eggs down into the ridges of *Hour* and sugar, swirl, and wait.

But what do I wait for? For company? For another widow woman to draw me to her? These women seem to surround me like a great cloud of witnesses, and they breathe love into me like I'm worthy of it. I want to sit with them again, tuck myself into the folds of their work dresses and breathe back. To say something of blessed comfort for their mourning. To eagerly hold my youth open, like a puckered jeans pocket: They can slip secrets in that I won't forget.

What am I holding breath for? I push "Play," and my mixtape fills the stifling quiet kitchen, and I turn it up loud and sing alongside the woman's vulnerable voice: "In the thick of the night, get me out of the cold, let me sing inside like a radio. In the thick of the night, before we grow too old, let me sing inside like a radio." The other women in the house can hear me when I sing it at the sink, loud, with Eliza Jeffers. With a whole chorus of women singing inside with me, as in the days of our youth, the days of our betrothal.

I live among women. I go to their doors, out of breath from climbing the hill, and I offer up my cool, wrapped package, as though asking: *Is this all we need?*

DAVID JAMES DUNCAN

# Valmiki's Palm

*"In the beginning,"* say the *Upanishads*—a scripture composed, according to the rishis of ancient India, by no one; a scripture self-created, found floating like mist, or the bands of a rainbow, in the primordial forest air, *"there was nothing here at all. . . . Death alone covered this completely, as did hunger, for what is hunger but death? Then Death made up his mind: 'Let me equip myself with a body'* (Sanskrit: *atma*). *So he undertook a liturgical recitation (arc), and as he was reciting, water (ka) suddenly sprang from him. Amazed, Death thought: 'Recitation caused water to spring from me!' This is what gave the name to and discloses the hidden nature of recitation (arc-ka). Truly, water springs up for he or she who knows the secret of recitation. Recitation is running water."*

## I. ADORATION OF A HOSE

I was born in a hospital located on the flanks of a volcanic cone. This cone, named Mount Tabor, looks innocent as an overturned teacup as it rises over densely populated southeast Portland, Oregon. Decades before my birth, scientists declared the cone unimpeachably extinct. The hospital, however, afforded a nice view of another cone, thirty-five miles away in the same volcanic system, also declared extinct in those days: Mount St. Helens. Forgive my suspicion of certain unimpeachable declarations of science.

My birth cone's slopes were drained by tiny seasonal streams that, like most creeks in that industrialized quadrant of Portland, were buried in underground pipes long before I arrived on the scene. There were also three small reservoirs on Tabor's slopes, containing the water that bathed me at birth, water I'd drink for eighteen years, water that gave me life. But

this water didn't come from Mount Tabor, nor from the surrounding hills, nor even from the aquifer beneath: it came, via manmade flumes, from the Bull Run River, which drains the slopes of the Cascade Mountains forty miles away.

I was born, then, without a watershed. On a planet held together by gravity and fed by rain, a planet whose every creature depends on water and whose every slope works full-time, for eternity, to create creeks and rivers, I was born with neither. The creeks of my birth-cone were invisible, the river from somewhere else entirely. Of course millions of Americans are now born this way; some of them grow up without creeks, live lives lacking intimacy with rivers, and become well-adjusted, healthy, productive citizens even so.

Not me. The dehydrated suburbs of my boyhood felt as alien to me as Mars. The arid industrial life into which I was being prodded looked to me like the life of a Martian. What *is* a Martian? Could Mars support intelligent life? I had no idea. My early impression of the burgeoning burbs around me was of internally-combusting hordes of dehydrated beings manufacturing and moving unnecessary objects from one place to another in order to finance the rapid manufacture and transport of more unnecessary objects. Running water, on the other hand, felt as necessary to me as food, sleep, parents and air. And on the cone of my birth, the running waters had been eliminated.

I didn't rebel against the situation. Little kids don't rebel. That comes later, along with the hormones. What I did was hand-build my own rivers, breaking all neighborhood records, in the process, for amount of time spent running a garden hose. . . .

In the beginning, in Southeast Portland, there was nothing much there at all. Dehydrated Martians seemed to run the place completely. So my *atma* and I fastened the family garden hose to an azalea bush at the uphill end of one of my mother's sloping flowerbeds, turned the faucet on as hard as Mom would allow, and watched hijacked Bull Run River water spring forth in an *arc* and start cutting a minuscule, audible river (*ka*) down through the bed. I then camped by this river all day. As the Hose River ran and ran the thing my mother understandably hated and my *atma* and I loved began to happen: *creation*. The flowerbed topsoil

washed away and a streambed of tiny colored pebbles appeared—a bed that eventually looked like that of any genuine river, complete with tiny point bars and cutbanks, meanders and eddies, fishy-looking riffles, slow pools. It was a nativity scene, really: the entire physics and fluvial genius of Gravity-Meets-Water-Meets-Earth incarnating in perfect miniature before me. I built matchbook-sized hazelnut rafts and cigarette-butt-sized elderberry canoes, launched them on my river, let them ride down to the gargantuan driveway puddle that served as my Pacific. I stole a two-inch tall blue plastic cavalry soldier from my brother's Fort Apache set, cut the stock off his upraised rifle so that only the long, flexible barrel remained, tied thread to the end of the barrel to serve as fly-line, and sent the soldier fishing. I'd then lie flat on my belly, one cheek to the ground, and stare at this U. S. Cavalry drop-out, thigh-deep in his river, rifle-rod high in the air, line quavering in the current; stare till I became him; stare till, in the sunlit riffle, we actually hooked and landed tiny sun-glint fish. "Shut off that hose!" my mother would eventually shout out the kitchen window. "You've turned the whole driveway into a mudhole!"

*Poor woman*, I'd think. *It's not a mudhole. It's a tide flat. . .*

I'd gladly turn the hose off, though: that's how I got the tide to go out. I'd then march my river soldier out onto the flat, to dig for clams.

## II. WOE V. WADE

The undisputed matriarch of my large suburban family was my maternal grandmother, Ethel Rowe. Gramma Rowe was 4'11", but insisted with such vehemence that she was 5'1" that most of the family felt her missing two inches were an oversight on the Lord's part and should be imagined as real. For my part, I wished Gramma Rowe was 3'11", or even 2'11", since at 4'11" she could be overwhelming. In those days we called people like her "firecrackers," but firecrackers explode once and that's it. Gramma Rowe could just keep exploding. She was more like a 4'11" Uzi. When a young nephew who had trouble with *r* sounds one day referred to our matriarch as "Gwamma Woe," it was too perfect. I called her nothing else ever after.

Gwamma Woe's lovingly despotic rule, like her mystical Five-Foot-Oneness, was based on an interpretation of scripture that corrected count-

less oversights on the part of the Bible's authors. All this "God works in mysterious ways" stuff, for starters, was hooey. Gwamma Woe knew exactly how God worked, exactly how humans should work in response, and atmas, garden hoses, rivers and US Cavalry dropouts had nothing to do with it thank-you-very-much. A fiercely devout Seventh Day Adventist, Gwamma Woe had, per her self-bowdlerized Bible's instructions, turned herself into a crackerjack real estate sales lady the better to serve the Lord: she was now spending her life getting rich by the sweat of her brow and enjoying all but a tithe of those riches, just as God ordered, after which she might agree to die, or at least briefly slumber, until such time as Jesus woke her, gave her body the complete rebuild that would make her a true 5'1", and whisked her up to the gold mansions and permanent riches of heaven forever.

I had only one objection to Gwamma Woe's Gold-Mansion-Track plan for her life: it was her plan for my life too. There were just two incarnational options for a Woe grandchild:

1) you became a staunch Adventist like Gwamma, spent your life pursuing wealth like Gwamma, and later retired for eternity to the infinite wealth of heaven with Gwamma, or,

2) surprise, surprise: YOU BURNED IN HELL FOREVER!!!

Ah, Gwamma Woe! If only I'd been able to embrace her plan for my life, I'd have saved myself a lot of heartbreak. Capitalist fundamentalism, I still believe, is the perfect Techno-Industrial religion, its goal being a planet upon which we've nothing left to worship, read, eat, or love but dollar bills and bibles. My boyhood worry, though, was that this world might not be techno-industrial. Maybe only the human world is techno-industrial. Maybe the world God made is natural, its 'industry' a bunch of forces like gravitation, solar rays, equinoctial tilt, wind, tides, photosynthesis, sexuality, migration. And if the world is natural, I'd fret, if it was the natural world God loved enough to send His son to die for it, then it might not be such a God-pleasing thing to spend my life converting that world into industrial waste products, dollar bills, and bibles.

Needless to say, my matriarch disagreed with every iota of this. She recognized natural beauty in a way: a "beautiful day," for instance, increased

the likelihood of selling a house. But the word "nature," to Gwamma, had an unwashed unsaved ring to it. Wild Nature, she believed, was basically a bunch of naked, dirty, heathenish creatures having sex with, stalking and devouring each other—more or less like realtors, she admitted, only in Nature's case there was no post-prandial Gold Mansion to give purpose to the earthly gizm and gore. The Natural World's duty, Gwamma Woe was certain, was to be knocked down, processed and converted ASAP into Industrial Christian World. And she was a force: I was convinced by age six that I'd eventually become a well-heeled Adventist doctor or lawyer not because I wanted to, but because a less highly paid, more nature-loving career would result in that formidable annoyance: eternal agony in hell.

One day when I was still six, though, my religious advisor committed a fatal tactical blunder. Everybody likes doing what they do best. Gwamma Woe also liked showing off while she did it. As a combination matriarch/ real estate whiz, she had an exhibitionistic love for hauling my siblings and me to "Open Houses" at various properties she had listed for sale, and letting us eavesdrop while she hooked and played prospective buyers like fish. Between clients she delivered impassioned sermonettes on Salesmanship, a biblical virtue that ranked right in there with Cleanliness and Godliness in its power to convert penniless wretches like us kids into Gold-Mansion-track sales experts like her. No matter how many times she explained the key concepts, though—terms like "earnest money," "commandment," "mortgage," "Holy Ghost," "immaculate interior," "redemption," "FHA-approval"—I couldn't wrap my nature-smitten mind around them. After a single Open House spent cross-eyed with boredom, I became an extremely reluctant companion.

Like I said, though, Gwamma Woe was a great saleslady. One day in October she drove her snappy red Rambler convertible down our driveway, spotted me merged with my garden hose river and fishing soldier, but instantly conjured three words that made me leap into the car's Immaculate White Interior with pure anticipation. The words were: "*Creek-front property!*"

I don't remember a thing about the drive, the sermonette en route, the layout of the home. All I remember is hearing—the instant Gramma parked beside a For Sale sign and shut off her engine—the unfamiliar

song of unpiped, non-hosed water flowing somewhere behind the house. In the lost Celtic recesses of my bloodstream a bagpipe and drum immediately answered. I told Gwamma to holler when she needed me, shot round the house, scrambled down a riprapped embankment into a ribbon of ancient fir and alder—and the world of mortgages and immaculate interiors vanished as a remnant slice of green and ancient world suddenly shimmered on all sides.

It was just one of Portland's dying creeks, really. One with a much needed but long-lost Indian name. "Johnson Creek" was now its anemic title. But it was twenty-six miles long, hence a little too big to bury. And when you fail to bury Northwest creeks, or to poison them quite to death, a few of them, even now, receive unimaginably non-Adventistic visitors from wild and distant realms. Gwamma Woe had not foreseen this.

I found a walking stick. I began walking and wading a stone streambed for the first time in my life. Because of what ensued, thirty or so pairs of wading boots later I'm walking them still. Love, it turns out, is for me something slippery, arrived at on foot, via lots of splashing.

Kids tend to befriend creeks the way adults befriend each other: start shallow, and slowly work your way deeper. So: skippers; water striders. That's what I noticed first. Inch-long, spraddle-legged, white-walled black-topped creatures embarrassing Gramma Woe's man, St. Peter, by demonstrating that mere bugs not only walk on water, they *run*. Next, deeper down: caddis fly larva. Driving their glued-gravel RV's back an' forth, back an' forth all day across the bottom like it was Arizona down there an' they were sick o' golf, dang it, an' maybe shouldn'a took early retirement after all. Deeper yet (I had to turn submerged stones to flush these) crawdads: designed right there in the '50s by staunch war hawks, it seemed, judging by their attraction to bombproof rock shelters, their preference for traveling backasswards, their armor, Cold War antennae, and oversized Pentagon-budget claws.

Then I came to water too deep to wade, or to even see bottom: a shady black pool, surface-foam eddying like stars in a nebula. And though I wanted to keep exploring, the big pool proved a psychic magnet. . .

Its surface was a night sky in broad daylight. Its depths were another world within this one. The entire frenetic creek stopped here to rest. I was

seventy-eight percent water myself. I felt physically ordered to crawl out on a cantilevered log, settle belly-down, and watch the pool gyre directly beneath me, the foam-starred surface eddying, eddying, till it became a vision of night; water-skipper meteors; sun-glint novas. The creek would not stop singing. I spun and spiraled, grew foam-dazed and gyre-headed. Pieces of the mental equipment I'd been taught to think I needed began falling into the pool and dissolving: my preference of light to darkness; sense of rightsideup and upsidedownness; sense of surfaces and edges, sense of where I end and other things or elements begin. The pool taught nothing but mystery and depth. An increasingly dissolved "I" followed the first verb, gravity, down, and found that depth, as a dissolved "I" sees it, is also height:

Up from the sunless depths, or down from foam-starred heavens, a totem-red tartan-green impossibility descended or arose, its body so massive and shining, visage so travel-scarred and ancient, that I was swallowed like Jonah by the sight. I know no better way to invoke the being's presence than to state the naked name: *Coho*. An old male coho, *arc*ing up not to eat, as trout do, but just to submarine along without effort or wings; just to move, who knows why, through a space and time it created for itself as it glided. And as it eased past my face not a body's length away, the coho gazed—with one lidless, primordial eye—clean into the suspended heart of me: gazed not like a salmon struggling up from an ocean to die, but like a Gaelic or Kwakiutl messenger dropped down from a realm of gods, *Tir na nOg*, world of deathlessness, world of *Ka*, to convey, via the pure fact of its existence, a timeless message of sacrifice and hope. The creek would not stop singing. My bagpipe heart could not stop answering. When you see a magnificent ocean fish confined in small, fresh water, it is always like a dream. And in our dreams, every object, place and being is something *inside* us. Despite my smallness, ignorance, inexperience, I felt a sudden immense entitlement: this creek and its music, secret world and its messenger, belonged to me completely. Or I to them.

The coho vanished as serenely as it had come, back into depth. But not before its shining eye changed the way I see out of my own. I'd glimpsed a way into a Vast Inside. A primordial traveler through water and time had said, *Come*.

So now I had an interior coho compass. *Find water*, it told me daily. But mine were not a culture, church and family whose members employ salmon as compasses by which to direct their lives. A salmon, in my culture's view, was a "resource" placed on earth by God, so that human beings (which in our suburbs meant white folks) could "convert the resource"— via a process of commercial fishing, cooking, chewing and swallowing— into ever-larger and more numerous white folks. To admire the flavor of the "resource" was allowable. But *to revere it? To believe the resource in some sense lived inside us? To fuel this belief by worshipping the waters that spawned both the belief and its salmon?* This was all a lot of unsaved unwashed heathen nonsense.

Yet Gwamma Woe's grandson was suddenly full of just that.

I became the Hamlet of the Adventist church, lurking in back pews, haunted by a suspicion that something was rotten in the State of Rote Worship. I managed not to blame the followers on the Leader: I saw Jesus as an expert fisherman and non-Christian, same as I longed to be. But I did notice, as a born river-lover and tree hugger, how Christ never really got cracking till John the Baptist dunked Him in a river, and never saved the world till He died on a tree. Jesus, as I saw it, needed Christianity and churches the way an ocean needs sailors and ships: that is, not at all. It made no sense to me to demote the Cause (Jesus, or the Ocean) of an effect (churches, or ships) to the level of a mere occupant of the effect (Christians, or sailors). So I didn't.

And with that conclusion, church became a stagnant pool in which I waited for rain, fresh flow, and escape. The real sacrificial dramas of the Northwest, the truly Christlike activity as I saw it, were taking place not in the buildings where Christians so brackishly tried to worship but in the lives of the wild salmon I spontaneously *did* worship, for the way they poured in from the sea in defiance of every threat, predator and pharisee, climbed increasingly troubled mountain streams, nailed their beautiful bodies to lonely beds of gravel, and died there not for anything they stood to gain, but for the sake of tiny silver offspring.

Longing to bust out of burbs and churches into the natural, God-given world that helped me explore the world within me, I realized: *I need to fish*. And not just in the River Hose. My intuition blasted me daily with

the sense that real rivers contained living denizens of fluid darks and deeps: I needed to lay literal hands on the life of these deeps.

### III. THE TROLL BOY'S SECRET

My family moved twice during my boyhood. The first time was from the foot of the volcanic cone to a country lane nine miles east of Portland, called Rockwood Road. We had a huge garden there, a cherry/apple/peach orchard, eight long rows of three kinds of berries, fifty chickens, a yard big enough for baseball if it hadn't been for windows and foul balls, a rose garden, a thick laurel hedge between us and the quiet road, and a row of stately maples just inside the hedge. Several neighbors owned little Jeffersonian farms and a fourth owned two hundred acres of ancient fir forest, which I roamed freely. Our front window faced Mount Hood and the sunrise. It took no effort on my part to consider our home an earthly paradise and me the luckiest bounder alive.

Then, one calm country morning, a chunk of basalt the size of a football crashed through the front window and landed on the couch. Blown there by the dynamite of a new kind of creature called "a developer." I marveled at the rock on the couch, not yet knowing what a metaphor was. Over the next few months I found out.

First, we learned that federal highway planners had designated Rockwood Road as the main artery connecting Interstate 84 and US Highway 26. Next, our country road's name was changed to NE 181st. Next, the highway department cut down our maples, tore out the sheltering laurel hedge, widened the road to four lanes, ran a concrete sidewalk through our rose garden, traffic increased a hundredfold, and a car ran over my dog, Hunter. My parents got me another dog. I named it Hunter the Second. Two weeks later a bus ran over Hunter the Second. The Jeffersonian farms vanished beneath a multicolored acne of the dynamite developer's housing. Another developer snuck up from behind, converting the two-hundred-acre forest into another vast housing tract. There was suddenly no woods to wander, no dog to wander with, and we no longer knew our neighbors. Bikes began to be stolen, homes robbed or vandalized, the words "rape" and "abduction" entered our vocabularies. A sicko in an old Pontiac tried

one day to steal me out of our hedgeless, unprotected yard. Another jolly old soul wagged his penis at my little sister while she stood waiting for the school bus. We learned never to leave the yard, never to talk to strangers, never to go anywhere alone, always to lock doors.

In recognition of our changed circumstances, my father bought my brothers and me boxing gloves. First time I tried them I was still just gawking at the bizarre look of them on my hands when a sizable new neighbor kid hit me flush on the jaw, I fell to a concrete floor, hit my head, and was knocked out cold. When I awoke, I no longer wanted to box again, ever: what I wanted was our country road, dog, trees, gardens, forest, knowable neighbors, farms, and freedom back.

Amazingly, I got them. When I was eight my parents moved us to a fir-tree-lined street twelve miles east of Portland. One June day, riding my bike to the general store in the postage-stamp-sized town of Fairview, I purchased my vices of the era—1¢ Bazooka bubblegum and 5¢ bags of sunflower seeds—jammed my face full of this chaw, and set out for home when I heard, seemingly under the pavement of the street, a gruff voice yell, "*Son of a bitch! Gotcha! Ow! You shit!*"

I stopped for several reasons. One: I didn't cuss (yet), so the dialect interested me. Two: the voice was a boy's. Three: the boy was invisible. Four: despite his choice of words he sounded unusually happy.

Further oaths drew me to a barn-red barbershop. "You *bastard!*" yelled the boy from nowhere. "*Come 'ere ya lil' fuck! Ha! Gotcha!*" I followed these sounds to a cave-like opening in the briars covering the west wall of the barbershop. I peered in and under. There in the dim light stood a rough-looking lout about my age, holding a galvanized bucket in one hand and a coat-hanger spear in the other, surrounded by the source of his happiness: he was standing knee-deep in clear, lively creek water.

"Wanna see?" the troll asked me, holding up his bucket.

Without a thought of shoes or clothes, I waded in beside him, and saw that his bucket was crawling with speared and dying crawdads. The troll boy informed me (as I contemplated multicolored skeins of intestine trailing out of shattered shells) that their tails and claws, once shelled, boiled, and dipped in French's Mustard, were delicious. I laughed. Yeah right.

Then I heard splashing downstream of us, and was alarmed to see a big-

ger, wilier-looking troll boy who in one hand held not a spear but a fishing pole, and in the other held not crayfish but a fresh-caught, still-flopping trout. No Christmas or birthday moment had ever compared: a mile from my house, beneath a magic barbershop, True North on my coho compass: *a secret trout stream.*

I tore back home, grabbed a pole, hooks, and split shot, rode back to the creek, caught crawdads barehanded, crushed the life out of them without compunction, used the tails and claw meat for bait, and by suppertime had caught my first two wild cutthroat trout.

## IV. NATIVE TEACHER

Fairview Creek, it turned out, was five miles long, two-thirds wild, and amazingly full of life. Over the next six years I probed it from the gravel-pit source to the Mud Lake mouth, catching hundreds of its cutthroat. In the gravel pits at the headwaters I caught stocked rainbow trout. Near the greyhound racetrack in Fairview, in a pond hidden by a raspberry farm, I plunked for bullhead catfish. In the plunge-pool below the I-84 culvert I caught a thirteen-inch Giant Pacific Salamander that flared and hissed at me like something out of Gwamma Woe's hell till I apologized, cut my line and freed it. In the cottonwood-lined meanders down near Mud Lake I moved aside the sheep herds and caught channel cats, enormous carp, bluegill, crappie, perch, bass and a cutthroat approaching two pounds.

Giving way to full obsession, I fished the creek an easy fifty or sixty times a year. There were interesting problems to work out. I was chased by police many times at the gravel pit ponds, arrested for trespass near the Mud Lake mouth, and run out of yards and off farms by irate landowners, teen bullies and a variety of militant dogs. Did these chasings and arrests combine to "teach me a lesson?" Absolutely. I learned to be *much* sneakier. The moral ambiguities of private property issues, though, were resolved for me in a 1964 publication called *Trout Fishing in America*, in which Justice Richard Brautigan gave this verdict:

*No Trespassing*
*4/17 of a haiku*

My fishing koan, ever since, has not been whether to trespass but how not to get caught.

I learned to fish the gravel pit ponds on moonlit nights to avoid watchmen and cops. I learned to clean up a pile of creekside garbage and hold it under one arm before knocking on the porch of a landowner to ask permission to fish. I used the mailman's trick—a pocketful of Milk-Bones—to tame the dogs. I learned to drift a worm and bobber down into the backyards of those who forbade trespass, skiing fish back up to where I legally stood (which twice so amazed people who had no idea their creek held trout that they gave me permission to trespass for life.) I grew ever wilier as a fisherman. I plied the creek's skinny headwaters in April and May, before buttercups closed over the surface, and plied the creek's Mud Lake terminus in summer heat, when trout had gone into hiding but big warmwater fish, especially carp, were on the prowl. I took pruning shears to impassable tunnels of briars, cutting my way back into sunless holes out of which I snaked nearly black cutthroat trout. I learned an array of lessons from the creek's confounded wild and "civilized" worlds: learned, for instance, via a few terrifying encounters, to spot and duck hoodlums before they cornered me, but also learned to build lean-tos in a rainstorm, to forage hazelnuts, apples, and berries in tossed Dairy Queen cups, and to make small smokeless fires and cook fare found along and in the creek, my best such meal ever a borscht of filched corn, green beans, onion, and catfish simmered in a tossed Van Camps bean can.

To spend so much time on a single small stream is to encounter every life-form it sustains. My presence in marshes and thickets untrod by humans enabled me to catch baby killdeer, baby mallards, baby cottontails in my hands. I stood face to face with one of the last blacktail deer ever sighted in East Multnomah County, and glimpsed perhaps the very last fox, which a teen idiot named Booth, no doubt related to John Wilkes, soon shot. I stumbled onto wood ducks, raccoons, ringneck pheasants, possums, turtles, horned owls and herons, and once, via an accident that soon became a nonaccidental riveted gape, a pair of joyously fucking teenagers. I once lay so quiet on a low wooden sheep bridge that a muskrat swam into my monofilament. Thinking myself hilarious, I lunged forward and went *BOO!*, inspiring a lightning quick flip-ass dive that drove dirty

water in under my eyelids. I bewildered my father, every Opening Day of trout season six years in a row, by refusing his invitations to the famed Deschutes River. I then dissipated his bewilderment, six years in a row, by bringing home ten-fish limits of Fairview Creek cutthroats while he often returned home skunked.

In this era of rapid-fire, unconsidered change I suppose anyone older than five or six is the relic of some sort of "lost era." For my part, I'm one of the last Americans raised on the edge of a major city who knows what he knows not just from desks in eight successive daily classrooms, from tough night streets, or from TV screens, but from six years as the Huck Finn-style lover and terror of a five-mile long ribbon of life. I stuck my hands, feet, nose, eyeballs, tongue, ears and body into a thousand places they did and a thousand places they didn't belong. I learned by poking at things, and gathering, stalking, killing, cleaning, cooking and eating things; I learned by letting things mesmerize, dazzle and hypnotize me, forming the million impressions which, when I'd collapse in bed at night, became an equally informative scramble of impression/ nightmare/vision/dream/ prayer. I learned from Tri-Met bus exhaust and Union Pacific locomotive smoke, from Crown Zellerbach paper mill stench and Reynolds Aluminum effluent, from cottonwood fluff on May pools, tractor dust in July bean fields, October cricket songs waning and geese songs waxing. For six rich years the living *ka* that was Fairview Creek flowed unmediated through my brain-halves and heart-valves, teaching me that this world is peaceful and dangerous, wild and artificial, beautiful and wounded, obscene and sublime. For six years, in other words, I studied with the most perfect teacher I can imagine for life in the America I've inhabited ever since.

## V. BODIES OF BLOOD AND WATER

Two weeks before my fourth consecutive Fairview Creek Opening Day, my eldest brother died, at seventeen, of what his doctors called "complications" after a series of failed heart surgeries. The little creek's presence, its flow, its ability to keep generating life, helped me a little with this grief. The ten Opening Day trout I caught that year felt different than any I'd caught before: their deaths especially felt different: the concept of

sacrifice had begun to invade my fishing. I could articulate nothing, but big feelings swept over me as I snapped each neck—and what an eerie version of fisherman pride I felt when my family and I, we "survivors," sat down to eat the little bodies whose lives I'd taken. Men, women and children, I suddenly realized, were dying, and no one seemed to notice but the funeral parlors who'd turned death into an industry. But each time I bloodied my hands, killing a trout as innocent as my dead brother, I noticed. Each time I killed a trout the pain would ease for a time inside me. Why? Christ. You tell me. I sensed a depth, in the act of killing fish, that spoke to my grief. A consciously snapped trout-neck was like a blues-string consciously bent against the day-to-day industrial harmonies. And a bent note, in the ears of the sorrow-bent, rings truer than a note clean-struck. Nothing soothes quite like the blues. A little trout stream, if played for keeps, can be a miles-long blues tune.

By my seventh Fairview Creek Opening Day I'd grown so confident in my abilities and creek that I bet a high school pal five bucks I'd take a seventh straight ten-fish limit. My five-mile teacher had a strange lesson for me.

At 6:30 on a rainy April morning I crept up to a favorite hole, threaded a worm on a hook, prepared to cast—then noticed something impossible: there was no water in the creek. I gaped at mud and exposed rock, then up at the falling rain. The sky was doing its job, had been doing it all April. How could this be?

I began hiking, stunned, downstream. The aquatic insects were gone, barbershop crawdads gone, catfish, carp, perch, crappie, bass, and sacrificial cutthroats not just dying but completely vanished. Feeling sick, I headed the opposite way, hiking the emptied creekbed all the way to the source, where I found the eminently rational cause of the mass killing. Development needs roads and drainfields. Roads and drainfields need gravel. Up in the gravel pits at the Glisan Street headwaters, the creek's entire flow had been diverted for months to fill two gigantic new settling ponds.

My native teacher was dead.

I was sixteen, and drove a car now. I didn't know enough to grieve. I felt so panic-stricken by Fairview Creek's death that I tried, as if keeping a stranded fish alive in a bucket, to transfer my need for water to the other

stream within easy driving distance: Johnson Creek—source of my first glimpse of a coho and an inner realm. But ten years and fifty thousand industrious industrious new human inhabitants had been murder on this friend too. I encountered none of the magic of Fairview Creek, little wildlife, no native fish, few birds. Johnson Creek's trout were now drab hatchery rainbows, planted in March by Fish and Wildlife to entertain local yokels on Opening Day. By May no one fished for them because the same Fish and Wildlife department pronounced them too toxic to eat.

I kept after them, though. I was old enough, now, to know a metaphor when I hooked one: I was fascinated by the trout's growing discoloration, growing scarcity, growing weakness. I entered a zone, fished Johnson Creek hard. By June it was low, warm, filmy, and the trouts' living skins had burst out in a pox of strange clear bubbles. By midmonth the rainbows stopped taking any kind of bait or fly, but I'd still see one drift past now and then, in a sudsy foam-line, sometimes belly-up, sometimes weakly finning. One hot June day I managed to catch a few suckers near the creek's terminus with the Willamette: they were on a spawning run, hadn't been in the creek long enough to be dead yet. One July day, near the 55th Street bridge, my catch was a discarded car radio and a woman's dress (red, with small white polka dots; short; sexy; poisonously sopped). Another day it was twenty bags of rotten meat and vegetables floating along in ziplock bags, looking like twenty disembodied stomachs still trying to digest their meals. By August, and drought, my new native teacher was an oil-scummed, fetid, foam-flecked sewer, there were warnings posted on phone poles telling kids not to swim, and even the hatchery trout of June seemed like a comparatively beautiful vision. The last day I fished Johnson Creek I waded into a nice-looking run, knelt low, cast a fly up into the riffle, noticed a more-offensive-than-usual stench coming from the creekbank behind me, turned—and gagged at the sight of the crawling, maggot-filled head of a horse.

## VI. CRASH TEST DUMMY

My two boyhood mentors were a brother and a creek, both now dead. My coho compass seemed to die with Johnson Creek. I still loved rivers,

But river don't come with you to school or ball games, don't brother you when you're haunted, don't speak English, don't intellectualize. So— linguistically, socially, fraternally, intellectually—I felt alone and unguided. The fishing talk of the best anglers I knew—honest working stiffs, men I guardedly liked—was a lingo of technique, conquest and gloat. The rivers within driving distance—the Columbia, Clackamas, Sandy—were the domain of fishermen who on their workdays helped destroy rivers and on their off days plundered them. There was no one to whom I could even mention such perceptions. Love for animals, birds, wilderness, led to no A's on report cards. If Henry Thoreau or Gary Snyder had attended my giant high school they'd have dropped out if they hadn't been expelled. If they'd taught there, they would definitely have been fired. There would be no coho questions on my S. A. T. exams. Free-flowing streams made no campaign contributions to senators—and look what happened to them as a result. A big trout sipping a mayfly may be a veritable hymn to the health of a watershed, but no TV or newspaper covered that hymn. On TV and in the papers I watched businessmen, economists, politicians place a dollar value on everything on earth and discount anything that lacked such a value. I knew this was wrong—knew that if everything was material then everything was negotiable and one's body, home, friendships, honesty, honor, could all be bought or sold. I then watched democracy itself be bought and sold; watched the TV war escalate in Asia, the campus and race riots escalate at home; watched a patriotic foster brother die almost the day he set foot in Vietnam; watched Martin Luther King and Bobby Kennedy die in the midst of expressing compassion and love of justice; watched people who define things in the crassest, most material way get what they wanted over and over; watched evil, mortality and stupidity win and win and win.

There came a time, in adolescence, when I questioned every last thing my heart had intimated to me since childhood. All this "nature stuff" suddenly felt too hard to articulate to bosses, teachers, parents, too airy-fairy to share with red-blooded three-sport pals. My unchecked river-love suddenly struck me as a way to achieve numbnutted poverty, cultural irrelevancy, and maybe a stint in Vietnam. I began to want to get what *I* wanted. And what I'd begun to want, I came to believe, was not richness, not meaning, not interior truth or depth: I wanted a skin so thick this

world couldn't hurt me. A skin I'd open, now and then, if the right looking kind of girl wanted in. But only briefly.

Hoping to create such a skin, I began to crash-test everything I'd ever loved or trusted, then pick through the wreckage to see what survived. I crash-tested my connection to creeks and rivers in the simplest way possible: I abandoned them. Quit seeking wild water. Quit yearning for it. I even quit crying, for any reason, since tears too are a bit wild and all too wet.

Taking aim at nothing I couldn't eat, feel, fool, fuck, or buy, I became a pathologically common brand of high school student, landed a series of the best-paying jobs I could find, became a cog in the purposeless box of industrial gears that had appalled me as a child, and "repaid myself" for this purposelessness by granting myself every pleasure I could grasp.

I began to grow that thick skin. The sensation scared me for a bit. But life, as I was living it, thickened me so fast that I was soon unable to feel even my fear.

### VII. VALMIKI'S PALM

At seventeen I took a full-time summer job at a plastics factory in the industrial heart of Portland. I then began, after work, to wander the city in the company of my fine new principle of depravity, seeking whatever pleasures I could physically grasp.

One day I dropped into a disheveled little used bookstore: the cram-packed, cigarette-singed '69 vintage Powell's Books, as it happens. I read books as a hedonist in those days, read them to trip. Looking for the wildest but least expensive possible ride, I impulse-purchased a musty verse translation of the *Ramayana*, and headed home.

I knew, from having read *The Odyssey*, that epics were a trip. I knew, from reading a remark made by Snyder or Tolkien or somebody, that the *Ramayana*—story of the prehistoric king, Rama—was India's greatest epic. But the translation I'd purchased in a post-work stupor told King Rama's story in wrenched, rhyming Victorian couplets that made even epic battles and ancient wisdom sound like the chuggity-chugging sentiments of an interminable Hallmark card. I soon threw the book away. Before I did, however, I took one small wonder to heart:

The *Ramayana's* author—the forest poet, Valmiki—states in his opening verses that he did not use his imagination while composing King Rama's story. He didn't need imagination, he said, because at dawn each day he took an urn to the nearby river, filled it, carried it to his hut, sat down on an eastward-facing mat, then scooped a little river water into his palm: in this tiny body of water Valmiki saw first King Rama, then Queen Sita, then every god, demon, bear, monkey and hero, and every love dalliance and bloody battle in his timeless epic. Fragrances and sounds, too, rose from the water: the smoke of brahmanic sacrifices, stench of demons, cries of warriors and victims, hissing flight of arrows, blood-burst of every wound. The poet then sang what he saw. All twenty-five-thousand *Ramayana* couplets were born in the water pooled daily in Valmiki's palm.

I was smitten by this. That an epic could spring from a palmful of river brought a jolt of the liturgical joys a garden-hose river and two-inch fishing soldier once gave me. Thanks to the Victorian prosody and my cynical teen self, this joy didn't blossom into anything life-changing. In honor of Valmiki, though, I did develop an odd tic: I took to glancing at my own palms, dozens of times a day, as if at a watch I expected to tell me more than the time. Just a nervous habit I suppose. Because of it, though, I came to see that palms have skin like no other part of the body: the moisture; visible texture; almost legible-looking lines. I learned the palms' topography—four ominous little canyons in which palm-readers claim to see secrets of the head, heart, fate and lifespan. I saw that palms, compared to fists or fingers, have no agenda: they're not a weapon, a tool, a talon: they're just a handy portable shelf revealing exactly what it holds.

I soon tossed the *Ramayana* and wandered off in search of more sensual or phantasmagoric trips. But I couldn't shake that little palm-reading tic.

The plastics factory that employed me produced a tough red polyurethane, dubbed "Redskin," from which we made indescribable geometrical gizmos we simply called "parts." These parts were shipped to other factories to be attached to larger indescribable gizmos, which were shipped to still other factories and attached to indescribable machines that were in turn shipped and fixed to larger machines. Five or six removes from us, rumor had it, our Redskin gizmos became part of something you could actually name: a raspberry-picking machine. We had no way to verify

this, but our bosses told us so and we believed them. We were Americans after all. What could be more American than manufacturing plastic crap called "Redskin" to produce a machine that put the real, destitute, flesh-and-blood "redskins" who in those days picked Oregon's raspberries, out of work?

I lived next door to a raspberry farm harvested, for the most part, by impoverished Indians. I liked those Indians when I worked with them. But I didn't feel sorry for those our "Redskin" helped put out of work. The reason I didn't was: we were being killed for our crime; Redskin Plant management had deemed the slow killing of workers to be an acceptable cost of the Redskin manufacturing process. What better revenge could the real Indians want?

The murder weapon was not an object, but a lack of objects. In the time I worked at Redskin I saw no blue-collar employee spend a single hour working with materials that weren't toxic, yet I never saw a respirator, an exhaust fan, a gauze mask, never heard or read a single warning. We spent every day stoned on carcinogenic fumes. Yet no one complained. In fact, plant morale was high. I think it had to do with Vietnam, which in turn had to do with childhoods in suburbs, in arsenals, in pews, immaculate interiors, fake democracies, everything and everyone destined to be sold, uprooted, bound in burlap, shipped out. Every Redskin worker had an *America: Love It Or Leave It* bumper sticker on their vehicle and seemed genuinely grateful to be spending their health and allotment of heartbeats making incomprehensible polyurethane gizmos. The typical Redskin Plant attitude was, "I'm non-union, I'm underpaid, I'm making nothing I understand, I'm breathing shit, I'll be dying young—and I'm *proud of it!*"

My job as plant lackey was of a janitorial nature. I cleaned up spills mostly. Redskin started out as a stew of toxic liquids which were mixed together in vats, poured into molds, placed on racks, rolled into a huge walk-in oven, baked to hardness, rolled back out, and removed as hardened "parts." There were spills at every fluid stage of this process, and spilled polyurethane quickly fuses with anything it touches. Once hardened, the only way to remove the stuff is with an acetone solvent—also toxic. I spent my Redskin career blitzed on solvent.

One of my daily tasks took place in Dumpster bins. Even after they'd been emptied into garbage trucks, the sides and bottom of our bins remained caked with enormous slabs of waste Redskin. It was my job to climb in the Dumpster, pour solvent on the slabs, let it work awhile, then attack the now-gooey Redskin with a giant C-clamp. The clamp was hooked to a steel cable, which attached to the overhead hydraulic lift. Blinded by tears from solvent fumes, terrifically stoned by them, I'd screw my C-clamp to the biggest meanest flap of Redskin I could find, hit the "Up" button on the hydraulic lift's remote, and hope the weight of the Dumpster and me would together tear the slab free while I was still fairly close to the ground. When the slab didn't tear I'd just continue toward the ceiling, too fume-ripped to tell the "Up" button from the "Down." It was a thirty-foot ceiling. I don't recall dropping a Dumpster from the top—management really didn't like that. But when a Redskin slab tore loose even at eight or ten feet, the Dumpster crashed to the floor with a force that brought a roar of laughter from the other workers, knowing I lay in a swamp of half-dissolved plastics inside. I laughed too, if brokenly, to show 'em I was tough.

Another job was cleaning the walk-in oven. Every time a rack of fresh-filled molds was rolled in, liquid Redskin dripped onto the oven floor. These drips built up after each firing, creating bumps that caused more spillage. My task was to pour solvent on the bumps, then hack them free with a garden hoe. Since "time is money," though, and cooling and reheating the oven took time, the plant foreman considered 140 degrees Fahrenheit "Can Do" cleaning conditions. At 140 degrees, my solvent vaporized the instant it touched the floor, turning the oven into a blinding, brain-fogging sweat lodge. The foreman would stand by the open oven door, watching me scamper into the lodge, throw solvent on bumps, run back out, take a breath, run back in, hoe bumps, run back out, take a breath, run in, hoe, run out, till the floor was smooth. His vigilance was not a kindness. Dead workers waste time, which is money.

Most Redskin parts had thin, sloppy edges created by a skin of plastic that had overflowed the mold. We removed this skin by hand with X-Acto knives. Six weeks into my job, after yet another toxic sweat and hoe in the oven, I sat down at my work station, fetched my X-Acto, and began

trimming sloppy edges from a box of Redskin parts, feeling as if time and space were drunk and my mind was dipped in plastic and indispensable parts of me were dying and so the fuck what. I was making eight hundred dollars a month to feel this way. I was tough.

I fetched another part, trimmed away another edge. Fetched another. Trimmed. Then something happened: feeling a faint swirl in my left palm, I glanced down—and saw a silver fin crease the surface of my skin.

"Trout," I murmured, too oven-stoned for surprise.

A trout had risen in my left palm. Hmm. My Valmikian tic was finally producing the goods. The trout's dorsal lazed up into sight and stayed there; broke the surface, making no ripples, and stayed there. I'd seen a lot of fish in my day, but never one rising from inside me. Half-forgotten river thoughts began to swim through my head. *How did a trout get inside my hand? And what did it do in there all day? Had it risen to sip some kind of fly or just to move, who knows why, through a space and time it created for itself as it glided?*

I had no idea. But a second wave of notions slopped through me. That something as fragile as a trout could survive inside the Redskin Plant seemed even less likely than that one could live inside my hand. So what were my hand and I doing in the Redskin Plant? I grew vaguely aware of a throbbing that never left my body, realized it was the dark digestive rumbling of the entire unventilated building, felt the Plant sucking at my limbs, my lungs, my life—and grew less vaguely aware. I looked at the men with whom I worked and joked all day, saw the black rings beneath their eyes, the lethargic movements, the dissolved plastics slopped on clothes and skin. Then a third wave struck:

Turning back to my trout-inhabited palm, I began gasping for life. My entire body was suddenly dying for clear running water, moss-trimmed cedars, clean-pebbled streambeds, the vast, preacherless church of the wild. I gasped so hard that my eyes filled not with fume-tears but with real tears and my palm—could this be happening?—began to bleed, right from the rise. I watched blood stream down my fate-line like water down a defiled stream, watched it fall, then pool, on the factory floor.

It took me the longest time to realize I'd stuck the X-Acto through my hand from the opposite side and was staring at the tip of its blade in

my palm. It took so long that, in the end, I reacted not to a blade but to a trout's rise—and began trying to rise myself.

Taking fresh aim at life and water, I bandaged my hand, told my Redskin cohorts that we were dying, and quit my job that day. I stopped at an Army/Navy surplus store on the way home, bought a box of 39-cent trout flies, an inexpensive fiberglass fly rod kit, and a stack of Oregon wilderness maps. I embraced poverty—and the freedom it buys. I built the fly rod. I then began, like a blind man with a nine-foot cane, to feel my way back toward things I fully loved and trusted.

The palm of a hand is impassive. Fists and fingers have their agendas, but what rests in a palm is free to tell its silent truth. In the years since a steel dorsal rose in my fate line I have waded hundreds of wild streams, held thousands of trout and salmon in my hands, watched millions of silvery rises. To this day I sometimes cup a little river in my pierced palm, flood the tiny scar, and check for signs of life there. To this day I keep thanking Valmiki.

LAURIE RACHKUS UTTICH

# Do Not Read
# Out Loud

He will write about his mother, a broom handle, a belt, a coat hanger. He will write about his escape route, a six-foot fence, a neighbor's house. He will write about the times that he makes it and the times that he does not. He will write in the present tense using his eight-year-old voice, *My fear is a living, wild thing that quivers like my own dog does not.*

You will write: *The pacing is strong throughout* and *I'm not sure if this metaphor completely works yet.*

She will write about her father, a constant bottle of Jack D in his hand, a cigarette burn on her chest. She will write about how love is imperfect and describe the raised, red circle still alive on the white page of her skin. She will write at the end, *I was three and today I wear scarves around my neck. My friends find me fashionable. My father does not apologize. He has never apologized.*

You will write: *The concrete details are powerful* and *Is the conclusion as solid as it could be?*

Both of them will write on the top of their papers: do not read out loud. And you will not. You will walk into class and you will pass back these small writing assignments. And even though the work is brave and beautiful, a search for meaning in moments both large and small, you will not hold up their words as examples of "good" creative nonfiction. Instead, you will talk about lyrical essays. You will ask them to focus on an object. *See where it leads you and how it can connect to your life. Surprise yourself.*

You will think about her scarf, his dog. But you will not look at her

neck. You will not lower your eyes when he watches you. You will smile at all of them: *Do we want music when we write?*

But at night—at 3:00 a.m. after two glasses of wine make you wake in the dark—your student is eight years old again and you are his neighbor. You open the door, lock it behind him. You pour him tea with milk and sugar, the way your own mother did. You rub the back of his head, near the base where his hair ends and you breathe him in, the way you do with your own sons. You whisper *I'm sorry* into his shoulder. You pull his pain into your chest.

You become the mother of your student's three-year-old self. You lift her off her father's lap. You buckle her into a car, drive away fast. You leave a wake of booze and burns and you don't stop until it's safe. You turn in your seat. You reach for your daughter. You smooth the hair out of her face, tuck it behind her ear. You press three fingers to your lips, rest them on that cooling circle. You see it is still red, but not yet scarred. *You are so lovely*, you tell her. *You are such a gift to the world.*

Still, you cannot sleep, so you compose lists of comments you cannot write. You speak as if your words are your own and not the person's you play in class: Gay is just who you are. You couldn't have stopped him from hurting your mother. You are so much more than the "fat friend." It's rape, even if you're drunk. I thank my God the rope slipped that day. To all of them, you don't write: If only you could see what I see. If only.

But even as your blue ink would like to rise and reach toward the writer, you know the space between you is too wide, the water deep with words that can drown your students' voices. They wade where truth waits, their feet flailing until the past settles and they push off into a new place. It is so tempting to tire early on, to float to the surface, to click Save, and sink into shallow shores. You know this. You have your own stories. You know "I'm sorry" would stick in your students' throats, forcing them to spit truth out or swallow it whole. This worries you, this fear that you may silence them, because you still believe that writing can save them. You still believe writing can save you. So you hold their words, heavy with hope, in your open palm and you do not—you do not ever—read out loud.

BRIAN DOYLE

# Playfulness
## *A Note*

Thesis: the essay is the widest fattest most generous open glorious honest endlessly expandable form of committing prose not only because it cheerfully steals and hones all the other tools and talents of all other forms of art, and not only because it is admirably and brilliantly closest to not only the speaking voice but the maundering shambling shuffling nutty wandering salty singing voices in our heads, but also because it is the most playful of forms, liable to hilarity and free association and startlement, without the filters and mannered disguises and stiff dignity of fiction and poetry and journalism, respectively.

Discuss.

Let me give you an example right off the bat. Just riffing for a moment with the typewriter, borrowing a small son and dragooning him into burbling over this way and banging with one finger, we get ffff and rrrr and bmbmbm, which immediately sound jazzy to me, and send me off thinking about the gleaming glimmering horns in the velvet dark of the jazz club in New York that my sister took me into when I was a teenager, and thinking about the jazzy phonemes my kids started off language with when they were little and spent a lot of time humming consonantal bursts and vowelacious arias, and thinking about how maybe typewriters remember what you type with them, maybe they actually steer you in

certain directions for their own devious entertainment, and this sets me thinking about my dad teaching me to type with two furious fingers on his old tall black steel typewriter, and the sheaves of love poems he typed to my mom in blazing dripping afternoons in Manila just before he was sure he was about to die in the invasion of Japan. So here, in the space of two minutes, we have leapt from jazz to jazzy infants to intelligent type-writers to a lanky young sergeant hammering words onto infinitesimally thin sheets of onionskin paper as parakeets and bulbuls yammered outside in the dense heat, words he thought for sure would be his last, words he desperately wanted to get down before he never saw the girl with the hair to her waist and that irresistible overbite ever again. I mean, there, in two minutes, are a whole bunch of essay starts. Is there any other form that can go so fast and piercingly and honestly and nattily, cutting holes in your heart along the way?

Naaaah.

Or here's another example. My grandfather John Francis Clancey, who was raised in Hell's Kitchen in New York City, not far from where we sit today, had a heart attack on the train one day, and I always wanted to try to write about that, and I tried to write it as fiction, but fiction was too mannered and arty and remote for me somehow, so finally I tried to write it like it really and truly happened, and I couldn't write it as straight reportage because it sounded too flat and confessional, but thank God Plutarch invented the essay, because I *could* come at it in an essay, like this:

"... a savage raging pain explodes in his chest so suddenly and cruelly that it knocks him to his knees and only by shooting his arms out blindly and landing on his hands does he avoid smashing his face on the floor o god o god he he thinks faintly from far far away he can't breathe uh uh uh uh uh uh gasping uh uh uh uh but desperately raggedly he gains a half a breath uh uh uh and gulping uh uh a whole one uh uh then another uh and greedily aah he fills aaah his lungs as deeply as he can aaaah he would eat all the air in the world if he could aaaaah he would suck it dry the blessed air aaaaah and somehow the friendly air aaaaah forces the

fire in his chest down aaahh and the rage retreats snarling aaaaah and he kneels there aaaah breathing aaah his shoulders shaking aah his knees throbbing ah his sweat dripping freely to the floor ah his mind whispering o god o god o god . . ."

You see what I mean? The essay gets there on the express train, you know? I mean, fiction can get there too, but there's always a polite conductor standing there with fiction; the gatekeeper, the man you cannot ignore, the guy who whispers *this is all made up, remember that,* even as the very best fiction, while invented, is utterly true. It's a puzzle, eh?

The essay is a jackdaw, a magpie, a raven. It picks up everything and uses it. It borrows everything and bends everything to its nefarious porpoises. The quick sketch of character and moodiness and evocativeness and action of fiction, the musicality and cadence and swing and rhythm and crisp imagery and line-cracking power of poetry, the play and banter and battle of voices of the theater, the camera eye of film, the shapeliness of sculpture (I always wanted to write an essay about weight that would actually get skinnier as you went along, with occasional binges where it bulges out again, wouldn't that be cool?)(or an essay about mountains that parades up and down alpinically, or an essay about caribou migration, say, that goes along for fifty pages but only two inches high, or an essay about windows with windows in it: seems to me you have a bigger playing field physically with essays than you do with poems), the athleticism and grace of dance, all these things are meat for the essayist—and the essay because of its form and size lends itself more to playfulness in terms of speed and pace and timing than other written forms—poems are bursts (and really, if we are being honest, all long poems, especially book-length poems, don't really work as *poems,* do they? They're just too . . . looooooong, you know? I mean, who really thinks of the *Odyssey* or the *Iliad* or God help us all that incredibly boring prison sentence called *Paradise Lost* as a Poem?), and plays and novels and nonfiction books are long. *Songs* are playful—think of Joe Cocker's "You Can Keep Your Hat On"—but songs, when you think about it, are two art forms married to each other. Which is

why music with lyrics is perhaps the greatest art form of all, seems to me; but of written art, I think essays are the coolest widest broadest biggest form. Everything fits in the essay, and it's nearly naked.

Right about here scholarly-type people will say, yeah, well, got any examples, got any documentation, got any illustrations? And being a happy student of the glory of the essay in the greatest of hands I say, sweet Jesus yes, think of Natalia Ginzburg's chant and cadence and swing, the tennis match of her great essay "He and I"—"He is hot and I am cold. He loves libraries and I hate them. He loves travelling. I would like to stay at home all the time . . ." She steals litany and music from poetry. Or think of Robert Louis Stevenson's glorious furious "Open Letter to the Reverend Doctor Hyde," the blunt terse judicial accusatory tone—you you you—echoes of the courtroom speech, the case for the prosecution—and then it flies up and away into an extraordinary prayer at the end, one of the greatest closing passages in the history of essays, bless his soul, that poor man, dead at forty-four. He crams fury and spiritual genius into what seems for a while like straight reportage or notes from a deposition and makes it dance, yes? Or the genius Annie Dillard, with her broken-whiskey-glass-and-ten-packs-of-cigarettes-day voice, in her extraordinary essay "Living Like Weasels," which begins like any old "nature essay" (man, what a reductive and thus dismissive term that is) about paying attention to that which we hardly pay any real attention to (this being the subject of all essays, really), and suddenly goes *flying into the brain and soul of the weasel,* o my god o sweet jesus wow. Doesn't she steal the imaginative fire of the best fiction, in a hundredth of the space, and make a dart to the heart?

And, you know, not to be rude or anything, and not to try to start a fire, but just to try to gently say, hey, are we totally sure the emperor is wearing his undies today, isn't one of the great virtues of the essay that it's short?

I mean, with total respect for doorstop novels, and muscular nonfiction epics like Peter Matthiessen's *The Snow Leopard* or Jan Morris' brilliant *Pax Brittanica* trilogy, isn't short almost always better than long? I hear everyone gasping with horror, but c'mon, let's be honest, isn't an arrow better than a tank when it comes to hitting hearts and heads? And isn't hitting hearts and heads the point? And isn't using the arrow that might hit the most hearts quickest perhaps the best idea? So if lots and lots of people will read a brief talkative odd funny pointed cheerful testy voice talking at them from a page, or a screen, or a radio, or whatever cool toy our children will invent next, but not so many people will spend a week with a really big book, or try to decipher a poem, or endure the dental work that is an awful lot of journalism, or see through the glittering neurotic screen that is so much short fiction, well, doesn't that mean perhaps that the essay is the form with the most pop and verve and connective electricity? Could that be? Could it be that we are gathered at what today is actually a team meeting for the form that could maybe most change the universe as we know it? Could it be that maybe I am right for a change, and for once am not a complete and utter doofus and bonehead?

And a last note about shapeliness. If we grant for a moment that I am right that essays are glorious because they are for the most part unfiltered, and so a direct and unadorned and naked form, which is good; and we grant also that the essay is the closest form to the human voice, which is good, because we listen easily and naturally to voices, and don't have to strain and labor and work and digest, we just dig the voice, as we were trained to do since even before we were born; and if we grant also that the essay is particularly cool because it's short and direct and a dagger and a dart rather than an epic or labor or doorstop or something you really are going to get around to next summer when you have time which you won't—that still leaves that nagging question that I get all the time from smart-ass high-school sophomores, what's the difference between an article and an essay? Hey, Mister, all these cool things you say about essays, don't they apply to articles in the best hands, articles written by great storycatchers

and storytellers like Mike Royko and Tim Egan and Murray Kempton and Dexter Filkins and Anna Quindlen and the late great Molly Ivins? To which I say, well, yes, except that journalism in general has to stay on a road, has to have an aura of information, has to at least pretend to be reasonable, whereas essays run anywhere they like; and essays, I would maintain, are also shapelier, more attentive to beginning and middle and end, more attuned to the ways and means by which we tell stories. Essays maybe are a little more carpentered, you know? and more liable to be more vehicles for discovery rather than mere knowledge. Think how many times in your own work you were typing along happily, cursing and humming, and suddenly you wrote something you didn't know you felt so powerfully, and maybe you cried right there by the old typewriter, and marveled, not always happily, at what dark threads your typing had pulled from the mysterious fabric of your heart. Maybe that happens the most with essays. This could be.

To return to the original thesis: the essay is the most playful and coolest form because it is the most naked. It is without much artifice, in the end; only enough to build a lean-to on the page for the reader and the writer to live in, for a few minutes. It is not a song by the fire, as poetry is, as poetry was certainly born as; it is a not a vast house in which are many mansions, as novels and other prose tomes are; it is not the terse ostensibly neutral (or neutered) reportage that journalism is, or the casual shaggy gossipy confessional that a letter is at its best; nor is it a song, a rant, a note, a blog, a speech (although a great speech is sometimes eerily close to a great essay, yes?), and along with all that it is not, it is not usually disguised or mannered in any way. As a general rule the essay is a clap on the back, a hand outstretched to be grasped, a blunt voice in your ear. Every other genre has some filter, some jacket it wears, some attitude it is supposed to have, some definition that hovers around it like a nimbus, but not the essay; the only definition that applies to the essay is that it be an adventure, a walk in the woods, an idea pushed and prodded and poked and played with. If an essay leans too much toward the scholarly, it becomes

a doddering avuncular article; too far over toward mere parade of facts, and it smells like journalism; too stern and instructive and scoldacious, and it morphs into lecture and sermon and homily; too spitting mad and uncontrolled and it is a rant, or Ann Coulter's diary; too uncontrolled and wandering and it is perhaps a blog entry, a letter, notes for an essay to be made. Direct and unadorned, for the most part—that is the essay. No frills, no filters, no manners, no capering motley, not much ego, it is not only closest to the speaking voice, which is why I love it so, but perhaps closest to the inner voice we all have in the deepest chambers of our hearts. Maybe that is why it is finally such a powerful form, the essay; not because it's closest to us, but because it *is* us.

ROBERT ATWAN

# Notes toward the Definition of an Essay

Anyone who has attempted to write about the essay knows how difficult the genre is to define. Yet essayists over the centuries have sought some sort of definition, despite the fact that the first modern essayist, Montaigne, the writer who gave the form its name, had the good sense to avoid defining the strange sort of prose he was in the process of inventing.

I'm not saying that poetry, fiction, and drama are any easier to define than the essay. My point is simply that anyone writing about these forms, unless of course the goal is explicitly critical genre theory, will not feel under a similar obligation to propose definitions. So, what is it about essays in particular that makes us nervous?

Before I boldly and perhaps foolishly propose a definition of the essay, I want to explore why the form seems to demand one. The reasons are historical, critical, and educational. I'll begin with a brief examination of these, and then focus on the practical problems I face as the editor of the annual *Best American Essays* series and of numerous college anthologies that feature essays.

First, the historical problem. As most readers know, the origin of the essay is usually traced to one writer, Montaigne, who began composing his peculiar prose pieces in the 1570s. At first, he has no literary category to describe what he is doing, nor does he appear to even possess conventional rhetorical aims. In nearly all previous prose compositions, the act of writing remained in the background; Montaigne is perhaps the first to foreground the writing process. In his prose, he refused to adopt, as did

his sixteenth-century contemporaries, a professional, scholarly, clerical, or judicial authority. He allowed himself no authoritative posture—only that of being an author.

As his pieces accumulated, Montaigne settled on the word *essai* to characterize his literary efforts. The word was an ordinary term that at the time had no literary resonance. Like most common words it carried a broad range of connotations. The etymology of *essai* can be traced to the late Latin *exagium*, which meant "to weigh" or "a weight." By the fourth century, the term had spread to the Romance languages with the additional and modern meaning of "to attempt" or "to try." Though we normally translate the title of Montaigne's book as *Essays*, suggesting only the genre, we should remember that in his time the term suggested no literary genre and would be read as "attempts" or "trials," or, since the verb *essayer* had a wide spectrum of synonyms, it could also suggest: to sample, taste, practice, take a risk, to experiment, to improvise, to try out, to sound—and these are only a few ways we might understand the term. As Hugo Friedrich says in his splendid book on Montaigne, the word also implied modest beginnings and a learner's first attempts. The word *essay*, then, served as a caution not to take the work too seriously; these weren't, after all, airtight arguments or conclusive treatises. The essays had an unfinished quality; I hear in the original use of *essay* something akin to a sketch or rough draft.

Montaigne deliberately pursued an anti-systematic and anti-rhetorical method of composition. He purposefully defied the formal conventions of classification, division, logical progression, etc. that characterized serious prose. And he thus established an ironic authorial posture: the art of his essays would be grounded in the illusion of their artlessness. His essays would reflect the mind in process. The writer will not worry about main points and thesis statements, as digressions lead to further digressions and his thematic destination disappears. A practicing Catholic, he doesn't even try to avoid the mortal sin of inconsistency. For Montaigne, the essay essentially came to represent a compositional subversion of the established rhetorical order, as his fluid thoughts appear to be generated solely from the act of writing and not from a preconceived plan. From this brief description of Montaigne's method we can see how far first-year

college writing programs, with their emphasis on clarity, coherence, and rhetorical patterns, have distanced themselves from the original meaning of an essay.

No sooner had Montaigne launched this new literary form than imitations appeared throughout Europe at an astonishing rate. The English philosopher and statesman Francis Bacon would be the first to take Montaigne's casual term and use it as a label for a distinct genre. But Bacon was reluctant to give his French rival full credit for the literary innovation. In 1597, Bacon noted that though the term *essay* came late (he was careful not even to allude to Montaigne), the form Bacon pointed out was ancient, going back to such works as Seneca's *Epistles*, which, he claimed, were really essays, or "dispersed meditations." Yet, despite Bacon's decision to cite the essay's prehistory and to downplay Montaigne's founding role, the essay by the beginning of the seventeenth century had clearly come to be recognized as an independent—and modern—literary genre.

Throughout the next two centuries, the English essay in particular would enjoy great popularity with an expanding reading public; the essay, in fact, not news reporting, was one of the chief reasons for the rapid development of the daily newspaper. It was a favorite form of such gifted authors as Daniel Defoe, Joseph Addison, Jonathan Swift, Oliver Goldsmith, and Samuel Johnson. Henry Fielding admitted that he introduced various chapters of *Tom Jones* with essays because he wanted to discourage imitations of his fiction by proving he could also write in a more difficult and intellectually challenging genre. The essay's literary significance would last roughly until the end of the First World War, reaching perhaps its apex in the Victorian era, that great age of critical and intellectual prose.

Now to my second point. Although the essay attracted many talented practitioners and was highly regarded as a literary form, it drew little serious critical attention: what little it did receive was largely biographical and impressionistic. To make matters difficult, Montaigne—as I said—had never formally defined his creation, and had used the word *essay* with so many different shadings that the term seemed applicable to all sorts of literary productions. It was not long before philosophers, scholars, scientists, naturalists, critics, and even poets would title their various works essays. When earlier writers did attempt to study the typical essay, they

usually did so with a Montaignean disdain for fastidious, scholarly distinctions. This situation did not change amid the explosion of criticism in the twentieth century. As a vast body of professional, academic criticism rose to meet the challenges of modernist fiction, poetry, and drama, the essay found itself merely a quaint, middlebrow genre, a holdover from Victorian times. The newspapers and magazines that had flourished as a result of the essay now abandoned it in favor of hard journalism and informative articles. In fact, it is no coincidence that the rise of objective and detached journalism went hand in hand with the decline of the subjective and familiar essay.

And in the academy the New Criticism, led by John Crowe Ransom, was busy developing a special definition of imaginative literature that deliberately excluded essays and ended once and for all the belletristic tradition that had nourished previous generations of readers. Certainly by the 1960s, the essay was an endangered literary species, hanging on here and there, but increasingly defined in nonliterary terms along with journalism and commentary. America's most popular modern essayist, E. B. White, often considered one of those middle-brows, would legitimately complain around this time that the essayist had become a second-class citizen in the Republic of letters.

Now to the essay's pedagogical problems. Neglected by publishers and marginalized by literary studies, the essay managed to find a home in the expanding field of university writing instruction, which for a time made a last-ditch effort to continue the belletristic tradition. In general, it was decided fairly early in the development of such programs that students would be required to write essays—not translate classical chestnuts or compose stories or poems—and they would write their essays by adhering to models of good prose.

The high school (many early anthologies were assembled by high school department heads) and college courses that sponsored essay writing did so primarily to stimulate and improve student prose for purposes of practical communication. Understanding the essay as a creative literary genre rarely entered into the picture. Even today, my guess is that the essays used in first-year courses are taught primarily for content, relevant issues, and rhetorical models—but rarely for the appreciation and analysis

of their literary form. Though loosely called "essays," they could also be termed "themes" or "compositions"—words that perhaps more accurately characterize their instructional nature. A few of the early leaders in the field of writing seemed to avoid the term *essay*, apparently not wanting to suggest that students were being asked to produce literary prose. Certainly, with their emphasis on unity, coherence, and organization, these compositional pioneers knew that introducing an essay such as Montaigne's "On Coaches" would drastically undermine their educational objectives. Still, the models supplied by early textbooks and anthologies were more often than not chosen from the best essayists of the past and present. That selection standard invariably led to a disconnection between what students were asked to read and what they were required to write. In short, they were asked to read essays but required to write compositions.

As the status of the essay declined in mid-century (and I would argue that one indication of its decline can be seen in its disappearance from literature courses and its emergence in composition studies) so did the critical standards by which the genre could be identified and evaluated. The scholar Lynn Bloom pointed out a decade ago that as freshman essay anthologies proliferated with the growth of writing courses over the past several decades, the traditional sense of what constituted an essay was stretched to its limits. Briefly put, freshmen anthologies will include any sort of nonfiction prose and call it an essay: speeches, manifestos, editorials, criticism, snippets from larger nonfiction works, scientific analysis, academic papers, and so on. I should note that I'm not speaking here of the few freshman collections designed explicitly to offer an in-depth treatment of major essayists. I'm referring instead to the large, all-purpose thematic readers, the rhetorical textbooks, and the cross-curricular collections that usually for editorial convenience classify nearly all of their nonfiction selections *essays*, regardless of the work's original genre or its author's intentions. But editorial convenience isn't the only reason; there's a historical reason as well. As I mentioned earlier, the essay's literary identity was almost totally lost early in the century and the word has, as Lynn Bloom aptly noted, become a catchall for any sort of nonfiction prose. A collection designed for a short-story course, for instance, would not contain memoirs and creative nonfiction, nor would a poetry anthology feature

journalism and reportage. But in Alice-in-Wonderland fashion, an essay can be whatever anyone claims it is.

My central point is that the essay today does get taught in composition courses but it does not get taught as literature. For the most part, the essay remains largely undefined and un-discussed as a literary medium. I doubt that instructors are even using the nonfiction mix offered by most collections to help students discriminate between real essays and other varieties of nonfiction. Surely, there's a qualitative difference between a work deliberately conceived and composed as an essay and a series of paragraphs excerpted from a nonfiction book and given an arbitrary title. Yet many anthologies don't even differentiate between the two; they casually label both selections essays, to the artistic detriment of the true essay and to the confusion of the student. In fact, by using the term *essay* indiscriminately, many anthologies perpetuate the genre's diminished and nonliterary status. This is an important issue in the relationship between the literature and composition divisions of English departments. By continually neglecting the literary qualities and history of the essay, composition programs have lost a significant educational opportunity, one that would have allowed them to establish a critical and theoretical foundation for the revitalization of the essay as a literary genre.

Now I come to my own personal stake in formulating a definition of the essay. Back in 1985, when I decided to launch an annual series that would celebrate the contemporary essay as a literary form, I realized I would need to develop some practical criteria by which I could filter out genuine essays from all the other sorts of nonfiction that crowded our current periodicals. I quickly discovered that this would not be an easy task. The difficulties arose mainly from magazine-publishing practices, which rarely distinguished essays from other nonfiction, and from the increasing use of hybrid literary forms that blurred conventional generic distinctions. Though I found plenty of writers back then who wrote essays that were undeniably essays (Joan Didion, Elizabeth Hardwick, Joseph Epstein, Phillip Lopate, to name just a few), I also came across a growing number of emerging writers who grafted elements of fiction, poetry, reportage, criticism, and especially personal memoir onto the familiar essay, creating some wonderful works of mixed or impure forms that back

then I personally considered "The New Essay," (as in the "New Journalism"), since these writers use various literary and nonliterary resources to reshape the essay rather than the other way around.

A definition draws boundaries between the included and excluded characteristics of the entity in question. So what types of prose do I see as falling outside the boundaries? I usually omit most dominant types of newspaper and magazine journalism: news reports; informative articles; interviews; profiles that are heavily based on interviews; editorials and commentary; book, film, theater, music and art reviews; service articles (every men's and women's magazine published in America contains a monthly article on ways to spice up your sex life). I also eliminate any excerpt from a nonfiction book. As you can guess from these exclusions, I can usually go through an entire year of America's popular magazines and find at best only one true essay per periodical a year. This is because America's major periodicals are mainly in the service, news, and information business and are reluctant to publish personal or reflective literary prose.

You can find genuine essays in the literary and intellectual quarterlies, and, with few exceptions, those are my primary sources. I should add, however, that many of the quarterlies show a marked preference for fiction and poetry—often devoting entire issues to these genres—and will very frequently lump literary criticism, book reviews, and interviews within their essay departments, if they have one. Though I don't automatically exclude writing about literature and the arts, or other forms of intellectual writing, I do find that in its art and craft most literary criticism or critical commentary falls short of genuine essayistic standards.

So what is an essay? Back when I started *The Best American Essays* series I worried mainly about an operational definition that would help me sift through the perplexing variety of nonfiction I found everywhere in the literary marketplace. In the first few volumes of the series, I hazarded a few critical distinctions. I wanted to privilege essays that were not merely responses to occasions or assignments but that grew out of what Annie Dillard nicely called the writer's "real work," essays that met a literary challenge and demonstrated individual craft and style, and that transcended the daily press or monthly magazine and left a permanent impression. My primary concern then, as now, focused on the distinction

between an essay and an article, a distinction that has had a fairly long critical history. As I continue to see it, the article is a piece of nonfiction in which a timely topic takes precedence over everything else; style is subordinate to subject, craft to coverage. But when the writer's reflections on a topic become as compelling as the topic itself, when he or she searches for the larger theme behind an isolated issue or event, or when the craft and handling of material reveal a keen sense of a subject's true complexity, then I believe "essay" is the most accurate designation. I don't mean to foster an invidious comparison here. I read informative articles all the time and the good ones perform the way they should, with their own generic formulations. Their main limitation, from my perspective, is that they are created with a sort of built-in obsolescence. They are made for the month, not the years. As a rule of thumb, I know that I'm inside an article when I find a large proportion of interview quotations, names in the news, catchy subheads, teasers, call-outs, bulleted lists, statistics— plenty of statistics—abbreviations, and acronyms. In this sense, essayists are just like poets, novelists, and playwrights—none of them, regardless of their celebrity or obscurity—deliberately sets out to compose works that are by their very nature perishable.

I'm sure I'll come to regret this, but I'll conclude with the definition I promised at the start. I've come to think that the genuine essay has certain persistent core features that have helped distinguish it over centuries, from its late sixteenth-century inception to its most recent post-modern examples. The essay has always been experimental, experiential, exploratory, and open-ended. It is hardly ever categorical, dogmatic, systematic, or conclusive. It resists narrow professionalism and academicism. In trying to summarize all of these features into a one-sentence definition that embraces the essay's essential literary characteristics as I understand them, I would say, ideally: "The essay, whether long or short, narrative, expository, or polemical, is a literary genre that enacts the processes and possibilities of thought and self-disclosure in a distinctive prose style." But don't quote me.

ANDRE DUBUS III

# Writing & Publishing a Memoir
## *What in the Hell Have I Done?*

It was early September at a college in upstate New York. The maples in
the quad were still in full bloom, and the grass was clipped and dozens of
young men and women walked along the paved pathways, carrying books
and backpacks, a cell phone in one hand, their iPod in the other, many of
them with an earbud in one ear so they heard music on that side of their
head while they carried on conversations on the other. I was there to give
a talk to the entire incoming freshman class, all of whom had been sent a
copy of my memoir, *Townie*. By nightfall it had begun to rain, and I'd just
eaten dinner in a room of raised panels and deep carpet with twenty or
so members of the faculty. Many carried umbrellas as we hurried across
campus to the hall where I would give my talk.

Like many published writers, I give a lot of talks. Sometimes to crowds,
sometimes to small groups. Sometimes I'm nervous beforehand, other
times I'm not. Tonight, I was nervous. Over five hundred eighteen-year-
olds had just read all about my youth, and now I was expected to say
something important to these young people, something that might inspire
them as they began their first tentative steps into their college years. I was
anticipating the kinds of students I often encounter on campuses across
the country, a baseball-cap wearing, gadget-addicted mix of earnestness
and glazed distraction, of intense desire for something real and helpful
and a standoffish world-weariness that comes not from the world itself
but from far too many cyber-simulations of it. Whenever I'm in their
presence, I feel a deep need to give them something worth showing up

for, a story or a quote or a line of thought and feeling that comes from years of trying and failing and trying again to write truly about human beings—in this case, myself.

But when we village elders stepped into the cavernous hall, nearly every seat taken by a young man or woman from various parts of the country, some from other parts of the world, something strange happened. We started walking down the aisle and I heard, "Hey, that's him." "Lookit, there he is." And then came applause, loud and sustained, then a few kids were standing up, and the applause grew louder. What *was* this? I kept moving to the front, but I was glancing around at these young faces. In so many of them was an expression of acknowledgment and recognition, many of them peering around others to get a closer look at me. And then it became clear what was happening; they weren't clapping for the middle-aged author of a book they'd been required to read; they were clapping for the boy and violent young man I'd been; they were clapping for the kid who'd grown into the man walking up to the stage to greet them; they were clapping not for Andre, the writer, but for Andre, the main character in a story called *Townie*. I may as well have been Jake Barnes or Harry Potter or Captain Queeg. And as I waited to be introduced, I stood there feeling as if I'd lied to them in some way, that I had somehow misrepresented myself. But had I? Yes. And no. Not at all.

In my hometown of Haverhill, Massachusetts, the mill town where I grew up and the setting for *Townie*, I'm told it's referred to as "The Book."

"Hey, have you read The Book?"

"You shittin' me? I'm *in* The fucking Book."

Just weeks after it was published, I was to give a reading at the Haverhill Public Library. Over five hundred people showed up. The librarian introduced me, and there was enthusiastic applause, a few raucous whoops and shouts from the rear of the room. I looked out over the crowd and took them in. Many were my age, in their late forties or early fifties. Behind aging skin and hair and a few extra pounds, I recognized a face here, the eyes of another there, people I hadn't seen in over thirty years, when we'd all attended the same high school with its undercover narcs and drug dealing, its high-achieving jock kids from across the river, the leather-wearing, pony-tailed losers like me on the mill side, the kids or

grandkids of immigrants from Ireland and Italy, Greece and Puerto Rico and the Dominican Republic. And there were older men and women there, too, the parents of those of us who grew up in the shadow of the Vietnam War and Watergate and Nixon flying away from the presidency in his helicopter, an echo image of what so many of our own fathers had done, though they'd driven away in Chevys or hopped a bus or just hit the road with a thumb out.

I thanked everyone for coming, then I read a few brief passages and took some questions. Mostly, though, the audience offered comments, and mostly these were words of thanks for telling our story. "Our story." I liked hearing this and was grateful for their gratitude, but I was also confused by it. I knew what they meant, that I'd written about that in-between generation we were members of; ten years younger than the Vietnam baby boomers but ten years older than Generation X, we were kids who grew up listening to early Aerosmith on eight-tracks in Z28s, drinking Haffenreffer tall boys and smoking angel dust. We grew our hair to our waists and carried pints of Southern Comfort in our Dingo boots like Janis Joplin, but the party had moved on years ago and so we were left wearing costumes, having sex too young, drinking too much, fighting in barrooms and in the street, our broke single mothers too overwhelmed to do much about it. I knew what they were thanking me for, but still, wasn't *Townie* essentially *my* story?

Years ago I read an interview with the writer Janet Burroway, in which she says that when readers go to the novel, what we're really saying to it is this: "Give me *me*." Most of us know this to be true. If the writer goes deeply enough into her characters and their stories, then they'll go deeply enough into us too, their own natures resonating with ours, like an easterly breeze moving wind chimes on a porch we'd never even known about. But with creative nonfiction/memoir, the breeze seems to be even more direct, the wind chimes closer to the front door of the house in which we live.

"Hey, don't tell me, but I know who the Murphy brothers really are. The Pecker Street gang."

The man who said that wore a dark sweater and Dickie work pants, broken capillaries blooming across his upper cheeks. He was my age, and looked pleased with himself, and I liked him right away.

"You got it," I said.

"Andre." A woman was raising her hand from the crowded center of the room. She had short gray hair and a plump, warm-looking face, her eyes lit with a street-savvy light I wouldn't want to mess with: "Now when I want people to know about my life, I just have them read your book. But what do you think of what the mayor's saying about it?"

Just days before, the mayor of Haverhill had written on his Facebook page that I was "embellishing details" and that Haverhill had never been the tough mill town I wrote about in *Townie*. If this were a novel, his words wouldn't have bothered me at all, but this was a memoir, and when that word is printed beneath the title of a book, the contract between its writer and the reader is this:

Dear Reader,

Everything you read in this book happened, at least to the best of my memory, which like everyone's is seen through a deeply subjective emotional lens. Still, I have tried to be loyal to the facts as I remember them, which isn't always the truth, but it is my truth.

I was on tour when I heard about the mayor's postings. I called him and told him I was concerned, that a charge like that against a memoir could very well undermine the authority of that book. And I had not "embellished." He apologized and told me he'd only begun to read my book that morning, that he'd been reacting to published reviews and interviews that referred to 1970s Haverhill as a "depressed crime-ridden mill town."

"But Mr. Mayor, it *was*."

"Not in my neighborhood."

"Where'd you live?"

"Riverside."

"Well, I lived across from the Avenues. A much different neighborhood."

We talked a while longer. The mayor said he'd read the first hundred pages of my book, and he could see I wasn't writing so much about the town as I was about my boyhood and my family. In fact, he said, it was clear to him that I hadn't called Haverhill any of those things the newspapers were calling it, and he had to admit, there were parts of our city

then, especially the bars along the river of an almost entirely boarded-up downtown, that were pretty rough.

"In fact, when I was a young lawyer, my first clients were drug dealers from near where you lived."

"Thank you."

"And my wife did remind me that I took boxing lessons to defend myself then."

"That's all I'm saying."

But the mayor, who has worked diligently to make downtown Haverhill a much more vibrant place than it was forty years ago, had every right to worry about how it was being described by the national press now. I told him I would make sure to mention things are different today. He promised to stop posting charges of embellishments on his website.

I told the woman in that library crowd that I respected the mayor, and now that he'd begun to actually read my book, he was taking back what he wrote about it.

A man standing near a window raised his hand. He looked over six feet tall and well over two hundred pounds, and he wore a black beret and a black sweater and black pants. He was my age or younger, but he was leaning on a cane. His goatee was wispy and just beginning to gray.

I called on him.

"You know your friend Cleary? Your best friend when you were kids?"

His voice was reedy and restrained, like he was trying to hold back an emotion that wasn't all good.

"Yeah? What about Cleary?"

"He was my brother."

Cleary, always clowning and stealing and drinking and getting high, the son of a hopelessly alcoholic mother and distant father, my best friend when I was thirteen, fourteen, and fifteen, stabbed to death at age twenty-five by the common-law wife he used to beat.

"Mark? Is that you?"

He nodded, and I left the podium and walked down the side aisle to Cleary's younger brother I hadn't seen in years. I hugged him and he hugged me back, and then the crowd began to clap, and I walked back to the microphone and told them just who he was.

Later, at the book-signing table, he asked me to inscribe a copy to their father. Mark told me how happy his old man was to hear that his oldest son, dead far too soon, had made it into the pages of a real book, that his son would live on now, that he wouldn't be forgotten. On the title page of the book, I wrote how much I loved and missed his son, and I wrote his son's real name and wished the father well, and signed my own.

But a week or two later, I received an email from Mark's girlfriend telling me Mark's father had read the book and that he was very, very upset. And why wouldn't he be? How could I not have thought of this earlier? I described his son as having been a wife-beater in his last days; I described how deeply alcoholic his mother had been, this woman who died of her disease not long after her oldest child had been stabbed to death; I wrote how absent he, the father, had seemed to me during those years. My God, what had I *done*?

I'd written as truly of that time as I could, that's what I'd done, but my intention never was to hurt anyone. Ever. These things rarely happen when what you write and publish is fiction.

Not long ago, my sister Suzanne walked into my kitchen holding up three or four stapled sheets of paper.

"Andre, have you seen this interview? It's one of the guys from your book. He says he's gonna kill you."

It was like hearing that a character who dies violently at the end of your novel has risen from the fictive dead to have a word with you. Or that a character you've worked hard to make three-dimensional and real is angry because she's just not likable enough, and now she's on talk shows saying so.

"Let me see that."

My sister handed over the interview pages. I put on reading glasses and sat down. I don't usually read much of what people write about me or my work. It's not that they have nothing valuable to teach me; quite often, I'm sure they do. I avoid it because writing daily is challenging enough without having a flurry of voices in your head, most of them negative, telling you what you do wrong and even sometimes right. I've come to believe that if there's any single enemy to human creativity, it's self-consciousness, and while criticism can of course be instructive, it almost always comes

after the fact, when it's too late to do anything about what has apparently failed, so over the years I've found that true and sustained artistic growth comes solely from the sweet and not-so-sweet daily labor of writing itself.

But I had to read this, especially once I'd read the title: "Maligned Character in *Townie* Challenges Andre Dubus." This comes from a blog dedicated to "Book and Author Information," and it's a sit-down interview with one of my "characters," who the interviewer (GTC) describes as "Devin Wallace, a tall, beefy man now sitting next to me in a dim and ominous place, stinking like hot panties and stale perfume, near where Wallace fought the future author thirty years ago."

> GTC: Dubus writes that he changed everyone's name except those in the immediate family. What's your real name?
>
> DW: None of your business.
>
> GTC: Okay, no problem. Have you read *Townie*?
>
> DW: Obviously. That's why you're here.
>
> GTC: Why's that?
>
> DW: To let people know what a prick Dubis is.
>
> GTC: I believe he pronounces his last name Duh-BYOOSE.
>
> DW: We don't go for that French shit around here.
>
> GTC: I can see why Dubus decided to get ready.
>
> DW: Ready for what? To become the biggest sucker puncher in history. Even Dubus admits it, the half that isn't fiction. He says he ran over and hit a guy sittin' behind his steering wheel and who wasn't even lookin'. And he kept hittin' the guy. Come on.
>
> GTC: The guy'd been nudging the bumper of a limousine where Dubus' girlfriend was riding.
>
> DW: Girlfriend? Sounds like he went out with her four years and didn't get anything. Or he's lyin' since she's one of those Muslims.

You may have noticed that I've put quotation marks around the word *characters*. Why? Because these are actual people, aren't they? This is nonfiction, right? Isn't Devin Wallace the same man who beat me up so badly one night thirty years ago he almost killed me? In fact, later in his interview, he even corroborates exactly what I wrote about him in *Townie*:

DW: Look . . . I weighed at least two-fifty and he must've been about one-sixty. When we got outside, I went right after him and stuck my head into his chest and drove him into the frozen sidewalk. He couldn't lie about that with a hundred witnesses around us, yellin' for me to kill him. I punched his face until he grabbed my wrists and then I grabbed his hair above each ear and started slammin' his head into the concrete and he was lucky the police came and pulled me off.

Here's that same scene from *Townie*:

He feinted away from it, his head ramming into my chest, and I was lifted and there was the back-slap of pavement, a weight on my sternum. The first punches were almost a surprise, hard and fast from the right and left, sparks behind my eyes. I opened them, and there he was on my chest. His face was in shadow, and it was hard to breathe and he kept punching and my hands grabbed both wrists and wouldn't let go.

*"Kill him, man. Fuckin' kill 'em."*

There were more words out there in the air around us, men's voices, then Jeb's. "That's my *brother*." His hands on the shoulders of the one on me, but then other hands pulled him away and there was yelling, had been for a long time, from the one on me who had a handful of hair on both sides of my head, my fingers still locked around his wrists, and he began to lift my head and slam it back down, lift it and slam it, the concrete beneath me felt like a betrayal . . .

One dictionary definition of the word "memoir" is this: "a record of events written by a person having intimate knowledge of them." Certainly "Devin Wallace" and I had intimate knowledge of that particular fight, and it was gratifying for me to read that his memory of it dovetailed precisely with my own. Or did it? Maybe his own recollection of that fight was shaped by my having written about it in *Townie*. Maybe he only remembered it after having read about it. But even if that was the case, why was he so intent on showing what a "prick" I was? Because he truly thought I'd been "the biggest sucker puncher in history"? This is coming

from a man who freely admits that he had ninety or a hundred pounds on me and still he straddled my chest, grabbed my hair, and began slamming my head against the concrete again and again. But later in the interview, there's a clue about what might really be bothering him:

> DW: Don't you just love the way Dubis spends pages settin' up his excuses? He claims he spent the day paintin' inside a closed room and his brain was stewed and his balance was so bad he shouldn't have been drivin' and he could barely see. Then, in the bar, he says a pretty lady named Hailey told me to fuck off 'cuz I was hasslin' her and had "predatory" eyes. That's bullshit. She wanted me and Dubis was jealous.

*Predatory eyes.* That's probably what pissed him off more than anything. But they *did* appear predatory to me, at least in my memory of that scene thirty years later. And even if there was nothing predatory about his eyes, his behavior certainly was; the college girl he was hitting on was telling him no, and he was ignoring her no. But I had a hunch it was something else that was making "Devin" want to kick my ass again three decades later: I had written my story, and he had not written his. Now mine was recorded in some way, and his was not. Why did I get to have this happen? How did I get to be the main character in a book, and Devin Wallace, who was still drinking in those same bars on that same dirty river and had story after story to express about his own life, why would his go untold?

And then there are my "truths" versus other people's "truths." Some of my childhood friends look back on that time and place much differently; one is Jimmy Quinn, a "character" in the book. His real name is also Irish, with a two-syllable first name and a one-syllable last name. By the time he was sixteen, he had a reputation as being a very tough and dangerous kid, a guy who'd easily beaten up grown men. He was over six feet tall and just under two hundred pounds, and he was handsome, even with a chipped front tooth. For many years in my youth, he was the only kind of guy I wanted to be, one who could defend himself and anyone he was close to. A few weeks after the book came out, my publisher forwarded to me an email from him, and we began to correspond. I hadn't seen or spoken

to him in years. He wrote to me that he was reading the book and that he especially liked the parts about him. Every few days, I'd get a new email from him telling me where he was in the story and what he thought of it. He told me about his life now, about his wife of many years and their three nearly grown children. I enjoyed these emails, and was struck by how reflective he'd gotten, how he was no longer that kid I remembered, though I heard that he still occasionally got into fights downtown and consistently came out ahead, the way he always had.

In one of his last emails to me, he told me that when he looked back on all those house parties and bar fights and street fights, even the one at the high school when he got stabbed and almost died, that he couldn't stop laughing at all the fun we'd had.

"Why was your book so *dark*?"

What could I say to this? He was the oldest of nine kids. They all lived with their mother and father in a big house on Main Street. He was an athlete who played football and baseball. Other boys respected him, many feared him, and most girls were drawn to him. We both lived in the same depressed town, but for him it was a playground. For me, it was just one more manifestation of the home I lived in—unsafe, unclean, wild, gray, and unhappy.

I wrote all of this back to him, and there was the strange sense that I was writing not to the man still living in Haverhill, Massachusetts, just nine miles from where I was raising my own family, but that I was writing to Jimmy Quinn, the young, handsome brawler in my book: Jimmy Quinn, the character.

He wrote back: "I thought you were going to say that. Makes sense."

The following Christmas, a woman from the Haverhill Chamber of Commerce asked me if I'd be willing to sign some books at an outdoor booth at their "Santa Stroll" through downtown. I told her I would, then promptly forgot about it. The night I was supposed to be there, my friend walked by and saw my booth unmanned and heard I wasn't coming. "No problem," he said. "I'm Jimmy Quinn. I'll sign 'em."

I heard he signed quite a few like this: "Merry Xmas! Best wishes, Jimmy Quinn."

I had never planned to write a memoir in the first place. It was the summer of 2007, and I had just delivered to my publisher my novel, *The Garden of Last Days*. I was contracted to follow this up with a collection of personal essays, a form I respect deeply. My wife and I are blessed with three children (Austin, 19, Ariadne, 17, and Elias, 15), and when our sons were very young, they began to play baseball. This was a sport I knew nothing about and had never followed or played, but because they were interested in it, I became interested in it, too. Now, years later, because of them and their years on the mound as Little League and Senior League and high school pitchers, I've become a devoted fan of baseball. I began to write an essay about this, and the question fueling it was: how as a kid did I miss this game I now love so much? What was I doing instead? These questions led to what ultimately became my accidental memoir, *Townie*.

But in those first drafts I was hiding something. Somewhere, sometime I'd read this from a writer whose name escapes me: "If you're going to write a memoir, you should be able to sue yourself for libel." Because so many years had passed since my youth (I was turning fifty writing the book), I felt there was enough emotional distance that I could write honestly about my own flaws—my early paralyzing fears and physical cowardice, my rage and eventual violence perpetrated against others, etc.—but I was not prepared to write about my family. Wasn't that *their* story to tell? Who was I to shine a light on their privacy?

My editor at my publishing house told me that she knew very little about my family, but it felt to her that I was leaving out some significant details about having grown up with them. I told her I was and why. (I did not tell her what, precisely, I was leaving out, that my younger brother was suicidal and had been sexually abused by his female special-education teacher for six years in our house, that my older sister had been gang raped and was selling drugs, that my younger sister was isolated and deeply depressed, that my exhausted, overworked and underpaid mother was just barely holding on with her fingernails, that my father was largely absent.) She told me that whatever I was leaving out, it was all part of my story, too, and that if I couldn't write completely honestly, then this shouldn't be a published book.

A few days later, I told a friend—a gifted and accomplished novelist—

my dilemma. He told me that if it were him faced with the same challenge, he'd ask himself this: Am I trying to settle any scores with this book? If the answer was yes, he wouldn't write it. Or he might write it, but he wouldn't publish it. If the answer was no, then he'd go ahead and write it. I knew then I wasn't trying to settle a score with anyone. I wasn't angry at my parents. (Though there were years when I had been, when I felt they could have taken better care of us four kids than they had, but the decades had fallen away and then came my belief that we all get out of bed each day trying to have the best day we know how to have, which is not the same as the best day we *can* have, and that's where all of us have room to grow, and so by the time I began writing *Townie* I had largely forgiven my parents.) I did not even feel sorry for the boy I'd been or the childhood I'd had. Certainly, there are far worse out there, generation in and generation out; I simply felt pulled to try and capture that time, that early-1970s mill town, growing up with a low-income, single mother and all that entailed, as truly as I possibly could.

Months of revision later, I had written the last line and knew this was a much more honest book. I had gone into my house and revealed whatever I felt it was important to reveal. For years I'd thought that the reason I'd become an effective fighter was this: I was the bullied boy who learned how to throw punches that then became fueled by all the pent-up hurt and rage of the victim. But opening those doors back to my family taught me how wrong I'd been: I couldn't stop my younger brother from wanting to die; I couldn't protect him from the grown woman suffocating him; I couldn't save my older sister from getting raped or keep her from selling drugs or hanging with scumbags who didn't love her and never would; I couldn't talk my little sister out of putting a padlock on her bedroom door and her heart; I couldn't lift my exhausted mother off the living-room floor where she'd fall asleep every night after her fourteen-hour days; I couldn't get my father to call or come over more than the brief times we saw him on Sunday afternoon or every fourth Wednesday night; and I could not stop myself from believing that, as the oldest son, all of the above was my job. It was every bit of this that I'd been putting into my fists in those fights.

And there was more, too. I, like many young men, had turned my hurts

and disappointments into rage and aggression. My brother had turned his inward and become depressed. I had become homicidal. He had become suicidal. This alone seemed an important note to hit in my memoir, and after I'd written it in, I was not going to give my brother, or any of my family, veto power. (I'd done that once with a personal essay about the birth of my daughter. In it, I had written briefly about my brother's first child, born out of wedlock, and after Jeb had read the manuscript, he said, "You can write about your own life, but leave me the fuck out of it." At the time, over twenty years before I'd write *Townie*, I didn't even question whether he was right or not; I assumed immediately that he was, and I cut those references to his first child. Later, when the essay was published, Jeb read it again and said, "I should've let you keep that in. The essay was better with it.") So now I was simply going to warn my family of what to expect, and I started by giving my sister, Suzanne, a copy of the manuscript that she would then pass around to the others.

Suzanne finished reading it in two days, and she surprised me by saying she had the exact same emotional memory of those years, and then she said: "But did you have to put in the part about my selling drugs? I have a pretty important job, you know." I do know. My sister has become a national leader in the prevention of domestic violence, and right now she's working closely with the Obama administration. I said to her, "Honey, you were *sixteen*. Besides, it gives you street cred!"

My younger sister, Nicole, responded next. She told me her childhood had been too shitty for her to want to visit it again and so she will continue to read my fiction, but not this. I told her I understood that completely.

At this point, the manuscript was still at my sister's house, and the actual book was moving into production. It was time to tell my brother and mother what was coming.

I was pretty worried about Jeb, probably because of what had happened with that essay years before, and because sexual abuse and attempts at suicide are deeply personal and entirely his business. And yet it was part of my story, too, and I felt compelled to keep the few pages I'd written about him. I'd wanted to meet in person to talk about this, but Jeb was working on a restaurant he'd designed down in Salem and couldn't get away.

One afternoon, sitting in my truck outside the grocery store, I called

his cell phone. When he finally answered he sounded tired and distracted, and I could hear the sounds of construction behind him—men's voices, a drill bit whirring into wood or concrete, the *pop-pop* of a nail gun.

I told my brother I'd finished this accidental memoir thing.

"Yeah?"

"And I—"

"What, brother? Just say it."

"I've put in your sexual abuse and suicidal years. It seemed like a lie if I didn't."

I heard only those construction sounds, nothing else. And it occurred to me that my brother could be so unhappy about this that he might sue me to try to stop it.

"Jeb? You there? Are you okay with this?"

"Well, brother—" I could hear him draw deeply on a cigarette. "I would never want to step on anyone else's tube of paint."

My eyes filled up, and I was thanking him, and he interrupted me and asked me if I could at least make it clear somewhere in the book that he's *not* that fucked-up boy anymore? That he's a very successful designer?

"I mean this could hurt my business. I've got my *kids* to think about."

I promised him I would, and the following morning I wrote an acknowledgments page about him and the rest of my family, each of whom *is* doing well all these years later.

My mother was next, this woman who stayed and raised us and did the best she knew how, this woman who—like so many before and after her—could very well have crumbled and descended into alcoholism and drug addiction, verbal and physical abuse of us, who could have driven away, even for one night, but never did. She was the absolute last person I wanted to hurt in any way, yet in *Townie*, I'd described a woman who had essentially given up being the one in charge, someone who felt to me and my siblings less like a mother and more like an older sister rooming with us and surviving any way she could.

I seemed to pick a moment to tell her when I didn't have to look her directly in the face. We were in my truck driving up the highway to an academic conference on the masterful work of her dead ex-husband, my father. I was behind the wheel, and she was in the passenger's side. We

were each sipping from cardboard cups of hot coffee, though I needed no extra jolt.

"Mom, you know I just finished writing a, you know, a—"

"I know, honey, your memoir."

"Yeah, well anyway, there's a part in it about you and how—I don't know—you kind of, you know, gave up for—"

She reached over and squeezed my forearm.

"Don't you *dare*—" (Oh, fuck, I already had; what was I going to do *now*?) "Don't you dare not write anything because you're worried about me. You write your story, damnit. It's your story, and you should write it the way you need to write it. Besides, honey, I'm too old to give a shit what people think about me anyway."

I laughed and wiped at my eyes and thanked her. We began to talk about other things, then soon we were seated side by side at a conference on the work of my dead father, the one I was most worried about reading my memoir, even though he'd been dead twelve years.

I had naively assumed—semi-consciously—that because he hadn't lived with us, I wouldn't have to write about him much at all. But as I wrote my way back into those years, I learned otherwise. The word "to remember" is the opposite of dismember and means "to put back together again." As I was putting back together the years of my growing up, my father's absence in our daily lives became a major presence in the book.

For a while, a few weeks or a month, I resisted it. I knew that if I were to continue writing as honestly as I possibly could, I wouldn't be able write about him in the most flattering light. He had wonderful qualities: he'd been immensely gifted, a true and humble artist, generous, funny, attentive to the suffering of friends. But as a young father, he also had been largely AWOL, and it hurt me to know that my writing was already showing this; I loved him, I missed him, I was proud of the art he had created with his time on earth, and I did not want to betray him.

Years earlier, when I'd just begun to publish my fiction, my father and I did a reading together in New York City. I read first and then it was his turn. As he wheeled himself up to the microphone, there was boisterous applause, and a woman sitting next to me leaned in and asked: "Was he just the *perfect* father?"

What could I tell her? That no one is? That it was my mother who raised us, not our father? That when he was around, he really wasn't? But she was clearly doing what I'd seen so many other readers of my father's work do; she was confusing the writer with his beautifully wise writing, the flawed artist with his nearly flawless art. I think I smiled and nodded and turned my attention toward my father, who'd begun to read.

People who read his stories tend to love them to a degree bordering on worship. Art of this caliber can change lives. The last thing I wanted to do was to paint my father in such a way that I might somehow damage that nearly sacred relationship between his devoted readers and—not *him*—but his work. But neither could I idealize him in any way; in *Townie*, I was trying to stay as loyal to my subjective memory of those years as I could, and in those years, my father was a deeply flawed one.

But if my father's own art sought to do nothing else, it sought to illuminate truths, and all my writing life I'd been trying to do the same thing. So I held my nerve, stepped into my fears, and tried to capture my father as he'd been.

I was in a bookstore in Ohio on the paperback tour for *Townie*. A Catholic priest sat in the front row. After my reading and talk and a few questions from others in the audience, the priest raised his hand. He was wearing his Roman collar and looked to be in his late sixties. He also looked troubled. The section I had just read showed how oblivious our father had been to the kinds of lives we children were living on the other side of the river from where our father wrote and taught. The priest said: "But your father wrote so insightfully about children in his fiction. How could he have missed this about you kids?"

"My old man, if he were here, would be the first to tell you that the writing is larger than the writer."

"But what about everything he wrote about being a man of faith? How could he have written those things and then behaved so consistently badly?"

I may have quoted D. H. Lawrence: "It is not I who writes, but the wind that blows through me." The conversation continued, and I could see that this priest was no less troubled. Then he said this: "In the mid-seventies

I was a stock broker on Wall Street, then I read you father's novellas, and I—" He paused, seemingly unsure about whether or not he should continue. "I quit and joined the seminary and became a priest."

"And now that you've read my memoir," I said, "you're wondering if the man whose work put you on your path was a fraud."

The priest half-nodded and said no more.

I told him and the others gathered there that my father was no fraud, that his work was genuine and authentic and far wiser than he, a mere man, could ever have been. I told that priest he should never think otherwise. He seemed semi-comforted, but that night, lying in my hotel room wide awake at three-thirty in the morning, I kept seeing my own death and possible reunion with my father, and what did I see? I saw him sitting before me, his trimmed beard as white as it had been in life, and he looked hurt and confused. He looked betrayed.

In his essay "The Magic Show," Tim O'Brien argues that successful characterization in fiction is not a pinning-down process, an act of "nailing" a character, but quite the opposite. The deeper we go into character, the darker and more mysterious it gets. In this sense, he asserts, we are all unknowable. *Townie* is not fiction, but when I wrote it, I was using tools I try to use as a novelist: sensory detail, direct dialogue, and real-time scenes, essential brushstrokes that make more textural and alive a moment. In the earlier part of the book, when I was a young boy, I tried to write deeply from that perspective, without judgment or commentary. As I got older, I allowed the voice to change, but again, I tried to stay emotionally who I'd been at the time. And one of the things I had been was largely fatherless, something that came as a surprise to the older me writing all this.

I was giving a talk at a university on the West Coast. Afterwards, a big, gray-haired man in a red sweater stood in the audience and said, "I read your book, and I think your old man was a friggin' prick. How come he never took you guys to a *ball* game, for Christ's sake?"

Hearing this was like getting slapped across the eyes. I took a breath. I sipped some water. I did not believe my father had been a prick, but what I had written, and no one else, had given this man standing in the audi-

ence—all of whom were now looking at me to see how I would react—this picture of my father.

I told the big man in the red sweater what I truly believe, that the book is out of my hands now and he's entitled to any emotional reaction he may get from it. (I did not tell him, but I'd been thinking it, that his story with his own father might be resonating here, too.) "I don't think my old man was a prick, though."

"Then why didn't he take you guys to a game? Why didn't he ever call you on the phone or take a drive over to your house on a weekday?"

I told him the truth. "I don't know. He'd have to tell you that, and he's not here to defend himself."

The man sat down, and I was relieved the next question had to do with one of my novels.

Again, late that night, I lay in my hotel bed wondering just what I'd done. I'd been hearing that the reviews of my book were positive, but many of the reviewers went after my father for having "abandoned" us. But had he? In the town where I now live, I know a woman whose husband drove away ten years ago, leaving her to raise their five kids alone: no phone calls, no visits, not one penny in child support. The last she's heard, he's living somewhere in Japan. Now that's abandonment. My father never did *that*. But I also had to stand by my remembered portrait of him, the very one that got that man and many other readers, apparently, to dislike my father. That he simply had not been present for much of our growing up. But he'd been so much more in life than this absent father I'd painted; by describing him only through the eyes of his oldest son who'd needed him, hadn't I reduced him in some elemental way? Hadn't I done the opposite of making him a mystery? Hadn't I nailed him and nailed him badly?

Man, I hoped not. I sure as hell hoped not.

A Barnes & Noble on the Upper East Side of New York City. A handsome middle-aged woman raised her hand and said: "I guess I like your new book, but you don't seem to know much about *women*. There's hardly any in there."

A few people laughed, a few others looked uncomfortable for me. I

laughed too, then told the woman that that's because *Townie* is a memoir, not an autobiography. If it were my life story—and who wants to read the life story of some fiction writer from Haverhill, Massachusetts?—then it would have three hundred pages about all the women in my life, but it's a memoir, a memory of a time in my existence that has a shape and narrative arc of its own, the way so many moments of our lives do: my young mother and father divorced; we lived in poverty and my mother was left to raise the four of us as best she could; we moved from one cheap rented house to the next, and I was always the new kid and I got bullied till one day I began to fight back till that was all I ever seemed to do, and I was on a road that would either get me killed or put in prison; and it was my finding creative writing that put me on a more peaceful and constructive path.

This *is* my story. I did not make it up. Nor did I put in any moments that did not happen in my life, but still, there's the vaguely shameful feeling that I've cast in stone something that should stay fluid, our ever-evolving and changing memories of who we and the people we love really are. And walking up to the podium of that stage of that college in upstate New York, the cavernous hall filled with applauding young people, I wanted to tell them that I was glad I had written my story, that I was grateful to them for reading it, but please don't confuse me with that Andre in the book; he's a character, and I'm real. That was then, and this is now.

But then they stopped clapping and the hall grew quiet. I could hear the rain on the roof and against the windows, and I could see so many of their faces—expectant, slightly wounded, hungry for something helpful, many masking this hunger, and I felt the younger Andre, the only one they knew, descend into my legs and arms and chest and face. Then we were both stepping toward the microphone, and together, we began to speak.

JESSICA LIND PETERSON

# Tall, Straight Sisters

"A tree is not a metaphor.
A tree is a tree, and we are both only
one strong wind away from falling."
ANGELA PELSTER | *Limber*

It is cold as I walk behind him on the trail. But not the kind of cold that shakes you, that steals your breath and turns it into haze. No, the good kind. The kind of cold that awakens and sharpens you and helps you breathe just a little bit better. As we walk, weightless yellow leaves fall softly overhead like a gentle confetti. We are quiet. The leaves are quiet. Only the birds are having their say. We came here to these Northwoods, these winding groves of birch and poplar, because we had to. This is where we met and fell in love: here in this friendly cold, here in this earthy smell, where we first saw each other and loved each other, under this wide net of glistening branches. Fifteen years ago we made love here and made plans here; the gnarled roots of these very trees dug into our backs, the sharp grass leaving a happy rash across my thighs. But we are not happy now, and today is not for making love. We have run here, the two of us, to these well-known trees, desperate for the healing they might bring.

More finished leaves fall quietly to the earth.

Ahead of me my husband tramples the newly fallen leaves with his hiking boots and I think of his hands in her hair and wonder if he touched her face the way he touches mine, one hand spread open against a cheek, his fingers slowly tracing her lips. I stop on the trail and double over. It is too much for me, this knowing. I am a good wife, I think. I am a pretty

wife. Suddenly I want to be spread thin on the decaying forest floor. I want to be the leaf and seep into the dirt and moss and be forgotten and reborn again next spring, a fresh and quiet green unfurling for the first time. But I am not a leaf and this is not a leaf story. A lonely, aching howl erupts from my mouth and stops the birds. I rest my back against a small birch tree and she holds my weight without protest like a tall, straight sister.

I think about the birch trees on the North Shore and how they are dying by the thousands. Their bare, forsaken trunks lean together in giant clusters along Highway 61, a silent choir of lifeless wood. No one understands what is happening to them. I read somewhere that a tree can be dying from the inside for many years before showing any sign of disease. A beetle or a parasite will eat away at it, laying its eggs and leaving entire colonies of itself behind, slowly poisoning and suffocating it. Sometimes a tree can fight them off by pushing its own sap through the tunnels they dig or by temporarily cutting off its own water supply in an attempt to drive the invaders out. You wouldn't know a fierce battle was taking place inside, you wouldn't look long enough at a tree to know that. But sometimes a tree is not strong enough. Sometimes a tree cannot fight back and the beetles get in and have their way. No one knows of the blackened rot inside until it is cut open.

The trail begins to open up and I see the pale blue beginnings of Lake Superior in the distance. Not far below this line of trees is the church where my husband and I were married in West Duluth. A sweet little house of worship with wood paneling and forest green carpet, the same church where my mom and dad had gotten married, where I had been baptized as a baby. My grandmother still plays in the bell choir there, still organizes the church rummage sale every summer, the lutefisk dinner every Christmas. It still smells faintly of old coffee and meatballs. Five years after our wedding, the pastor who married us was caught on camera by the local news station in a prostitution sting and his wife died suddenly of cancer only one year later, her body, I imagine, succumbing to the grief of his betrayal. They stand behind us in our wedding photo, smiling, their bodies pressed lightly together, united for a moment by our sweet and naive beginning, pronouncing us man and wife.

For my wedding present, my husband had dragged branches from

these woods to the basement of his college apartment, where he spent countless hours whittling two knotty chairs by hand. He had never made a chair before and improvised their design as he went along. The grooves don't quite fit together and they are uncomfortable to sit in, but they are beautiful in a rugged way, though one was broken beyond repair when a careless dinner guest leaned too far back in it and it collapsed. But we still have the one chair, and it sits in our bedroom in the corner, where it serves as a nice resting place for my laundry basket. I sometimes wonder, though, if it is lonely without its mate.

We are walking with more purpose now and I struggle to keep up. My husband turns back and points out an eagle flying in a slow circle above us. I don't see it. I look and look, but it's nowhere. I can never find the things he sees in the sky. He laughs at me uneasily and then catches himself. A tight ball of hot pain rolls through my chest, threatening to break open my rib cage and swallow me. I stop to let it pass and my husband waits on the trail ahead, giving me the time I need. He is good inside, I know this. Even the trees know this. (They remember him from before, the way he breathed me in and brushed the dead leaves from my back when we were done.) I hold the crisp, cold air in my lungs, exhaling slowly, the way I was taught. I think of our two little boys and the lie I told them about Mommy having a stomachache this week. My littlest one bringing me glass after glass of water, telling me to maybe eat more apples.

For now the only thing that does help is this rustling, mossy quiet. Putting one foot in front of the other and walking on a well-worn path in these familiar woods; knowing that just up ahead is a stunning view of the harbor, and that we might sit together on a warm rock, our knees touching, and remember that there was a time before this pain. We walk past two waterfalls and I notice their thin, dying streams reaching toward each other, waiting for rain.

JOE MACKALL

❖

# By Force, Threat, or Deception

On Friday the thirteenth, just twelve days before his forty-second birthday, a birthday he swore he'd never see, Don pulled out of his parking space at a job he hated and turned into eastbound traffic. As he headed down Detroit Avenue to one of his favorite bars, he turned on his headlights to combat the disappearance of daylight, on one of those winter afternoons when darkness comes before supper, when evening subsumes late afternoon, when all that is known of daytime bows to the early night.

As he drove toward the Driftwood Inn through the rain and snow, mixed and falling, perhaps Don thought of ways to spend the paycheck neatly folded in his wallet, or of his dream of becoming a painter; or maybe he conjured up images of his past: of his time as a dance instructor at Arthur Murray's, guiding couples through the steps of the waltz or the gyrations of the jitterbug, or of his time in the service during the Korean War. Or maybe thought of his recent past crept into his mind with the stealth and skill of a cancer cell: of his leaving his kind wife and doomed marriage of twelve years, the look on the face of the ten-year-old daughter he loved as he drove away from their home, to his new home five miles away, with his belongings carefully packed in the truck of his Lincoln Continental.

He had popped in the bar merely to have a drink and cash his check. Bars did that then. Maybe some still do. While he was in the bar, Don no doubt talked easily to strangers; he was friendly, well liked by men and women. Especially women. They could always talk to him. And his dark brown hair, aquiline nose, easy manner and penchant for dressing above

his means seemed to draw women to him. On this day maybe he bought a few drinks for friends, feeling that familiar working-class flush of Friday riches: riches tentative, hard won, well-deserved, riches here on Friday afternoon and gone on Monday morning.

When Don walked to his car, having stayed no more than an hour, just long enough to get out of the cold, have a warm drink, enjoy the reflection of himself in a barroom mirror, he made the mistake of letting strangers see his wad of money. As he braced against the light breeze blowing in off Lake Erie, two young men—two Hispanic kids, Spanish or Puerto Rican—surprised him. One pushed a gun in Don's back and forced him into his car.

The men wound up at the northwestern edge of Edgewater Park in Cleveland at a place called Perkins Beach, where the lake became part of the night. Lake Erie's latent waves crashed and fell against the rocky shore of Edgewater Park. The temperature hovered just above freezing. The older kid who did all the talking, got in the passenger seat; the other kid got in the back. The boy in back was only sixteen.

The punk sitting shotgun pointed a .38 in Don's face.

"Hand over the money or I'll kill you," the punk said.

Don lunged for the gun. The kid fired: two bullets in the neck, one in the side of the face, one in the temple.

For years this was the story the family believed. A convenient story. Ugly, but safe. Horrible, but ordinary. But it wasn't the whole truth.

Somehow I always knew much of what happened to my uncle had become a family fiction. Maybe it was the way the story never changed, as if one detail out of place would cause the entire narrative edifice to come tumbling down, resembling a collapsed cathedral, its glory betrayed by the sudden clutter of its bricks. It could have been the way my father, a former Cleveland homicide detective and my uncle's good friend, mysteriously lost interest in the case. He simply didn't want to know anything he didn't want to know.

I, however, have never been able to let it go. I've encouraged the family to talk about it. Not because I thought it would do any of us any good, but because aspects of my uncle's murder had been mired in mystery for so long that rumors and innuendo had begun to seep into holes of doubt.

I needed to know more. For twenty-five years I have remained selfishly, seriously curious. I am now the age my uncle was when he died. I'm probably not even entitled to dig around in the ruins of my uncle's murder. We were not bound by blood but by marriage. He taught me how to play tennis; he talked to me often and always treated me well, assuring me that when it came to women, I wouldn't have a problem. As an awkward and unhappy teenager, I appreciated the apparent sincerity and wisdom of his words.

I know I loved him, and I'm hoping this love is enough to attempt to tell his story.

You're at Uncle Don's house not long after he and your aunt separated. You watch the maroon Lincoln Continental pull in the driveway. You see him kiss his ten-year-old daughter good-bye. (Was it the last time he ever saw her? She him?) You run through the kitchen and down the steps. When your aunt sees you she asks where you're going. You tell her you want to talk to Uncle Don. "You don't have to," she says, picking up a laundry basket filled with women-only whites. "Okay," you say, hearing something in her words you feel you should obey. You turn your back on the door that leads to him. You never see your uncle again.

The night after the murder, my uncle's smiling face from better times appeared boxed in the corner of the TV screen. The newscaster mispronounced his polysyllabic Polish surname. After a day or two his picture was replaced with an icon meant to represent murder in the abstract: a cartoonlike drawing of a gun superimposed on a chalk sketch of a body strewn on a street, a faceless, nameless body. It could have been anybody. Which it was. Which it wasn't.

In order for members of my family to get at what really happened twenty-five years ago this fall, we'd have to give up at least a modicum of the memory of the man we thought we knew. We'd have to take a fresh look at the man we called husband, brother-in-law, father, friend. The man I called Uncle Don. And, finally, we'd all have to learn a little something about a few strangers—strangers even to my uncle. We'd also have to get to know a guy named Alan G. Barnes.

You have appointed yourself the person who has to get at the truth. After 25 years, you still believe the truth is out there. In buried police reports and in the distant memories of aging detectives. In secret, stolen family moments. In the hidden history of people you claim to love. You want to tell your uncle's story. No matter what. Why is it so important that you know what happened. Who are you to believe you have a right to the truth—or even the facts?

On Friday the thirteenth, just twelve days before his forty-second birthday, a day he swore he'd never see, Don—whose father died at forty-one—pulls out from his parking space at Alan Pack and Rubber Co. and away from the steeple-shadow of the Methodist church on the corner, which must have hovered over him on this day the way the Catholic church had his entire life. As he turns into eastbound traffic and heads down Detroit Ave. to one of his favorite bars, he switches on his headlights and settles restlessly into the leather seats of his Lincoln.

As he drives toward the Driftwood Inn through the rain and snow, mixed and falling, perhaps Don calculates the division of his paycheck, wondering how much he'd have left after debts and other bills. Surely enough for the extra gas for the long, out-of-the-way drive to Perkins Beach.

Alan G. Barnes also felt the promise of Perkins, albeit in a more sinister way. Barnes must have been feeling the oncoming weight of his twentieth birthday, which at the time of his becoming a murderer was only three days away. Perhaps he foresaw his dimly lit future, which looked a lot like his present. He was nineteen years old, living in his parents' W. 87 St. Cleveland home; he had minimal education, no job, and a shared, fledgling criminal enterprise with a sixteen-year-old who would soon become his accomplice in a kidnapping and murder.

But Barnes had stumbled onto something interesting and potentially profitable back in August of 1974 when he'd assaulted his first victim; and it was then he must have begun noticing the population frequenting Perkins Beach. It was the same population that frequented other Cleveland hot spots like West 25th, West 32nd (where the gay bathhouses sat), West 45th, West 65th. Barnes viewed the gays who congregated at these spots as easy marks. A lot of them were married. Even if they weren't married,

they didn't want to report to the police that they had been cruising when robbed. A lot of people could not care less what befell homosexuals. They probably asked for it anyway. They were the perfect marks.

Some members of the Cleveland and Lakewood police departments even had a name for Barnes and those with a similar modus operandi: "tulip vultures." Barnes quickly became a tulip vulture extraordinaire. Although Barnes lived in Cleveland, the then sixty-four-year-old city of Lakewood began only thirty blocks from his house, and even in the early 1970s, the city was know at the "flower patch." Just five miles west of Cleveland's downtown sat what was once a forest along Lake Erie, now a city fertile with homosexuals, mostly male. And near the border of Lakewood and Cleveland sat Perkins Beach, which already had a reputation as a lovers' lane, a place where gays could hook up, hang out and not be hassled by the police.

The border separating the two cities was symbolic as well as geographical, serving as a dividing line between decent living and decadence, moving up or going down. The Cleveland police were too busy with homicides (350 a year at that time) and other big-city crime; and neighboring Lakewood police had an arrangement with the city's large homosexual population, which in 1974 was just over twenty thousand "card-carrying homosexuals" in a city of around seventy thousand. The arrangement, simply stated, was: "We won't bother you guys, but don't lie to us. If you're cruising and get beat up, just say that. Don't make up a big story that's impossible for us to believe."

Perhaps because they were left alone by the police and didn't want to jeopardize that relationship, or their marriages, or their reputations, more than ninety percent of gay victims of crime never filed reports.

With all this in his favor, Barnes figured he was onto something good. He assumed that at five feet ten inches tall and 170 pounds, young and lithe, with brown hair and hazel eyes, the correct moves and the right clothes, he just might be able to make this work.

It's bad enough you have to pry into your uncle's life, but you soon learn that to discover what happened to him, you'll have to investigate a string of robberies committed by the murderer just prior to the

murder. And in the robbery reports are the names of other victims. Were they all lured by the unspoken promises of Perkins Beach? Suddenly you're reading the names of others, names, attached to men, men attached to lives and families. In at least one case you'll know more than his wife and family ever knew about a particular autumn day. You wonder if you know more than your aunt does. You worry about the talk you'll soon have to have with her.

Michael McEntee was ten years out of college. He had a wife and two young children, a good job in Cleveland, and an urge he couldn't control. At least he couldn't control the urge on November 1, 1974.

McEntee left downtown Cleveland at 1:00 p.m. and headed west. He later told the police he wanted to grab lunch at the Blue Fox, a restaurant that for a generation had served fine dinners and businessmen lunches on the boundary of Cleveland and Lakewood. But he needed some cash first, so he pulled up in the auto teller line at Cleveland Trust for some lunch money.

Enjoying a free hour, McEntee cranked up the car radio as he waited in line. He wasn't in line very long when a guy without a weapon jerked open the driver's door and pushed McEntee hard on the left shoulder so he'd move to the passenger seat. The perp got behind the wheel.

"Give me your wallet," he said.

The perp took McEntee's wallet. Disappointed by the few dollars he stole, the guy eventually forced McEntee to write several checks.

Detective Michael Flynn of the Lakewood Police Department couldn't understand why a guy looking to rob somebody would choose a car sitting in an auto teller line, where the car could easily be trapped.

"I remember talking to this guy [McEntee]," Flynn said twenty-five years later as he looked over the police report, running his fingers through his thinning gray hair. "I knew I was being hosed. I knew he had cruised somewhere. He had to have been at Perkins."

Flynn remembers McEntee making a composite of the suspect. He remembers him mentioning several times that he was married.

Detective Flynn, whose still handsome, angular face and mustache conjure images of former TV cops, knew it was time to ask the question he'd been holding back.

"Why did you pull off at Perkins Beach?" McEntee wouldn't answer.

"Are you a homosexual?" Flynn asked, his experience telling him that crime at Perkins Beach always involved homosexuals.

"I'm a heterosexual," McEntee said. "I told you. I'm married."

At this time Flynn brought up the possibility of McEntee taking a polygraph test.

Flynn waited.

"One time. In college. A group of us from Ohio State went out and had a homosexual commit fellatio on us," McEntee said.

Flynn waited. He wanted to leave McEntee a respectable out.

"I'd like to change one thing in my story, and then I'll take a polygraph."

McEntee informed Flynn that the crime did initiate at Perkins Beach, not in an auto teller line.

McEntee left downtown Cleveland at 1:00 p.m. and headed west. He wanted to grab lunch at the Blue Fox, a restaurant that for a generation had served fine dinners and businessmen lunches on the boundary of Lakewood and Cleveland. Instead of going to lunch, however, McEntee decided to waste a little time at Perkins Beach, maybe catch a little shut-eye before heading back to work. He drove his gray 1971 Camaro up the long road leading past Edgewater Park and into the more secluded Perkins Beach area.

He draped his suit jacket over the back of the passenger seat, undid his top shirt button, loosened his tie, leaned his back against the drive's door and stretched his legs across the Camaro's console. Finally, he dozed off.

Suddenly McEntee jerked awake. Some guy ripped open the driver's door and grabbed McEntee's arm with one hand and his tie with the other.

"Move over," the guy demanded.

McEntee scramble to the passenger seat.

Barnes, clean-shaven and neatly dressed in brown from his zipper-down shirt to suede zippered boots, hurried behind the wheel and threw McEntee's suit jacket into his lap.

"Give me your wallet," Barnes said.

McEntee removed his wallet from his jacket and handed his money, eleven dollars, to Barnes. Barnes took the wallet, checked it out and handed it back.

"You got a checkbook, right?" Barnes asked. "Then write a check for fifty dollars. Where's the closest auto teller?"

McEntee told Barnes where he could cash the check.

With McEntee still in the passenger seat, Barnes left Perkins Beach and drove east along the Cleveland Shoreway. Frustrated by construction, Barnes turned and took an alternate route, pounding the Camaro over a dirt road filled with holes. As he drove, Barnes flipped through McEntee's checkbook.

"Is the balance in here right?" Barnes asked.

"No."

"Write another check for fifty dollars."

"Why?"

"Because of that," Barnes said as he pointed to another branch of Cleveland Trust bank.

McEntee wrote another check for fifty dollars.

"When can I get out of the car?" McEntee asked.

"In a couple of minutes. Write another one for two hundred dollars," Barnes said as the Camaro idled in the Cleveland Trust auto teller line. Barnes took both checks and edged up in line.

"It's dumb to have two checks because they'll only cash one of them," McEntee told Barnes, either because he was trying to win him over or because he was frightened of what might happen if the bank refused to cash the checks.

Barnes agreed, ripping the smaller check into tiny pieces and tossing the scraps in the car's ashtray.

Losing patience, Barnes suddenly began pounding on the horn and rocking the car back and forth as he tried to get out of line. When he managed to escape the line, Barnes darted to the front and parked right by the lobby.

When Barnes informed McEntee that they were going inside the bank to cash the check, McEntee figured this would be the best time to get away. He too got out of the car and walked in front of Barnes into the bank. "Look at the crowd," McEntee said when he opened the bank door.

"Get in the car," Barnes shouted. "Get back in the car or else!"

McEntee opened the car door as if to get in, but then he slammed the door and ran into the bank.

Barnes started the car and drove away, the dual white walls on the Camaro's front tires blurring in the afternoon. The police later found the car in the parking lot of a Cleveland bar.

"The only reason this guy filed a report is because the check was out there, and he knew he'd have to tell his wife something," Flynn said. "He had to come up with an explanation. If it was money only, we'd have never heard from him."

> You recall your recent conversation with McEntee's wife. "My husband died four years ago," she said. "Cancer. He was only fifty-one. I don't think I want to talk about this over the phone. For all I know you could be the guy who did it. Anyway, I don't think I can tell you anything about your uncle's murder," she tells you. "All I know is that my husband was in line at an auto teller and the guy jumped in his car."
>
> You thank her and tell her you will not call again. You hope you can keep your promise.

Over the next six weeks, Barnes picked up his pace. Shortly after the McEntee kidnapping and the bungled check-cashing scheme, Barnes kidnapped Thomas Walker on November 12 under similar circumstances. He abducted Michael J. Palmison on December 4 and Alan W. Rounds on December 11. All of these men were picked up in or around Perkins Beach. All of them had been taken "by force, threat or deception."

Don pushes the accelerator down as he picks up his speed, driving faster now, hard. As he drives toward Perkins, he passes apartment buildings built in English Tudor style, and cruises beneath the shade of the maples and oaks lining Clifton Blvd., which once was home to Cleveland's wealthy families of industry.

Although Don at times may have lived as if he were from a wealthy family, he was not. With only a high school education, he had worked as an elevator repairman, a street sweeper, a shipping clerk. For a time he even trafficked in cigarettes. Don would drive his Lincoln down to North Carolina where he'd pull up in front of a barn at 3:00 a.m. The barn door opened and he drove in. Immediately the door shut behind him and lights went on. Without much being said, three or four guys would load the

Lincoln with one thousand cartons of cigarettes, ensuring that not a single carton showed above window level. Don would pay the sellers one dollar a carton in North Carolina, drive back to Ohio and sell them for two dollars a carton when cartons regularly sold for four dollars. The only tax that went unpaid was the Ohio tax, so it looked to be a good gig. Unfortunately, Don never had money in his hands for long. Instead of turning around with the one thousand dollars profit and going back for another cache, Don blew the money and had to borrow cash from friends and family in order to make another run, which was why the paycheck stub found in his wallet on the day of his death was for $282 for two weeks of work.

Don doesn't stay long at the Driftwood Inn, just long enough to get out of the cold, feel the wet heat of Cutty Sark, enjoy his reflection in a barroom mirror, and cash his check.

No minorities—no Spanish or Puerto Ricans—spotted a wad of money. Barnes waits miles away, eating chicken and holding a gun.

> You once watched Uncle Don wash his wife's hair, carefully brushing it out, blowing it dry, gently foraging through it with his fingers as if searching for the secret of the static electricity he created. Her hair billowed. He was electric; he had the touch. As he brushed his wife's hair, he had everything in its place: brush here; gel there, comb here. Twice you playfully rearranged his tools. The second time that he told you not to move anything again, you heard something in his voice—anger, simple and clean—that you'd never heard before.

A guy named Allen Gump lived on Cleveland's west side and had an acquaintance named Barnes. Barnes and his minor sidekick Michael visited Gump often enough to know he owned just the help they needed to upgrade their business in a hurry without a cent of overhead. Gump owned a .38 blue-steel snub-nosed revolver. Barnes needed the gun, so he broke into his friend's house and took it.

On December 12, 1974, just about twenty-four hours before Barnes would become a murderer, he decided to step things up. Now he had a gun. All he needed was another so-called tulip ready to be picked.

Richard Wilkinson stopped his silver two-door 1972 Mercury XR7 at a red light near Perkins Beach. As he waited for the light to change, his

passenger door flung open and Wilkinson stared into the two-inch barrel of a .38 caliber revolver.

"Freeze or I'll shoot you, you bitch," the gunman said, his hazel eyes flashing. "If you move I'll blow your balls off with this gun."

Barnes, with his hair slicked back and greasy under a black leather cap with a brim, a green field jacket and light-colored plaid pants, forced Wilkinson to drive to Perkins Beach.

You visit Perkins Beach, take pictures, time distances to get things right. On the way home you go out of your way to drive past your aunt's house. If you see her outside you'll stop and visit. See if she feels like talking about her dead husband. Surely a quarter of a century has eased the pain. After all, they were on their way to a divorce when he was killed, you tell yourself as you pass duplex after duplex. You see her outside. She's playing with her grandchildren in the rear of her narrow driveway. It's a beautiful summer afternoon. You keep driving.

When they arrived at Perkins, Barnes forced Wilkinson into the back seat. Barnes's accomplice sat in the passenger seat. The minor, referred to only as Michael, who stood no more than a few inches over five feet tall and weighed less than 140 pounds, wore a black sweater with blue stripes, shoulder-length brown hair parted on the left. He held the .38 Titan Tiger on Wilkinson while Barnes did the driving.

Barnes drove Michael and their victim to an apartment complex, where he stopped the car and got out to inspect the trunk. He reached into the trunk, produced a tire iron and got back in the car.

"You better come up with fifty dollars or we'll kill you," Barnes said, brandishing the weapon.

"I don't have any money," Wilkinson said.

Barnes then dragged him out of the back seat, smacked him on the head with the barrel of the gun and threw him into the trunk.

Barnes and the kid sped around enjoying the power and speed of the XR7. Every half hour or so, Barnes would pull the car over, open the trunk and crack Wilkinson in the head with the tire iron. By the time Barnes

freed Wilkinson from the trunk, the young kid was gone and Wilkinson was forced back up front.

"I really just want to be friends" Barnes said as he held the .38 on Wilkinson. "You should come and see me . . ."

After his bizarre comments about becoming friends, Barnes stopped the car in the parking lot of a dry cleaner's and got out, telling Wilkinson to head west and to keep going.

Weeks before you were to make the sacrament of Confirmation at St. Bridget's Catholic Church, you asked Uncle Don if he would be your sponsor, somebody willing to stand for and with you as you became a soldier of Christ. Uncle Don said he'd love to, but that he could not. At the time he felt he was not a good Catholic. He wasn't even receiving Communion. He refused to be a hypocrite by playing the role of good soldier. He apologized for letting you down. You admired him for his honesty. You hoped you had the courage one day to follow his lead.

Just after 6:00 p.m. Don maneuvers his 1971 Lincoln into the entrance to Edgewater Park and moves slowly up the drive to Perkins Beach, where unbeknownst to him, Barnes waits, finishing take-out chicken and sipping a can of RC Cola.

Perhaps Don checks himself out in the rearview mirror, slips his glasses into their black case, nods in a knowing way that he looks good. Although he's still wearing his work clothes, light gray pants and matching work shirt with Houghton Elevator sewn over the right shirt pocket and his name stitched over the left, he looks fine, dapper even. His brown dress shoes ease up on the accelerator as he nears the portal to Perkins. The temperature this close to the lake is only a couple degrees above freezing; Don's lucky he wore his blue nylon work jacket.

He backs into a spot along the cul-de-sac, turns off his headlights, and then the engine. To his left and across a more inland section of the shoreline the lights of Cleveland shine through the oncoming darkness. He sees the Terminal Tower. Behind him sit leafless trees, and beyond the trees a black drop-off to the shallowest of the five Great Lakes. On

the other side of the cul-de-sac stands a sixty-three-year-old statue of German composer Richard Wagner. Wagner's beret-topped head angles away from Perkins Beach; his coat looks as though it has been blown open, and he holds a sheaf of music in his left hand. Don gazes around casually, noncommittally, perhaps clicking the ballpoint pen in his shirt pocket or fingering the yellow-handled pocketknife in his pants.

Barnes licks three chicken bones clean, throws them into the black plastic box they came in and drops the box to the ground. Another tulip. And this time Barnes is ready. He's tired of playing around.

When he sees the young man approaching his car, does Don's heart pick up speed? Does he quickly rehearse his lines or does he know the drill? Does he check his hair one last time, frustrated by the tinges of gray growing above the ears? Does he lower his power windows a bit to convey a welcome? Is this his first time, the time he's fantasized about, the time he's been forbidden to fantasize about? Forbidden himself to fantasize about? Does his conscience tingle with the electric knowledge you get when you know something's wrong and you do it anyway, as if you're moving through everything you are and know to enter another place, whose passage you'll only worry about once you're safely back from the other side? Is this why, when Barnes pulls out his gun and demands money, Don can't possibly give it to him? Can't possibly give in to him?

Surely Don knows the fantasy is over when the minor accomplice gets in the back seat and he's forced into the passenger seat. Barnes is once again behind the wheel, still sipping his pop.

From the passenger seat Don lunges for the gun. Barnes pulls the revolver's trigger six times; two of the six hit the firing pin but do not fire. Two bullets rip through Don's right upper chest and lodge in his back. Another hits the upper left side of the neck and exits from the right side of the back. The final bullet enters in front of Don's left ear and exits through the back of the same ear. In the confusion windows are busted, blood and glass sprinkle the black vinyl roof, the seats, the maroon carpet on the floor, the door panels. While Barnes fires, Don attempts to get out the passenger side of the car. Frightened, Barnes flees, drops the gun on the front seat. Don dies before he can get away; he dies lying half in, half out of his car, his right lung perforated, specks of gun powder in the

wounds, massive internal hemorrhaging, seventy-five feet away from a police call box.

The lady at the Cuyahoga County Coroner's office warns you about one of the autopsy pictures. She says you don't have to pay for that one if you don't want to. You thank her but insist on seeing all seven of them. She says okay and hands them to you, back first, so the photographs face her. "What relation was he to you?" she asks. It should be a simple question but has gotten considerably more complicated. Story to storyteller? Subject to writer? Nephew to . . . ? "He was my uncle," you tell her. "Three and a half years ago my daughter came through here," she tells you. "That was hard." "I'm sorry," you say. "You do what you have to do, huh?" When she says this you almost think you hear her ask, "Why are you doing this?"

Around 7:00 p.m. on December 13, 1974, Edward Chomiak drives west on the Shoreway. Although he had hoped he could make it to his destination without having to stop, he finally decides he'll have to pull over and relieve himself. This isn't the first time he hasn't been in complete control of his body; it had betrayed him years earlier with boyhood polio.

Looking for a secluded place, Chomiak finds a darkened drive where he can relieve himself privately and be back on his way. But then he notices something. Although it is already dark and the weather's becoming more miserable, a light attracts Chomiak's attention. Walking with difficulty, he moves closer toward the light until he can make out its source, which is a dome light shining in the evening in what appears to be an abandoned car. He looks toward the middle of the cul-de-sac, to the third tree west of the center. Getting closer, he sees that the driver's side window has been smashed or the glass blown out, something. Because of his lack of agility, he heads carefully toward a Ford Falcon parked across from the Lincoln, where a man in his twenties with dark curly hair and slight beard sits alone.

"You better go call the police," Chomiak tells the curly-haired man. "I think there's a body by that car over there."

"I'll call from a gas station on Detroit Ave. And then I'll be back," the young man says before driving away.

It's almost 7:30 p.m. now. The police have still not arrived and the curly-haired young man has not returned. Chomiak assumes that the kid has taken off without ever calling the police, apparently not wanting to be associated with a crime at Perkins Beach.

Chomiak drives the short distance to Detroit Ave. to make the call. At 7:51 p.m. Det. Bob Shankland and Det. Jimmy Fuerst arrive. Shankland, muscular, with a reputation as a tough, brave and gutsy no-holds-barred kind of cop with reddish-brown hair, heads directly to the Lincoln, where he'll collect pop cans and soil samples. His partner, Fuerst, a fun-loving, well-liked, stocky guy, gets Chomiak's story and then, noticing he's partially paralyzed, gently takes Chomiak by the arm and walks him over to the Lincoln to see if he can identify the body.

Although Chomiak remembers looking into the upturned and bloody face of the dead man, the police report it differently. The victim was found lying outside the passenger door, face down, feet together and pointing south, left arm under the body and the right arm outstretched along the right leg, head pointing north. No mention of his soul leaving his body, tumble-drifting down, above and across the lake, flying fast and safe to the far north beyond the water.

Chomiak, who still thinks of the dead man and says a prayer for him whenever he passes by this place, stares at the once-handsome now blood-smeared face of the stranger.

> You take one look at the autopsy pictures. One. The woman with the dead daughter was right. You should have thought twice about acquiring the pictures. The wounds, both entrance and exit, are confirmed. Chomiak's right about the blood-smeared face. You glimpse Uncle Don through the façade of the murdered man. Yes it's him. No it isn't. Both equal and separate truths. You should have spent more time with the woman from the coroner's office, the one with the dead daughter. You should have listened to her tale of love and loss. You need to talk to your aunt, your deceased mother's closest sister. The time has come.

In the middle of the front seat, strewn cold, were car keys, and next to the keys, hot and spent, rested the .38 blue-steel revolver, an Arminius

Titan Tiger, serial number 023805. Because Gump had reported his gun stolen, the trail led easily to Barnes. He and his minor accomplice were arrested while sitting on a couch the day after the murder. Barnes confessed immediately.

Uncle Don was taken to St. John's Hospital where he was pronounced dead at 10:05 p.m. on Friday, December 13, 1974.

My aunt asked if we would mind keeping the Lincoln at our house for a time. Perhaps she asked because my father was not only my uncle's friend but an ex-homicide detective. At first it simply took up space in our driveway and in my imagination. Soon we investigated it, my father piecing together clues, explaining to his young sons the likelihoods and probabilities: the shards of glass told one part of the story, the blood another part, the smell—in its utter indescribability—yet another. Soon we sat behind the wheel. Fearing a dead battery, my dad and I began driving the car, leaving the pieces of glass and splotches of dried blood where they lay. High school friends flocked to the car the way they were expected to. Soon the car was gone, at least from the driveway.

Good friends of my aunt and uncle—friends who lived directly across the street from them—bought the Lincoln; my uncle's then ten-year-old daughter saw it every single morning she left for school, each day she went out to play.

You call your aunt and ask her if you can visit. You ask her if she's willing to talk about Uncle Don. She says she will but that she will not do it over the phone. "He was a free spirit; that's for sure," she says. You stop at a local deli and pick up sliced turkey breast, Swiss cheese and a loaf of Italian bread, as is a family custom—not the specifics, just the gesture. Her oldest sister is also in town. They both want to talk about their parents. How one came from Italy as a twelve-year-old, about the hardships their lovely, strong and gentle mother, your grandmother, endured. You love these stories and let them lull you away from what you want to talk about. Soon they produce boxes and bags of pictures of family and its extensions.

"The guy who killed Uncle Don got released from prison in 1989," you say when a photo of Uncle Don comes up. "He served fifteen

years. There wasn't even a trial. He pled to a lesser offense of murder, aggravated robbery and kidnapping."

You don't tell her that you located Barnes, that he's been living in the same house for about the last seven years. That you tried to talk to him. That he's living with at least two other men, including a chiropractor with a bad back. You don't admit that your repeated phone calls enraged a guy running interference for Barnes. 'I know Alan. I'm friends with Alan. I will talk to Alan, but if I were you I wouldn't hold my breath.' You don't tell her about the letter you wrote him, asking about the murder that "rightly or wrongly" he was convicted of committing, asking about that night in December, twenty-five years ago, for information that only he can supply. You don't bother telling your aunt that the guy who killed her husband never responded to your request for information.

"That's horrible the way Don died," Aunt Manny, the elder aunt, says. "Being shot and all like that."

Uncle Don's wife is silent for a moment and it makes you want to turn and run in shame. You know at that moment that you won't be able to ask her the questions you came prepared to ask. You're sitting in her kitchen, which looks exactly the way it did twenty-five years ago. You remember one Saturday night, probably thirty years ago now. Your aunt and uncle sit with your parents playing Pinochle in this very kitchen. Hand after hand. Cigarette after cigarette. Drink after drink. Laughter. Friendship. You're in the living room watching "Mannix." Never before or since have you felt so simply loved, so perfectly safe. Your aunt's a good woman and an even better aunt. She's your godmother. And in a generation and a religion that took godparenting seriously, she took it more seriously than most.

"Here's some pictures of Don," she says.

You take up one of him in tennis whites standing next to his Cadillac. Another where he's lounging on an army cot during the service; he's wearing his uniform and a huge smile. You wonder how many points of view it takes to tell anything about anybody.

"This is your grandpa," my aunt says to her oldest grandchild, whom she babysits a couple of days a week.

The boy, holding a stack of baseball cards in his fist, stops for a second and looks at the black-and-white picture. Of course the statement is as true as it is false. There is no doubt that the blood of the man is coursing through the body of the boy. Yes, that's his grandfather. No, it isn't the whole picture.

What do you do with all the circumstantial evidence? All the other pictures? All the rumors about the guys Uncle Don moved in with after he left his wife. A family member asking him, 'Why are you hanging out with these queers?' Uncle Don's response, 'Don't knock it if you haven't tried it.' And what about Perkins Beach? What about the tulip vultures? What about going miles out of his way on a miserable evening to sit in a dark park with a reputation as a homosexual hangout? What about the other strangers? Did he die because he couldn't live as an openly gay man? Would there have been less pressure if he had lived anywhere but Lakewood, anywhere other than "gay city"? Was his death ultimately caused by force, threat or deception? All three? Threats from whom? Who was deceived?

> But who's the real person? How vain and egomaniacal is it to think you know? How foolish? How wrongheaded? Does loving somebody and being a writer give you a right to his story? You cannot tell your aunt what you've learned, and you hope she never reads this story.

In one photograph Uncle Don and Aunt Dee stand in front of the fireplace in their Christmas-tree lit living room in the early 1960s, not long after their wedding. Flowers adorn the wooden mantel, as do a bronze plate and a candle. Two snowmen stand sentry, flanking the flower arrangement. Two Christmas stockings—a few years away from being three—hang from the mantel. In the background, in front of a window covered with a soft, white cotton curtain, a saint with a crown of gold and a gown of white stands atop a corner cupboard with glass doors. Small, light blue designs decorate Uncle Don's white, short-sleeve shirt. He wears navy blue slacks with a thin black belt. Aunt Dee's green dress curves perfectly with her form; there's a gold pin above her left breast.

Uncle Don's arms are wrapped around his wife's waist. Her right hand holds his left wrist. My aunt's smile at his holding makes her beautiful. Uncle Don's smile rules and lines his face.

Their smiles appear to be evidence of something. Of something good. Something worth telling. They seem, at this captured moment in time, two people possessed of all the love that can possibly exist in a world where people are murdered.

ANN HOOD

# The Best Fried Chicken

I have massaged it with herbs. Bathed it in buttermilk. Immersed it in water, sugar, and salt. Rolled it in corn flakes, panko, seasoned crumbs. I have spent three days tending to it, double dipping and double dredging and double bathing. Ham has been involved. Also, hot pepper flakes. But now I know that the finest way to make fried chicken is to dust it with heavily salted and peppered flour and fry it in lard until crisp. That's the way my father did it, and his mother before him. That's the way they still do it in his part of Indiana, which is to say the southeast corner whose Hoosiers are more Kentucky than Midwest. But like all children when they grow up, I doubted and questioned him and his chicken. I grew too sophisticated, and turned away from everything I once believed to be true. I tasted too many others that had been fried by the likes of Edna Lewis and Sean Brock. I forgot the crunch of that Indiana chicken, its moistness and peppery kick. I forgot until a yearning for people and things I no longer knew forced me backward, and brought me home.

I have read that Virginia Woolf's earliest memory is of a close-up view of the pattern of flowers on her mother's dress on a train trip to St. Ives. The English poet Edwin Muir's first memory was of his gold and scarlet baptism suit. American historian Henry Adams remembered the yellow of a kitchen bathed in sunlight. Tolstoy's first memory is of being swaddled and crying out for freedom. Me, I remember fried chicken.

I was three, or maybe four, lying on my back in what we called the *way back* of our green Chevy station wagon, watching the trees that lined the Blue Ridge Parkway in Virginia speed past. Every weekend we would get in that station wagon and take a long drive. To the Luray

Caverns or Monticello or a glass factory outlet somewhere in West Virginia. And always on these day trips there was a picnic, eaten at a picnic table beneath mountain pines. Always potato salad, bread and butter, plums and peaches. Always fried chicken. My brother Skip, older by five years, tall and solid (our mother bought his clothes in the HUSKY section at Heck's department store), wore his summer buzz cut and a striped shirt. A Four Seasons song played on the radio—*Rag Doll* or *Big Girls Don't Cry*—and my mother sang along softly and off-key from the front seat. My father drove. His left arm, the one with the tattoo of an eagle in front of a blazing red setting sun, rested on the sill of the open window, and his fine blond hair fluttered in the hot breeze.

We four were displaced. I didn't know it then, but ever since they'd married a decade earlier my parents had been moving at the whim of the US Navy, for whom my father was a proud Sea Bee. They'd lived in Naples, Italy and Annapolis, Maryland, with long stretches in between in which my father was at sea. My mother was homesick for her small hometown in Rhode Island, for the house where her mother still lived, for the nearness of her sisters and brothers, all of them within walking distance of that house on Fiume Street where they'd all been born. I didn't know that she was still grieving the sudden loss of her favorite sister, Ann-Marie, who had died six years earlier during a routine wisdom tooth extraction. I only knew that my mother had sad eyes, and that it wasn't uncommon for me to walk down the long hall of our apartment and find her staring out the window and crying. To me, my world was that apartment in Arlington, Virginia and my family was the four of us—Mom, Dad, Skip, and me.

So I am on my back in the *way back* of our green Chevy station wagon and my brother in his buzz cut and striped shirt is beside me, both of our heads on the pillows taken from our beds, and we are staring out at the trees rushing past us. Then the car slows and everything out the window is brilliant blue and green. My father parks and takes a red cooler with a white lid from the back seat. He opens the wide door of the *way back* and we crawl out. My mother, in a pretty red dress, her eyes large and brown and sad, has already hurried to the wooden picnic table, which is painted green. When she sees us spill out of the car, she smiles, and opens the white lid of the cooler, and pulls from it a large yellow bowl.

"Fried chicken," she says.

It is fried chicken made from my father's recipe, which is to say Indiana fried chicken. No buttermilk. No spices. No brining. As I said, but it is worth repeating, the chicken is simply dusted with heavily salted and peppered flour, then fried in lard. It is crispy and moist and the best fried chicken in the world. I am three years old, wearing a dress covered in a pattern of yellow flowers, running toward my mother. And the world is perfect.

In her essay, *A Sketch of the Past,* Virginia Woolf links the memory of her mother's flowered dress to a memory of lying in bed in the nursery in St. Ives and listening to the sound of the ocean, on that same trip to St. Ives from London. But Woolf admits that the light in the train of this memory is such that the journey was an evening one, which means that it was not on the way *to* St. Ives but rather *from* St. Ives on their return to London. Therefore the memory of lying in bed and listening to the sea can't be right, an inconvenient fact that questions the voracity of her early memories, or their connection to each other. But Woolf wrote, "If life has a base that it stands upon, if it is a bowl that one fills and fills and fills—then my bowl without a doubt stands upon this memory."

What then of my own earliest memory, the one on which my own bowl stands? Although this particular picnic on this particular day is not part of my family's lore, what I remember happening later is this: It's dark, and we are heading (back) home to Virginia from wherever we spent the day, still full of fried chicken. The car smells of the lemony moist towelettes my mother carries in her purse for us to wipe our hands after eating. My brother has fallen asleep beside me, and I am now watching the pattern the streetlights make as we drive past them. The radio is on, and there is a news bulletin: Marilyn Monroe has been found dead by her housekeeper in the bedroom of her Brentwood home. I remember those words. Marilyn Monroe. Dead. Housekeeper. Brentwood home. My mother starts to cry. Skip sits up and asks what happened.

Then there are bright lights, what I now know were the high beams of another car, and they are moving toward us fast, in our lane, hurtling head on toward us. There is the sound of metal upon metal, of glass breaking,

of someone screaming. For an instant, I am airborne, flying above the *way back*, over the back seat, over the front seat, hurtling toward the night. Until my mother catches me like a football someone has tossed her way. My brother, older, heavier, has not been lifted into the air by the collision, but rather thrown hard against the wall of the back seat, breaking several ribs and suffering a concussion. Surely an ambulance arrived and took Skip to the hospital after the car accident. My father probably went with him; my father was the one who swabbed our scrapes with Mercuricome and put on our Band Aids and brought us to the ER for stitches and casts. Yet I have no recollection of sirens or ambulances, of waiting—where? By the side of that dark road?—with my mother. All I remember is what came later back at home: the long stretch of white bandages on Skip's ribs, my mother's terrified expression, my father lifting a glass of Jack Daniels in his shaking hands.

We were instructed to keep him awake all night and check the size of his pupils every hour. Years later, when my brother was thirty and drowned in the bathtub of his Pittsburgh home, my mother would recall that long ago accident and wonder if it had something to do with whatever mysterious event had led him to die that way. It didn't, of course. We spend so much of our grief looking for answers to explain what cannot be explained.

Marilyn Monroe died on August 5, 1962. I wasn't three; I was five. A five year old who could read. In Virginia at that time, a child had to turn six by September 1 in order to enter first grade. My birthday isn't until December, so it was decided that I should go and live with my grandmother in Rhode Island where a child could start first grade as long as she turned six by December 31. So was I even in the car in Virginia the night Marilyn Monroe died? Or was I in Rhode Island awaiting the first day of school? *Big Girls Don't Cry* didn't come out until November of that year, and *Rag Doll* came out in 1964. Whatever my mother was humming, it couldn't have been either of those songs.

But I want to keep my bowl full of these images, these soft lovely memories. I want to keep the taste of that fried chicken on my tongue. Not just the fried chicken at that roadside picnic in the Blue Ridge Mountains, but years of it: hot from the silver fryOlator in a bright yellow bowl, cold in the backyard on a summer day, all you can eat at a chicken place

in Indiana with all of my Indiana cousins and aunts and uncles. When I drove to Florida every spring break during college, my mother fried up chicken for us to snack on during the long drive.

But somehow years passed. All that other fancier, more complicated fried chicken came my way. Then last summer I found myself craving the simple fried chicken of my childhood. No. I found myself craving my father's throaty laugh, the way he said *roof* like it rhymed with *hoof*, how being wrapped in his arms made everything ok. But he was gone almost twenty years, although the particular blue of his eyes had not faded for me. And my brother, dead at thirty, the science geek who had the first Betamax and CD player; what we think of iPhones and Netflix and everything the world has invented without him? How I wanted to have a beer with both of them, ask their advice on the big life decisions I was facing. And then I craved that fried chicken.

I was heading to a wedding in Michigan that August, and although not exactly on my route, I needed to detour to Greensburg Indiana. I sent out a message to my Hood cousins: *Coming through Greensburg. Want fried chicken.* A flurry of possibilities dropped into my inbox, and finally they settled on the Brau House in Oldenburg. We filled a room there, and in no time platters of all you can eat fried chicken covered the tables. My cousin Keith Hood took me back into the kitchen where the owner told me how she made that perfect chicken: lots of salt, lots of pepper—more of both than you think you need—in flour. Fry until crispy. So simple, this recipe. There were mashed potatoes and corn too, but it was the fried chicken I'd come for, and it was the fried chicken I ate, breast after crispy breast.

Every bite brought me back in time, reminding me that there is nothing as good as that fried chicken, especially when it was made by your mother and eaten at a rest stop somewhere in Virginia, at a wooden picnic table, with your older brother beside you and your father so young his tattoo is still vivid reds and blues. All of us so young, and happy, and full.

SAM PICKERING

# Dog Days

An aging man should not own an old dog. George turned thirteen in July. His dog days foreshadowed the doldrums into which I am slowly nodding. In past summers George loped down the lane behind the barn, air currents spinning salty fragrances around him, pulling his nose right and left. This summer George wallowed through troughs of grass, his hull slipping warped, no longer scudding in the bright sun. His head hung down, and the skin under his jaw looked like a flying jib stripped of wings. During days he wandered without purpose, one moment hunching by the steps leading to the backhouse, appearing to want to go outside, the next scratching the screen door on the porch asking to come in. Time has swept his helmsman overboard, and his tiller swung directionless. When not pitching and yawing, he clung to me, seeming to need assurance and affection. Occasionally I became exasperated and shouted, "Go to your bed." Immediately thereafter I imagined myself tottering toward the kitchen in slippers and bathrobe, weary children saying, "Go back to bed, Dad." At nine o'clock every night I carried George upstairs. I set him atop a pillow on the floor next to my bed, then I covered him with a blanket. At a quarter after eleven I lugged him back downstairs and took him outside so he could pump himself dry for the voyage through the night. Afterward I carted him back upstairs. Shortly before six in the morning, he stood and flapped his ears to awaken me. I took him back outside, after which I built a fire in the kitchen stove and he fell asleep on a pad beside my rocking chair.

"You live a dog's life," Vicki said one night.

"Not yet," I answered, "not quite yet."

In the past George resembled a trim bark. This summer he became a lugger. Heavily laden and lumbering, he bolted meals and lived, Vicki said, to eat. *Like me,* I thought. Once a week I went to Tim Hortons, a doughnut shop in Yarmouth. I drank a medium-sized cup of coffee, always in a ceramic cup, and ate a Dutchie, a rectangular wad of glazed dough, spotted with raisins and fat. Trips to Tim Hortons were the high points of weeks in Nova Scotia, and I looked forward to them eagerly. One Wednesday an old man sat across the aisle from me, a worn version of myself, I thought. The man's back curled like the upper half of a question mark. He wore a green and white checkered shirt, a red baseball cap, Canadian Tire sewed above the bill, boots, and dark khaki trousers held up by red suspenders. Time had shrunk the man's hips into coat hangers, and the trousers hung loosely from his waist, wrinkled like laundry bags. His two middle-aged daughters accompanied him, one sitting on his right, the other on the left. That morning they signed him out of "the home" for an outing and for a treat brought him to Tim Hortons. The man was deaf, and while he ate a sugar doughnut, the women leaned toward each other and talked over his shoulders. The man paid no attention to them and concentrated on eating. He held the doughnut tightly in both hands, head pushed up looking like that of a turtle sticking out of its shell. His eyes gleamed alertly, as if he thought someone might snatch the treat away. "No more Dutchies for me," I resolved. The resolution lasted only until the following week.

July was flush with beginnings. Four newly hatched red-bellied snakes lay under a slab of plywood near the bluff overlooking the Gulf of Maine. Tadpoles, big as thumbs, roiled the cow pond. A young muskrat swirled through rushes growing beside the bridge spanning the Beaver River outlet. Seventy yards above the bridge six ermine bundled across the gravel road. A robin lured a fledgling from its nest in the golden elder behind the backhouse. Hares no bigger than fists crouched under canes of rugose roses. Some mornings I got up at three thirty and, after brewing a pot of tea, wrote in the study, sitting at the desk in the bay window. One morning I watched a young hare thrust through periwinkle under the window. On reaching the front entrance, he tried to hop up the steps. The hare was so young that he moved awkwardly. Instead of forward its

big feet pushed its body sideways, and the hare tumbled over four times before he reached the top step.

Often while the green extravagance of summer nourished my eyes, my thoughts drifted to endings. Two days before watching the hare climb steps, I'd found tufts of brown fur on the headland, sweepings from the meal of a marsh hawk. I chased the hare off the porch into roses bearded with ferns. "Stay there," I said, "and maybe the hawk won't get you." Life, alas, is beaked. That morning I received a letter informing me that two days before his retirement party, a friend died in a car wreck. That night cirrus clouds curled fruity overhead, orange then pink and purple. Instead of imagining fair seedtimes, I thought about sad old women, dyeing and baking thin locks in hopes of disguising age, hiding not so much from others but from the people who stared at them from mirrors.

"More than two score years and ten have come and gone since that day when I, Benjamin Lathrop, put out from Salem harbor, a green hand on the ship *Island Princess*," Charles Boardman Hawes wrote at the beginning of *The Mutineers* (1920). Almost as much time had passed since I read such books. Late in life, though, a man returns to childhood reading, tales of butchery and cowardice on the high seas, of bravery and the improbable survival of virtue appealing more than great books in which meaning gapes like a bog, pages scratchy with leatherleaf. After dinner between journeying up and downstairs with George, I read three of Hawes's books: *The Mutineers*, *The Great Quest*, and *The Dark Frigate*. No matter the guttural cough of the foghorn at Port Maitland, I steered a straight course under blue skies to enjoyment.

"What do those books make you think about?" Vicki asked.

"Nothing," I said, "just the subject people my age should think about."

Returning to Nova Scotia every summer contributes to the illusion of smooth continuance, each summer not the first thread in a new fabric but another button on a cardigan, perhaps looser than buttons below but still familiar and comfortable. Every summer the songs of white-throated sparrows bounce from scrub like novelty tunes from the fifties. Early in the morning ravens grind woodenly. In the evening veeries perch in damp ruffs of spruce, their songs refracting and piercing the fog in beams of color, blue, green, and pale pink. Every summer I scythe Japanese knot-

weed growing at the edge of the side meadow. In the barn I split firewood. Early in July Vicki buys beet greens and strawberries at roadside stands. After a flick of time she buys potatoes, peas, raspberries, and Swiss chard. No matter how slowly I jog, on the headland butterflies spring from my feet in clumps, first azures and orange crescents, then wood nymphs, and finally, over the lowlands near the outlet, cabbage whites spiraling, dizzy with mating. Although the children now spend summers far from Beaver River and the arms that carried them down the sharp headland to the beach, occasionally a child telephones and memory lifts me. Late in July Eliza called from Minnesota where she was teaching Russian. She was weeping. Francis sent her an e-mail from Storrs. He said Harvard had written her. Because of an unanticipated high rate of acceptance, some freshmen, including Eliza, would have to live off campus.

"The university," Francis wrote, "will help you find an apartment."

"Daddy," Eliza sobbed, "I want to meet other freshmen. I have been so lonely in high school. I want to make friends and be part of college."

Francis's e-mail was a joke. "I must have forgotten to write 'ha, ha' at the end," he said. I explained that good jokes did not upset or create anxiety. Instead they provoked warm laughter, making people appreciate life.

Vicki and I do not agree on humor; the disagreement, however, long standing. This summer we didn't watch television. Instead we listened to the radio, on Saturday nights tuning in the CBC and "Finkleman's 45s." For two hours Danny Finkleman played pop songs from the '50s, '60s, and '70s, lining each record with quirky commentary, suggesting, for example, that the CBC construct a bowling alley in the basement of its building in Toronto. One Saturday while Vicki was outside emptying the slop dish, Finkleman told a joke. Normally I don't like jokes, but I enjoyed this one so much I was gasping for breath when Vicki returned from the compost pile. Golf provided the frame for the joke, any discussion of which makes me dream of holing out. Moreover the pesticides and weed killers slathered over courses have turned fairways into toxic dumps.

"The poisons pit even steel-plated shoes," my friend Josh told me, stepping forward to address an idea. "The only safe way to indulge in golf is on stilts. Even so, eighteen holes can reduce a pair of sixteen-foot titanium stilts to six inches."

"If sprays shrink stilts that much," I said, swinging my niblick at the idea, "a real sportsman would need several bags of clubs for a single round, the lengths of the clubs in one bag different from those in another. Caddy fees would be enormous. The game is doomed."

"No," Josh said, always up for the short game, "all a duffer needs is a set of clubs with adjustable shafts, the length of a driver at the top end, say, twenty-one feet. Of course bags would be expensive, and giants could charge monstrous fees for caddying."

Finkleman's joke hooked less than Josh's musings. At the bar on the nineteenth hole, a man described his new golf ball to a friend. "If topped into water, the ball floats," he said. "If sliced out of sight into deep rough, it beeps, and at dusk a light beneath the gutta-percha blinks automatically." "Good-bye double bogies," the friend exclaimed. "That's fabulous. Where did you get the ball?" "I found it," the man said. I laughed uncontrollably after telling the story, belly rising like a bunker then sinking into a divot. Vicki looked, as scratch narrators put it, teed off, her expression grittier than a sand wedge.

I expected silence, that being par for a 7,200-yard course of marriage. Often I don't respond to Vicki's remarks, and if I answer, frequently I chip only a word or two her way. Unlike Vicki I eschew fashionable discussion on the radio, particularly boutique programs that pander to the salacious. One chilly, July afternoon Vicki sat in the rocking chair by the stove, sipping Earl Grey tea, feet raised, resting on the seat of a kitchen chair. From the radio atop the table to her right a feline voice purred.

"Do you think," Vicki said as I strolled into the room, "our marriage could survive a sex change?"

"Yes," I said and striding into the barn split wood.

Next spring Michigan will publish two books I wrote. "I wonder if I will make a half million on the books," I said in the kitchen that night.

"I want to win the lottery," Vicki replied.

"I'm talking about the sales of my books," I said.

"I prefer to talk about something more realistic," Vicki said, "like winning the lottery." Years ago, Vicki would have allowed me a handicap and not responded to my musings. The most any of my books has earned is four thousand dollars, the half million simply the dream of a buccaneering reader.

Not all summer's doings dragged like anchors, stirring silt. I thought of titles for two essays, both from songs, the first, "Precious Memories," susceptible, I am afraid, to waterlogged melancholy. The second song, "Give My Love to Nell," told a story. Two close friends, Jack and Bill, left home arm in arm and sailed across the ocean seeking to better their lots in life. Besides home and family, Bill left his girlfriend, Nell. Jack made his fortune first. "Give my love to Nell," Bill requested before Jack returned home. Jack obeyed his friend, and later when Bill arrived home, he discovered that Nell and Jack had married. Instead of pining or behaving badly, as characters often do in sentimental songs, Bill wished the couple well and got on with living. Rather than mulling connection or opportunity missed, my essay would celebrate actual happenings. "In other words," Vicki said, "whatever is, is," adding, "that's a wallet stuffer."

Although the tides now look hackneyed, other summer doings seemed practically new. A boreal chickadee foraged alders around the cow pond, the second boreal chickadee I've seen. At my age sights and sounds are suspect. Not until a second sighting confirms the first do I claim seeing a bird. At the Beaver River outlet I found a dead loon. Salt had cured and sun dried the body. The loon died during winter, the feathers on top of its head dark gray and a white patch under its bill. I snapped the loon's spine at the base of the neck. The neck was long, resembling the butt of a pistol. When school starts in August, I'll take the head to class and use it as a pointer. "Students will think you insane," Vicki said.

"Exactly," I said, "a lunatic."

"Is everything a joke with you?" Vicki asked.

"Very little," I said, lifting George into my lap and rubbing him behind the ears.

Not every animal I held was dead or declining. "What's that?" Vicki said one night, switching on the lamp sitting on her bedside table. A little brown bat whirled overhead then, swooping low, flew out of the bedroom into the upstairs hall. The house resembles a barn. Ceilings are high, that of Vicki's and my bedroom being the highest, beyond my fingertips even if I stand on a stool. I closed the bedroom door so the bat could not return and hang himself high above my reach.

"I will find him in the morning," I told Vicki.

"I hope so," she said. "I'd feel terrible if the bat starved to death." Before

breakfast the next morning I searched the house. I began upstairs, scouring the long hall and the other four bedrooms. I peered under beds and looked behind headboards. I pushed chests away from walls and shifted clothes in closets. Downstairs I searched the hall and the study. I lay on the floor trying to spot droppings. I almost gave up and told Vicki the bat must have flown into the chimney in the study and escaped. But then I found it behind the door to the front parlor. The bat looked like a furry Mars bar. While Vicki peeled the bat's legs off the top of the door, I held a butterfly net over and below the animal. The bat clicked then slipped into the net. I carried the bat into the barn and set it atop the old sleigh, placing it on the rear seat, making sure it couldn't slip off. Eight minutes later when I returned to the barn, the bat was gone.

"We should have named it," Vicki said.

"Yes," I said, "it is our first house bat. What a thrill!"

This summer I spent more time than ever before stirring about purposelessly. "Like George," Vicki said. I wandered outside throughout the day hoping to glimpse an unfamiliar insect. I had spent fourteen summers in Beaver River. The chances of my spotting a creature not seen before were small, and so like those of George, my excursions were short, and I quickly returned to the kitchen and munched on cheese and crackers, prunes and peanut butter, muffins, and rhubarb flummery, in the middle of this last a mound of whipped cream as alluring as Treasure Island.

To prevent myself from dozing the summer away, I did things I had not done before. The first Saturday in August Vicki and I went to the Quilt Show and Tea sponsored by the Patchwork Pals Quilters Guild and held at Beacon United Church in Yarmouth. Over 150 quilts hung from railings or draped over the backs of chairs. The chairs stood in double rows on the tops of tables, eight, six, four, or two chairs to a table. For an hour and a half I roamed the hall studying patterns: bow tie, double wedding ring, flying geese, Dresden plate, city streets, winning hand, postage stamp, Ohio rose, Lady of the Lake, and Bargello rippling in waves. Color spilled from vases of Trapunto flowers. From the center of a radiant star, eleven pink and red eight-pointed stars shimmered outward. My favorite quilts were old, in particular grandmother's flower garden, its bright bouquets washed into pale delicacy. The three-dollar ticket not only admitted me to

the show but it also let me drink tea or coffee and eat as many homemade confections as I wanted. I sampled six. Culinary memory deteriorating almost as fast as nominal, I recall only two, a devil's food cake muddy with icing and cheese cake, a bush laden with blueberries drooping over the top. Few men attended the exhibition. On entering the auditorium I counted six men and forty-four women; on leaving, seven men, and seventy-four women.

Pasted to a wall in the men's lavatory was a yellow sign, black letters printed upon it. "Please wrap your gum in a piece of paper towel and throw it in the garbage not in the urinal." Under the request, someone scribbled, "as it tastes bad then." The impulse toward disorder runs deep in me, as in society itself, and I admired the person who wrote on the sign in the act not marring cardboard but making it reflect human nature. In contrast the quilts fostered the pleasant falsehood that life radiated design or at least that order could be imposed upon living, transforming chaos into the beautiful and the functional. In the house at Beaver River clocks tick like balm, generating the illusion that time is regular. In the attempt to control living, man created time. Now man deludes himself into believing he controls time when the truth is that man never masters his creations. Instead they master him, binding him and his offspring like serfs to ways of living. Studying the quilts led me to ponder education. Instead of attending university for four years and coming to believe that learning prepares people for life, wouldn't children fare better, I thought, if they mastered quilting? Although sewing might foster wrong-headed ideas about order and disorder, at least the children would belong to a community. Society has accepted the exaggerated claims of education for so long that place and family no longer provide identity. Instead schools furnish pedigrees, the bluer the educational lines the more admirable the person. Rarely do people mention family or birthplace when they intro-duce me. Instead they cite the schools I attended, almost never referring to Sewanee but not failing to mention Cambridge and Princeton.

Such ponderings are not for young but old dogs who have ground teeth away chewing at life. That aside, one Sunday Vicki and I drove to Salmon River and watched the stock car races at Lake Doucette, a day triangle sunk into a hilltop and bound on three sides by spruce. Berms, buttressed

curbs of tires, and wire fences surrounded the track. We sat at the base of the triangle just beyond the end of the straightaway below the start. Protection seemed flimsy.

"That fence couldn't restrain a sleepy cow much less an automobile," Vicki said after a car cartwheeled toward the grandstand, trunk over engine at the start of the first race.

"Right," I said, brushing clods of dirt from my shirt and trousers. Throughout the afternoon dirt rained upon us. When Vicki bit into a slice of pizza, she got "the works." Gravel had drizzled over us and covered her pizza, resembling nubs of hamburger. The cars looked like boxes wrapped in crumpled foil. Trucks towed them into the infield: dump, pickup, tow, and a pink and white Firestone repair truck. During races people sat in white plastic chairs on the roof of the Firestone truck. Throughout the afternoon tires smashed into berms, and the cars themselves whirled about like water beetles. I scanned the infield looking for an ambulance but did not discover one.

"What happens if someone in the stands is hurt?" Vicki asked.

"I don't know," I said. "The best you can do is learn from that woman in front of us," I said, pointing down to the right. Tattooed on the woman's left shoulder were two hands, palms pressed together in prayer.

Just after the start of the first race, three cars flipped. At the first turn following the restart, five cars spun out, smacking the berm beneath us. "Oh, shit!" Vicki said when a tire flew over the grandstand. Vicki said the word so many times during the first three races that I suggested she emend her exclamations.

"*Sugar* would sound more like a lady." "Fudge you," she said.

The cars raced in categories: those with four cylinder engines, six cylinders, then eights, followed by cars whose eight-cylinder engines had been modified. To muffle the storm of noise we stuffed cotton balls into our ears. Still, by afternoon's end, I recognized categories by the noises engines made: the heavy thrum of modifieds and the thin popping of four cylinders. Individual cars stood out, one with "Welcome to the Swamp" printed on a mud flap, and a 1989 Volkswagen Fox painted white and black like a Holstein. Rubber udders hung beneath rear doors on both sides of the car. Unfortunately the car needed freshening and did not finish a single

race. Local businesses sponsored racers, and their names appeared on doors and hoods, often sprayed on: Nighttime Auto Salvage, Howard Andrews Electrical, S&H Newell Trucking & Bait, Bishara's Garage, Waterview Machine Works, Andrew LeBlanc's Excavating, and D. J.'s Corner Store, this last in Salmon River where we bought newspapers and ice cream cones. Between races the Water Buffalo, an old tanker that once hauled milk, sprinkled water over the track. The announcer discussed cars and drivers. Sometimes he addressed the crowd, wishing Gerald and Christine a happy anniversary. At the entrance to the track, the Lions Club sold tickets for the half-and-half. Tickets cost a dollar, fifty cents going to the Lions, fifty cents to a winner-take-all pot. I bought three tickets, and we stayed until the draw. We arrived at the track at eleven twenty; the drawing took place at three fifteen, the winner receiving $954. "We must go now," I said to Vicki. "I have to let George out."

"I know. I know," Vicki said. "But we are coming back next week. This is the real stuff."

"Perhaps," I said, "but maybe you have been brainwashed."

"Washed!" Vicki exclaimed, brushing off her trousers; "I look like I have spent the day on my hands and knees in a garden."

"I read an article that accused the government of experimenting with mind control," I continued, ignoring the interruption.

"What proof did the article cite?" Vicki asked.

"The number of yellow cars in New York City," I said. "Mind control provides the only reasonable explanation for so many people driving yellow cars."

"Sugar," Vicki said.

On the way home Vicki didn't talk. Instead she stared at the dunes behind Bartlett's Beach. George moved so slowly when I let him out that I picked him up and carried him into the yard. "You're a good old fellow, my good old fellow," I said, suddenly unutterably sad.

MAUREEN STANTON

# Good Guys

### THE BEAUTIFUL PLANT

My brother Patrick and I speed down Route 9, a curvy, one-lane, luge track of a road, toward Buchanan, New York, where the Indian Point III Nuclear Generating Station rises from the east bank of the Hudson River, thirty five miles north of Manhattan. Through a friend, Patrick and I have landed temporary jobs as painters for a refueling outage and "plant beautification" project.[1] To work here, Patrick and I must join the International Brotherhood of Painters and Allied Trades. For this, we need a Good Guy letter from a union member vouching for our character. I have no idea who has signed for us—our friend has arranged that—but someone is willing to say we are Good Guys. (Incidentally, the Good Guy letter is an actual form with the words "Good Guy Letter" printed across the top.)

We pass a baseball diamond along the Hudson, then turn into a sylvan glade enclosed in chain link. At the guard station, Patrick offers the name of our employer, NPS Energy Systems, then we cruise past hunks of rusting metal and neolithic concrete forms in wire-mesh pens to a four-story, L-shaped training building. From the parking lot, we see only half a dozen modular buildings and two warehouses surrounded by woods. I'm amazed at how easy it is to hide a nuclear power plant.

Inside the training center, next to a mock control room that visitors peer into as if looking upon a nursery, is the windowless conference room where we will spend the next five days in Fitness for Duty training. Our group of trainees includes thirty construction workers-pipe fitters, elec-

tricians, insulators, carpenters, painters-and one executive who looks pink and priggish in his white shirt and tight tie. Patrick and I stand out too, with our uncalloused hands, our fingernails evenly trimmed white quarter moons, and Patrick's fleece pullover, evidently not a masculine fabric like denim or the brown Carhartt jackets everyone wears. Patrick's hair is resolutely short, unlike the "mullet" that is popular here, clipped bangs and sideburns with long hair in back, a schizophrenic style that shouts, "I may look like a citizen, but I'm a rebel at heart."[2]

Patrick would blend more easily if he weren't with me. Of the nearly three hundred construction workers hired for the outage, only eight are female. "It's nice that your brother brought you into the trade," a sixtyish electrician says to me before class. Then adds, "I just don't think women belong in construction."

Our instructor, Jack, a thin, ruddy-faced retiree who trains part-time, begins by administering a psychological exam, a series of statements to which we must respond *strongly agree, strongly disagree,* or *neutral.* Jack hands out number two pencils and answer sheets with rows of tiny blank ovals and instructs us to select *neutral* as seldom as possible.[3] The problem is that some statements I agree with slightly, but not *strongly.* For example: "Threats never bother me." Well, idle threats don't bother me. Serious threats do. The fact is threats *sometimes* bother me. I'm momentarily stymied, but finally choose *strongly disagree.* Now I worry they will interpret my answer as demonstrating paranoia. Haven't I just implied that "Threats *always* bother me?" Perhaps I am being paranoid. I move on.

"The pomp and splendor of any big state ceremony are things which should be preserved." I typically don't go for ceremonies, but who doesn't like a parade? I think I agree, but certainly not *strongly.* What choice do I have? "If plates are the least bit dirty, I feel too disgusted to eat." I do have standards, but I don't want to appear neurotic. I decide to *strongly disagree.* "I have disturbing thoughts that keep me awake at night." I've been an insomniac most of my life, and yes, *thoughts* keep me awake. Are they disturbing? Sometimes, otherwise they wouldn't keep me awake. I'm beginning to feel anxious. I can't respond to any of the statements without

a full-scale debate, then I come across this: "I would feel out a decision over a long period of time rather than make a quick decision using logic and reason." Naturally, I can't decide how to respond.

Around me, the other trainees are turning in their exams. I am the last one finishing; even my brother is done. In a panic, I select *neutral* for the remaining statements. Afterward, Patrick says, "I think I figured out the pattern behind the questions," as if he's fooled the testers. But why would you have to fool the testers if you aren't insane?

Jack passes out loose-leaf binders that we use to follow his lessons on everything from radiation waste ("which is shipped to North Carolina to pay for schools for the children," he says proudly) to hazardous materials to industrial safety ("Do not drive a vehicle with inoperable brakes"). Periodically during his lectures, Jack says, "This is informational," which makes me wonder how *that* information is distinct from other information he conveys that somehow *isn't* informational.

Perhaps he is following procedure. Everything at the power plant must be done by an approved, numbered, catalogued Procedure written by the Procedure Writing Group. Complying with procedures is even a Procedure. For example, you might be required to *read* each step of a Procedure before proceeding. A second level allows you to merely *refer* to the Procedure, and the final level, subtitled "Information Use," allows you to perform an activity from memory. If a task cannot be done by the Procedure, you must initiate a Deviation Event Report. "I think of standard deviation as a gay person," Jack quips.

Next, we watch a film on hearing loss. A female narrator invites us into an Inner Ear, a small dim room with panels of buttons. The voice-over: "It's 7:05 a.m. Carl is about to enter a loud environment." Within seconds, Carl's ears fall off his head and plop on the floor like two shriveled apricots. A colleague picks up an ear and says, "I think you lost this!" I marvel; this is pedagogy.

The narrator explains the signs of hearing loss-tinnitus, a constant ringing in the ear—and the names of the inner ear bones, malleus, incus, stapes, like tiny gnomes with woodwind instruments making music out of air and vibrations in their orchestral chamber, the tympanic cavity. Aside from hearing loss, workers face other job hazards. We learn the difference

between heat cramps, heat stress, and heatstroke. When the plant is operating, the temperature in the dome can reach 120 degrees Fahrenheit. We learn how to behave in confined spaces and how to prevent back injuries and electrical shock. We learn fire science, how *not* to start a fire, and of course, the Procedure for reporting a fire.

After several hours of reviewing occupational hazards, we learn about emergency evacuation. Naturally, the reasons for evacuation are categorized, beginning with NUE (notification of an unusual event), no release of radiation; an Alert, possible release of radiation; and a Site Area Emergency, during which a major function of the power plant fails. Topping the list is a General Emergency, when the core degrades, or "melts," as it did at Three Mile Island. (It was only *after* Three Mile Island that evacuation plans were required.) Jack outlines the evacuation route, and I'm certain I could never escape. I'm not good with floor plans or dance steps, make Ys backward, and sometimes mistake the letter F for the number five.

Jack gives us a quick rundown on bomb threats. If you happen to be the person who receives the threat, you are advised to ask the caller questions: *Where is the bomb? Why did you set the bomb? Are you part of some organization?* And my favorite: *What is your name?*

At the end of the day, we review the star system, not astronomically speaking, but acronymically. Stop. Think. Act. Review. We go over this endlessly until it becomes a bright shining constellation in our minds. "You wouldn't want to do something that would affect the configuration of the plant," Jack says. He gives an example involving a painter who hung up his jacket on an innocuous looking lever that turned out to be a switch that shut down a cooling pump. "He tripped the whole plant," Jack says, almost gleefully. Tripping the plant means that you do something that might cause the entire plant—a power source for New York City's subways, hospitals, police and fire stations, and rail lines—to cease operating.

## THE PERPETUAL MOTEL

Patrick and I find temporary housing at the US Academy Motel in Highland Falls. Because of the hordes of out-of-state workers in town, for the upcoming outage, this is the cheapest place we can find—eight hundred

dollars a month.[4] As the manager hands me the keys, I notice a box of petrified donuts on the counter and a perpetual motion machine, a contraption of balls and metal that moves back and forth mockingly. We have two rooms in our efficiency: a kitchen and bedroom. As Patrick and I walk through the kitchen, our shoes stick to the greasy linoleum so that each step we rake sounds like Velcro being pulled apart. Near the stove, the linoleum buckles into a six-inch-high wavelet that I will trip over daily. The bedroom smells of toxic fibers from new carpet, and stale beer and cigarettes, but I don't dare open the jalousie windows, which are held in place by duct tape. The curtains, soiled and falling down, are pocked with cigarette burns, as are the bedspreads and furniture.

When I close the door to the bathroom, I see an insect exuvium in a tumbleweed of dust settled into the corner. I step in the shower stall and close the plexiglass door, and a pink tile pops off the wall as if I have upset the building's structural integrity. I soon discover that the temperature of the water is completely unrelated to the position of the faucet. (In this hotel, there seems to be a shortage of *cold* water.) I attempt to adjust the scalding water throughout my shower anyway. All I require for sanity is the illusion of control.

At the Grand Union down the street, Patrick and I buy a rotisserie chicken, breakfast and lunch makings, and cleaning supplies. We sit on our beds eating plates of chicken dripping with grease, yet dry like jerky. We watch Homer Simpson spill coffee on the control panel at the Springfield nuclear power plant. *Jeopardy* follows, and this becomes our evening routine. After dinner, Patrick and I clean and scrub the efficiency, lay a bath mat in the shower stall. I'm amazed how a five-dollar-rubber mat and a can of Ajax can make me briefly cheerful. Uplifting, too, is Patrick's comment: "We've earned two hundred dollars already for doing practically nothing."

## NEUTRONS, ELECTRONS, PROTONS

On the second day we take a health exam. Workers are lined up in a hallway outside of the medical department, waiting to enter the waiting room in which only five people are allowed to wait. Those of us who enter thumb our noses at the rest in line as if admitted by a bouncer to a posh

New York City nightclub. Inside, a technician escorts me to a bathroom where I attempt the anatomically improbable task of peeing into a tiny cup. My hands are wet with urine, as is the cup, but the water in the sink is shut off so that people cannot tamper with their samples. I dry the cup with a sinful amount of paper towels, worrying that the technician outside the door is becoming suspicious. If you are suspected of foul play, you will be accompanied into the bathroom by a same-sex health department employee who will watch you pee.

Back in the classroom, Jack is discussing contamination. "You all know the movie where Cher was thrown into the shower," he says. Wasn't it Meryl Streep? Oh, what's the difference. We learn that radiation is a term for the energy that nearly all substances exude, and that indeed, radiation is floating around us, on land and in the heavens, in rocks and soil and building materials, from the sun and the stars, with levels increasing at higher altitudes. There is radiation in food, potassium specifically. Bananas have radiation. We study neutrons and electrons and protons, and I am back in sixth grade science class.[5] We learn what a Curie is (a measure of radioactive material) without learning about Marie, who coined the term "radioactive" a hundred years ago. Alpha radiation can be brushed off like dandruff. Beta penetrates your epidermis like lead paint. Neutron radiation penetrates skin and bones but, strangely, can be shielded by hydrogen-rich substances: water and paraffin. Finally, there is gamma radiation, which can only be shielded by lead, steel, or concrete and water. Patrick and I are the only trainees furiously scribbling notes for the quizzes. We feel like geeks, but we can't help it; we've been to college.

We learn about the effects of radiation on the body, starting with a lesson in basic cell biology: nucleus, cytoplasm, membrane. "Man's gestation period is nine months," Jack says, followed by words like mutation, cell death, chromosomal damage. "Thirty-three percent of Americans will contract some form of cancer," he warns, assuring us that our chances of getting cancer from radiation exposure are "less than the chance of drawing an ace four times in a row from a full deck of cards." I've never been lucky at poker. Perhaps that bodes well.

Jack asks the class where on our bodies we might pick up radiation. People shout answers: hands, face, feet, arms. I raise my hand. I have

something original to say. "If you're sitting down, you know, you might get some on you."

"You mean your butt?" Jack says. A big Italian man named Joe says, "I'll clean it off for her!" and the class howls. My brother smirks, not because Joe's comment is funny, but because we both know: I am an idiot.

### RANDOM INSANITY

The next day, Jack mentions that a few people will be called to speak to the psychiatrist. He makes a big deal of insisting the names are randomly drawn, and then calls my name. I think: Interviewing random people would be an inefficient, scattershot approach to sleuthing around for nut jobs. I'm on to their ruse. I have been singled out based on some character flaw made glaringly obvious by the clever test, which my clever brother has managed to deceive. Standing in line in the hallway with two other possibly unbalanced people, I suddenly regret my checkered past, experimenting with an array of hallucinogens in high school, involvement in activist groups in college. In fact, background checkers from the Wackenhut Corporation have been busy digging up my past.[6] The application form (which asks you to list your aliases) requires six references—excluding family members—who have known you for five years and employment history. For ten years prior to this, I worked as a fund-raiser for environmental groups. Carol, one of my former coworkers, had this conversation with a Wackenhut investigator:

Wackenhut guy: "Can you provide a reference for Maureen Stanton?" Carol (in her lovely Scottish brogue): "Oh, Mo is the best development director we've ever had. She's excellent at strategic planning." Wackenhut guy: "How is she at parties?" Carol: "She's great with major donors and board members." Wackenhut guy: "When she goes to parties, does she drink a lot?" Carol (growing confused): "No, she doesn't drink a lot." Wackenhut guy: "Is she the kind of person who might take a bribe? To your knowledge, has she ever been addicted to drugs?"

I am summoned into an office to talk to the psychiatrist, a kindly looking, well-tailored older man behind a desk. "Do you know why you were

selected?" he says. "No," I say, "but I'm pretty sure it wasn't random." He laughs, and explains that my test was kicked out because the responses that measure self-discipline fell outside the bell curve.

"Can you explain?" the psychiatrist says.

I'm a writer," I say. "But nobody pays me to write, so I have to be disciplined with my limited time and resources." I tell him I am painting to make some quick money and because it doesn't tax me mentally. The shrink says his daughter, an artist, waitresses for the same reasons. My lucky day; he has not discovered my neuroses. Instead, we chat amicably for ten minutes, and smiling, he says, "Go on, get out of here. And get that book written!"

## THE TRAILER WARREN

After five days of training, we are fingerprinted, photographed, and handed over to the contractors. From the training building, Patrick and I walk along a blacktopped strip that we think is a sidewalk until we notice bright yellow words stenciled on the asphalt: "Danger: High Voltage." We casually step off. Appearing not to be fools seems more pressing than possible electrocution. Down a fairly steep hill from the training center, a good eighth mile from the power plant, we come across a warren of trailers—contractor's offices—in the middle of which is a large corrugated aluminum building, like a rectangular Quonset hut.

The Quonset hut is divided into work areas for the insulators (industrial sewing machines and huge flat tables); the pipe fitters (welding stations cordoned off with translucent black sheeting), a shop for carpenters, and four small rooms for the painters. In the paint shack, each room is connected by huge swinging doors like those to a restaurant kitchen and lit by bare bulbs dangling from twenty-foot-high ceilings. The concrete floor is littered with cigarette butts, wrappers, and sandwich crusts.

The center room contains two Dumpster-sized gang boxes filled with brushes and rollers and sleeves and scrapers, and the desk of our general foreman, Arturo Castellanos, a quiet, fiftyish Peruvian with disarmingly attractive green eyes and a streak of white in his wavy black hair. Upon

Arturo's desk is a large mirror with a plastic mock rococo frame to which he has taped newspaper photos of Mother Theresa, one with a large, block-letter caption: "Bless Her."

Patrick and I think we are about to paint, but alas, we must fill out employment paperwork for NPS.[7] Then we sit in the contractor's office and read through technical procedures collated in two four-inch-thick binders. We are given a full day and a half to do this, though nobody *reads* the procedures. Instead they slowly turn pages in a show of reading, and when the supervisor leaves, rest their heads on the table and sleep. We must sign off after "reading" each section, so I make a solid effort. This only lasts a half hour, though, because none of the information has anything whatsoever to do with my job.[8] I begin to despise the blue binders and the tedious procedures. I can find no information related to "coating," the euphemism for painting. I begin to flip pages without reading; I rest my head on the table; I long for a cigarette, though I don't smoke. Sitting in the trailer pretending to read those unreadable notebooks is torture, even at our base pay of $26.70 per hour. This requirement makes me wish for hard labor. Perhaps that is its true purpose.

## ACTUAL WORK

Since my photo ID takes a few days to process, on my first day of actual work I am escorted by Hector, a middle-aged, paunchy yet suave Argentinian. Hector has sole responsibility for my actions and must keep me in sight at all times. He must enter the power plant before me, exit behind me, and stand guard while I am in the ladies' room. (This is a written Procedure, of course.) That morning, Hector goes to the men's room and leaves me alone in the hallway with my bright green visitor badge. A manager passing by asks, "Where is your escort?" I point to the men's room. The man waits until Hector returns, scolds him, and informs us of the procedure for peeing if you are escorting someone of the opposite sex.[9]

Finally, my badge arrives and I am free to roam about the plant, feeling a bit giddy for the havoc I have the potential to create. A typical day goes something like this: We arrive around 5:45 a.m. and sit in the paint shack until 6:00 a.m., when we are officially on the clock. Then we get a

fifteen-minute break. When I ask everyone why we get a break *before* doing a lick of work, Angela, a thirteen-year veteran of Indian Point, says, "It's something the union negotiated."

En masse we walk down the hill to the plant, which is surrounded by a chain link fence topped with a garland of razor wire. Across the Hudson, small but steep jagged mountains funnel the air, so it's often windy at the security entrance, where the plant, at sea level, dips its toes in the Hudson. The brackish river water is sucked into the plant's cooling system, then pumped downstream. Fish are channeled through a passageway and released into the river.

We enter the security building, pick up our badges, and pass through an Explosive Detector and a metal detector.[10] We swipe our ID card into a reader and punch in a PIN that unlocks a turnstile for eighteen seconds. We are warned: You must never let someone else pass through with you, though we find piggybacking is treated like a venial sin. Our first stop is the tool room to pick up disposable brushes and earplugs, lime-green, miniature marshmallow-like foam bullets you squish into your ears to muffle the steady locomotive-like roar of the plant's huge turbines.

Except for the administration building, the plant is divided into elevation levels instead of floors, the highest being the 95-foot level inside the dome. The painters' staging area is on the 15-foot level, in a corner of a gymnasium-sized room that, except for walkways, is dense with pumps and valves and tangles of pipe of varying lengths and widths through which lubricants or boiling water and steam continuously pass.

At the staging area, we stand around waiting for Arturo to issue assignments, a process reminiscent of kids choosing teams. In school, Patrick and I were either captains or chosen early, but here, to our dismay, we are routinely fingered last, along with the oldest painter, Henri Leblanc, a little French Canadian with white hair and pale blue eyes who looks like he is made of sky. Even his five o'clock shadow is pure white; he reminds me of angel food cake.

Once you get an assignment, you gather tools and paint, which takes another fifteen minutes.[11] By now, 7:00 a.m., we've been paid for an hour. At 9:00 a.m., we get a fifteen-minute break. We paint until 11:30 a.m., then clean up for lunch. Lunch is officially thirty minutes, but by the time we

pass through security and walk up the hill to the lunch trailers and repeat in reverse after, it's 1:00 p.m. We get our afternoon break at 2:30 p.m., then clean up for the day at 3:30 p.m. We punch out at 4:00 p.m. for a ten-hour day, seven of which are actually spent painting.

### THE LUNCH TRAILER

There is a politic to the lunch trailer that takes me a few days to intuit. The first morning, I boldly take a seat at a table toward the front of the crowded seventy-foot-long trailer, near the refrigerator and microwave and the bulletin board where employees pin flyers for pig roasts or used trucks. I'm sitting with a half-dozen sixtyish men. I notice a tacit unease and when I turn around, I see a fellow loitering behind me. He seems at a loss as to how to handle this strange woman who has taken *his* seat with *his* friends. For all I know, the man has been sitting in this seat since Indian Point's start-up in 1976. "Oh, this is your seat," I brilliantly surmise. "Keep it," the displaced man says unconvincingly.

"No, it's your place, I'll find another." I walk away as the man is razzed. *You're going to make the lady stand? Taking a seat from a woman. There's a real gentleman.* I cruise the alley between the columns of picnic tables in search of an empty seat. My objective is to blend, to *not* be noticed, a fairly impossible task if you are the only woman in a trailer of a hundred or so men, with the exception of Pamela Anderson Lee, who's on a five-by-seven-inch postcard strung to the ceiling, and the many nameless naked women on the walls at the far end of the trailer, one whose legs are spread and who has a coke bottle inserted into her vagina. (To the credit of some manager, this photo is removed quickly, but Pamela Lee remains, floating and swaying above our heads like a busty angel.)

My subsequent lunchroom blunder is not as bad, but only because there are no witnesses. I pause strategically and scan for empty tables. Joy! A vacant spot. I unpack my lunch and take a bite of egg, then realize I am sitting directly across from Floyd Grabowski and he is, in fact, the reason the table is empty. Floyd heralds my presence with a trumpeting of his large rubious nose, the contents of which he issues into a hanky, momentarily studies, and then stores in his back pocket. The nose blow-

ing precipitates a tuberculoid coughing fit that generates expellations of a substance I have heard called "lung butter."

I examine Floyd, a man whose lifelong project of ruining his body is in its final stages. At six-foot-three and probably four hundred pounds, Floyd is the oldest Grabowski brother working at the plant, Duane and Earl being the other two. Together they weigh half a ton; there are bridges I imagine they cannot cross in unison, elevators they must take turns riding. Floyd's head, a good thirty-pounder, rests on a goitrous collar of flesh. He has a cartograph of veinlets on the landscape of his enormous face with an alcoholic's ruddy, hamburger-like complexion and red, watery eyes beneath which are puffy aprons of skin. I studiously avoid lunching with Floyd again, but a bond has been established between us, and we smile and nod whenever we pass each other. We are alike, Floyd and I: the ogled, the joked about, the outsiders.

Once a week after lunch we have a "tailgate," a meeting of all hands at which a manager reads to us from *Fatal Facts*, a publication of the US Department of Labor. One day we hear of a worker who slipped on icy scaffolding and fell to his death. Another day this article:

A crew of ironworkers and a crane operator were unloading a twenty-ton steel slab from a low-boy trailer using a fifty-ton crawler crane with ninety-foot lattice boom. The operator was inexperienced on this crane and did not know the length of the boom. Further, no one had determined the load radius. During lifting, the load moved forward and to the right. The boom twisted under the load, swinging down, under, and to the right. Two employees standing 30 feet away apparently saw the boom begin to swing and ran. The boom struck one of the employees—an ironworker—on the head, causing instant death. Wire rope struck the other—a management trainee—causing internal injuries. He died two hours later at a local hospital.

The article is accompanied by a line drawing of the crane and outlines of the two bodies. Safety talks usually have a theme such as proper lifting or ladder safety, though one day a manager announces, "A woman jumped off the Bear Mountain Bridge, but they haven't found her body yet, so if you're down by the water you might keep your eye out for anything unusual." Different managers give the talks, so occasionally there is

repetition. The week before Christmas, I heard the same memo three times, which I recall because of this curious advice: "Keep dangerous objects away from children—guns, knives, and ornaments."

## DON'T GO CRAZY

From day to day, we don't know what our assignments will be. Usually, Arturo will say something like, "Get some black and follow me."[12] He'll point to a machine or pipes we are to paint and in the way of nuance, say, "Don't go crazy." Work is confusing at first. Some days we are told to "stretch" the job, and other days we move at a frenzied pace. Days we paint floors are hectic; pot-time for floor epoxy is forty-five minutes so we must move quickly before the paint hardens. My job one morning is to "cut in" which means that I must crab walk under pipes and machines to paint the juncture where the floor meets the wall. Once Part A and Part B of the floor epoxy are blended with a huge electric mixer, I spider along the base of the wall in a space about two feet high, inhaling vapors, sweating in stiff polyester coveralls, trying to stay ahead of Hector "rolling out" the floor. We finish the job and post "Wet Paint" signs and signs that read "Fumes: Do Not Linger," cordon off the area with caution tape, wash brushes, dispose of cans and thinners, and dean up in time for lunch.

After lunch that day, Patrick and I are assigned to paint a living room–sized section of floor underneath a snarl of pipes on the fifteen-foot level. Patrick gets a Shop-Vac to prep the area. My job is holding the cord. I decide I've had enough of the "girl" jobs (sweeping, scraping, opening cans), so I untie a second shop vac.[13] My idea is to work twice as fast. (It takes Patrick and me a while to realize that this is not the modus operandi. We must pace ourselves to neither appear idle nor out-perform our fellow workers. "Slow down," Hector says to me one day. "You'll paint yourself out of a job.")

I plug in my vacuum cleaner but it doesn't start, and now Patrick's vacuum has quit. Turns out, I've blown a circuit. Strange, I muse. In a power plant that generates enough electricity to send commuter trains careening past the Bronx and sixty miles to Poughkeepsie every ten minutes, I can't

run two vacuums off one outlet. Now Patrick and I must use a tiny house type vacuum cleaner plugged into a distant outlet, trailing an extension cord one hundred feet, thus creating a tripping hazard.

For the "plant beautification project," we paint everything: pipes and valves and snubber attachments; channel iron, angle iron, and electrical boxes; pumps and floors and walls. "Don't stand still or they'll paint you!" workers joke daily. The crew of forty painters is an anomaly, the multi million-dollar beautification project a rare expenditure.[14] We paint pipes large enough to crawl through in the Rock Room, a subterranean grotto resembling the Bat Cave, its granite walls graffitied with dates and initials (I add mine). Patrick and I paint fist-sized bolts and flanges in the Zurn pit, a strange small cell we must swipe our badges to enter. We paint floors in the Havoc room, the Iodine Labyrinth Room, the Water Factory, the Polisher Building. One morning I paint dozens of valves of various sizes—silver dollars to dinner plates—bright orange like blooming flowers; they're almost pretty.

For a week, I paint in the electrical tunnel—a long winding corridor so narrow you can't help but rub bellies when you pass a coworker. It's windowless and dimly lit, but cool and quiet, relief from the constant thundering of the turbines. Various widths of piping run along the walls of the tunnel in between racks that house sprinkler spigots that we must prime, being extremely careful not to paint any moving parts, a serious transgression that could prevent the system from functioning. Hector painted a moving part once, which earned him a Deviation Event Report. The morning after, Arturo gathered all the painters and one by one we filed past Hector's besmirched slide bolt.

For two weeks Patrick and I are assigned to the Pump House, a small brick building atop a hill, inside the chain link fence but outside the main building, perched next to two water tanks three stories tall. Here we are sequestered, scraping floors and washing grime off the pumps before painting. To get hot water for cleaning, I must carry two buckets a hundred yards down the hill into the Primary Auxiliary Building (an oxymoron, I point out to a group of coworkers, who stare blankly), and fill the buckets from the showers in the ladies locker room inside the plant-the closest source of running water-then schlep the buckets back up the hill. In the

building that houses the pumps necessary to extinguish fires should the core melt, I cannot fill a bucket of water to mop the floor.

## LADY PAINTERS

After two months, Patrick, my confrere, trades his blue hard hat for the white ones worn by management, working as a materials expediter.[15] (Every time he passes the painters, they taunt him about the white hard hat.) So I am partnered with Angela, and thereafter we are referred to by our fellow workers as the "lady painters." My friendship with Angela develops slowly, in fifteen-minute increments sitting in the women's locker room before work. "It's been seven years since I took a punch in the face," she tells me our first day together. My chest goes numb imagining someone slamming his knuckles into Angela's heart-shaped, intelligent face, pretty despite a faint patina of *tristesse*. Angela broke the mold in the early '80s when women in the trades were rarer, enduring daily crucibles like a foreman assigning her to move fifty cans of paint from one side of the room to the other, then back again. Angela is a foreman now, though not immune to mistreatment.

One day, the union representative, Leo Lacognata, is discussing the sexual harassment policy with some workers joking about the "threefoot rule." Leo turns and bear-hugs Angela. "Hey, is this three feet? Is this sexual harassment?" he says, pinning her against the building. Angela laughs as she pushes Leo of trying to be a good sport. The men laugh. It's all a big joke, like when Leo positioned himself behind his young secretary bent over a desk and mock-humped her.

Shortly after, a manager announces at a tailgate meeting that the sexual harassment policy will be posted on the bulletin board. Angela asks him why the policy isn't distributed.

"If I hand them out, they'll just throw them away. If I read it, they'll fall asleep."

"So you'll wait for a lawsuit before you'll do anything?" Angela asks.

"Yes," the manager says.

The New York Power Authority, which owns Indian Point and eleven other power plants in the state, treats sexual harassment more seriously

than NPS. When the secretaries complain about the stares and catcalls from construction workers on break in the plant cafeteria, a wall of green tarpaulins is erected to shield the women, a kind of crude containment.

## ZOOMIES

A blue inflatable hard hat the size of a Volkswagen appears one day at the plant entrance blazoning the start of the refueling outage as it bobbles in the breeze. That morning, Bob Barrett, the highest-ranking executive on site, peptalks employees. "It's been 342 days since our last Human Performance," he says. He means Human Performance *Error*. A running tab of days without a Human Performance Error is tallied on a dry-erase board in the cafeteria. But his *faux pas* characterizes the atmosphere inside the plant while it's operating; you don't see many people working, *per se*, aside from the janitorial staff. There are no lines of workers assembling motherboards, or mechanical arms and robots fabricating widgets. Energy, the plant's product, is invisible.

Occasionally men in ties with immaculate white hard hats pass through the plant, bigwigs from the New York Power Authority or inspectors from the Nuclear Regulatory Commission. They always smile at me. It seems to warm their hearts to see a woman in the trades, as if they are responsible for the laudable diversity that I represent. Or maybe they are amused by my too big overalls and slipping-down safety glasses (protective apparel is often unavailable in small enough sizes). Or perhaps those clean, tall executives were smiling because they saw me on the day I painted a railing and then promptly leaned against it, yellow stripes across my backside broadcasting my blunder.

When the outage is scheduled to start, plant capacity is gradually reduced to ninety percent, then seventy percent, and so on. One day I arrive and it's quiet and eerie like the hour after the villagers have slain a terrible groaning dragon. After four months of adjusting to the roar of the turbines, the awesome silence seems disturbing and wrong, yet a welcome relief. We can talk in normal voices. We can remove the miniature marshmallows from our ears. And now workers are everywhere: hundreds of construction workers, engineers, Health Physics workers who

staff control points, and nuclear cleanup crews, a coterie of out-of-staters who travel between nuclear power plants during outages.

Angela and I switch to the night shift, 7:00 p.m. to 3:00 a.m., which is less hectic and cooler, especially as we work mostly in Radiologically Controlled Areas, "controlled" being the operative word. To enter a Radiologically Controlled Area, you must stop at a control point and pick up a Self-Reading Pocket Dosimeter, which resembles a small pen flashlight. When held up to a light, a hairline needle shows how many millrems of radiation you've picked up, known to workers as zoomies.[16] Next, a Health Physic hands you a ThermoLuminescent Dosimeter (TLD), assigned to you by a five-digit code. Roughly the size of a microcassette, the TLD clips onto your clothing and keeps a cumulative count of gam ma (whole body) and beta (skin exposure) radiation.

You scan your badge into a small keypad, enter your social security number, the work permit number, the baseline reading on your pocket dosimeter, and hit a "yes" button when the keypad screen asks you if you've read the work order, whether you have or not. You push through a revolving gate into a long, winding hall, ascend several sets of stairs, and access locked steel fire doors, a sequence akin to Agent 86 entering the headquarters of Control in the opening sequence of *Get Smart*.

Entering a Radiologically Controlled Area is like being in the lobby of a bank; penetrating Vessel Containment, the dome, is breaking into the vault-a steel-lined, four- to ten-foot-thick concrete shell purportedly strong enough to withstand the impact of a 727 jetliner. The reactor inside the dome is further shielded by a seven- to twelve-inch-thick carbon steel barrier. It's behind that shield that the nuclei of uranium atoms are splitting and splitting and splitting, like dominos falling, in a controlled chain reaction. It is there that the dragon is harnessed, where the Lilliputians have strung up Gulliver. A controlled chain reaction seems as oxymoronic as a beautiful nuclear power plant.

To access the dome, add to your gear a half-face respirator and a Merlin Gerin Alarming Electronic Dosimeter, which, at the push of a button, gives a digital readout of radiation dose. At a second control point, you don protective clothing, enter more codes, and unlock more turnstiles and steel doors. Finally, you step into what looks like the antechamber of a subma-

rine, an air-locked passageway with heavy steel doors at either end that a helmsman-like employee opens and closes by slowly cranking a giant metal steering wheel, Charon ferrying souls across the river Styx. You walk up a set of stairs and there you are, staring up at a ceiling that looks, perhaps, like the Sistine Chapel before Michelangelo's paint job, bowl-like, blank except for huge flakes of cream-colored paint threatening to flutter down.

Our goal is to locate the site we are to paint and work quickly to minimize radiation exposure. Angela is a genius at locating the job sites on the work order, finding the right sections within the dome, which has several levels below the 95-foot and a labyrinth of hallways and concrete sarcophagi-like cubbyholes. One night we paint a small crane the height of a giraffe that stands on three gangly legs. A young pipe fitter says to me, "I see you got that thing all painted and looking beautiful."

"I wouldn't exactly call it beautiful," I reply. After all, we're surrounded by steel and concrete.

"I think it's beautiful," the pipe fitter says.

"Beauty is in the eye of the beholder," I say. I envy his ability to see pleasing images where I see ugliness, but after a few weeks of working in the dome, I too see a kind of beauty: The curve of the ceiling is smooth and sensual; the rectangular tank in the middle of the floor, slightly smaller than a backyard swimming pool, is filled with absolutely clear turquoise-hued water that cools the zirconium rods filled with uranium pellets. The water is perfectly still and deep, calming. The giant forty-foot crane that rotates every so often on a groove that circumnavigates the floor is enormous and powerful. Size impresses. I'm a person who dreams of living in a modest hut in Maine, but I can't help being awed by the grandeur of the power plant and its workings.

Or maybe it's the lure of danger that appeals to me, though the *miseenscene* inside the dome is more surreal than perilous: workers in silly looking, oversized yellow rubber boots, yellow surgeon caps, elbow-length rubber gloves, and slack white jumpsuits, faces the only visible skin, like Teletubbies. A constant metronomical beeping, like an EKG monitor or a submarine radar detector, creates a sense of encapsulation, free-floating twenty thousand leagues under the sea or lost in space. You can forget that land is just outside.

Outside, workers stroll around the cafeteria or the smoking area in shorts and muscle shirts, breeding a peculiar intimacy. Hairy bodies, pale flesh, flabby arms, bowlegs, callused knees, freckled shoulders, birthmarks; we know each other a little better now, though not by name.

## TRANSMOGRIFICATION

I learn more about physics from painting than I recall from my high school course: gravity, friction, viscosity. Different paints have different properties. "Watch out for the red," Angela says to me. "It walks." Like no other color, red appears everywhere you don't want it to be. Before I leave the gang box one day, I have dribbled red paint on the floor, stepped in it, trailed footsteps like telltale bloodstains. That day Angela and I paint steel fire doors. The paint, no matter how thinly I apply it, puddles. I push and drag with my brush and roller, but the paint gathers itself and drips again. I wipe, brush, dab. "The paint is cold," Angela says, but I know it's a poor worker who blames her equipment.

In painting, you are attempting the impossible, trying to control or defy the substance's natural property: flow. It's a somewhat ridiculous endeavor, but satisfying when you succeed. Transformation by paint is immediate. Paint beautifies. Paint redeems. It cleans and camouflages and lies. I am never as fast as the fastest painters, but after several months I can flick my wrist in one fluid motion to create a perfect arc around a doorknob. Painting becomes a meditation, a quiet, steady motion that I get lost in, a wide-open space where I can think and dream, lying under a ganglion of pipes with a bucket of Alaska Blue. Painters call missed spots "holidays," as if you were absent while painting. It's the right word. Hypnotized by the repetitive act of brushing or rolling, your body takes over, your mind checks out. You're split in half as neatly as the nucleus of an atom.

My original plan was to work two months and pocket a few thousand, but I become addicted to the money, drawn into the plant like a fish from the Hudson. I adapt easily to different environments, a beneficial survival trait perhaps, but it means that I settle or rise to the environment around me. I begin to change on a cellular level, transmogrify into a creature I only half recognize. After two months I can lift hundred-pound bags

of coal sand for the sandblast machine. I feel strong and agile crawling behind Angela on scaffolding and underneath pipes, in tight, dark corners, somehow forgetting about my fear of heights and confined spaces.

On break, I take puffs from Angela's cigarette, one of those feminine brands, long and thin, with a purple logo. The lure of blowing hot sluggish streams of smoke, something to do between assignments, to squelch the boredom, is overwhelming. There's a natural bond among the smokers: the raw addiction to nicotine; the quasi-sexual pleasure of sucking; the perception of being outré, banished from the air-conditioned cafeteria, corralled outside by an arbitrary yellow line; the fearlessness of mocking emphysema and cancer. One wants to be part of this group.

I begin to wear makeup, investing in a stock that is valued here: conventional femininity. When some guy makes a flip remark, I retort hastily instead of blushing. I stop using words that nobody understands, like oxymoron. The foreman, Arturo, observes, "You know a lot more than these guys, but you don't use it to belittle them. That's power." Restraint is power. Control. But that's an illusion. I've lost control. The half-life of this job is already longer than I imagined, and there's work for a small crew for months to come, years maybe. I keep postponing my end-date a week at a time to collect another fat paycheck. The problem is, I haven't written anything in months. I am a painter, I fear, no longer a writer.

Finally, I select a date to quit—my six-month milestone—and stick to it.[17] On my last night, after my terminal body count for radiation, before I have punched out for the final time, Hector decorates my jeans Jackson Pollock-style. He flicks blue and red across my pants, splashes yellow and white as I rotate, then brown and seafoam green. He dips a brush into aluminum paint, which has a consistency similar to mercury (it wiggles), and spatters the canvas of my clothing using his brush like a magic wand. I drive through the security gate, past the giant hard hat now half-sunk and barely recognizable, arrive home at 4:00 a.m., and fall into bed. The next morning, I discover that the epoxy has bled through my clothes. Splotches of blue and red and faint yellow spots like old bruises stain my thighs. There's a patch of white in my hair that prematurely ages me, and on my arms, I have shiny, shimmering silver freckles.

## NOTES

1. For the previous few months, I'd been living in my mother's cottage on Cape Cod and writing a novel. I'd quit my career as a fund-raiser and was answering a customer service hotline for Papa Gino's, Inc., a chain of two hundred pizza joints. For twelve hours a week, I listened to gripes about rude clerks, cold pizza, late delivery, and once, a call from a patron who complained that he could not "stop burping and farting." The painting job is an infusion of much needed cash for Patrick, too, who for years has been squirreling around with various inventions.

2. See *The Mullet: Hairstyle of the Gods* by Barney Hoskyns and Mark Larson.

3. The test is a version of the Minnesota Multiphasic Personality Inventory, which evaluates characteristics including masculinity and femininity, cynicism (two types—misanthropic beliefs and interpersonal suspiciousness), college mal-adjustment, brooding, need for affection, ego inflation, and poignancy. The test measures dozens of other personality traits; I've only listed the ones for which I might register as abnormal.

4. The plant is shut down every two and one-half to three years to replace spent fuel rods and complete repairs in "hot" areas. The outages draw hundreds of short-term workers, increasing Indian Point's employees from approximately eight hundred to about two thousand.

5. FIRST ATOM: "Hey, I lost an electron." SECOND ATOM: "Are you sure?" FIRST ATOM: "I'm positive!"

6. The Wackenhut Corporation operates in every state and fifty countries. Revenues for the most recent twelve-month period were $2.1 billion. Their investigations division promises to "utilize the latest approaches to tell you if you have employees who are stealing, using drugs, not doing their jobs, abusing authority, engaging in discrimination or sexual harassment, committing fraud—and who they are."

7. NPS's beneficiary form asks for "wife's name." I righteously cross our "wife" and write "spouse," though I have no name to scribble there.

8. For example, ISP 3.14, Revision 0, Attachment 1, Title 5–1, 5.15–11 of the Electrical Work Practices and Procedures Book reads: "Intermediate voltage dis connecting potheads shall not be used to break or pick up load or to energize or de-energize feeder cable, feeder mains, transformers, regulators, or capacitators."

9. Hector must fill out a form to transfer me to a temporary escort, then reclaim me after. Security must fear that I, a possible subversive, will outwit Hector, locate the control room, and sabotage the plant. I must confess, every time I pass a panel of switches and knobs and flashing red buttons, I get an urge to reach out and push one.

10. Each employee steps into a portal and places her feet on two adhesive footprints—like those rubberized bathtub flowers popular years ago—and waits six seconds for a green light. This is a walk-through Explosive Vapor Detector, which operates twenty-four hours a day and can process six hundred people an hour. There are two at the security entrance. Three more will be added for the outage at a cost of about $350,000 per unit. Certain perfumes can cause the explosive detector to alarm. (A perfume can contain over a hundred ingredients, including acetophenone, also used in tear gas.) More sophisticated machines can differentiate benign substances. A Dualscan-85600 from Spyworld, Inc., can measure one part per trillion of an explosive vapor in the air. The increase in terrorist activity worldwide has spawned a competitive market for formerly classified explosive detecting technologies. One can order a Dualscan-85600 over the Internet.

11. Buckets, screens, rags, an assortment of brushes, rollers and sleeves, drop cloths, ladders, sandpaper, scrapers, drop lights and extension cords, dust pans and brushes, and bottles of Spray-Nine, an industrial cleaner, which, its label declares, kills HNr virus.

12. Or Authority Green, Alaska Blue, Spectrum Yellow, Dark Red, Albert Orange. I often wondered about the Albert in Albert Orange. When I called the paint manufacturer, Keeler and Long, a representative said, "Do you mean Alert Orange?" though he admitted that they name colors specifically for Indian Point, so the label could have been a joke on some employee named Albert. "That happens," he said, "or it could have been a misprint." Now I wonder: Was it a misprint, or was it I who was not too albert when reading the can?

13. Equipment is tied down in case of an earthquake. The plant is designed to withstand a quake with a magnitude of 7.0 on the Modified Mercalli Scale (difficult to stand, hanging objects quiver). The largest quake in the vicinity of the plant was in October 1985, a 4.0 on the mms (standing automobiles rocked, windows rattled).

14. Shortly after my employment, the New York Power Authority sold Indian Point III to Entergy, a private energy company based in New Orleans, for $967 million, the highest purchase price of a nuclear asset in the industry to date. The plant was the largest single asset of the State of New York.

15. Daily, Patrick must face surly construction supervisors demanding supplies. There is pressure to complete jobs on time, especially during the outage when the plant loses nearly a million dollars a day in revenue.

16. A millirem is a measure of the biological effects of radiation absorbed in human tissue, or greatly simplified, dose. The maximum allowable Total Whole Body Dose at the plant is 1,500 millirems less than the Nuclear Regulatory Commission's ceiling of 5,000. An average American might pick up 400 or so millirems a year from "background" radiation (rocks, soil, sun, foods, consumer products).

17. Patrick, having greater responsibility as a manager, sticks it out for another two months until the outage and his position officially end.

SARA CURTIS

❧

# Daughter of a Gun

When my father was twenty-two, he wrote number 177 on *Rolling Stone*'s list of the 500 greatest rock 'n' roll songs ever written. My father's name, Sonny Curtis, is not well known, but the song, "I Fought the Law," is. Since Bobby Fuller plucked it from B-side obscurity and made it a hit in 1964, hundreds of artists have covered it, from The Clash to Bruce Springsteen to Johnny Cash to me, once, in my twenties. At Lonnie's Western Room karaoke bar in Nashville, I confused the tempo with my father's blues version—the only version I'd ever heard him play at home—and rightly bombed.

A quick YouTube search unearths another female cover, this one by an all-woman Japanese street punk band unsubtly named Thug Murder. Pierced and clad in the universal stylings of disaffected youth, the women run through concrete city lots hurling the song like a tight fist, a screaming declaration of war—not quite the anthem of resignation I've always heard. Other than our two versions, few women have touched it. It's a masculine song, and men are drawn to it. It's a violent song, and each man who covers it stamps it with his own brand of violence. Bobby Fuller didn't rob people with the original version's "zip gun"—a crude firearm that made its rounds among 1950s teenage gangs—but rather a "six-gun." In concert, the Clash changed the line "I miss my baby and I feel so bad" to "I killed my baby and I feel so bad."

Five years ago, a historic letterpress company in downtown Nashville designed a poster commemorating my father, to advertise a show he was performing at the Country Music Hall of Fame. His manager called him after he'd seen the print.

"They put guns on your poster, Sonny," he told him. "Is that okay with you?" When my father later told me about this conversation, we both laughed, sharing the same unspoken thought. *What a silly question.*

It's no accident that my father wrote a song mythologizing guns. He hails from West Texas cotton farmers and cowboys, Dust Bowl survivors and victims of a lawless land. Guns play a crucial role in his family's mythology, as stories hinge on whether or not the protagonist had a side arm. If I begin unspooling the thread at the spot where the gun mythology was formed in my father's family, I can see the places where it looped and knotted, spinning on and on, until it reached me.

My Texan grandparents were poor, and though I didn't inherit much, I did inherit these stories. They are spoken heirlooms, subjective truths hammered out in living rooms after Sunday suppers, one brother's feelings and observations fused with the thing his sister overheard—memory as alchemy, or sculptures chiseled over time to form the contours of my family's reality. They have been told to me by my grandfather Arthur, written to me by my father, and corroborated by my father's brother, my uncle Pete. They are the stories I tell myself as I grapple with my own complicated heritage, to answer the questions of why I sit under that gun poster every night as I eat dinner with my family, and why, though I consider myself a pacifist, it inspires in me a feeling of pride.

I have two main stories to tell. Every mythology, including this one, has a genesis. The first story, the genesis story, does not contain a flood or a birth, but rather a death, a murder. The second story is one of redemption, a righting of wrongs, and the place where the myth took root in the dry West Texas dirt, alongside unending rows of cotton. Through the ages, its branches spread, sprouting habits and convictions that still exist in my family today. And on one branch, if I look closely enough, I can even see a song about a gun.

May, 1913

The house was unusually quiet when my great-grandfather Will Curtis awoke that Sunday morning, alone. The familiar morning clamor—Pearl

banging a pan onto the stove to fry the hoecakes, the children's small, hungry voices—was gone, replaced by the soft rustle of breeze through Indian grass, the raspy call of a lonesome chickadee. Throughout his life, Will would replay that day in his mind so frequently that the neural pathways became as dusty and trodden as the Arkansas backroad he called home in those days. Was his memory of the event framed by the initial stillness it shattered?

The kids were gone and his second wife Pearl was visiting family nearby. Will had the place to himself—not that the Ol' Bob Place, as it was known throughout the town, was his to begin with. He was only a tenant farmer on this scruffy patch of land in the backcountry of Paron, Arkansas. The town lies smack in the middle of the state, among the rolling hills west of Little Rock, just before the land grows thick with hardwoods ridging the flinty peaks and valleys of the ancient Ouachitas Mountains to the east. There is beauty there, though the Ol' Bob Place was just a one-mule homestead with a rickety shack, nothing much to speak of. Still, it could have been Will's soon enough, if the drought eased up and that spring's crops cooperated. Finally, he could be a landowner.

The night before, Will's ex-wife Ida had sent word that she wanted their three children to spend the night at her house a half mile up the road. One night wouldn't hurt, Will had figured. It was May, peak planting month for cotton, and he could get a lot more done without the kids underfoot. Maybe it was even good for them to see their mother every once in a while, crazy though she was. He'd agreed to let them go for one night only, and had sent seven-year-old Freeman, five-year-old Arthur, and four-year-old Etta over the hill to their mother's.

Harrowing the land with his mule and plow for hours on end that Sunday, Will must have let his mind wander to Ida's house. She and her husband Henry—a "common-law husband," according to my father—were rumored to be housing transient hillbillies, reprobates. It wasn't the kind of atmosphere he wanted his kids around, though should it keep them from seeing their mama? Will had no guideposts on this road; he was just trying to do right by his kids, better than any parent had ever done by him. Ida, on the other hand, had never made decisions with the children in mind, which is why Will had asked for custody of the kids in

the first place. She hadn't fought him on it; of course she hadn't. The only emotion she'd shown was relief.

The day wore on until suppertime, and the kids were due home. Will was outside working a stubborn patch of ground, watching for them to come over the hill. Before long, sure enough, two small figures emerged. Just two? "Whoa," he signaled the mule, steadying its chain in order to get a better look. He made out the pant legs of the boys—no sign of Etta. She'd probably stopped to pick daffodils or collect a sparkly rock. She was often straggling behind like that, distracted by God knows what, never minding instructions. Just like her mama.

"Where's Etta?" he called out when the boys reached earshot.

"Mama wants to keep her another night," Freeman answered. Arthur shuffled his feet around, unable to meet Will's disapproving eye. A sensitive boy, he felt his father's moods before they landed.

"The hell she will," mumbled Will. He chained up the mule and walked into the house. *Damn that Ida, what's she up to now?* he wondered. She never made anything easy for him. He should have known better than to take her at her word, he thought, fishing through a desk drawer for a slip of paper. On it, he wrote down a clear order: "Send Etta home."

"Freeman, run back up the hill and give this to your mama," Will said, handing over the note. Maybe he hoped the written word would carry more weight than his little boy could deliver, an official decree of sorts. Or did he have a darker premonition? Did he send Freeman because something told him that going himself would only bring trouble? Freeman did as he was told, while Arthur stayed back at the house with Will.

Before long Freeman returned, this time bearing a new note, one written in Ida's shaky scrawl. "You want Etta, you come and get her," it read. *Damn Ida.*

As Will set out to retrieve the little girl, his younger brother Dick happened to pass by on his way to Sunday evening church service. Dick was twenty-four, almost fifteen years Will's junior, and not yet married. His devotion to Christ during their mutually hungry childhood was a faith that would elude Will until later in his life. In those days, Will worshipped more immediate gods, ones foretold in his precious, dog-eared Old Farmer's Almanac: early frosts, new moons, and spring rains.

Will told Dick where he was headed, and asked his brother if he'd like to join him on the walk. Dick paused. Something about the situation made him wary. "You expectin' any trouble?" he asked Will.

"Naw," answered Will. He was telling the truth. He had decided to leave his gun at home. Dick, on the other hand, sensed a danger that Will did not. Perhaps Will was just worn down, tired of dealing with his ex-wife's folly. What kind of mother leaves her three kids to shack up with a band of hillbillies? Perhaps he thought he was used to Ida's brand of trouble by now. He was wrong.

Dusk was falling as the brothers approached Ida's house. Dick stopped under a tree about thirty yards away, perhaps still uneasy about accompanying Will to resolve such a private family matter. The moment Will touched his right hand to Ida's picket gate, the first shot rang out. The bullet struck Will in his wrist before lodging in his chest. Doubled over, he frantically scanned the house for a sign of the shooter, and there it was—the unmistakable shape of a rifle emerging from a front window. Before Dick could run to his brother's aid, Will saw a second gunman lean around the back corner of the house. He yelled for Dick to run, but it was too late. The gunman fired a bullet straight to Dick's head.

The gunmen were coming for the brothers now. Will dashed fifty yards to a nearby creek bed, where he scrambled under a downed tree, shrouded in the newly fallen darkness. He huddled there all night, his thumb stemming the bullet hole in his chest. Around midnight, he watched the long silhouettes of the gunmen pass by with their rifles as they called his name. *Come on out, Will. Here, kitty kitty,* they beckoned, their lantern light sweeping the brambles. Along the embankment above him, his brother lay dead.

Freeman and Arthur spent that night at the Ol' Bob Place alone. At some point, word of the ambush reached Ida's uncle Henry Garrett, who had remained friends with Will after the couple divorced. Garrett gathered a team and a wagon and drove to Ida's house, where they set out on a search. This time when Will heard his name called, he answered.

The search team lifted him up the hill to where Ida's house now stood empty, she and the gunmen having deserted it in the dead of night, Etta in tow, after they were unable to track down Will. The team carefully laid

him on Ida's bed and summoned Pearl, who arrived with a country doctor. The doctor removed the bullet from deep within Will's chest, then asked Pearl for her silk scarf. As the story goes, he threaded it through Will's chest and out his back, weaving it back and forth to clean the wound. Will lay on his ex-wife's bed in a laudanum fog for several days, his life still a question hanging in the air, until he was well enough to be moved back to the Ol' Bob Place.

The day after the ambush, the *Muskogee Times-Democrat* in nearby Muskogee, Oklahoma, ran an article all but pronouncing Will dead. Under the headline "Child Leads to a Killing," it read, "Henry Coburn, a young farmer, shot and killed Dick Curtis and probably fatally wounded his brother, Will Curtis, in Saline County . . . Trouble over a young child of Will Curtis and Mrs. Coburn, from whom he was divorced two years ago, caused the shooting. Coburn surrendered today, claiming self-defense."

But Will survived. Later, the doctor told the family that he was lucky to be alive on two counts: the bullet had barely missed his heart, and the cold creek water had likely clotted his blood and kept him from bleeding to death. That was the only good news. Will stayed in bed recovering for months, and by the time he was able to work again, he'd lost crucial wages that cost him the Ol' Bob Place. Among his injuries was a permanently closed right fist that he would thrust in the air to wave hello to people, much to his future grandchildren's curiosity.

Four months after the shooting, Henry Coburn was indicted on two counts: assault with intent to kill Will and the voluntary manslaughter of Dick. Whatever happened to the second gunman—the one Will saw lean around the back corner of the house and actually shoot Dick—remains a mystery.

The trial began nearly a year later, on the morning of Thursday, March 5, 1914. Henry and Ida showed up for court looking like refugees, in a covered wagon bulging with furniture, clothes, and kitchenwares, seemingly all their earthly possessions. They had something else with them too: Etta. The little girl had been staying with her mother and her uncle's accused murderer ever since the shooting.

It took less than three hours for the jury to deliver its decision. For Dick's murder, Coburn was found not guilty of voluntary manslaughter.

As for the second charge against him, assault with intent to kill Will, the court reporter's slanted longhand declared it "nol-prossed," a misspelled attempt at the Latin term "nolle-prossed." In other words, the state dropped the case.

The court adjourned for lunch. Ida walked outside and climbed into the waiting buggy, her makeshift home on wheels. Henry picked up Etta and handed the little girl to her mother. Ida held her in her lap as the couple drove away from the courthouse to start a new life in East Texas.

Will stuck it out in Paron for a few years after the trial. He moved off the Ol' Bob Place and onto a different rickety one-mule homestead. He took any tenant farming job he could find to support his family, which was growing. Two years after the trial, Pearl welcomed a new baby boy they named Alvin. But the tragedy had cast an indelible shadow on the family. In early 1918, almost four years after the trial, Will looked at the unlucky cards left in his hand and decided to fold. He and Pearl packed the boys into a covered wagon and got the hell out of Arkansas.

They headed west, like so many farm families of their time, lured by soaring agricultural prices brought on by World War I and the dream of an open range. The pilgrimage was a grueling, five-year journey of stops and starts aimed for the promised land of California. A year in, the family crossed over to Texas, and began making their way along the fabled Red River Valley. They survived on sharecropping jobs in towns along the river, settling briefly in Annona, then moving on to Quanah, named after the last great Comanche chief, Quanah Parker, though the Comanches were fifty years gone. There, Will bought some livestock and another wagon. The next year, he and Pearl welcomed a baby boy they named Kenneth, who died in infancy. The couple drove his body through a lonely stretch of pasture twenty miles east and they buried him in a cemetery near the tiny railroad town of Chillicothe. After two more years of grinding labor in Quanah, the family still had nothing to show for it. They loaded up again and headed south, the dream of California growing ever more distant.

Will had heard about the town of Lubbock, where there was rumored to be cheap, uncultivated farmland for sale. Deciding to take a chance, he and Pearl bought the boys train tickets and sent them ahead with the

family's possessions. When the family arrived in Lubbock, they saw prairie grasses and tumbleweeds for miles on end. It was raw earth, perfect land for planting cotton. Will took yet another sharecropping job until the following year, when the owner of the sprawling L7 Ranch west of Lubbock sectioned off 640 untouched acres, located in a tiny town aptly named Meadow. The L7 owner, an old gold miner from Illinois, was asking two thousand dollars for the property. Will managed to come up with half for the down payment. The year was 1925—the war was over, agricultural business was booming, and Will, finally, was a landowner.

Once in Texas, Will never again left the house unarmed. He carried two guns wherever he went: a side arm on his body, and a rifle in his car. It's unclear how much of that choice was cultural—gun carrying was more prevalent in Texas, partly because so were snakes—and how much was situational—he'd vowed never to repeat the Arkansas tragedy. What is known is that Will got into street brawls in Texas, a lot of them. His son, Arthur, my grandfather, used to say that he learned to avoid going anywhere with his father, for each time he did, he came home with "knots on his head," the after-effects of spontaneous fist fights.

The second story is about one such altercation that took place in the summer of 1925, a few months after Will acquired the farm. The family's status had been upgraded from tenant farmers to landowners, though now they were mired in cultivating the ground to plant cotton. It was West Texan ground, riddled with mesquites. Will and his boys hadn't gotten much farther than rooting them out, a punishing task that had to be done with shovels, axes, and grubbing hoes. Arthur and Freeman were the main grubbers, fated to spend decades bent under the paltry shade of those barbed canopies, digging away at the deeply interlacing roots.

After he cleared the mesquites, Will would turn over the sod. In this endeavor, he wasn't alone. Farmers throughout the Western frontier—migrants and sharecroppers and cast-offs, all turned landowners now like Will—were doing the same, ripping out the thick Texas bluestem and the rest of the native grasses. Between the years 1925 and 1930 alone, farmers plowed an area twice the size of Yellowstone National Park, 5.2 million acres. They would soon learn the error of their ways; how, without the

grass, the topsoil couldn't hold. The Dust Bowl was just around the corner, the decade where the ground became the sky.

But all that would come later. On this morning, Will and Arthur had driven to the trading post in town, and Pearl was home with seven-year-old Alvin. She looked up from her washing to see a wagonload of cowboys from the L7 ranch drive up, the previous owners of Will's farm. Will had bought the land with a fence on it, and he believed that owning the farm meant also owning the fence. The ranchers disagreed. Pearl watched as several men stepped out of the buggy and began yanking the six-foot cedar posts out of the ground.

"Alvin!" Pearl hollered for her son. "Hurry down to Brownfield and get your daddy and brothers!" The road ran eleven miles to Brownfield, but the little boy knew a shortcut and ran as the crow flies, six miles across the sun-scorched pastures. He found his father and half brother at the trading post, where he reported the news of the ranchers between desperate gulps of air. The family jumped in Will's Model T and sped back to the farm, where they found the men still tearing out the posts.

"Stay in the car with the gun, son," Will instructed my grandfather Arthur, fifteen, before he jumped out of the car and ordered the ranchers to stop removing the posts, as well as to return the ones they'd loaded up in their wagon.

"He was a scrappy old guy," my father tells it. "Not afraid of anyone."

One of the ranchers, armed with a two-by-four fence stay, charged at Will. He swung it high and landed it hard against Will's side, knocking him backward. Arthur watched from the front seat as the rancher steadied his footing and planted his legs wide, rearing back for another blow.

Arthur looked down at the .22 rifle lying on the floorboard at his feet. There was no moment to think, no choice to be made. He got out of the car and aimed it at his father's assailant. "Stop it or I'll shoot you!" he yelled. To Arthur's surprise, the rancher dropped the post. In that moment, Arthur knew that the men were unarmed. Emboldened, he took a step forward, adjusting his aim. "Now y'all do exactly as my daddy told you," he instructed, summoning a lower register in his voice. "Give him back the posts you took."

The ranchers begrudgingly unloaded their wagon as Arthur stood guard under the gaze of his father. The boys from L7 never returned.

"Would you have shot him, Daddy?" my father used to ask my grandfather.

"Well, I reckon I would have," he'd shrug.

It was hard to imagine my grandfather hurting anything other than a rattlesnake. Quiet and unassuming, he walked with shoulders permanently bowed from decades of crouching in the fields, his eyes steady on the ground two feet ahead of him, as if scanning the milkweeds in a row of cotton. At times, his mannerisms evoked a punished dog, but when he spoke, there was an unexpected levity about him. He ended most of his stories with a jokey turn of phrase and a tremulous chuckle. When I grew older and learned more about his childhood, I wondered where he got his mirth.

I've wondered other things as well. Why didn't Will have a gun on him the day he went to retrieve Etta? It seems uncharacteristically naive of him to have gone unarmed, given his later reputation for street fighting. How could he not have seen that Ida's note was a trap? Her deception is not only obvious from my privileged perch a century later; his younger brother felt it as well. *You expectin' any trouble?*

Or maybe I'm approaching Will's story backward. A better question might be: Did Will's guilt for not carrying a gun that day lay at the root of his proclivity for violence? By the time my father was a child, Will had found a religion that softened him. But in the early years after his brother's murder, did he turn combative, in the same way the bullied becomes the bully? In seeking the answer, am I, to paraphrase Joan Didion, imposing a narrative line upon disparate images? A careworn father with cotton to plant, hoping the drought eases up. A mother, hoping for another night with her daughter. A young man on his way to church, hoping to meet a girl. Three small children, already proficient at silencing their own hopes.

Will's experience in Arkansas became a story his family—my family—told itself in order to live. Each time the story was passed down, its rough edges and inconsistencies were sanded and honed, until it took on the sheen of a parable. The lesson it teaches—*A gun will protect you*—was the one Will learned that night, too late, as he lay fetal in the cold, black

creek. How he must have longed for a gun, a god, anything that could have saved him and his brother. When he emerged the next day from those frigid waters, he was baptized into a new mythology.

That mythology is the reason Arthur had the rifle at his feet when the L7 ranchers came to call. It's also the reason I recently saw a Facebook photo of my nine-year-old second cousin, posing with a toy shotgun on a playdate. His two playmates are clearly brother and sister; they have the same pudgy smiles frozen obediently for the camera. *Smile.* The siblings sit innocently at a breakfast table, the girl finishing what remains of her lunch, a half-drunk glass of milk and a grilled cheese sandwich nibbled around the crusts. My cousin's son stands behind her holding the gun, one hand gripping the barrel and the other curled firmly around the trigger. His eyes have my Grandma Violet's hooded lids; they're my father's eyes too. He glares menacingly into the camera, twisting his mouth into a mirthless tough-guy smirk.

*Well, isn't he a Curtis* was my first thought. My second was *but so am I.*

Snakes lurked everywhere on the rural Tennessee cattle farm where my parents raised me—especially copperheads, hidden under the tall timothy grass. Two pastures from our house, the Piney River gently glided over glossy brown rocks that I longed to skip, but my father deemed the path too snakey and I was only allowed to go there after he cut the grass for hay. I learned at an early age to walk through the pastures head down, ever alert for snakes with diamonds on their backs.

Down the country street we lived on, a pack of hungry dogs would cut me off if I ventured too far past where the pavement crumbled to gravel. There was a tiny stone bridge I liked to sit on there, dipping my feet into the shallow stream below and collecting sticks and acorns for my fairy house, or wild watercress for my mother's salads—if the dogs did not stand guard, that is. I never knew until I rounded the corner past an ancient country cemetery that stood on a hill opposite our pasture. My mother and I sometimes wandered through it, two grave detectives solving mysteries in the knotty etchings. Twenty steps past the headstones and

the dogs would emerge, one by one, teeth bared, ribs protruding through their mangy brown coats. I'd pivot slowly on my heel and walk calmly back to the house, *always calmly*, my father warned, *otherwise they'll give chase*. I could hear their shallow panting trailing me home, but like Orpheus leaving the underworld, I dared not turn my head.

Our farm was an encyclopedia of peril, my father its chronicler. For almost every danger, we had a gun. For the copperheads, rattlesnakes, and puff adders, we owned a slender .410 gauge shotgun with the words "Snake Charmer" printed on the barrel. A single-barrel shotgun, it only fires once before it needs reloading, so the shooter must take careful aim before firing—just right, to quote my father, "for snakes and suicides."

After I left for college, my parents sold the farm and moved to a pristine white clapboard house overlooking a less threatening road, one closer to town. The cowboys, copperheads, and wild dogs are gone, but the mythology remains. My father suffers from lifelong insomnia, and when I visit him, I wake to find the television invariably tuned to the late-night Western channel. Though he no longer lives in a Western, he still sleeps with two rifles under his bed and a snub-nosed black pistol in his bedside table. I find that most of my father's guns come complete with a story, and this pistol's is my favorite. It once belonged to a friend of my father's from his Hollywood days, a character actor best known for his role in the television show *Gunsmoke*. The man's wife had left him and their two small children to hole up with her lover in a high desert bungalow. One night, the actor showed up at my father's house, drunkenly raving that he planned to drive up there and kill them both. My father managed to wheedle the gun away from his friend before the actor drove off in a fit of rage. Soon afterwards we moved to Tennessee, and though my father never saw his friend again, he keeps the pistol in his bedside table, equal parts protection and souvenir from his youth.

My father doesn't display his guns; it's not his style to show them off. He hides them, sometimes accidentally from himself. As with any protective amulet—a crucifix or rabbit's foot—the awareness of its presence matters more than the object itself. For my father, that knowledge is vital, and enough.

Sometimes after we have dinner together, the wine blurs our boundaries

and warms our blood, and my father will lean into me. "I know you don't believe in them . . ." he'll trail off before narrowing his eyes and slowing his speech for effect, "but you should really think about owning a gun."

And so he instills the mythology that was long ago instilled in him. It isn't rote instruction. It's his truth—the truth of his experiences, and the experiences of those who came before him. My truth is different. I suppose I followed in the footsteps of my Wisconsin-born mother, a stranger to his Texan lore. Now that I too am a mother, one raising children in the wake of Columbine and Sandy Hook, my terrain is fraught with terrors hidden like the copperheads in the timothy grass—only on paths I can't avoid, or arm myself against.

For now, the guns I own are made of paper: two tawny letterpressed revolvers, framing my father's name on his commemorative poster. It hangs above my dining table where my husband and I nightly feed our family, spinning more peaceful mythologies for our children to keep or discard as they choose. Sometimes my eyes rest upon those six-guns, and for a split second, I hear a gunshot drumbeat, like the pounding heartbeat of a frightened teenage boy, forever frozen in time. He is watching through the windshield as the rancher raises the fence post, as his father cowers, unarmed. It's time for him to make his debut.

DANIEL W. LEHMAN

# Proper Names Are Poetry in the Raw
## *Character Formation*
## *in Traumatic Nonfiction*

"Proper names are poetry in the raw. Like all poetry they are untranslatable."
**W. H. AUDEN** | from *A Certain World: A Commonplace Book,* 1970

As literary nonfiction has shouldered its way into the longstanding generic trinity of fiction, poetry, and drama, writers and theorists have argued about what sorts of allegedly truthful narratives quality as nonfiction. A few years ago, these intermittent squabbles about classification broke into open war with the publication of *The Lifespan of a Fact,* in which essayist John D'Agata, a professor in the University of Iowa nonfiction writing program, sparred with an exacting fact-checker named Jim Fingal, who was probing the facticity of D'Agata's essay about teenager Levi Presley's suicidal plunge from the observation deck of the Stratosphere Tower in Las Vegas. Their debate ranged from the mundane to the vital. For example, D'Agata admitted that he changed the color of a pink dog-grooming van to purple, explaining, "I needed the two beats of purple, so I changed the color. I don't think it's that big a deal" (39). More seriously, D'Agata conceded that he altered the actual suicide of an unrelated Las Vegas victim from jumping to hanging "because I wanted Levi's death to be the only one from falling that day. I wanted his death to be more unique" (18). Ultimately, Fingal proved that many of the surreal events that D'Agata

said happened the day that Levi Presley died did not, in fact, happen at all—or at least not the way that D'Agata had essayed.

Challenged on these points, the Iowa nonfiction professor protested: "I'm tired of this genre being terrorized by an unsophisticated reading public that's afraid of accidentally venturing into terrain that can't be footnoted and verified by seventeen different sources" (22). An exasperated Fingal was moved to respond: "Basically it sounds like you're saying that an essayist can write things with arbitrary truth value and make quotations out of whole cloth that are attributed to real people in the real world. Is that right? And if so, isn't that what people call fiction?" (53). And so the debate was on. One *New York Times* review called D'Agata "a fight-spoiling dodobrain" and added, "[J]ust trying to sneak and bully his work into magazines is a disingenuous strategy; it borrows the prestige of a credibility he forsakes" (Lewis-Kraus). Another charged that D'Agata "shimmies too close to the flame. In pursuing his moral questions, he plays fast and loose with a verifiable historical date, one involving a kid's suicide. He does this just for the sake of a tight narrative hook. . . . [I]t damages the moral authority of D'Agata's voice, which is his narrative's main engine" (Bock).

Perhaps the most perceptive response came from Salon.com's senior writer Laura Miller, who argued that D'Agata's and Fingal's set-to in *The Lifespan of a Fact* "is a travesty of the fact-checking process." She noted: "Any lingering impression that Fingal is a put-upon toiler in the boiler room of journalism dissolves as he introduces more and more tedious digressions and unfunny wisecracks into an ever-burgeoning pissing match." In fact, D'Agata and Fingal *had* staged and embellished much of the argument that became *The Lifespan of a Fact*, disclosing as much in an interview with Weston Cutter on his *Kenyon Review* blog. D'Agata called the book-long debate over the facts of Levi Presley's death "a bit of a reconstructed performance" while Fingal revealed that his six months of part-time fact-checking were inflated in the book to an increasingly obsessive seven-year debate with D'Agata. Yet, to his credit, D'Agata seemed to understand that their discourse—even if substantially staged— did foreground some essential peculiarities about what we commonly call

creative nonfiction, literary essays, or narrative journalism. By whatever name, this form of nonfiction is intertwined with the characters, events, and memories that precede the written text. Uncovering the deep relationship between sources and texts—particularly when real names are used—explodes more formalist notions of writing style. "[A]s embarrassed as I was by what Jim had revealed, I was dazzled by his thoroughness," D'Agata told Cutter. "He was as obsessed with nailing down the facts of the essay as I was with the rhythm and imagery and what-not."

Beyond those sorts of insights, the entire discourse—which threatened to devolve into a post-structural inside joke and ultimately created its fifteen minutes of buzz in the literary universe—did seem to confirm some of its critics' worst fears. And to think that you, oh dear reader, were moved by the spat, that you ever believed it actually concerned the tragic facts of a sixteen-year-old's life and how to write truthfully about such a loss.

On this occasion, I want to rekindle our desire for the complex truth of a written life. To do so, I wish to refocus our attention to what I believe matters about nonfiction, particularly nonfiction about trauma. I would never argue that facts don't matter in nonfiction (I'm as offended as anyone by people who make things up and pass it off as truth). Yet I hope to prove that what really counts is the tangible human presence outside the text that competes with the nonfiction character inside the text.

Technical arguments about what can or cannot be done in nonfiction hit dead ends because they normally are obsessed by the *taxonomy* of narrative rather than by its *power*. Therefore, ostensibly nonfictional texts about private events, especially when names are altered or obscured, turn out to be largely indistinguishable from fiction. The genre distinction in these cases depends mostly on the author's goodwill promise to live up to some standard of factualness. So when "facts" inside the nominally nonfiction text cast little or no shadow on the world outside the text, the traditional generic boundary largely becomes a distinction without a difference. What really counts, I would argue, is not a safe realm of generic certainty, but the dead reckoning of nonfiction's potential ability to affect actual lives. And much of that power derives from what W. H. Auden has called, in another context, the raw poetry of a name. Precisely because real names leak over the edge of text in nonfiction, their enactment

eludes the final control of author, character, or reader. Three texts—Richard Hoffman's memoir *Half the House* (2005), Terri Jentz's testimonial investigation *Strange Piece of Paradise* (2006), and Eli Sanders's "The Bravest Woman in Seattle," a harrowing piece of literary journalism that won the 2012 Pulitzer Prize—will help me reveal in varying ways how names and naming matter, particularly in testimonial nonfiction about memory and trauma.

Hoffman sets the stage for our discussion in an author's note heading his memoir *Half the House*. "This is not a work of fiction," he writes. "It contains no composite characters, no invented scenes. I have, in most instances, altered the names of persons outside my family. *In one instance, on principle, I have not*" (emphasis added). The unaltered name is that of Tom Feifel, Hoffman's sandlot football and baseball coach in Allentown, PA. Hoffman's book reveals that Coach Feifel molested and raped the then ten-year-old Hoffman, luring him with pornographic slides and 8 mm movies. "I wanted to cry but I didn't dare," the author recalls of one episode. "I bent over with my arms folded over my belly, pretending to watch the ballgame. Why was I unable to understand what was going on? The more I learned, the more confused and ashamed I became" (53). What the ten-year-old learns is that "sex was sinister, clandestine, hot, and universal. I may have even known that my childhood was over" (53–54). Much later in the memoir, a now-adult Hoffman confronts his own father over physical abuse (being punished by his dad with a belt or slotted spatula) as well as the father's failure to protect him from the coach/predator Tom Feifel. In this written scene, Hoffman's father looks away, "his mouth hanging open, tears rolling down his face." Hoffman presses on: "I have more to say, Dad. I didn't come here to hurt you. Thirty years ago I stopped telling you the truth. I couldn't. Now I have to, and it hurts like hell, but I have to tell it and you have to listen" (111–12).

What follows is an astonishing interchange about "what happens to a little boy's soul" (119) when he is raped by a man like Tom Feifel. The son's anger and the father's culpability emerge truthfully and unflinchingly within a painful discourse of fact and implication that reveals the insufficiency D'Agata's and Fingal's staged dialogue to get at the real power and dangers of truth-telling. To the narrative taxonomists, I would

proffer that it may not really matter so much if Hoffman recounts each and every word of this long-ago confrontation, but that he and his father are alive, named, on the record, and that the criminal presence of the accurately labeled Tom Feifel hovers over them like an oily cloud. Facts are adduced, names are named, and responsibility is pinned and accepted.

Ultimately, the book's publication with Feifel's name set off a chain of events spurred by Hoffman's father, who made sure that someone associated with the youth organization where Feifel was now coaching saw the book and sought out the families of vulnerable lads. "It was the decision, on principle, not to change the name Tom Feifel that proved to be fateful," Hoffman writes in an afterward to a new edition of the book. "There was simply no reason to protect him. I did not foresee anything like what happened" (180). What happened is that more and more boys and families came forward; this time the law stopped winking at Feifel (as had twice happened in earlier decades), and he was prosecuted, convicted, and imprisoned. Feifel died in prison a day after a Dateline NBC report about the case. "The death certificate says heart failure" (195), though Hoffman has his doubts.

The lasting power of Hoffman's testimonial memoir—as elegantly written and shaped as any modern novel—astonishes even its author. "No one, however, taught me more about the power of the written word than an 11-year-old boy named Michael," he writes in his afterward. "He was one of four boys selected by the district attorney from among many more to testify against Feifel" (189). After Feifel's conviction, Hoffman telephoned the youngster, essentially a doppelgänger of the boy Hoffman had been when Feifel had attacked him. Michael tells the memoirist: "I mean thanks for, you know, for writing the book. You made it stop" (190).

Testimonial nonfiction, therefore, not only *reflects* but may directly alter history precisely because of the power of nonfictional identity and naming to leak outside the written text, as it did with Tom Feifel's name. A second example, Terri Jentz's *Strange Piece of Paradise*, illustrates an opposite flow: the power of extra-textual discourse to overwhelm an author's management of names and identity within her narrative. Anchored by far more detailed fact-gathering and reporting than is Hoffman's book, Jentz's testimonial memoir concerns the June 22, 1977, attack on her and

a female companion at a campground in Cline Fall State Park near Red-mond, OR. Cycling across the United States while Yale undergraduates, the two young women were sleeping at the Oregon state park when a pickup truck drove over them and its driver attacked them with an axe. Names are crucial here, as in Hoffman's book. Promising the reader that she has "checked and cross-checked facts" and included no "probable" dialogue (539), Jentz then addresses naming:

> I have changed many names and some minor details to guard privacy. Not everyone wants to be under public scrutiny, and this is under-standable. Changing names does not compromise the veracity of the whole. Most specifically, I have changed the name of the alleged perpetrator. The reason I have done so is that I do not want to feed into the cult of celebrity granted by this culture to charismatic vil-lains. (539)

And so she pens an alliterative pseudonym, "Dirk Duran," for her attacker, which fairly closely mirrors the alliterative real name of the man who she believes slashed her and left her for dead at the campground in 1977. Jentz's meticulous search for "Dirk Duran"—commencing some fifteen years after the attempted murder and spanning more than a decade—builds over a riveting five-hundred-plus pages in Jentz's book and culmi-nates in a series of confrontations between Jentz and "Duran." Read as a series, the scenes enact a struggle over the power of the gaze and, indeed, for narrative meaning itself. In the first scene, Jentz rigorously controls the surveillance as she spies on "Duran" when an acquaintance maneu-vers him into a restaurant where Jentz is sequestered. "Dirk looked up, cocked his head, and his light blue eyes met mine for a space of a second," Jentz writes. A few moments later, "I sat sideways in my booth. I had a box seat now. He was only five feet from me. I felt my heart race, but not from fear. I felt not a quiver of terror. I waited for a sensation arising from my past" (361). At the time, "Duran" knows that someone may be interested in that long-ago crime, but does not yet know it is Jentz or the extent to which she will haunt his life. His once-quarry essentially has become his tormentor.

The two next meet in a courtroom for an unrelated witness tampering

and weapons case in which "Dirk Duran" is the defendant. Jentz high-lights the axe-inflicted scars on her arms with lipstick and first watches "Duran" from a row close behind him. "I savored the leisure to watch him for hours, drill holes into the back of his head with my eyes. I thought, I'm feeling good here in my boots observing my prey. Strong and calm." During a recess, "Duran" rises and ambles back into the courtroom so that he can in turn eye Jentz. She is ready for him. "I felt his eyes. I rolled up the left sleeve of my denim shirt . . . landing my scarlet scar just in front of his eyes. A few pregnant minutes passed in this pose. I willed my scar to show its savagery. I imagined it springing to life, a fresh cut" (474). Clearly, through her narrative, its imagery, and its arrangement in her words, Jentz reasserts some of the power and autonomy that her attacker robbed from her and her companion in that long-ago Oregon campground. The scene culminates with a dramatic stare-down that reinforces Jentz's agenda: "[T]hen a moment came—I knew it would—when he looked back over his shoulder and we locked eyes. I stared back at him with confidence and an attitude of dominance. . . . His eyes were like two empty holes in a mask . . . I held his gaze steady. He looked away" (475).

A careful reader of *Strange Piece of Paradise* cannot help but con-clude that Jentz's reporting has solved the attempted murder case that the authorities had bungled more than two decades before. Although Oregon's statute of limitations for attempted murder had long since run out (a statutory loophole that Jentz's case helped to overturn, but which could not be retroactively applied to her case), she gains some measure of actual revenge by seeing "Duran" found guilty of coercion and a serious weapons charge at the end of the trial. "That outcome loosed in me a relief so deep that my menses started to flow," she writes. The two lock eyes once more as "Duran" is led from the courtroom. When he is gone, "I burst into tears, leaned over and covered my face. I could feel hands, many sets of [comforting] hands on my back" (483). Yet her story's impli-cations do not fade as the author and her character, the once-victim and her would-be killer, wrestle for identity and control inside and outside the text. On the twenty-year anniversary of her attack, the author goes public with her evidence against "Duran" and begins to feel "the weight of responsibility" to the man/character she has reported and created. "I

felt locked into mortal combat with him. I was under his control, in his hands, totally vulnerable, exposed on all fronts. Skinned alive" (489). Friends take her to a tiny inn across the mountains in coastal Oregon where she can calm down. "Then as suddenly as it began, the spell broke. I rejoined the present, calmed down, drove into the desert again" (489) toward Redmond, OR.

While it is easy to see how Terri Jentz's narrative trajectory is working—even in this brief discussion of her nearly 550-page book—the special power of nonfiction ultimately bursts from its covers and reverses its gaze on the author. Working from the case facts that Jentz had unearthed and published—and combining them with the protected court records of the unrelated case—a CNN report broadcast on May 9, 2006, disclosed that "Duran's" real name was Dick Damm and that "the nickname Dick Damm the hatchet man came out almost immediately" in town gossip after Jentz and her companion were attacked at the campground ("Survivor"). Thus, Jentz's narrative control over Damm's identity was breached despite her attempts to manage the character's name with a pseudonym. Chillingly and somewhat ironically, the man we now know as Dick Damm was released from custody the day before Jentz was scheduled to read from *Strange Piece of Paradise* at an Oregon bookstore less than twenty miles from Redmond. "I had three deputy sheriffs and one retired member of the state police protecting us," the author said in a later interview (Cook).

Though no further menacing encounters have been reported between the author and her character/attacker, the case of *Strange Piece of Paradise* in this and many other instances (for instance, the ramifications of Jentz's decision to change the name of her young female companion on the cycling trip) easily demonstrates the power of nonfiction to implicate author, character, and reader in ways that dwarf similar encounters even in roman à clef fictional narrative. And at the core of that transaction, I would contend, are decisions regarding naming, truth, identity, and disclosure.

A third narrative of deep trauma, the 2012 Pulitzer Prize winner for literary reporting, further complicates and culminates this discussion of the complexity and power of naming in nonfiction. Like Hoffman's *Half the House*, the Pulitzer winner is a riveting testimonial of violence and sexual abuse, though it is less reflective and more immediate in that

it was produced from the courtroom reporting of Eli Sanders for the Seattle alternative weekly *The Stranger*. And like Jentz's *Strange Piece of Paradise*, a character's actual name breaks out of the narrative beyond the original intent of the author, though for different reasons. Sanders' article/essay, "The Bravest Woman in Seattle," stems from a rape and murder case in Seattle's South Park district, in which a lesbian couple was brutally attacked during a home break-in that left one of them dead. As we have seen, narratives of this sort normally include some author's note or aside about naming: "[O]ut of respect to her wishes, *The Stranger* is not publishing her name," (2) Sanders writes of the surviving woman who testified at the trial. In withholding the name Sanders follows standard journalistic procedure for cases involving sexual assault, though he and other reporters did disclose the name of her companion because she is now deceased. Still, while he protects the survivor's identity, Sanders exposes her emotions, the facts of her case, and its impact on her life and future.

In part, Sanders manages this effect by building an indirect spoken voice for the rape survivor free of the enclosure of quotation marks or actual courtroom testimony. "This happened to me. You must listen. This happened to us. You must hear what was lost. You must hear what he did. You must hear how Teresa [her companion] fought him. You must hear what I loved about her. You must know what he took from us. This happened" (2). In this manner, Sanders can render what he believes to be the actual emotions of the survivor with direct quotes even though the survivor had tailored her actual words to fit within the more conventional discourse of prosecutorial questioning and witness response. Thus, the survivor's defiant mind provides a conceptual framework for the truth of what happened, some of it too horrifying to recount here. Generally, Sanders tips these moments of indirect testimony with signal phrases ("as if to say"), which disclose a deeper emotional truth than anything the survivor may have testified directly. One of these moments recalls the emotions of Terry Jentz in *Strange Piece of Paradise*, both women scarred, but unbowed. Sanders writes in his character's inner voice: "[F]or all of you who are looking, the four slashing scars that run from below my left ear toward my throat, the scars from when the man cut and stabbed me with his knife. I am not scared. I have nothing to hide here. Not anymore" (3).

Now a fact checker such as Jim Fingal (whether reenacted or on the actual job) would find no such words within the trial transcript, and he and other generic taxonomists thus might be tempted to dismiss Sanders's narrative strategy as at least quasi-fictional. But what counts in the way I read nonfiction is that Sanders implicates himself by the testimonial quality of his publicly available story, specifically by the risk that his character might step outside his written text and contradict him in real life, (*I did not say that*, she might claim. *I would never say that*.) Therefore, the inner/outer relationship of character and construction, and the potential struggle over voice and meaning, matters much more than safely factual certainty. In signaling that a real person lies behind the protagonist of his story, Eli Sanders seems careful to endow her with humanity, even though he withholds her name. In his story, he paints the tender real-life details of the survivor and her deceased companion. They grill steaks together, join Weight Watchers, share dreams, hope to open a movie theater/bistro named the Reel Café, and plan a commitment ceremony that will seal their love for one another.

When they awaken in the middle of a warm summer evening to a naked intruder, one Isaiah Kalebu and his hunting knife, the narrative turns brutal, though Sanders mostly shields his readers from the most horrific details. Instead, he describes the reactions that her testimony (of rape, sodomy, and almost unimaginable violence and degradation) produces in the courtroom. "The horror of what happened next made the court reporter's eyes well up, made the bailiff cry, had the whole room in tears," he reports. "The jury handed around a box of tissues. The prosecutor took long pauses to collect himself. The family and friends in the courtroom cried (though, truth be told, they had been crying throughout). The *Seattle Times* reporter seated next to me cried. I cried. The camerawoman who was shooting video of all the television stations in town cried" (6).

Ultimately, Sanders's decision to render the emotional truth of his protagonist—in essence to deduce what was on her mind and to form the words that relayed her deepest emotion—leads him, however subtly, into the realm of imaginative literature, but not, I would argue, into fiction. As I have maintained throughout this essay, his narrative is anchored by and even competes with the actual presence of a woman, her testimony,

and the events outside his text. Simply put, if she disagrees with his interpretation, she can show him up. The events he recounts are too public and too detailed. He cannot finally silence her in this narrative any more than her attacker could silence her actual testimony in the courtroom. As compellingly created and realistically envisioned as a fictional character might be, a fictional character normally cannot escape the text in quite the same way: hence the implications and power of nonfiction that builds actual characters and recounts public events.

As it happens, the rape survivor in this case *did* talk back, *did* disclose her name, and *did* reclaim her story. Published by *The Stranger* two months after Sanders' Pulitzer-winning piece, her essay, "I Would Like You to Know My Name," is remarkably candid and deliberately anchors her textual identity in actuality. "My name is Jennifer Hopper, and I am the survivor of the South Park attacks of July 19, 2009," it begins. "My family calls me Jenny. My friends call me Jen. And my late partner, Teresa Butz, often called me J-Hop." Why would Hopper breach the veil of anonymity that had been so scrupulously protected by Sanders and other journalists? Simple: "I no longer want to give the impression that I'm afraid to be known, or that I might be ashamed of anything that happened that night. I am not afraid. I am not ashamed. I am still here."

Like Hoffman and Jentz, Jennifer Hopper thereby reasserts control of her own story, snatches it from the predator, and reverses the ability of abuse to define her. And, as it happens, in this case Hopper finds Sanders and his Pulitzer-winning nonfiction to be her ally, not an impediment: a conduit to her inner truth. "His writing brought humanity to my personal horror," Hopper writes. "And I will always be grateful to have been interpreted by his honest voice." Yet what makes nonfiction special is that Sanders could not guarantee her reaction. All he could do was bet on his own honesty and talent. Hopper could have contradicted him, exposed him, shamed him. What sets nonfiction apart is that these sorts of characters in literary nonfiction can talk back to their authors, can endorse them or undercut them. Writers and characters become living partners and/or contestants in the production of historical meaning.

Interestingly, for all the sometimes-contrived squabble over the "truth" of Levi Presley's death, fact-checker Jim Fingal did fairly accurately

describe this sort of author/character transaction. "You are writing what will probably become the de facto story of what happened to Levi," he reminded D'Agata, "and so, every detail you choose to do that with will become significant, because your account will be the one account anyone is ever likely to read about him" (107). Moreover, Presley's death had silenced him in a way that Hoffman, Jentz, and Hopper have not been silenced—though any number of Presley's family members or acquaintances could contest D'Agata's depictions. For his part, when confronted with the powerful implications I have been tracing in this essay, D'Agata in his own words seemed to slip into the safe harbor of studied narrative indeterminacy despite his often stunning prowess as a wordsmith. "Now, is it crass to call a dead boy [Levi Presley] whom I never knew an 'idea'?" he asked his interlocutor and fact-checker Fingal. "Probably. But would it be better to call him a 'subject'? A 'character'? He is going to be 'used'—or 'defiled,' as you put it—the moment he's written about" (118).

Yes, he will.

The lasting implications of testimonial nonfiction set in motion all these possibilities. No one who has honestly reported and written about tragedy or scandal—and understood the power and responsibility of real names and details—would argue otherwise. Yet, when faced with the bracing specter of that responsibility, D'Agata ponders a solution that would sidestep these implicating questions and that reveals perhaps more than he intended: "So maybe the most ethically appropriate thing for me to have done is to have completely made up a suicide victim so that I could use him however I wished" (108). As Jim Fingal already had noted elsewhere in the dialogue, the name for that sort of narrative sidestep is *fiction*. One need not insist on a reductive binary classification to note that the "completely made-up suicide victim" would thus evade the sort of implicated reporting and naming that I have traced here through the nonfictional examples of Richard Hoffman, Terri Jentz, and Eli Sanders. At the conclusion of *The Lifespan of a Fact*, after the combatants have agreed to disagree and after John D'Agata has discounted "moral responsibility in nonfiction" (111) and sought solace in "a better work of art—and thus a better and truer experience for the reader—than I could have [written] if I'd stuck to the facts" (112), the somewhat wistful fact-checker Jim

Fingal cannot seem to shake the power of the human life behind their story—anchored by the power of a name. And to the extent that the book becomes an artful dialogue over fact and meaning, his partner D'Agata probably also understands that power at some level.

After all, the author and fact-checker of *The Lifespan of a Fact* ultimately give to Fingal the last word in the book they have contrived together: "[E]ven if I could definitively determine to the fraction of a second exactly when it was that Levi left his house and from how high it was that he jumped, and in what direction the wind happened to be blowing," Fingal muses, "and how hard and at what temperature and whether there was dust or not when he dove off the tower at 6:01:53 p.m. and plummeted for a total of 8 seconds onto a sidewalk of brown-brick herringbone . . . well, then . . . I don't know. I'd have done my job. *But wouldn't he still be dead?*" (123, emphasis added).

Exactly.

Ultimately, the fact checker seems to understand that the material presence of Presley's body and name fuels the narrative power that outwits the artificial divisions of factual taxonomy. And Jennifer Hopper, the survivor in Eli Sanders' Pulitzer-winning literary journalism, seems ultimately to rejoice in that very power in the responding essay where she reclaims her own name. "Yes, this happened," Hopper exclaims. "This happened and Teresa is dead. This happened and I somehow made it to the other side. It's a very strange place to be . . . All I can say is that I think there is tremendous power in testifying, in saying, 'This happened to me.'"

Therein lurks what may be the truest power of nonfiction—writing that dares disturb the universe with the raw poetry of a name.

## WORKS CITED

Bock, Charles. "American Wasteland." NYTimes.com. *The New York Times,* 28 Feb. 2010. Web. 29 Jan. 2013.

Cook, Emily. "An Interview with Terri Jentz." Bookslut.com. *Bookslut,* Aug. 2006. Web. 30 April 2012.

Cutter, Weston. "Doubling Down: An Interview with John D'Agata and Jim Fingal." Kenyonreview.org. *Kenyon Review Blog,* 23 Feb. 2012. Web. 29 Jan. 2013.

D'Agata, John, and Jim Fingal. *The Lifespan of a Fact*. New York: W. W. Norton, 2012. Print.

Hoffman, Richard. *Half the House*. Morehead, MN: New Rivers, 2005. Print.

Hopper, Jennifer. "I Would Like You to Know My Name." *The Stranger*. n.p. 10 Aug. 2011. Web. 31 Jan. 2013.

Jentz, Terri. *Strange Piece of Paradise*. New York: Farrar, Straus, and Giroux, 2006. Print.

Lewis-Kraus, Gideon. "The Fact Checker Versus the Fabulist." NYTimes.com. *The New York Times*, 21 Feb. 2012. Web. 29 Jan. 2013.

Miller, Laura. "In Defense of Fact Checking." Salon.com. Salon Media Group, 9 Feb. 2012. Web. 29 Jan. 2013.

Sanders, Eli. "The Bravest Woman in Seattle." *The Stranger* 20:41 (2011): 1–8. Print.

"Survivor of Hatchet Attack Confronts the Past." Transcripts. CNN.com, 9 May 2006. Web. 30 April 2012.

JERALD WALKER

❧

# Captain Love

From the time my siblings and I were very young, our blind parents taught us to assist them in ways they could not assist themselves. So we accompanied them grocery shopping. We read their mail. We sat next to them in theaters and whispered what we saw on the screen. We told them when they were wearing porn. They did not wear porn often, as far as I know, and it could be that our mother never wore it at all. Perhaps our father wore it only once. All I know for certain is that he arrived home from work one day so wet from a summer storm that his white dress shirt had turned transparent, revealing his T-shirt beneath, on which was a picture of a naked man and woman.

At first I thought the couple was wrestling, with the man having pinned his smaller opponent to the floor. *No,* I concluded, *this is something else.* I closed my comic book, rose from the couch, and moved toward my father to get a better look, and my father, blind since the age of twelve, the age I was at the time, asked who was there. By then I understood what the couple was doing. I also understood that my father had mistakenly put on my eighteen-year-old brother's T-shirt and that, if this mistake were made known, my father would explode.

The last time my father exploded was three months earlier, on a late afternoon in March. There was precipitation that day as well: large droplets of freezing rain that pelted us as we walked along 79th Street, arguing about my new shoes. The shoes were in the box I carried under the arm opposite the one my father held, and at issue was the fact that they weren't the current fashion. They were flats like my father's, like every-

one's father's, I suspected—the footwear of old men and of nerds. I *was* a nerd, it is true, but the growth spurt I was experiencing included not only my body but also my sense of who I was and of what I might become. I might become cool, it had recently occurred to me, but for that to happen I needed platform shoes. My older siblings wore them, as did most of my friends, as did Don Cornelius and the *Soul Train* dancers. "When you're a dancer on *Soul Train*," my father responded to this last point, "I'll buy you platform shoes. Better yet, I'll buy you *stilts*." He laughed, and I regret that I did not simply laugh with him. Instead, I led him off the edge of the curb, where his feet plunged into the four inches of slush that, at the last moment, I had cleared with a short leap. My father shoved me aside, telling me to get away from him, although later, when we were home, he called me back. I found him in his bedroom, removing his belt. He ordered me to lower my pants and bend over. The pain on my backside lasted two days. But despite the heavy price I paid, I have not forgiven myself for what I did. I never will.

But my father forgave me. He forgave all of his children for our transgressions, the many violations of his and our mother's trust that provided a counterbalance to our assistance, like how we gathered our vegetables in our hands during dinner and, under the pretense of getting more milk, dumped them behind the refrigerator; how we kept our lights on in our bedrooms well after lights-off time; how we tiptoed into the kitchen to sneak cookies; how when told to turn off the television, we put it on mute; and how, if we were in the front of the house playing a particularly captivating game beyond our curfew, we remained silent as our father stood on the porch, his hands cupped to his lips, calling our names—transgressions we might have gotten away with if lights and televisions did not hum, vegetables did not rot, neighbors did not snitch, if cookies ate themselves. But sometimes we were so guilt-ridden that we voluntarily confessed our crimes. And sometimes, feeling mischievous, as I was that late afternoon when my father came home wearing porn, we threw each other under the bus.

"Who's there?" he asked again.

"It's me," I said.

"Hi, Jerry," he responded. "Really coming down out there." He set his briefcase on the floor before folding his cane and putting it in the closet. "I'm soaked."

"Right down to your T-shirt," I noted.

"And to my socks." He knelt and began unlacing his shoes. "As soon as I left work it started and it hasn't stopped since."

My father was a high-school teacher. His school was an hour and a half away by public transportation—a trip that required two subway trains, a bus, and a three-block walk. During the course of his return commute, he must have encountered hundreds of people. What had they thought upon seeing him? I wondered. That he was a hippie? A swinger? A madman? An undercover cop? Had they scampered to get away from him, as people often do when a blind person approaches, or had they, like me, moved closer to get a better look?

"How was the trip?" I asked.

"Long," he said. His shoes were off now. He turned and walked through the living room, navigating the furniture as if by sight. I followed him, stifling a giggle.

"Anything . . . you know . . . um . . . *bizarre* happen along the way?"

The question must have struck him as odd, if not because it was odd then because of the halting way I delivered it. He paused and faced me. We were in the hall, his bedroom just to his left. I could hear my mother's voice carry from the bedroom's opened door as she talked on the phone. "No," he responded. "Why do you ask?"

"Well . . . your T-shirt's sort of . . . visible."

"And?"

"There's a picture on it."

"A picture? A picture of what?"

"A man," I said. "And a woman."

"Who are they?"

"I don't know."

"What are they doing?"

I hesitated, trying to think of the most delicate way to break the news. My father lost his patience. "*What are they doing?*" he demanded.

I said, "Making love."

I could not recall having ever spoken those words before, but in that age of Motown and Rhythm & Blues I surely must have sung them. It was such a beautiful phrase, I believed, one associated with tenderness and caring, and that made the contrast between it and my father's reaction all the more stark. He swore and began removing his dress shirt, fumbling with the buttons before giving up midway and yanking the remaining ones free. When the shirt was off and balled at his feet, he snatched the T-shirt over his head so violently it tore, which set in motion a tearing frenzy. By the time he went into his bedroom, the culprit lay on the floor in quarters. I picked them up and threw them away, smiling at the thought of my brother's fate, though not yet knowing that, despite my father's rage, he would one day forgive this too. I went back to my comic book, and while I can't remember who was on its cover, I sometimes imagine it was my father—stance wide and hands on hips as he rode the bus in his pornographic T-shirt, and his eyes, functioning now, scanning the faces of the commuters, taking in their wonder that he—Captain Love, the world's greatest superhero—was actually there.

JILL CHRISTMAN

# Going Back to
# Plum Island

The decision to return to the island began with the dreams. Ted was back, and this time he hadn't come just for me. He was after my nine-year-old daughter Ella.

Part of me had always known this would happen.

In my twenties and thirties I had tried to write Ted, if not into complete obliteration, then at least into insignificance. Here are the facts: as close as I can align the memories and the photographs with the markers of time—birthdays, moves, my mother's sequential boyfriends and waitressing jobs—Ted molested me, regularly and sometimes violently, from the time I was six or seven until age twelve, when the arrival of my period and the fear of pregnancy scared me so much I finally made him stop. I locked myself in the only room with a phone and I hissed through the crack that I would tell if he didn't stop. I would call my mother at the restaurant if he didn't stop.

And he did. He stopped.

Was it that easy?

Ted was our neighbor and a regular fixture in our home—seven years older than me and twice my weight. He carried his wallet on a chain and a folded knife in the pocket of his saggy jeans, which is the feature I remember most about Ted's body. He had no hips, no ass, nothing to hold up his pants, and so he wore a thick, brown belt with a buckle he'd forged himself (it had something menacing on it—a serpent? a skull and crossbones?), cinched tight on the bones of his pelvis. When I think of

Ted physically, I see two things: first, his hands, which were never clean because of the work he did on engines. Even there, I *feel* the hands more than I see them, sandpapering the soft skin of the child's body I inhabit in deep memory, scratching audibly across the denim of my overalls—and in close-up, the black whorls of his fingerprints, as if he'd come, every time, from a booking at the station.

And I see him walking away. I think this is from all the times he'd cross the sandy field between his garage and our house, a straight view from my bedroom window, and I would hide in my room while he knocked on the front door, hide without breathing, a rabbit in the grass, and then, when I thought it was safe, I would peek out from the lower edge of my window.

I wanted to watch him go.

I don't know how tall Ted was, but he loomed, a shambling Lurch from *The Addams Family*, shoulders hunched forward, pants hanging in a straight line from his belt down to his dirty sneakers, long legs moving in pendulum swings across the sand. He could cross a lot of ground with what appeared to be very little effort. Is there such a thing as an ambling lope? A stride both low-energy and efficient? Yes, I think so. This is the locomotion of a wolf, or a big cat—a predator.

Watching Ted walk away in memory, I see the animal in him, and from this perspective, and the supposed safety of over thirty years, I can almost find a fragment of empathy. He looks so broken and lonely, barely more than a kid himself.

And then I remember that the sag in his shoulders is disappointment. He hadn't found me. Now what would he do to get off? The empathy is gone and the rage is back.

Once, when I was in graduate school, a fiction-writing professor said to the class: *You should know everything about your characters. You should know what your characters look like walking away.* And in that seminar room in Alabama, the lemony smell of azaleas drifting in through the cracked windows, so far away from that cold island in Massachusetts, the image of Ted walking back across that field hit me like a blow to the gut. *Yes*, I thought. *Okay. I know.*

The dreams I could not shake had their roots in the days I escaped. In the dreams, he's outside, and I'm in, and he's trying to see if I'm in there.

It's the most fundamental of nightmares: he's trying to get me. That's it. And no matter what I try to do, he can see me. I try to press myself up against the wall under the window, away from any possible line of vision, but my foot splays out to betray me, or he pushes right through the window and looks straight down to find my curled body, as small as I can make myself, but not small enough. And then at some point in the dreams, I realize he's seen me, the jig is up, but he leaves me there. It's not me he's after.

Oh, no. *No no no.* This time, Ted is back, and he's come for Ella.

Night after night, I burst from these dark dreams with the feeling that someone had cracked through my chest and was squeezing my heart. I couldn't get a breath, I felt like I was going to throw up, and I was so *mad.* I thought I was done with all this. I really did. "Oh, honey," my husband Mark would say in the morning when I told him, holding his arms open for me. "I'm so sorry."

But Mark didn't know what to do to help me, and at first, I didn't either. The dreams started in the summer and stayed with me through the fall and into winter. Crap. These intrusive fucking nightmares didn't fit into the recovery narrative I'd crafted for myself, and I was pissed. I thought I had written myself through all of this. Isn't that what I'd been telling people? Telling *myself?* That the writing had healed me? And hadn't I thought my recovery, once achieved, would last forever? Didn't I consider myself a kind of superhero of sexual-abuse survival? Me with my wonderful family and happy sex life? The bulimia and binge drinking of my young adulthood now a mere vestige of a former self, I knew how to love and be loved. I'd moved from being a victim of my own sad brain, a captive in a body that remembered more than I did, to being a mother and wife, a friend and a teacher, a woman with a big smile and a big heart who could stand steady and do the good work of helping others tell *their* stories. While I'd had my share of therapists in the beginning, I confidently attributed the mother lode of my emotional and psychological health to having written myself through childhood trauma in my first book.

In grad school, I had denied that the writing did me any good. My MFA program didn't have a nonfiction track, but one day I brought the first chapter of the memoir I was working on into a fiction workshop. A few of my

peers accused me of perpetrating something they called "therapy writing." That made me furious—and nervous. I was afraid, of course, that maybe they were right. So I denied it. I denied that writing my childhood did me any good at all. Stamping my outraged feet and downing beer after beer at the bar after class, I insisted that my art was as legitimate as their art, that I was as distant from the Jill in my book (a typographical mark! the letter "I"!) as they were from the characters in their purportedly made-up stories.

But three years after the memoir was published, I visited a class of high school students, and a girl with eyes I recognized from the mirror asked if writing my memoir had helped me, and I looked at her, and instead of releasing the tired lie that was waiting in my mouth like a dog by the door, I thought about her question: Had writing *Darkroom* helped me?

And I said for the first time: "Yes. Writing *Darkroom* saved my life." And when I heard myself say that, I knew it was true, so I kept talking. "In order to write that story, I needed to look into all the dark corners of my brain. In order to find something true that would matter, I needed to think hard about things I'd avoided thinking about all my life. And now? Now the dark corners are lit up. Now I'm not carrying around this brain that holds things I'm afraid to look at." The girl smiled. "Try it," I said, and I hope she did.

What I wasn't ready to articulate then is my understanding that good writing and good therapy share similar goals and methods. In both, our objective must be to make some sense of a disorderly world. To do this, to find peace in the mess of it all, to make art out of anecdote, we have to *look closely*. We have to look past what we've grown comfortable with seeing, beyond the easy representations we allow to stand in for the real deal. We have to locate patterns and connections we didn't know were there. In this way, in both (good) therapy and writing, we work our way to a kind of cohesion, an order in the senselessness that we can live with.

To survive, we might bury our traumas or skirt the edges of our grief, but to *heal*, we have to go right through the middle. We have to know what's in the dark places. We have to point to who scares us and see what makes us sad—give them all names. There's no other way through. I thought I had done this and emerged on the other side into the light. And, yet, all through the winter, the dreams kept coming.

"Have you ever seen a match burn twice?" Ted asked, striking the wooden match on the rough bricks of the fireplace, both of us watching the flame between us, orange and blue.

"No."

He blew out the match and held the fading tip to my forearm. A blond hair sizzled and crimped.

"Oww! Hey!"

"Now you have."

I can never see his face. I know he had big glasses, and the outline of those frames stands in for the rest of his features, a kind of comic-book representation for both memory and dreams.

In the year Ted came back, Ella's favorite pajamas were a soft white cotton printed with hundreds of tiny pink ballet shoes, close-fitting in the way that the manufacturers would have us believe will save our children in a fire. When I tiptoed into her room to make sure she was sleeping, Ella looked as if someone had come and stretched her in the night, pulling our little girl from a chubby, bookish child into a lean, preteen body, muscled and limber from hours of dance classes. She looked so impossibly beautiful, her dark eyelashes fringing her pale cheeks, her every limb a study in form, the tiny ballet shoes patterning her body in the crack of light from the door like the last pixies of childhood who did not want to leave. And that's when I started to think. *Nine. By the time I was nine . . .* and that's when Ted returned.

I imagined what I would do. I would kill to protect Ella. I would rip him limb from limb.

Some weeks, he would come every night, looking for Ella in the corners of my own damn brain. This could not be. This could not stand.

That's when I decided I needed to go back. I had to do something. And going back to Plum Island, where it all went down, was all I knew to do. The timing was perfect. In early March, I would be attending a conference in Boston. I could slip away a day early, get a rental car, bring a friend who loved me enough to hear my problem and my proposal over the phone and climb onboard, and drive the hour north to Plum Island.

That was the extent of my plan. I should have thought it through. What exactly did I think I was going to do when I got there?

There is so much about this story that is hard to make clear. In the months after the I'll-call-my-mother confrontation, Ted evaporated from our lives. Poof. Gone. Where he had once been a fixture, he was an empty space, nothingness.

*Was it that easy? Would it have always been that easy?*

My mother asked about him from time to time. "Where's Ted? Seems like we haven't seen him in a long time." And my brother Ian, who was a couple years younger than Ted, shrugged his shoulders. "He's over there," he'd say, meaning in the double garage behind Ted's mother's house, where Ted had set up a metal and woodshop on one side—he'd been a student at the vocational technical high school—and a creepy living room/drug den/bedroom on the other side. The bed in the way back was built right into the wall, and there were wooden platforms to hold incense and candles. "He's over there," my brother said, and I, knowing more, said nothing at all, marveling at the possibility that my threat, a twelve-year-old girl's scared whisper up against a nineteen-year-old boy's rough hands on the door, had made a difference.

For months, I startled at every sound, even silence. This was a new reality that I feared could not hold. He must be planning something. He must be angry. Under the fear was the spark of something else: if it was that easy, if all it took was a single threat, why hadn't I made Ted stop years ago?

The answer to this question was simple: I didn't know I could. I had no idea I had that kind of power. I was a child. How could I have understood what I now know about how pedophiles choose their victims? When my mother left me alone to go to work, I had been vulnerable, an easy target. My threat to tell had changed everything. But at the time, in addition to the precarious sense of relief I felt in Ted's absence, I felt two more things—shame (I could have stopped him and I didn't, so therefore I must have wanted it) and regret (I could have stopped him, I could have stopped him, I could have stopped him). Having Ella, and watching her grow up, turned my perspective once again.

At nine, I had felt so . . . *grown up*. In my early twenties, when memories of Ted had first surfaced—not exactly the *recovered memories* the media likes to debunk and call false, but *insistent* memories, memories

that would no longer permit me to look away or forward—I had felt as if perhaps I'd participated in something that was at least partially my choice, a very early consensual sexual relationship. These things that Ted did to me were mine to accept, mine to conceal, and thus, my shame to hold. Since memory, always, is suspect, I was forever running over the years in my mind, wondering if "sexual abuse" was a mislabeling of my experience. But as I watched Ella, the first child I have ever truly seen grow up, I was able to align birthdays with human socio-sexual development. I saw her at nine, growing into this new body, but still so profoundly innocent, a child who despite her preternatural interest in current events, civil rights, and the welfare of animals, wanted a meticulously accurate Harry Potter-themed party, complete with sealing-wax invitations, Quidditch, and—the highlight—a potions class.

"*Veritaserum*," I had explained from beneath the wide brim of my witch hat, "impels those who swallow it to tell the truth. If your potion turns green, you'll know your recipe has been a success. You can ask your friend anything you want, and your friend will *have* to tell you the truth."

The black-robed kids gathered around the ping-pong table on the second floor of the YMCA, and I watched as they poured their medicine cups of yellow vinegar and blue baking-soda solutions together, the potions bubbling up over the rims, and they turned one to another with questions that needed answering. Ella's cheeks glowed a happy pink with the success of her party. Every child's oobleck brew frothed a gorgeous green, and I thought, *Actually, veritaserum extracts the truth as the teller understands it. That's not the same thing.* Truth is complicated and we all know that facts can lie. There is always a level *more* true: true, truer, truest—and then some truth beyond that we will never reach. How true is true enough? Was I afraid of Ted? Yes. Truth. Was I more mad than afraid? Yes. Maybe. Was I going back to Plum Island to protect Ella or to save myself? Yes and yes. Was there a better way? I just didn't know.

All this to say: I don't know what makes Ted go away and what brings him back. But that spring, he was back, and I needed to find a way to banish him for good.

The summer after I unleashed my desperate, furious power, and Ted stopped coming around, my brother graduated from high school and my

mother sold our house. I don't remember moving day, or even the weeks leading up to it—the sorting and the packing and the decision to leave our dog, Tigger, with the new owners of the house. But move we did—leaving Tigger and Ted behind on the island—and I don't remember Ted coming over to say good-bye. I never saw him again.

When we were thousands of miles away, all the way across the country, I let myself relax a little, and then I did myself one better: I let myself forget. The repression of memory is never as simple as its pseudo-scientific detractors would have us all believe. The process of uncovering traumas from our past that we have managed to avoid really seeing for many years is not some kind of therapeutic voodoo. Far from it. Pulling out the psychological shovel and burying what hurts us isn't a quackish anomaly; it's human nature. Look around. Look inside.

Our house on Plum Island had been the very last one before the Parker River Wildlife Refuge. Our backyard was the entire refuge, with its salt marshes and dunes and beaches. I can't imagine a more beautiful place to grow up, and yet somehow, in the seventies, our island was still undiscovered, undeveloped. Like so many of the houses on the island at that time, the house my mother bought for fourteen thousand dollars was no showplace—wide-plank floors, unfinished walls, visible studs and insulation—but my mom made it beautiful, with staple-gunned fabrics over the ugly bits, a new coal-burning stove that formed the cozy center of the house, art made out of sea glass and driftwood and shells.

To the kids at school, in the town across the bridge where we traveled on the bus, we were "the island kids," which translated to the poor kids, the grubby kids, the good-for-nothing kids. Our island was a kind of a ghetto, the wrong side of the river, but man, what a *location*. We picked wild cranberries from the bogs and gathered buckets and buckets of bayberries to melt down into a single candle. We fished in the marshes and made elaborate forts in the dunes. We swam, we climbed, we ran free.

Friday nights began with a bicycle ride to the island store with a dollar to stock up. A penny a fish. That's one hundred Swedish Fish in yellow, red, and green. Sometimes we stopped short of the full paper bag of fish for an Atomic Fireball or a comic-wrapped powdery pink block of Bazooka bubblegum, for tongue-on-fire excitement and longevity, respectively.

The only TV in the house was balanced on a wooden fishing crate in my room—an old ten-inch RCA sporting rabbit-ear antennae, tips flagged with aluminum foil.

Friday night was the best night of TV—first *The Love Boat* and then *Fantasy Island*. Sometimes my brother must have been with me, but mostly I watched alone. How I longed to be Julie with her clipboard, beaming at the top of the gangway as she welcomed that week's guests to the *Pacific Princess*, keeping everything straight and in order—her uniform and hair, each passenger's name and quirky predilections, an elaborate schedule of fun and enriching activities and destinations. And as if *The Love Boat* weren't escape enough, next was a show with a wish-fulfillment premise, a show with *fantasy* right in the title, a show in which hearts could be unbroken, fortunes recovered, and childhoods replayed. There was much time travel. Complete do-over. Did I cringe when Tattoo climbed up on his tower to throw his insubstantial weight onto the bell rope and shout out in his much-parodied French accent, "De plane! De plane!"? No. No, I did not. I laid out what was left of my Swedish Fish, rationed for the second part of my Friday-night double feature, and felt a shiver of pure pleasure.

It sounds lonely, but it really wasn't. Being the kid who was me on Plum Island in the seventies had dangers, but it wasn't all bad, and that's important to remember. On Friday nights, while my mom was off serving chili and beer to keep our small family afloat, I fell into the fantasy on the screen with uncomplicated joy, and now I wonder if I'd always known I would get away from Ted. Maybe even more than once.

In Boston, the day before my friend and I were supposed to get the car and drive north to the island, the winds were whipping and the snow was coming down. According to the voicemail messages from both Mark and my mother, conditions on the island were much worse. Mark was fairly calm: "It sounds like there's another storm coming through. You might want to take another look at the forecast." My mother, who had never before called me on my cell phone when I was working, sounded panicky: "You can't go to Plum Island! There's a *terrible* storm! They've called in

the National Guard. On TV, they're showing a house that fell into the ocean. *Fell into the ocean!"*

*Really?* I thought. *Really? And then: Now you worry, Mom? Now?*

My friend Sherrie had signed on to this trip months earlier, after I told her about the dreams. Sherrie is a poet and a genius with fabric and beads, a dear friend whom I met at my first post-MFA job and who has managed to appear like a kind of steady angel in my greatest moments of need since then. Sherrie didn't think I was nuts for needing to physically return to confront the past. Adopted as an infant along with her twin sister, Sherrie had recently made the decision to search for her birth mother, despite her twin's objections. Her sister wanted to live only looking forward, but Sherrie needed to look in all directions—including back. Sherrie and I understand each other.

Back in the hotel room, I checked the forecast for the next day—clear, sunny, and cold. The storm that had gotten my mother and Mark so worried had passed on through. Then I pulled up the news. Sherrie and I sat shoulder-to-shoulder on the bed and watched footage of a house along an eroded stretch of beach, pounded by the waves, slowly slowly slowly tipping over the edge. Geez. Was this an omen that we should stay away?

Ninety percent of me was relieved. Here was the perfect excuse. The weather had cleared, but the island had sustained heavy storm damage. I had *wanted* to go back, but maybe now wasn't the time. Too bad.

The remaining ten percent of me was scared: did this mean Ted had won? Did this mean the dreams would never stop? Was it possible that chickening out would somehow leave Ella vulnerable? Does the world work like that?

The weather wasn't the only thing I checked online before the trip. Months earlier, when the dreams intensified, I had done what I could to find Ted, hoping—forgive me, but it's true—hoping I would learn that he was dead, something which, if his teenaged lifestyle choices (drugs, alcohol, fighting, motorcycles) had continued unchecked, seemed fully possible. I'm no private detective, but I was able to determine from some online record searching that his mother had been dead for over a decade, and I was pretty sure Ted was still alive. I couldn't find a record of sale

for their Plum Island house, but it looked as if his most current address was in Salisbury, at least twenty minutes away. I knew my chances were good that I would not find him on the island, and I had no intention of trying to track him down in Salisbury.

How do I explain this? I wasn't looking for Ted himself, fifty years old and god knows what. I was looking for the memory of Ted—and then, somehow, I was going to find a way to slip free of its dark snare.

The next morning, when I pulled back our curtains on the twenty-seventh floor of the conference hotel, the sky had cleared and the world was *sparkling*. No excuses. We would go.

Newburyport is the last town before you cross the river for the island, and Sherrie and I started there. I needed to ease myself into the past, and breakfast in Newburyport seemed right. At first, I felt comfortably like a tourist in my own childhood, and this phrase looped through my head as we wrapped our scarves tighter around our necks to walk along the dock, edged by a park I'd never seen, and then navigated the slushy streets to Angie's Food: *I am a tourist in my own childhood*. A tourist is a visitor. A tourist gets to leave.

The last time I saw Newburyport, I was thirteen, so there was the thrill of rediscovery after so many years—the now-defunct Fishtail Diner where Fast Eddie had cracked our eggs, four at a time, before we struck out for the open seas on my mother's boyfriend's fishing boat; the toy store—the *same* toy store!—where I'd picked out wind-up toys and kites; the newsstand where my mother's friends had spent long hours drinking coffee refills and eating tuna melts, worrying napkins and the changing world; the dock with its giant scale for giant fish. So there was the excitement of recognition. And the horror of the same.

At Angie's, I ate the eggs Benedict recommended by the super-friendly Enterprise employee in Boston who'd helped us get our bags into the trunk of our rented economy Ford. He'd asked where we were headed, and I'd said, "Newburyport. I grew up on Plum Island and I haven't been back in thirty years." He smiled and nodded his head like he'd just passed me a joint and he was holding the smoke in his lungs, letting the high soak in. "*I'm* from Newburyport!" he said with a burst of breath and a grin, and

because this whole day, this whole journey, had a scrim of the otherworldly and predestined from the get-go, I thought, *Of course you are.* He told us what he loved about the island where I'd run wild as a kid, how when he was a teenager they'd drive out there at night and build fires low in the dips between the huge and sifting dunes—"Down where nobody could see us. It was awesome. And then we'd do things we probably shouldn't have been doing." He grinned again.

I told him I wanted to have lunch at a place called The Grog, where my mother used to be a waitress, how I'd ride my banana-seated yellow bike over the bridge and into town by myself every Sunday to visit her there, eating cups of chili heaped with shredded orange cheese and sipping an endless procession of Shirley Temples slid across the polished wood bar by Bruce the Bartender. "The Grog's still there," our new friend said, handing over his card and telling us about the Mexican restaurant on the main street. "But if you want a buzzy afternoon, just drop my name here and they'll hook you up with some free margaritas."

I'm old enough to think—*Wait. Aren't you renting us a car?!*—but *me* enough to appreciate his enthusiasm for our pilgrimage. "A lot of things have changed," he said, closing the trunk and shaking our hands. "You'll see. A lot of things."

As soon as we crossed over the drawbridge, I felt a kind of tingling in my bloodstream. Every molecule: fight or flight. Dark corners of the brain I hadn't known were still there. Language loosening, scenes intruding. Here. Under the bridge. Giving me a ride home, Ted had swung his car down this road, into the marsh under the bridge, a troll with his reeking, smoky breath. Scenes and images flashed. The nightmare felt real. Now I was back. But who was I? Why had I come?

I moved my lips to the words without sound: *I am a tourist in my own childhood.* Instead of turning right off the bridge, the road that would take us to my end of the island, I asked Sherrie to go straight. Just a block. I wanted to see if the island store was still there. The candy. I wanted to buy some Swedish Fish. This was an obvious stalling technique, but Sherrie obliged, looking at me warily. "I'm okay," I assured her. "I feel okay. If I'm not okay, I'll tell you."

Inside Dick's Variety (Grocery Deli Tobacco Ice Cream Subs News), the glass case under the cash register was still filled with candy: Jujubes, Boston Baked Beans, Now and Laters, Airheads, Nerds, Jolly Ranchers—and Swedish Fish. Just the red ones, prepackaged in yellow. Pulling out two dollars for what couldn't have been more than twenty fish, I joked with the cashier wearing the blue-and-orange knit cap. *In my day, the candy here was a penny*, and as she took the bills from my hand, she laughed a laugh deepened by years of smoking, the fact that I was back after thirty years not even really worth noticing, and flipped a thumb to the side: "Yeah. Things sure have changed, but we still have our pickle barrel!" An old-timer hanging out at the end of the counter joined in with a smoky baritone chuckle—*we still have our pickle barrel!*—and I peered down at the pickles jostling one another like fetal pigs in a formaldehyde bath, waiting for the ladle, the dissection. I swallowed back a gag, my tongue sour with memory before we'd even left the candy store.

I was no longer a tourist. I was ten, and I was going home.

On Google Maps, I'd confirmed that our old house on that prime real estate had been torn down, replaced by a three-story beauty, a million-dollar home where our glorified shack had once stood. We'd start with Ted's. Just as I knew my house was gone, I knew his was still there. Returning to one's childhood in the age of satellite and Internet means virtual reconnaissance is possible. I was armed with information—partial, uncertain, but still something—and yet I had no plan. The extent of my plan was to trust my gut and to show Ted I was not afraid. I was all grown up, and damn it, I was fierce. I was not to be fucked with by the likes of him.

"Okay," I said. "Okay." I directed Sherrie the half mile or so to Ted's street, the street before mine, which was the last street before the refuge. Navigating the narrow road between the snow banks—when had the roads shrunk?—Sherrie's toe barely tapped the gas pedal as we crept along. I felt furtive. It was as if I were turning the pages of my childhood, driving along sketched-in, charcoal roads in a real car. I wasn't supposed to be able to do something like this. My mother's best friend's old house wasn't the same. Somehow, it looked bigger. Had it always been two stories? I only

remembered one and an attic sort of space. Maybe the house had been renovated, pushed upward. The weathered gray New England shingles looked the same, the red trim.

Sherrie inched forward, watching me. Ted's house was next. "I'm okay," I lied. First I saw the front of Ted's house, seemingly the only structure on the whole island that hadn't changed at all. In a landscape of brown tones and shingles, the pale yellow siding of Ted's house was one of those things that was not like the others. White trim, black shutters, a door on the front I knew nobody used. Almost thirty-five years later, the fact that I knew the rules of this house was confirmed. In the deep snow of the postage-stamp front yard, there were no footsteps. No tracks to that unused front door.

I took a picture right then, and the photo is dirty snow, brown sand, gray roof, yellow house—all muted, tired—and then a flash of deep red in the side mirror which I recognize to be my wool coat. This fragment of me looks like a cardinal in a shrub. There was one real shrub in front of Ted's house and an assortment of shrubby-looking beach pines around the edges of the property. I remembered these, but now they seemed bigger. Of course those that survived would have grown. We have all grown.

In my mind, I could see the inside of the house. All the shades would be drawn. The real way to go in or out was through the side door attached to the small porch. The first room was the living room, with thick, stinky carpets, everything steeped in dense, stale smoke. The kitchen was really more of a kitchenette, with a cheap ridge of laminate counter separating its small appliances from the room where the TV was always on. Then a tiny bathroom, Ted's room, and his mother's room.

Theirs was more of a beach cottage than a place two people would live, but without the quaintness—a beach cottage out of some kind of apocalyptic hellscape. As children, we didn't go in there often, and only when Ted's mother—who worked long shifts at a mental hospital for the violently insane and told really creepy stories—wasn't there. I remember only one visit to Ted's room. He had said he wanted to show me something that was in the closet. I can see his hand on the door of the closet, the kind that slides to the side. White. That's all I remember. I don't remember

what he showed me. I try, but there is nothing there. Ted didn't sleep in that room in the time I knew him, anyway. He stayed in the garage. He did all his work in the garage.

The garage was Ted's lair, and as we crawled down Jackson Way, grisly images from inside the garage flashed in my brain—melting candles, burning incense, a giant vice with a throwing star clamped in its square metal jaws, sparks flashing from the file in Ted's big hand, heavy smoke over musky animal reek. I could smell him. My refrain was different now, and one I had trouble believing: *I am a grown-up. I am safe. I am a grown-up.* I was forty-three years old and locked in a rental car, for chrissakes. That's the kind of grown-up I was. I was the kind of grown-up who would attend a conference of many thousands of professionals, the kind of grown-up who would sit on the board of the association hosting that conference and then rent a car to drive up the coast before flying out the next morning to reunite with her grown-up professor husband and her two well-protected, beautiful children. I tried hard not to notice the thought that the kind of grown-up I was pretending to be, the kind of grown-up who would be safe in her rental car, would likely not be assessing her status as a grown-up. But never mind. I nodded wordlessly to Sherrie and she maintained our steady progress. The car crept forward. "I'm okay," I said again. "I'll tell you if I'm not."

And now I could see around the corner. Everything was occluded. My view of the double-garage was blocked by a jumbled assortment of vehicles and watercraft—a salt-eaten station wagon faced us, hooked up to a trailer bearing a sailboat, and next to that, a huge white RV and another trailer, this one with two boats, skiffs, stacked gunwale to gunwale like a giant clam. *Okay, okay,* I thought. *Breathe.* I didn't recognize the car or the boats, and ridiculously, I took this as a comfort, although of course, that was absurd. A man can buy a new boat in the course of thirty years, can't he? But then I got a clear glimpse of the garage through the tunnel of cold air between the sailboat and the RV, enough to see a window I knew, with an air-conditioning unit duct-taped into the bottom half. I was in my nightmare. I couldn't get a breath. I would have opened the door to vomit, but I was afraid to touch the door. I was afraid to move my hand.

"Go," I whispered to Sherrie, digging deep for air. "Go. Go go go go go."

When you return to a childhood whose story was told on the shifting sands of a barrier island—and your house has been torn down and replaced with a different house, another kind of life entirely—it's hard to find your bearings. Sherrie and I circled the block and pulled into the dead end that was my street: Temple Boulevard. "I don't remember the trees being this big," I said to Sherrie when we got out of the car. I was crying.

She reached over and squeezed my arm. "What do you want to do?"

"Walk around," I said. "I just want to walk around a little." *Fuck,* I was thinking. *Fuck fuck fuck. Ted wins. I ran. I got close and I ran away. I am still afraid.* I had been dismantled by one glimpse of an old garage. *Fuck.*

There was nobody home in the big new house that stood regally where our one-story cottage had once squatted, and I guessed it was a beach getaway, not the kind of place, say, where people would weather a storm that was pulling houses into the ocean. I remembered the Storm of '76. The great nor'easter. How the National Guardsmen had come to our door, knocked, told us it was time to evacuate, but my mother said no, we couldn't. She had cookies in the oven, she explained to the baffled uniforms, and she needed to fold the fortunes inside as soon as they came out of the oven, while the cookies were still pliable. Thank you, but we'd stay. The morning after the worst of the storm, the beach had been covered with galactic-looking, honeycombed chunks of ice as big as park benches—and we walked among them, snapping pictures. Back in our cozy house, we drank cocoa and broke open our fortunes. My mother had written them herself, so they were all lucky.

I climbed the dune behind what had been our house, but couldn't be sure if there was anything I really remembered. All the contours were different. The place where I'd sunbathed no longer there. At the top, I turned, and again, I was struck a physical blow—a clear shot of the back of Ted's garage, the same angle as the view from my bedroom window when he walked away—the same shingles, the same listing picket-and-wire fence, bent by the wind into a crooked spine, the same gray plywood nailed over the window in the exact corner where I knew the bed had been. It was as if this view had been preserved for me, not a blade of beach grass out of place. The boarded-up window was the thing I could not stand—so sinister. My heart. I was sick in my heart.

I raised my hand and pointed. Sherrie's eyes followed my finger.

"That's it," I said. "That's the garage. It looks exactly the same. That's it."

"Oh, Jillian," she said, moving closer to me. I rested in the circle of her protection. I knew if there was an attack—which is what every part of my body was expecting—she would be my fierce defender, and then I thought: *What if Ted is hiding from me? Could he be in there? What if he is crawling along the dirty baseboards, scared that some part of his giant body might betray his location? What if he is afraid of me?*

I needed to think. I needed a plan. I mean, how is a body supposed to know how to react in these completely bizarre scenarios? You've returned to the landscape of your childhood abuse: What are you supposed to *do?* I didn't know, but I knew I had to do *something*. I couldn't leave without doing something.

We drove through the gates and onto the refuge—and my mind let me play tourist again. I'd never had to *pay* before. All the beaches were closed because of the storm, so we drove a few miles down to a marsh walk, parking among the birders with their poised binoculars. *We are all looking for something*, I thought. For the tenth time that day, Sherrie and I wished for more serious boots, but we tromped through the snow on the boardwalk to reach the marshes, climbing the clanging metal steps of a lookout tower, and standing high in the brisk wind and bright sun—looking out. The blue of the river was deepened by the floating ice, so white in dark water, and where the river broke into tributaries, some so narrow a child could leap across to the other bank if she got a running start, the marsh grasses curved down the muddy banks like a velvet drape. I felt giant, huge, as if I could reach out a finger and smooth the edge of the grass tapestry down below.

"I need to go back," I told Sherrie. "I can't let him win. If I just run away, he wins. He still has me." High in the lookout tower, I got a grip, and I laid out my first real plan.

Back in the parking lot, I called Mark and told him what had happened, let him know we were about to go back. "You are *not* going into that garage," Mark said, his voice rising in my ear from one thousand miles away.

"He's not there," I said. "I'm sure he's not there." Pretty sure. Not totally sure.

"There could be someone even more dangerous living there now," Mark said. "I want you to promise that you won't go into the garage." Poor Mark. He sounded panicky. He wanted me to tell him the name of the street again.

"Jackson Way," I said. "Okay. I don't think I need to go into the garage anyway. That would just be like torture. I don't need to see that much. All I'm going to do is knock on the door and tell whoever answers the door that I used to know someone who lived there when I was a kid and I want to look around a little. Just outside. I won't go in anywhere."

"Call me as soon as you do it," Mark said. "I love you."

"Okay. I love you."

I needed to let that place and its shadowing ghost—the grown man or the memory of the teenager who had hurt me—know I was not afraid. We parked in a gravel lot two houses down from Ted's house and went over the plan. We'd walk back to the house together, Sherrie would wait in the street right behind me, but I would walk up to the house alone. And then I would knock. That was my whole strategy: I would knock.

The driveway had been cleared of snow all the way back to the boats, and the asphalt shone in the wet patches. From this close, I could see the dirt and mold that had collected in the ridges of the yellow siding. Everything except the shoveled ground, washed by the heavy snows, looked filthy. In my body was a war. Flight or fight, fear or courage, child or adult, 1979 or 2013. My body was the place two currents meet the ocean and rise up in a frothing ridge. I was the confluence. The storm door on the yellow house was a gate to hell. Sherrie's face at my side was the steadiest kind of love. I squeezed her hand and stepped forward. *Fuck it. I am not afraid. You don't scare me anymore, you asshole.*

Under this rage, I felt this giant upswell of love. I don't know what else to say. So much love. Sherrie, standing sentry right behind me, Mark back in Indiana with his hand on the phone, our kids safe in the room next to their father, building sturdy Lego towers with their interlocking blocks,

my friends at home, waiting to hear how I fared, my friend Nikki whom I'd seen at the conference, a sister survivor. I knew whatever I did in this moment, I would tell her, and I wanted my act to be the kind that would pull Nikki up with me. If I were in a movie, you would watch as my walk toward that door gained force and speed. You would see my hand raise, the fist already formed, and you would hear what happened next, the solid sound reverberating in the dark theater, my back in my red coat lit up by the white snow, standing at the door of the dirty house: knock, knock, knock.

The response was immediate.

Two giants dogs peeled out of the dark entry to the rest of the house, barking viciously. I jumped and took a step back, my heart startling in its cage of ribs, watching the black frame behind the dogs for whoever might come next, and hoping the rattling door would hold. *The slavering dogs throw themselves against the window, showing their flashing teeth, spraying hungry saliva on the pane.*

I looked beyond the dogs and into the dark space from which they'd emerged. Nothing happened. No one came.

I hadn't thought this moment through. Hearing the dogs throw themselves at the door—muscle on metal, concussive, so loud—I concentrated on my own body, noticing my feet in too-thin boots on the cold concrete, realizing I had planned only what I would say if a stranger opened the door. *Hello. I'm sorry to bother you, but I had a friend who used to live here. I wonder if you would mind if I just walked around the yard?* I didn't know what I would do if Ted himself emerged from the shadows, and yet, checking my body from my icy toes to my pounding heart, I thought, *I am not afraid. I am not afraid of you anymore.* And I knew how I could make this courage true.

Here we were again, each on our own side of a closed door, just as we had been over thirty years ago when I had told him to go away. And he had. Now that Ted was back, skulking into my night dreams, I had gone out in the bright winter sun to track him down where he lived—or where he used to live—and this time I would not cower. This time, I would protect Ella and save myself.

The dogs barked and growled. I stepped forward. *She steps forward and*

*she knocks again.* Yes. I knocked again. Behind me was all this love, this rising surge of love, and that love held me up and pushed me forward.

I knocked again. No one came. I had knocked—twice.

And that was that.

Whether I had found Ted himself, or my memory of Ted, this time, *I* would walk away. This time, I would leave and not come back.

As I turned to walk the ten steps back to Sherrie, I felt a smile come to my face. A smile? "Nobody's home," I said, shrugging, as if that were the most inconsequential thing in the world. And then, "Actually, I'm thinking that's the best thing I could have hoped for, you know?"

My blood was tingling again, but this time, it felt loose, freed, the dam opened and the water pushing past into the open sea where it belonged. I didn't cry until I heard Mark's voice on the other end of the phone. "I did it," I said, and I told him about how I'd felt the love, a protective buffer of love.

"Oh, honey," Mark said. "You're so brave. You're my hero."

Having finished what we'd come to the island to do, Sherrie and I decided to drive by and see the house that had fallen into the sea. I didn't have a good reason for wanting to look, except that I'd never seen a house sideways in the waves, and the metaphorical possibilities seemed rich. The National Guard had closed off a single stretch of road along the beach, right by my old bus stop, where the cranky old lady in the housecoat used to live with her tiny gray dog. Gawkers had been coming to the island to get a close-up look at the destruction, and the Guardsmen stood by their roadblock to turn outsiders away. This was somebody else's disaster to claim. When a Guardsman leaned toward my open window and asked if we were residents, it would have been easy to lie—I wanted to see the house in the ocean—but instead I told the truth: "I used to live here," I said. "But not anymore. I don't live here anymore."

The Guardsman in his fatigues didn't care about the details, didn't care that I'd returned to face disaster—or to change my vision of catastrophe, stare it down, grapple with my own domestic emergency. He shook his head, said nothing, took a couple of steps back, and made the universal gesture for *Turn it around and get the fuck out.*

Sherrie and I didn't care. I had knocked—twice. To celebrate, we went to The Grog and sat under the portrait of Duncan, a crazy old man I remember from my Shirley Temple–drinking days with Bruce the Bartender. I ordered a pint of IPA instead of an icy glass of grenadine syrup, but I still got the chili with cheese. It was as good as I'd remembered it, but one thing has changed: now they melt the cheese on top. In my day, it was a tumbling pile of shredded cheese that spilled over onto the glossy tabletop. You had to stir it in as best as you could. I liked the cheese better the old way.

And the dreams? Back in Indiana with my family, I had a new dream. I dreamed I could fly. In forty-three years of dreaming, I have never flown.

The place was beautiful, a kind of dream-flyer training camp staffed with carrier pigeons holding long colored ribbons in their beaks to show the dreamers in what order we would take off and land. At first, I was flying just below Mark's sister, Sophia, the athlete, and we were so far above the trees that wisps of clouds licked our cheeks. They didn't feel cold or wet. Sophia said, "Look, I use my left hand like this—to steer," and that's when I noticed she was a lefty flier and I was a righty, and when I reversed my own method, the one that was working just fine, to try it her way, I lost control and the fear of crashing was back.

So I went back to my method and again I was alone, swooping, swooping: I felt completely free and unburdened in a way I never had—*not even in dreams*. I practiced a few backward somersaults, a flipping, weightless joy, arching my back and letting the wind lift me higher. I wanted to stay here, safe and buoyant, forever or a very long time, but it wasn't as if this place was entirely without rules.

The pigeons flew by, holding their different colored ribbons in their beaks. The pigeons were the dreamy, avian equivalent of the dudes in the reflector vests with the wands down on the tarmac, coming to lead me home, and since I was pretty aware of how fantastic this all was, I almost expected a Red Baron wink from the one in the front holding the long crimson ribbon in her beak. I watched the pigeons circle and dive—red, orange, yellow, all the colors of the rainbow—and after violet, I turned my hips a bit, finding the wave of air I'd need to follow my pigeon friends, as

if I'd been doing this all my life, and when we dropped below the clouds and into the river valley where we'd begun, I saw people on the river beach under the shining sun, cooling their toes in the water, and I thought, *Now I'll crack. Now the undoing, the loss of control, the fear of failure, crashing* . . . But the wind held me up, so easy. No flailing and no effort, everything airy and soft. When I splashed down with the merest ripple in the water in front of the friendly people on the beach, they clapped and cheered and congratulated me on my wonderful flight. There was a baby propped up in a pile of towels. Her open, toothless smile was a kind of signal to wake up, and I thought, *Wow. Wowwowwow. Hey there, baby, I flew!*

I keep three tassels of Plum Island beach grass in a miniscule square glass bottle balanced on the windowsill above the kitchen table, where my children sit every morning to eat breakfast. Sometimes, when I'm spreading butter on Henry's bagel, or handing Ella a spoon for her grapefruit, the morning sunlight through the bottle catches my eye, and I follow the light up to the three disintegrating brown tufts. I'm pretty sure it's illegal to collect any artifacts—animal, vegetable, or mineral—from a national wildlife refuge, so in order to stuff the grasses covertly in my purse, I'd snapped off their frondy tips. While I was breaking the law, I scooped up an Altoids tin of sand and slipped that into my bag, too, making away with these relics of my feral childhood on this particular stretch of the Atlantic Ocean.

Why do I keep grass and sand? Why did I bring them home? I think I mean for them to be talismans of a time when I not only rescued myself, but also lived in a kind of natural freedom I don't think I've known since— not even in my reckless teenage years on the mountain. It wasn't all bad. There was much to love on the island, so much to see, so much to learn. Plum Island was a lucky place to be a kid. One bad guy cannot destroy it all unless I let him. And when I look at the beach grass in my window, I remember how many ways there are to be saved.

A few months after my trip to Plum Island, the kids and I shared the Swedish Fish I'd bought there in a way that was completely unceremonious, and exactly right. Mark was off somewhere—teaching, I think—and we were

sitting around the table after dinner. *What's for dessert?* Henry wanted to know, and I looked in the pantry for something sweet, but nothing popped out at me. Nothing looked good. "Oh! I know," I said, and I went back to my bedroom, dug to the bottom of my underwear drawer, and extracted the hidden candy and the Altoids sandbox.

"Swedish Fish!" I said, returning to the table and ripping open the package. The kids beamed. I dealt the fish out—all red ones—into three piles like cards, to be absolutely fair, and I told them about my trip. How Mommy had gone back to Plum Island where she was a kid, and Aunt Sherrie had gone along to keep her company, and how the first thing we'd done when we got to the island was go to the store at the center of the island. When Mommy was little, there were penny-candy counters, with all different kinds of candy in baskets, and *everything* was a penny. One penny.

What kind of candy could you get for a penny, Ella wanted to know, and I counted off on my fingers. *Well, Swedish Fish, of course—in three different colors. Bazooka gum, Atomic Fireballs, Bit-o-Honey, Bottle Caps, Gobstoppers, Laffy Taffy, Smarties, Peppermint Patties, Zotz . . .* The kids wanted to hear more about this magical world where candy was so abundant, and as we chewed and chewed our stale Swedish Fish, I told stories about Bazooka gum wrapped in pink-sugared comics, Atomic Fireballs so hot I had to spit them into my sticky fingers to give my tongue a break, and a TV commercial where a red-suited man on a trapeze platform chewed his incredibly long-lasting Bit-o-Honey until the stands cleared.

The night of the Swedish Fish was just a regular night, like hundreds of regular nights, sitting around the table with the kids, and on this night, there was no big ceremony, no melting of red fish on a smoldering sage pile to smoke out any lingering smudges of my nightmares. Why waste good candy? Because we had nothing else for dessert, and because I didn't need to hang on anymore, we shared the souvenir candy I'd carried home, prying the gobs of sticky sugar from the grooves in our teeth with our tongues, and telling sweet stories.

Henry, never one for delayed gratification, shoved all his fish in his mouth, cheeks bulging and eyes shining, while Ella arranged the fish in her own sense-making pattern and nibbled them one by one, nose to

tailfin, studying the curving gills, the seven letters disguised by bumpy scales. *Thank you for keeping her safe.* While we waited for Ella to finish eating, I snapped open the tin box and Henry and I pushed our fingers into the coarse sand, making paths and changing contours. The brown grains tumbled, turning up chunks of white shell shining like bones.

And this is where the story ends this time, around a real table with a real dream for real children: I want Ella and Henry to know, always, that it's okay to tell the truth, to name names and make noise, no matter what. I want them to lay down shame and be brave. I want them to be willing to go back when they know there is something they need to see or set free or reclaim—and then I want them to remember that the way is forward. I want them, always, to let the giving and the taking in of love and sweetness lift them up.

I want them to feel light.

I want them to know they can fly without crashing.

# Drowning Catfish

The rhythm of the mouth moves with me. The slow, regular work of impossible breathing should have been frantic, should have looked more like fighting death, but then, having come so far from the water, if a catfish wriggled free, where could it expect to go?

I was three. My first fishing trip to my grandfather's little pond he'd built behind his trailer—some peaceful place he could watch over after his "nervous breakdown," where he could be alone to nurse his country-widower's virulent paranoia while he waited to die. Keep your door locked. Brace it with this staff of wood. Wrap a rubber band around your wallet to make it harder to steal. Don't go to town unless you have to.

But he laughed sometimes. At the first tug of my line, he'd told me to "break his damn neck!" "I'll break his goddamn neck!" I said—a warm family moment we'd recollect for years after.

We don't talk about the after. I suppose we don't need to. Cleaning fish is a country boy standard and never demands conversation. In the after, we walked up the hill, me taking long strides to step in the tracks of my father, he easily walking in the footprints of his—good practice, he'd say, to conceal from trackers how many of us there'd been.

Daddy carried the five-gallon plastic bucket, our small mess of fish sucking the last little oxygen from the water that barely covered them.

Catfish are slippery, and hide sharp spines in their dorsal and pectoral fins. Cleaning them on a flat surface was the foolish man's way. Around here, if you weren't too lazy, you'd build a rack on which to skin them. And if you built things properly, they'd be permanent. Two steel posts sunk into the ground, secured with concrete. A four-foot crossbar eye level

with a grown man, but far too high for the clumsy work of a boy. Along the crossbar, Daddy had welded a row of ten heavy-gauge nails, curved and sharpened to fine points—barbless industrial fishhooks.

The hands looked very much the same—my daddy's and his daddy's. Wordlessly, they each took a fish—palming down the dorsal spine, sliding thumb and forefinger safely under the knifepoints of the pectoral fins— and lifted it to the skinning rack. The mouth moved, slow and calm, even as the eyes grew large with panic, then relaxed in resignation. Gills flared but drew in nothing. They moved at the pace of a schizophrenic, rocking on a dark filthy bed with his chin to his knees. The rhythm of the mouth moves with me.

The mouth will open. Lay the bony upper jaw against the hook. Pick a spot just below the point of penetration—between the eyes—and gently pound there with a ball-peen hammer. The hook breaks through. For a moment there is flailing. Fleshy whiskers, suddenly awhip, settle quickly. The rhythm of the mouth returns. The rhythm of the mouth moves with me.

Air-breathing catfish croak like weary frogs. Imagine ten at once in a hopeless choir of something that may or may not be pain as I know it.

Special clippers to lop off the spines, to strip the skin and make a sound like peeling tape. Knives that live in families for generations delicately part the bodyflesh from the head. Daddy's cuts so clean and precise they can be taken as evidence of love.

It takes gentleness to leave the organs dangling, respect not to mutilate. The heads live on for several minutes. Leave the right machinery intact, and the croaking continues. Leave nothing, and the sound goes, but the mouth keeps moving, the gills flare, the rhythm of it constant. One seemed not to notice when I poked her hanging roe sack with an exploring finger.

In this way I first watched something accept its own dying, and never did I refuse to eat what came of it. The lungshot deer. The vivisected fish. The winged quail and doves whose necks must be wrung in our mercy. If anything, it was more disgraceful to eat an animal whose death you hadn't known so intimately. Solemn butchery became necessary ritual, a way to honor the life of the food, a way to remember how the old folks had to eat when food was scarce.

A decade later, my grandfather knew there'd be no more fishing. Gradually, there'd been no more hearing, no more talking, no more breathing on his own, and no more leaving this tiny glassed-in room of the ICU. He'd been quarantined with a handful of cancers and hospital-issue pneumonia. Daddy brought me with him for our last look, though neither of us called it that.

Thin and knobby, a paper gown on a stripped carcass, Daddy's daddy lay on his back beneath the tubes and pulsing machines, the clear trachea tube flecked inside with the pink-brown moisture of his throat.

Daddy leaned a hand against the steel frame of the glass wall and tapped on it in a manly way, like a father trying to enliven his child's sleeping goldfish. "Hey, Pop," Daddy said, not that he could hear. The old man's cataracted eyes stayed wide, though I'd always seen them sharply lined and squinted by the sun, a look of wry wisdom never to be spoken aloud. He wearily lifted a hand whose dorsal side was spiked with an IV.

I'd mostly known him as a watcher of corks, a whittler of cedar turkey calls, a BB gun sniper of wasps. I'd seen him do little but sit and wait. The world had gone on without him years ago. He opened his mouth and closed it again, accomplishing nothing. Airway rerouted, he wasn't quite drowning, yet lay there, fishlike and flaring his gills.

We stood a long time watching one another through the glass. I watched them watch each other. Nobody cried. That never occurred to us. They'd never talked like they were close, but you could tell just by looking that they were whittled from identical wood.

So, I've discovered, am I, though I maintain some suppleness of the sapling, yet to dry rigid and hard against the wind and the world. Except for the care I take in doing it, the work of my hands is unrecognizable in his. These days, without the hunting and fishing, without my sharing of his careful work wrought from sweat, the force of will, and the weary breathing of paint dust, Daddy and I speak mostly with our eyes over holiday meals. "Yes," his gray eyes say, laughing. "I heard what your mother said." Though our works are different, we are too similar to communicate in ways other than this.

I've seen him more upset over having to leave his property for the

weekend than at the expected death of any person. Death to him seems natural. Leaving one's home, however, does not.

And when it comes time for his time, I imagine it will look like this. A fathomless conversation between their eyes. This is how I learned how to watch your father die. It is also how I learned to watch your father live.

They stood and watched each other with the bone-hard calm they carried at their centers, a calm so easily rocked at fears of robbery and crowds and traffic at complicated intersections; shattered by the lost feeling at watching the young ones, even your own, act like they don't need what you've got to teach, like there's no world in which to use it anymore; paralytic in terror for when your homestead will no longer hold out, when the work will stop working, when you'll no longer be able to bend the world to the will of your own hard hands. Dying is a natural comfort when you've been held for years too long in a world where you can no longer breathe.

Now it was peace, like life and death were passing in proper time, if not a long time coming. Daddy's daddy broke off the stare and aimed his gasping breathlessness toward the ceiling. A machine breathed into him at an unnatural pace, one unfamiliar to him that, as hard as he tried, he couldn't match to what his body had known. What a terrible time to be given this strange new list of mechanical and chemical fears. I felt sad that he didn't slip away sitting, didn't crack open planing down the red cedar that smelled like home, didn't fly away with the rich-scented breeze that promised cooler weather and better things, that he'd been brought so far from the place where he'd first sat down to die. We moved down the hall, Daddy's face as illegible as my own. And the rhythm of the mouth moves with me.

FLEDA BROWN

# Mirrored Transoms

Our neighbor has been renovating her condo for almost a year. Just cosmetic changes, she said, but the place has been gutted, the hundred-year-old chair rails and trim are gone. Now there are all sorts of soft gray built-ins, floors stained fashionably dark, wallpaper, and so on. I know because we live next door and I poke my head in from time to time to fret over what the workmen are doing.

It took me weeks to see what's been done to the high transom windows (our ceilings are eleven feet high) over the doors and the front entryway. I kept thinking there were lights on in there, but one day I just stood and looked. I got a flashlight and shone it on the windows. The light bounced back at me. She'd had them covered with mirrors! What I'd been seeing was the lit hallway.

If I stood on a ladder, I'd be seeing myself.

I can't help looking up every day as I pass, harboring a vague sense of being shut out. A general sense of a soft glimmer at the junction of what I can and can't know. I wish I had words for this feeling.

Not exactly glimmer. More like a thought that travels past the boundary, past the gravitational field, and thins outward until some distant source sends it back to you. More like the way you see a creek running under grasses when the sun hits it. Oh, there it is! Like when I head out for a walk behind our historic buildings, along the warren of trails up on the hill. I'm exploring, in a sense, another world: this summer a peace sign woven of vines hung from one of the trees. Who put it there? Who took it down? The flat old water tank in the woods is decorated with amazingly skillful graffiti, overlaid so thick on the old graffiti, the whole is a blast of

cartoon-fat signatures and designs from the secret world of teenagers, of gentle insurrectionists.

The path is soggy these days, leaves making the slopes, especially the rocks, slippery. Where the trail dips down into the cedars, the broken-down organic matter is black as tar and clings to my shoes. It is secret and dark in here. Now I am "in here." Wherever else my thoughts have gone, when I reach this stretch, I am entirely here. Alien and muddy, at the lowest spot.

There is something crucial about this: wandering to the low point, as if I have to feed on it. There are no words there, but that's probably the point. I have to stare into that, and later, the words are never right, but I have to try. There was my cancer, then the words for it, then words for me (*fear, sorrow*), and then the wordlessness beneath the words.

The same feeling from high up instead of low, when Jerry and I were standing on the Cliffs of Moher—cocooned up there, same as cocooned down there, for a few minutes, a strange and looser attachment to the mundane earth. The whipping wind—and my mind then turns to our condo, on the third floor. When the wind blows—as it does particularly hard off Grand Traverse Bay a few blocks away—the sound is eerie, otherworldly. Our huge building used to be the Northern Michigan State Asylum. I can imagine the mental patients living here long ago, hearing the sound of wild, uncontrollable spirits, trying to eat, dress, bathe, with the spirits raging in their ears.

Everything I write eventually bumps into that mirror. When I can't see any farther, there goes my mind, taking on the problem. When I was a child, at our lake there was Old Dave, who lived in a little house not a quarter mile up what's now called Woody Knoll Road. We walked all the way to the top picking wild blackberries for Old Dave, we said, wanting an altruistic reason for the picking. When our buckets were full, we walked back down and timidly knocked on his door. Very scary, a bearded old man in a ragged flannel shirt in the middle of summer. Inside his house it was dark, with magazine pages stuck on the walls from the Joe Louis/Max Schmeling fight. He'd thank us for the berries and tell us about the fight, which he remembered in detail from the radio.

Now I can tell you that Joe Louis was the most important Black athlete of his age, a focal point for Black pride in the 1930s. Schmeling represented

Nazi Germany. Against the backdrop of the Great Depression, the fights stood for the struggle between democracy and fascism. I can tell you that in the first fight, Louis was knocked out. Old Dave's magazine pages were probably of the rematch. The poet Maya Angelou, who listened to the fight over the radio in her uncle's country store in rural Arkansas, said that when Louis was on the ropes, "My race groaned. It was our people falling. It was another lynching, yet another Black man hanging on a tree. . . . It would all be true, the accusations that we were lower types of human beings. Only a little higher than the apes."

And then he won. Bands, dancing in the streets. How did Old Dave feel? Where was he, then? Not in his little house, but at the top of the hill in the old Airstream trailer that's turned on its side now, the one I used to explore and take away a cup, an old coffee pot, as souvenirs. Like Old Dave, I collect artifacts and press into them as far as I can.

Now I can tell you that his family moved him down the hill so that they could bring him food in the winter. He was a little crazy. He was a hermit. We children called him a hermit, loving that word. What did we know of a hermit? What does any of us know? Only that he—or she—exists at the bottom, or in a cave at the top. We don't know how to understand someone who won't conform. So we bring him berries. Sometimes we think he's a sort of god, because he seems to need nothing but himself. His mind furnished pictures enough to make him content, so it seemed.

The stone foundation of his house is still there, on Woody Knoll Road, in the front yard of a newer house and planted with flowers. I've thought of him often. Some neighbors at the lake know his history, his family. I have not asked very many questions because each answer seems to flatten the story, deflate my imagination. The work of the imagination is to press on, beyond the barrier of facts. Not to ignore facts, not to discredit them, but to see through them into the space where the separations into here and there, then and now, are no longer the point.

The management company for our condo association has sent our neighbor a letter, chastising her for what she's done to the historic space, although there's not much that can be changed, now. The mirrors are clever, though, and I commend her for that solution for privacy. Jerry and I argue a bit about this. He is an eighteenth-century scholar and lover of

all things historical. He doesn't like it when people mess with history. He's studied and written about the history of the novel, starting with Cervantes' *Don Quixote* in 1605 and springing to a wide and popular genre in the eighteenth century. The modern novel is intimate, private. You can burrow into its secret life. The novel—as is true for visual art, for all art—began as gesture, as mimic of "real" life, as close to a mirror image as possible. A play, on stage, on the stage of the mind. After photography, after the splitting of the atom, after the big Wars, when art began to turn inward, the direction of seeing reversed itself. Instead of mirroring the objective world, it was our own minds we thought we saw in the mirror—the textural excitement of Van Gogh, the balletic distortions of Matisse, the multiple angles of Picasso.

Our section of the building, we've been told, housed the seriously crazy patients. The whole huge complex was designed to allow patients to work, meet, socialize, in as attractive and supportive an environment as possible. Yet our section was a locked ward. I sometimes sit in our bedroom, which is also my study, and try to imagine what it was like to be a patient here, hearing the wind howl, the mind turned back on itself so that all it knows is the story it makes up, full of demons and spirits.

Spirits, being weightless, float upward. Demons are heavy, down-ward-urging. The concrete floors on the lower level of our half-mile-long building sit over joining tunnels, tunnels higher than your head, rounded at the bottom, arched at the top, just like the Romans built them. Before the renovation, kids used to sneak in and wander through, smoking, drink-ing, listening to their echoes. A forbidden zone. Tunnels used to connect all the buildings. Nurses, doctors, and workers could walk through them, and there were steam and water pipes, electrical conduits, bracketed to the walls. Some were shafts to pull fresh air throughout the hospital and out the spires on top. An ecosystem, a cosmos, literally a bricks-and-mortar version of Dante's universe.

Or of *Paradise Lost*, maybe. The height and depth and breadth of Mil-ton's cosmos was the height and depth and breadth of his mind, of the minds of the prophets, added together, so dense they curved space to make a safe enclosure.

Across the huge lawn from us is Willow Cottage Assisted Living, one

of the other renovated buildings on this 480-acre campus, where my ninety-seven-year-old father lives. The residents there are pretty much safely contained within their own ecosystems. Sweetly, for the most part. If they were hostile, they'd live somewhere else. Their minds have grown less limber, less able to maneuver in the outer world. So the front door opens with a code, the stairway doors with a different one. But even for us, who are still agile in that way, the stories we tell ourselves about what's true can easily admit no external world. That's what crazy means, isn't it?

For the patients in the locked ward, there is only the present. For those who live as external a life as possible, the sober fact of death can be held in a locked closet for a long while. Until a diagnosis, for example. Yet with or without our permission, the moment of death brings the interior and exterior to the threshold together.

My father has said for years he wants to die. But really, his talk about it is his way of warding it off. He's afraid. No point in trying to examine why. I know how it is, since my cancer. Isn't it sane, after all, to dread seeing our great good fortune of being born human, intelligent, and capable come to an end? Others at Willow Cottage sleep their way slowly toward their end. Others forget who they are, so fear doesn't know where to lodge.

Mother officially died from choking on a piece of Halloween candy. She'd been having mini-strokes all along, so probably she had a stroke as she was chewing. By the time I got to the hospital from halfway across the country, she was lying there unable to speak. But when her three daughters gathered around her and bent down to kiss her, tears ran out of her eyes. The MRI soon after showed no brain activity. I thought many times about her fear of the enclosure of the MRI scanner and imagined that she was still alert enough to feel that fear. I wondered what she felt when we were gathered in her room, waiting for death. She seemed unaware, but the nurse came in and shouted in her ear, "I'm going to aspirate your throat, Mrs. Brown, so you can breathe better." The nurse turned to us and said, "They can sometimes hear, you know." I keep that image with me, the trouble in my mind about what my mother knew and didn't know, when she fully crossed the threshold and what I might have done or said at that moment that could have held her gently in the passage.

Not that I ever knew my mother, not really. I've tried to see into her

and my heart hurts. She remained innocent. She was battered by a life she didn't know how to get out of or fix. She was kind and gentle. And cheerful by nature. When she threw herself across the bed in tears, she would recover like a child, with little residue of sadness. Or is that what I'd like to think? I had to ignore her suffering so I could grow up, myself. That's what it felt like. It felt as if, had I had been inside her mind, I would have died of sorrow.

Do unto others. I wanted to be good, and kind. I was offered that conduit between heaven and earth that Sunday School provided. I lifted mine eyes unto the hills and tried desperately to see beyond. To live beyond. I sat in a tiny chair in a semi-circle with the others and sang "What a Friend We Have in Jesus" to the flat notes of the piano. This was the group worship session with words read out of the booklet. Then our individual classes, where we trekked through the Bible stories, week by week. If we weren't sure what to make of them, the moral was printed at the bottom of the page. What was soaking into us during those years, those of us who were faithful?

We prayed. Sat in a circle and bowed our heads in submission to Something-Greater-Than-Ourselves. Something separate that we needed to reach. That's what I thought; that's what we thought. As if the thing greater were not located inside ourselves. As if there were anything separate from anything. Everything felt separate. My small athletic body, restless; my nose, with its own separate awareness of the musty smell of the wooden floors, the old classroom; my fingers playing with the pages that held each week's scripture, plus a prayer; my ears, tuning in and out. I was only marginally a believer by nature. I had inherited my father's atheism in my rational brain, but there was also my mother's irrational belief in something else, something called "out there." Called "Greater" by the Sunday School booklet. By the minister.

What was my Sunday School teacher thinking? How did her belief work? When her mind bumped against the unknowable, did it move on out into space, or did it stop at the border and turn back, turn the page and read to us what was written there. Look, these words stand for what I don't know. But the words know. They are words, and they must know something.

There was Bessie, who taught the adult women's class, had taught it for years. One morning she got up, went to church, taught her class, came home, ate dinner, took a nap, and died. I have thought about this as a good life, a good death. And then I think, I don't know. Is this life any better than the drunk's, the criminal's? What if the criminal sees the truth and can't get to it, keeps trying, by all the twisted routes he knows? Through whose eyes is there a judgment? Is there a point of reference out there that doesn't shift, that is the same now and forever? And what about the person whose last moments are filled with pain and anguish that aids the leaving in some crucial way? We can't know.

Who can fathom death? I ask this in all earnestness, as I've come up against it myself. But then, who can fathom birth? Ovum, sperm, an explosion of cells, each marked to build its portion of the structure. Then here comes the spark of life, out of nowhere, and the human mind that learns to say "This is life." Learns to mirror itself.

Our great water, Grand Traverse Bay, is often glassy-smooth this season, late into the winter with no snow. When it finally comes, and it will, I'm sure, the surface will cloud over with ice. Below the ice will be walleye, pike, and perch, and the fishermen will set up their huts, cut holes through, bring their kerosene heaters and beer and sit there for hours, leisurely fathoming what might swim up to their bait. Imagining. Their minds will be a mirror of their desire.

And I will be imagining them in their icehouses, and writing what I think goes on there. What is their cryptic male conversation? Are they retelling fish tales? I have one for them.

My grandson Zach was fishing from the pontoon boat, way up the Chain of Lakes. He was ten, I think. The water was very clear. He saw northern pike down there, hovering, as they do, huge submarines. Then the jerk on his line and oh lord, the fish to contend with, the terror of its rising with its prehistoric teeth, out of the other world, bent on destruction or return. Zach, his face gone white, pulled against the fearful thing, pulled until at last the line snapped. Shaky with relief, he looked down at the water reeds swaying, the fish gone already, the tale beginning to form in the absence of flesh.

Absence is a grand palette. When we moved in here, the huge, wide

halls had nothing on the walls. Now we have art. This year it's multicolored abstract paintings, with pieces of brightly colored wood planks and branches attached. A pleasure to see every time I walk down the hall. But ever since I figured out the mirrored transoms, my eyes turn to them instead. They're more fascinating than the paintings, the sculpture in the elevator foyer, the boots outside other people's condos. They can't look back at me because they're too high. I can't see myself. The light is a soft shimmer, almost like a window, but you can tell it isn't quite. And there's a slight telltale reflection of the wood trim at the sides. Not absence; not presence. It's enticing in a spooky way. Not a metaphor for anything, really, but still, I feel a bit floaty when I look up. Nothing is what it seems, and maybe I'm not, either.

# A Pilgrimage
# to Dennis Hopper

The first time I saw Dennis Hopper in *Easy Rider* I didn't think he was acting. I thought he was some stoned-out freak shoved in front of a camera to see what he'd do. When I realized later he'd written, produced, and directed the film, acting took a paradigm shift for me. He was brilliant *and* crazy as hell, his own kind of signature wacko that got in your face and howled like a hyena. Like Frank Booth in *Blue Velvet* on his knees inhaling gas, fondling Isabella Rossellini, crying, "Baby wants to fuck!" He'd called David Lynch after reading that script and said, "You have to let me play Frank Booth, because I *am* Frank Booth." Like Brando, Dean, Nicholson, he showed you what human beings were really like, *really* did, not some half-baked vanilla version. If you were afraid to offend, embarrass, horrify, mystify, disgust, or shock people, you were in the wrong profession. If you thought acting was about being pretty, you'd missed it. Not only was he going to show you what people were really like, he was going to reveal the bizarre truth you never imagined.

Once, Hopper was arrested, naked and raving drunk in public—a natural lineage of behavior from James Dean, his mentor, pulling a knife on a director. And there was the time the young Hopper worked with old-school director Henry Hathaway, who made him do eighty-five takes on a scene because he refused to do it the director's way, the old codger tiredly lifting his megaphone, saying, "Do it again," eighty-four times until Hopper finally cracked, did it the director's way, and stormed off the set.

Early in my film career I have an audition for a movie Hopper's directing in North Carolina called *Chasers*. I am instructed not to approach him or shake his hand. All right, I think, a rule from the rulebreaker. Expect the unexpected. I have a mishmash of early film pieces on tape I'd planned to hand him, but hearing these instructions makes me decide to wait to see what the vibe's like. Maybe it'd blow an otherwise perfect audition. I'm half-broke and have to drive five hundred miles in my old Volvo, which is acting up with electrical problems. My plan is to start out at noon, which would put me there around dinner time, when I'd get a cheap room, go over my lines, and grab a good night's sleep before reading in the morning.

Regional actors are used to these journeys, but they're drudgery. Richard Jenkins asked me on a set once, "Is it true you guys drive hundreds of miles to read down there?" To him it sounded like a military mission, and he wasn't far off. I'd made round trips on the same day as the audition, driving home afterward to save money, which always seemed pointless. When I arrived at the interview after eight hours on the road, my head was mush and I didn't have a prayer of getting the part. Casting would look at me quizzically like, what the hell's wrong with you? I'd drive home frustrated and pissed off, babbling to myself, pounding the dash and cackling, out of my mind, doing far better work in the car than I'd done in the audition.

This is before cell phones, so if there's car trouble I'm at the mercy of the road. The first stretch out of Atlanta is a monotonous corridor of rolling highway and unbroken tree line for a hundred and fifty miles through Augusta toward Columbia. It's late September and the leaves are turning, blue sky lifting and falling against gas stations, fast food restaurants, and fireworks billboards. I have a couple of peanut-butter sandwiches, an apple, a banana, and a Thermos of coffee, and I eat while listening to Atlanta stations fading, putting on some *War*, thinking about my wife and two boys, aged two and eight. I don't like to be apart from them. Business is business, you have to do it, but you'll never convince me there's anything natural about it. I feel more like this when I'm broke and have to spend the little I have to drive hundreds of miles from my family without any assurance it'll pay off. There's not enough work in town, so I go where it is; I'm the

hunter-gatherer, the fisherman heading to sea. I love my vocation and know I'm good at it, but trying to land it can be a lonely process. But hell, I'm a writer too, so I must love something about being alone.

When I gas up near Darlington, the car won't restart. Lovely, I think—then it sputters to life, and I say a prayer I won't get stranded on the road hundreds of miles from my family and not even get to read for the man. I wonder if he'd ever been broke with car trouble and trying to get acting work. Then I remember this was everyday business for Hopper. When he crossed Henry Hathaway, the old director had him banned from Hollywood for years. No one would hire him. Everybody got kicked around by somebody, and as one of the *enfants terribles* of modern filmmaking, nicknamed "Dennis the Menace," Hopper'd made himself a human soccer ball until he was making his own pictures. Just get me there and back, I think, let me deal with car issues when I get home. I have enough cash for the cheap room and food, and my wife's loaned me her Chevron card. If I had a credit card, it'd be maxed out already.

As soon as I hit I-95, the signs for South of the Border start up, a Mexican theme park just south of the North Carolina line. Sombreros and clichéd cheesy little mustached grinning Mexicans with chili necklaces barking at you from an endless string of trashy billboards. For fifty miles these garish signs blot out the landscape, which is more interesting now. Then I cross the Little Pee Dee River, which makes me miss my baby boy, who'll have no comprehension of why I'm not home tonight. Then I see the phony sad Mexican theme park off to my right like a city from fake hell, spinning sombrero rides and towers and restaurants with orange and yellow and black sombrero roofs, giant strings of chilies everywhere, and though I can't make out a soul there, I'm sure a few people are gobbling frozen bean burritos to the tune of piped-in Mexican standards.

I watch for Lumberton signs and my turn onto State Highway 74 for the last ninety-mile jaunt east to Wilmington as the light's fading. *Blue Velvet* was shot in Wilmington, which David Lynch called Lumberton, showing the big lumber trucks all through the movie, a radio DJ hawking, *"Time to get up, woodchucks, and get those chainsaws revving, a beautiful day for lumbering!"* As soon as I hit 74, the trucks are pounding past me heading the other way. It's a split four-lane for a while, which narrows

to two lanes, and I'm in farm country, with wide stretches of fields and ramshackle houses and barns in the middle of withering crops, falling down, leaning, glorified piles of lumber that saw the Civil War. A poor, humble, beat-up landscape.

I'm in good spirits on my last leg, running lines for tomorrow, an Air Force General I'm reading for, and another throwaway role, when my car starts to sputter and lose power. Finally it's not firing at all and I pump the gas, begging it to go, and it gives out completely, cuts off so I have to muscle it without power steering onto the shoulder. Oh, hell, I think, sitting a minute, trying to revive it, looking off into the dark swampy trees. Twenty minutes of light left and I'm stranded on a desolate bleak highway rivaled only by the Tamiami Trail I hitchhiked up one night with a friend out of Miami, so dark you couldn't see your hand.

This is bad though. It's the highway Michael Jordan's father would be murdered on years later when he stops to take a nap, or maybe just had car trouble. Every few minutes one of those thundering lumber trucks from *Blue Velvet* comes rumbling by, blowing me back a few feet, peppering me with debris and dust, the drivers not even glancing at me. Am I screwed? I've come all this way to be stuck here with a 10:00 a.m. call to read for Hopper in the morning. If I don't get there on time, the trip's shot and I have to fix my car and limp home defeated. Dues make you a better actor, I tell myself; *of course* they do.

With a flashlight I tinker with the distributor cap, trying to dry it off inside. This was the problem before, but nothing I do gives a spark, and the battery slowly bogs down, and I'm desperate. At last light a state patrol car pulls up and a grinning, crew-cutted young officer says, "Havin' trouble?" I've never been happier to see a cop. I tell him I need to get to Wilmington tonight and my car's shut down; he tells me to hop in, he'll run me over to Gabby's Gas in the next town.

"Old Gabby'll help you one way or another," he says. "This ain't the place to get broke down tonight. No tellin' who you'll run into on this bad man's highway."

In a few minutes we pull into a blue-plastered Pure Station from another time in a tiny town already closed down for the night. Some old character's yelling into his phone, slams it down, and the State Patrol kid

introduces me to Gabby and tells him my problem. Gabby says, "Hell, I got nothing else to do tonight but go home and fight with my wife. I'll tow you to Wilmington, no problem!"

I tell him I don't have any cash but can write him a check and promise it'll be good, and he says, "I trust you. And if it ain't good, I'll come down to Georgia and take it out of your ass, how 'bout that?"

I thank him, say good-bye to the State Patrolman, and Gabby and I are headed over to pick up my car with his tow truck.

Gabby's about five foot six, with wild long wooly-white hair, and looks like a cross between Will Geer and Wild Bill Cody. He has no A/C and growls and yells over the noise from his half-muffled engine, shaking his Lucky ashes out the window, George Jones droning on the radio. The side of his truck says, "GABBY'S GAS . . . YOU BLOW 'EM . . . WE TOW 'EM!" He's got the energy of a leprechaun, bouncing around the truck, rattling chains, hooking up the wench, lifting my car while he's yelling he'd rather do this than go home and listen to his wife piss in his ear, and we barrel east again for the sixty-mile haul to Wilmington. I figure I'll tow the car to my cheap motel, do the audition in the morning, then try to find a full-service Chevron for repairs, but Gabby says, "Hell no, I'm finding you a place to fix your car *tonight,* I ain't draggin' you over here to leave you in some goddamn parking lot. You married?" he shouts above the roar of the truck, his hair flying back in the wind as we tear along the dark four-lane, his dispatch radio popping off static.

"Yeah," I say, "nine years. How 'bout you?"

"Aw, hell, been married three times. My second wife tried to kill me five years ago. Swore I'd never remarry but my third wife was too damn good in bed. *Readjusted* my thinking."

Dennis Hopper'd love this guy, I think.

"My second wife was a wrestler, see. Got into an argument one night and she put me in a headlock and almost snapped my neck. Got two herniated discs." He points to his ruddy vertebrae. "A torn meniscus in my right knee. Had to get a restraining order against the psycho bitch and she's turned my daughter against me. Got kids?"

"Two boys, two and eight."

"Yeah, well, once she's got a kid with you, she's got you by the short

hairs. Not just for money. She can hurt you every which way. Your kid's a part of you, see, and then she finagles that part of you against you and then you're fucked, brother. Thank God for my new old lady. She likes to fight too, but what woman don't?"

"How long you been drivin'?"

"Thirty-eight years this November, since I left the Navy. Driven three million miles in that time, give or take a hundred-thou. Think I'll pick up a cold six-pack when we land over here for the trip back. Nice night for it."

We cruise into Wilmington, passing the ghostly USS *North Carolina* docked for tourism, with its hundred-and-thirty-five guns lit up against the harbor, and I give Gabby directions to the Greentree Inn on Market. It's a short walk to restaurants and a mile from the Screen Gems lot, where I'm reading in the morning. As luck has it, a full-service Chevron's next door, and Gabby unhitches and drops my car off while I write him a check for eighty-five dollars.

"Give it three days and it's good as gold," I say. "My number's on there if there's any problem."

He peels a 16 oz. Pabst Blue Ribbon off his six-pack and hands it to me. "Fill up a hot bath, sip on this baby, get a good night's sleep, and go show Mr. Hopper what for in the mornin'. *Do it for Gabby.* Tell him I'll be in his damn movie if he needs a wiry old Navy man."

"You'd be the best thing in it," I tell him, meaning it. "Drive safe, Gabby."

"I'm indestructible, brother."

It's not exactly the way I'd planned to get here, but as I write a note for the mechanic telling him I'm next door, I know the angels are still with me. I check into the Greentree, which has crater-like monster potholes in the parking lot as if the place had been bombed, call home, and take Gabby's advice about the hot bath and cold beer. I toss around half the night dreaming a montage of my General's scene, flying along in Gabby's truck, and standing out on that desolate highway, stranded in *Blue Velvet* with Frank Booth, those damn lumber trucks plowing past me like dark rolling Leviathans.

In the morning I'm told I need a new distributor and they can have it done by noon. I eat at the Huddle House, focus on my roles for an hour,

and start the short hike to the Screen Gems lot. It's a crisp fall morning, I'm feeling fresh, my car's being fixed, I'm reading for a notoriously eccentric Hollywood legend, and I'll be back in my own bed tonight, God willing. I check in at the guard station, sign in at casting, make sure I've got the right script, and join the nervous actors sitting in chairs along the hall, silently mouthing their scenes. A few actors drift out, looking flustered or relieved, then Dennis Hopper pops out wearing a tan sport jacket over a black T-shirt. He coolly shuffles down the hall. In a minute he strolls back with that relaxed, confident, cocky short man's gait, a quick rhythmic swagger, and everyone mutters and chuckles when he steps inside.

Somebody goes in, I don't notice who, and five minutes later the door flies open, and a chunky black actor leaps out on one foot with a big sweating grin and a loud clap, dancing the Skate down the hall, going, "All y'all can go on home now! *Yeah!* I got that one in the bag, baby! *I got it!*" He snaps and fist-pumps. "Don't even need to go in there. I got the part! Hell yeah, baby, Mr. Hopper done found his man, and it's me! All you suckers can take a hike!" He's completely sheened out, doing a combination James Brown-Ickey Shuffle that seems to go on endlessly. Men, women, children, black, white, and Hispanic, watching this jive clown dance down the hall and turn the corner, yelling, "*I got it! Got the part, damn right!*" until he's out of the building.

Of course he's completely full of it. The lamest trick in the book's trying to deflate your competition by making them think your part's been cast, so you'll lose focus and do a lousy audition. Casting rarely makes decisions while you're in the room—not until they've seen everybody—so it's silly, jive, bush-league bullshit. I have no idea what the fool's reading for, but the vision of him popping out of that door, putting on that strutting little show, is a small actor's perk, part of my own personal comical movie for the road. I never see this guy again in the real movie or anywhere else.

Finally my name's called and I go in feeling exhilarated and relaxed, which is good. Obviously fate wanted me to be here, I think. There are no accidents. This can be the best part if I let it.

It's a big room with seven or eight people, producers mostly, sitting behind two long *L*-configured tables. Someone greets me and I hand him my headshots and wave hello to Dennis Hopper, remembering my instructions not to approach him. I have my tape in my briefcase just in case.

"What you doin' for us today, Ron?" he says, and I tell him I'm reading the Air Force General. "Good, let's see it. Go ahead, roll it."

I run through the scene with the reader standing next to the camera. Leaning back in his chair, with his hands behind his head, Hopper tells me to take my time next take. I do it again.

"Yeah, yeah, that's better, all right." He half-shuts his eyes, leaning forward. "*This time.* This time I want you to do it the way Gene Hackman would do it. Do it like Gene Hackman would do it, yeah. *Yeah.* Do it like Gene Hackman this time."

Is he joking? I wonder. He seems dead serious. I've had some unusual directions, but this is one of the strangest. Dennis Hopper's telling me to do my role as if I'm Gene Hackman, his costar in *Hoosiers.* It isn't that I have a problem with the direction. I'll do it like an ostrich if he wants me to. And I'm crazy about Gene Hackman—who isn't? It just throws me for a second. I've never been told by a director to do a role as if I'm some other star doing it—and this is a star telling me to do it. At the same time I'm chuckling inside. This is Dennis Hopper. Did I expect a normal audition? Sometimes directors give specific notes to see if an actor will follow directions—and I'm not bad at impersonations—and it's the spirit of the guy I'm after anyway. So I give it my best shot.

"Not bad," he says, staring at me a minute, and I think he likes me. "You got anything else? Another role?"

I tell him I've got an MP role, and I run through that once quickly, and he's sitting back in his chair again, leaning back on two legs, hands behind his head, nodding, saying, "Okay, that's fine," and I think, what the hell, you've got some kind of connection maybe, who exactly made the rule anyway, and I take my tape out of my briefcase and approach his table. He looks a little surprised as I walk up, and he stands very slowly, as if we're doing a scene together, reaching across for the tape as I hand it to him. For a few seconds we're staring at each other like we're in some kind of movie scene, and I'm thinking he's thinking, whoever this guy thinks he is, I'll play along just to see what he does—sure, what the hell; and there's this moment, this brief suspension in time, when all the beautiful, insane, manic-headed and off-the-wall crazy roles he's done well up into a few seconds for me, to show him I'm connected if by no other means but appreciation for his colors and originality and boldness and in general

doing it his way and not giving a shit about anything else, and he gives back to me, a kind of awed respect at who I am, with a handshake, even if it's only just appreciating that I appreciate him—or else he's just amazed I'd have the balls to approach him like this—*didn't this guy get the memo?*—and he has respect for an actor who's not afraid to make a fool of himself, since that's been his bread and butter for his whole career. At the same time I'm thinking, I wasn't supposed to do this, was told not to—oh well, hell, it feels like I'm supposed to, so fuck it. Maybe he just thinks I'm insane to be approaching him and this is the best way to get rid of me, the way he stares at me, leaning forward, I can't tell, but I don't think so. No, we have a moment of some kind of recognition, whatever it is, and I mumble, "It's a true pleasure." I thank him and everybody else in the room, and I'm out the door.

It's a funny feeling early in your career when you meet a kindred acting spirit, one you've known for years who didn't know you. Actors mean something to people not because they're more important, but because they've made themselves completely vulnerable and let people live and die through them. What an actor does is like a dream people carry around in their heads for years, and sometimes it explains your life to you better than anyone else could, explains life itself and makes sense of the nonsensical, lets you know that all of your nightmares and fears and awkward moments and heart-rending are shared by everyone, pulls everyone together in a scene that lets you laugh at the absurdity of each of our lives. Actors have some of this too for other actors, but a whole lot more. It isn't star or celebrity worship, although everybody feels a little of that. You know these are just people who sweat, bleed, cry, have their hearts shattered and beaten down and die just like you do, and many of them have bigger problems *because* of who they are. It's like watching a great running back run in an open field. You think, I can do that, *I can see myself doing it.* You've been mentored by these people, been inspired many times, been told by their performances: look, you've got something you can do that nobody else can, it's as much yours as this is mine, so don't hold back— make it happen. I've paved new ground for you, let's see what you bring to the table. And for Godsakes, don't *bore* us!

I'm feeling high as I stroll back to the motel. I'd just done a damn good

read for—entertained, even—one of the best real-life characters in the business. Something had happened in there, though to this day I couldn't tell you what. And now I'm heading home. My car's ready, it's early, and I'm on the road wondering what the hell Dennis Hopper thought when I handed him that crazy tape. He'd looked at it like it was some illuminated object, a mysterious charm or amulet—a gift to me, him doing that—letting my tape have value for him for a few seconds because it obviously did for me.

A few weeks pass and I don't hear a thing. Gabby cashes my check and there's other work at home and after a while I'm let down, assuming I didn't get the part. Maybe approaching him did blow the whole audition, but I doubt it. He would've done the same thing. An actor has to deal with so much rejection he can't dwell long on one thing, but sometimes not getting a role will eat at you for months, and this one's a bit of a mystery.

When Chasers comes out in theaters I don't go see it. I wait until it pops up on cable. When I finally do see it I look closely for the parts I read for and they aren't in the movie. Which makes me feel better, but strange too, because all of that work and study and driving, breaking down, getting towed, car repairs, and everything else was done for ghosts of roles that weren't going to live anyway.

As time goes on, I realize this trip wasn't made for me to play some insignificant role in Dennis Hopper's film. It was made for him to play a lasting one in mine. I sit back with a tall 16 oz. Pabst Blue Ribbon, watching him run through his forgettable movie, playing a goofy, comical character named Doggie, driving a fat red Cadillac, and I laugh thinking about being told by Dennis Hopper to "play it like Gene Hackman." Knowing he had a small independent movie in his head of me. Wondering what he thought of my tape—if he even looked at it.

In The Last Movie, Hopper tries to help a Mexican filmmaker make a western in which they use real bullets, and his character surreally gets killed making the thing, gets shot on camera filming a movie of a shootout. It didn't do very well at the box office, but it's one of my favorite Hopper films. It's a sort of signature film of his, a perfect metaphor for Hopper's surreal and dreamlike life. If films are an actor's life, what better way to die than to pretend to be shot on film and actually get shot and die there?

Someone once said, "We must follow the film wherever it takes us," and Hopper made his life like he made his movies, with total abandonment, insane commitment, and irreverence, breaking all the rules as a matter of course, becoming Hollywood's "greatest survivor." Considering he started huffing gasoline from his grandfather's truck at age seven, you have to marvel at how a career like his was possible.

The short film I have in my head of going to see the wild auteur was for me better than the film I went to read for. It was the real reason I went to read for him. It's not always about the celluloid film and our role in it, although we think it is, the permanent record and performance that everyone sees, that pays the bills. Sometimes it's about that odd little random piece of flickering brain footage that keeps on spinning out forever for us of the wild-headed people we spent time and space with, if only a few moments. People who had already changed our lives in unknown and derelict ways, as human beings and film actors alike.

# Acknowledgments

Although faithfully giving thanks to all the people who have helped us over twenty years would be impossible, we'd be remiss by not thanking a few. First, we would never have made it half of a decade without our first managing editor, Sarah Wells. Sarah's intelligence, exuberance, ambition, and dedication made our jobs easy. As rare as it is to have one outstanding managing editor, we at *River Teeth* have been blessed with two. Cassy Brown assumed the role after Sarah. Cassy, too, allowed us to do the work of editors and made us believe we did it all ourselves. The truth was far different. Cassy not only made the trains run on time, but she also did every job expertly and with a smile on her face, even while doing the work of two or three people. Surviving the transition from Ashland University to Ball State would have been utterly impossible and impossibly painful without Cassy's earnestness and dedication, long after she had officially left her job. Thank you, Cassy. We'd also like to thank one of our most faithful readers, Mike Hupfer, who not only read every piece of every issue, but who also helped us out early and often in his role as an assistant dean. Thanks also to David James Duncan, Steve Harvey, Tom Larson, Matt Tullis, Ann Glaviano, Jill Christman, and Mark Neely.

We owe a huge debt of gratitude to Elise McHugh at the University of New Mexico Press. Along with being our partner in the River Teeth Literary Nonfiction Prize series, Elise believed in this collection from the beginning. She and her team have been a dream to work with over the last few years.

We also have to thank our wives, Dandi and Barbara, who for twenty years have put up with and supported their husbands giving time and energy to a dream.

# Contributors

**ROBERT ATWAN** is the series editor of *The Best American Essays*, which he founded in 1985. His essays, criticism, humor, reviews, and poetry have appeared in many professional and literary periodicals, including *The Atlantic Monthly*, *The Denver Quarterly*, *Image*, *The Iowa Review*, *Kenyon Review*, *River Teeth*, *Creative Nonfiction*, *Publisher's Weekly*, and *America Book Review*. For years he reviewed poetry and fiction for *The Los Angeles Times* and *The New York Times*. The editor of numerous college and literary anthologies, he has written on a wide variety of subjects, which include a history of precolonial American literature, Shakespearean tragedy, dream interpretation and divination in ancient literature, nineteenth-century photography, prose aesthetics, and the cultural origins of American advertising. "Notes Toward the Definition of an Essay" was originally a talk Atwan gave at a *River Teeth* conference. He lives on New York City's Upper West Side.

**KIM BARNES**, a Distinguished Professor of English at the University of Idaho, is a recipient of the PEN/Jerard Fund Award in nonfiction for *In the Wilderness: Coming of Age in Unknown Country*, which was a finalist for the Pulitzer Prize. Her novels include *In the Kingdom of Men*, named a best book of the year by the *San Francisco Chronicle*, *The Seattle Times*, and *The Oregonian*; and *A Country Called Home*, winner of the PEN Center USA Literary Award in fiction.

**FLEDA BROWN**'s *The Woods Are On Fire: New and Selected Poems* was chosen by Ted Kooser for his University of Nebraska poetry series in 2017. She has nine previous collections of poems. Her memoir, *Driving with Dvorak*, was published in 2010 by the University of Nebraska Press. She is a professor emerita at the University of Delaware and the former poet laureate of Delaware from 2001 to 2007. She is on the faculty of the Rainier Writing Workshop, a low-residency MFA program in Tacoma, Washington.

**JILL CHRISTMAN** is the author of two memoirs, *Darkroom: A Family Exposure* (winner of the AWP Prize for Creative Nonfiction) and *Borrowed Babies:*

*Apprenticing for Motherhood* (which inspired a play by the same name), as well as essays in magazines such as *Brevity, Creative Nonfiction, Fourth Genre, TriQuarterly, River Teeth, True Story,* and *O, The Oprah Magazine*. She teaches creative nonfiction writing at Ball State University in Muncie, Indiana, where she lives with her husband, writer Mark Neely, and their two children. Visit her at www.jillchristman.com and @jill_christman.

**SARAH CURTIS**'s work has been noted in *Best American Essays 2018*, has been nominated for the Pushcart Prize, and has appeared in *Creative Nonfiction, Salon,* the *American Literary Review, Assay, River Teeth*'s "Beautiful Things" column, and elsewhere. She holds an MFA from the Vermont College of Fine Arts and is currently working on a biographical memoir.

**BRIAN DOYLE** was a dad, a dad, a dad, a husband, an editor, a son-brother-friend-citizen, and the author of thirty-one books of essays, fiction, "proems," and explorations of hearts and vineyards. His first sprawling Oregon novel, *Mink River*, birthed its own movement, and his last novel, *John Carson in Several Quarters of the World*, is a love letter to Robert Louis Stevenson and San Francisco, not to be missed. His essays have been reprinted everywhere. Among various honors for his work is a 2008 Award in Literature from the Academy of Arts and Letters—a total puzzle to him, although he got a free steak dinner out of it in a lovely jazz club in Harlem, complete with a wonderful and engaging dinner companion. What could be a better date than that, you know what I mean? He also made the all-star team in a tough basketball league in Boston, but that was long ago when the world was young and dewy and there were no smartphones yet. Even though Brian physically left the world as we know it on May 27, 2017, his star-filled soul *is;* he soars and spins and seeks for all of us to strive to reach our higher selves, which his stupendous scribblings inspire us to do. What an honor to carry his torch. Namaste MaryBrianLilyJosephLiam.

**ANDRE DUBUS III**'s seven books include the *New York Times'* best sellers *House of Sand and Fog, The Garden of Last Days,* and his memoir, *Townie*. His most recent novel, *Gone So Long*, was published in the fall of 2018. Dubus has been a finalist for the National Book Award and has been awarded a Guggenheim Fellowship, The National Magazine Award for Fiction, and two Pushcart Prizes. He is also the recipient of an American Academy of Arts and Letters Award in Literature. His books are published in over twenty-five languages,

and he teaches full-time at the University of Massachusetts Lowell. He lives in Massachusetts with his wife, Fontaine, who is a modern dancer, and their three children.

**DAVID JAMES DUNCAN** is the author of the best-selling novels *The River Why* and *The Brothers K*, several books of stories and nonfiction, and two fast-response activist books, *Citizen's Dissent* (with Wendell Berry) and *The Heart of the Monster* (with Rick Bass). His work has won three Pacific Northwest Bookseller's Awards, a National Book Award nomination, the Western States Book Award, the American Library Association's 2004 Award for the Preservation of Intellectual Freedom, an honorary doctorate from the University of Portland, a Lannan. It also has appeared in more than fifty anthologies, including *The Pushcart Prizes, Best American Sports Writing, Best American Essays* (twice), and *Best American Spiritual Writing* (six times). Duncan is wrapping up a novel called *Sun House* that fuses his loves for world wisdom traditions; acoustic folk and blues music; and the mountains, river valleys, and openhearted people of the American West. The closed-hearted are on their own. "Valmiki's Palm" is the first of twenty in Duncan's 2003 National Book Award–nominated, Western States Book Award–winning nonfiction collection *My Story as Told by Water*, available in trade paperback from Counterpoint Press.

**STEVEN HARVEY** is the author of a memoir, *The Book of Knowledge and Wonder* and three collections of personal essays: *A Geometry of Lilies, Lost in Translation*, and *Bound for Shady Grove*. Two of his essays have been selected for *The Best American Essays*: "The Book of Knowledge" in 2013 and "The Other Steve Harvey" in 2018. He is a senior editor of *River Teeth* and the creator of *The Humble Essayist* website.

**MARY WOSTER HAUG**'s book *Daughters of the Grasslands: A Memoir* was published in 2014. She has been published in several literary journals and anthologies. She is currently writing a memoir about a murder that shocked her small South Dakota hometown in 1962. She is Professor Emeritus of English from South Dakota State University.

**RICHARD HOFFMAN** is author of the memoirs *Love & Fury* and *Half the House*; the poetry collections *Without Paradise, Gold Star Road, Emblem*, and *Noon Until Night*; and the novel *Interference and Other Stories*. He is a Senior Writer-in-Residence at Emerson College and an adjunct assistant professor at Columbia University.

**ANN HOOD** is the author of the best-selling novels *The Knitting Circle: A Novel*, *The Obituary Writer: A Novel*, and *The Book That Matters Most: A Novel*; three memoirs; and books for young adults and middle-grade readers. Her new book, *Kitchen Yarns: Notes on Life, Love, and Food*, was a *New York Times* Editors' Choice and a *People Magazine* book of the week, and it was named the best memoir of the month by *USA Today*, Amazon, and *The Washington Post*.

**JON KERSTETTER** completed three combat tours in Iraq as a combat physician and flight surgeon. He obtained his MD degree from the Mayo Medical School in Rochester, Minnesota. He also holds an MS in business from the University of Utah and an MFA in creative nonfiction from Ashland University. His essays have been published in *Best American Essays* and other literary journals. His essay "Learning to Breathe" won the Normal School Nonfiction Prize in 2014. Kerstetter is the author of *Crossings: A Doctor Soldier's Story*, which was selected as one of the best reads in military literature in 2017 and was a finalist for the 2018 Colby Award. He currently lectures on PTSD, stroke recovery, and nonfiction writing.

**JUDITH KITCHEN** was the author of six books: *Perennials* (poetry, Anhinga Press); *Writing the World: Understanding William Stafford* (criticism, Oregon State University Press); *Only the Dance: Essays on Time and Memory* (essays, University of South Carolina); *Distance and Direction* (essays, Coffee House Press); *Half in Shade: Family, Photography, and Fate*, a book of nonfiction that was published by Coffee House Press in Spring 2012; and *The Circus Train*, published by Ovenbird Books in 2014. She edited or coedited four collections of nonfiction: *In Short: A Collection of Brief Narrative Nonfiction, In Brief: Short Takes on the Personal*, and *Short Takes: Brief Encounters with Contemporary Nonfiction* (all from W. W. Norton); and, with Ted Kooser, an anthology, *The Poets Guide to the Birds* (Anhinga Press).

**TED KOOSER**'s most recent book is *Kindest Regards: New and Selected Poems* from Copper Canyon Press. His fourth children's picture book, *Mr. Posey's New Glasses*, came out this past spring from Candlewick Press. He lives in rural Nebraska.

**SYDNEY LEA**, a former Pulitzer finalist, founded and for thirteen years edited *New England Review*. In the summer of 2018, Green Writers Press reissued his collaborative book of essays with former Delaware laureate Fleda Brown, *Growing Old in Poetry: Two Poets, Two Lives*.

**DANIEL W. LEHMAN** is the author of *John Reed and the Writing of Revolution* and *Matters of Fact: Reading Nonfiction over the Edge*; the coeditor of *River Teeth: A Journal of Nonfiction Narrative*; and the series editor of the River Teeth Literary Nonfiction Prize series for the University of New Mexico Press. He was a Fulbright Senior Scholar at Stellenbosch University near Cape Town, South Africa; was a visiting professor in Taichung City, Taiwan; and has traveled widely in Southern Africa, where he studies how narrative nonfiction and traumatic memory have implicated African writers and characters. Lehman's more recent publications include a *Best American Essays* notable essay on naming in nonfiction, a chapter on the social history of the New Journalism for Cambridge University Press, and a study of Raymond Carver, as well as essays and interviews on South African nonfiction, fiction, film, and documentary.

**JOE MACKALL** is the cofounder and coeditor of *River Teeth: A Journal of Nonfiction Narrative* and of the River Teeth Literary Nonfiction Prize in partnership with the University of New Mexico Press. He is the author of the Book of the Month Club selection *Plain Secrets: An Outsider Among the Amish* and of the memoir *The Last Street Before Cleveland: An Accidental Pilgrimage*. His work has appeared in a variety of publications, including *The New York Times, Brevity*, and *The Washington Post*, as well as on NPR's "Morning Edition."

**LEE MARTIN** is the author of the novels *The Bright Forever: A Novel*, a finalist for the 2006 Pulitzer Prize in Fiction; *River of Heaven; Quakertown; Break the Skin*; and *Late One Night*. He has also published three memoirs, *From Our House: A Memoir, Turning Bones*, and *Such a Life*, in addition to a craft book, *Telling Stories: The Craft of Narrative and the Writing Life*. His first book was a short story collection, *The Least You Need To Know: Stories*, and his most recent book is another story collection, *The Mutual UFO Network*. He teaches in the MFA Program at The Ohio State University, where he is a College of Arts & Sciences Distinguished Professor, and where he was also the winner of the 2006 Alumni Award for Distinguished Teaching.

**BRENDA MILLER** teaches in the creative writing program at Western Washington University. Her latest collection of essays, *An Earlier Life* (Ovenbird Books, 2016), received the 2017 Washington State Book Award. Her individual essays have received six Pushcart Prizes.

ANGELA MORALES is the author of *The Girls in My Town*, published by the University of New Mexico Press in 2016. Her essays appear in *River Teeth, The Baltimore Review, The Los Angeles Review, The Harvard Review, The Southern Review, The Chattahoochee Review, The Pinch, Hobart, Under the Sun, The Indianola Review*, and *1966: A Journal of Creative Nonfiction*, and other magazines. Her essay "The Girls in My Town" appeared in *Best American Essays 2013*, and her essay "Bloodyfeathers, R.I.P." appeared as a notable essay in *Best American Essays 2015*. Morales lives in Pasadena, California, and teaches at Glendale Community College. She holds an MFA from the University of Iowa and is a recipient of the San Francisco Foundation's James D. Phelan Award for nonfiction, the River Teeth Literary Nonfiction Prize, and the PEN Diamonstein-Spielvogel Award for the Art of the Essay.

CHRIS OFFUTT is the author of *Country Dark, Kentucky Straight, Out of the Woods, The Same River Twice, No Heroes: A Memoir of Coming Home, The Good Brother*, and *My Father, the Pornographer*. His work has received a Pushcart Prize and is included in many anthologies and textbooks, including *Best American Short Stories, Best American Essays, Best American Food Writing*, and *Modern American Memoirs*. His writing has received awards from the Guggenheim Foundation, the Whiting Foundation, the Lannan Foundation, the National Endowment for the Arts, and the American Academy of Arts and Letters. The international magazine *Granta* included him in its list of the Top 20 Young American Writers. His books have been translated into eight languages. For seven years Offutt worked in Hollywood, writing screenplays for *True Blood, Treme*, and *Weeds*. He grew up in the hills of eastern Kentucky and currently lives in rural Lafayette County near Oxford, Mississippi.

JESSICA LIND PETERSON is a playwright and cofounder of Yellow Tree Theatre in Osseo, Minnesota. Her essays have appeared in or are forthcoming in *Seneca Review, Alaska Quarterly Review, River Teeth, Passages North*, and *Anomaly* (formerly *Drunken Boat*). Visit her at jessicalindpeterson.com.

SAM PICKERING grew up in Nashville, Tennessee. He spent sixty-seven years in classrooms, beginning with kindergarten and ending with thirty-five years at the University of Connecticut. He is now retired, but he remains his own yardman and a tediously slow jogger. Pickering has written thirty books and hundreds of articles. The subjects of the books range, but most are collections of familiar essays, providing his take or perhaps "untake" on things. His most

recent collections are *Parade's End: Essays* and *The World Was My Garden, Too: Travels of a Plant Explorer.*

**RON CLINTON SMITH** is a writer of poems, stories, songs, novels, and screenplays, and an actor who appeared in such films as *We Are Marshall, The Mist, Parental Guidance, True Detective, Hidden Figures, Boy Erased,* and *Just Mercy.* He began his acting career in standup comedy before moving to theater, and later to film and television. In 2012 he published the literary novel *Creature Storms.* His story "A Pilgrimage to Dennis Hopper" first appeared in *River Teeth: A Journal of Nonfiction Narrative,* was nominated for the Pushcart Prize in 2014, and was listed as one of the most notable essays in *Best American Essays 2015.* Smith has published poems and stories, fiction and nonfiction, in *Upstreet Magazine, 2 Bridges Review, Litro Magazine, The Legendary, Zoetic Press/NonBinary Review,* and *Soft Cartel.* He balances his time between writing and film acting.

**MAUREEN STANTON** is the author of *Killer Stuff and Tons of Money: Seeking History and Hidden Gems in Flea-Market America,* winner of a Massachusetts Book Award in nonfiction, and *Body Leaping Backward: Memoir of a Delinquent Girlhood.* Her nonfiction has been widely published, including in *Fourth Genre, Creative Nonfiction, New England Review,* and *Florida Review.* She has received an *Iowa Review* prize, a Pushcart Prize, and the *American Literary Review* nonfiction award, as well as fellowships from the National Endowment for the Arts, the Maine Arts Commission, and the MacDowell Colony. She teaches at UMass Lowell.

**JASON TUCKER** has published essays in *Pleiades, The Common, The Southeast Review, Cream City Review,* and *AWP Online,* among others. His *River Teeth* essay "Drowning Catfish" was a Pushcart finalist. An instructor at Suffolk University in Boston, Tucker has written for newspapers and magazines and earned his MFA in nonfiction from The Ohio State University.

**LAURIE RACHKUS UTTICH**'s prose and poetry have been published in *Fourth Genre, Creative Nonfiction, The Missouri Review, Rattle, Superstition Review, Brain, Child, Sweet: A Literary Confection; Iron Horse;* and others. She teaches creative writing at the University of Central Florida in Orlando.

**JESSIE VAN EERDEN** is the author of two novels, *Glorybound: A Novel* (WordFarm, 2012), winner of the Foreword Editor's Choice Fiction Prize, and *My Radio Radio: A Novel* (Vandalia Press, 2016), as well as the essay collection *The*

*Long Weeping: Portrait Essays* (Orison Books, 2017), winner of the Foreword INDIES Book of the Year Award. Her work has appeared in *Best American Spiritual Writing, Oxford American, Willow Springs,* and other magazines and anthologies. She has been awarded the Gulf Coast Prize in Nonfiction, the Milton Fellowship, and a Mid Atlantic Arts Foundation Fellowship. van Eerden holds an MFA in nonfiction from the University of Iowa and directs the low-residency MFA program at West Virginia Wesleyan College.

JULIE MARIE WADE teaches in the creative writing program at Florida International University. Her most recent collections are *The Unrhymables: Collaborations in Prose* (Noctuary Press, 2019), coauthored with Denise Duhamel, and *Same-Sexy Marriage: A Novella in Poems* (A Midsummer Night's Press, 2018). Wade's collaborative essays with Brenda Miller have appeared in *River Teeth, Tupelo Quarterly, Creative Nonfiction, The Kenyon Review,* and *The Normal School,* as well as in two recent anthologies of contemporary collaborative work.

JERALD WALKER is the author of *The World in Flames: A Black Boyhood in a White Supremacist Doomsday Cult* and *Street Shadows: A Memoir of Race, Rebellion, and Redemption,* winner of the PEN New England Award for Nonfiction.

JOE WILKINS grew up in eastern Montana, where he spent his summers working on a wheat and cattle ranch deep in the Bull Mountains. He is the author of a memoir, *The Mountain and the Fathers: Growing Up on the Big Dry,* winner of a 2014 GLCA New Writers Award, and three collections of poetry, including *When We Were Birds: Poems,* winner of the 2017 Oregon Book Award in Poetry. His debut novel, *Fall Back Down When I Die,* praised as "remarkable and unforgettable" in a starred review at Book List, is now available from Little, Brown. Wilkins lives with his family in western Oregon.